CORNELL STUDIES IN CLASSICAL PHILOLOGY

EDITED BY

FREDERICK M. AHL * KEVIN C. CLINTON
JOHN E. COLEMAN * JUDITH R. GINSBURG
G. M. KIRKWOOD * GORDON R. MESSING
ALAN NUSSBAUM * PIETRO PUCCI
WINTHROP WETHERBEE

VOLUME XLVI

Odysseus Polutropos:
Intertextual Readings in the *Odyssey* and the *Iliad*
by Pietro Pucci

From Myth to Icon:
Reflections of Greek Ethical Doctrine in Literature and Art
by Helen F. North

Lucan: An Introduction
by Frederick M. Ahl

The Violence of Pity in Euripides' *Medea*
by Pietro Pucci

Epicurus' Scientific Method
by Elizabeth Asmis

The Rhetoric of Imitation: Genre and Poetic Memory in Virgil
and Other Latin Poets
by Gian Biagio Conte, edited by Charles Segal

THE TOWNSEND LECTURES

Artifices of Eternity: Horace's Fourth Book of Odes
by Michael C. J. Putnam

Odysseus Polutropos

INTERTEXTUAL READINGS IN
THE *ODYSSEY* AND THE *ILIAD*

PIETRO PUCCI

CORNELL UNIVERSITY PRESS

ITHACA AND LONDON

THIS BOOK HAS BEEN PUBLISHED WITH THE AID OF A GRANT FROM
THE HULL MEMORIAL PUBLICATION FUND OF CORNELL UNIVERSITY.

First published 1987 by Cornell University Press.

International Standard Book Number 0-8014-1888-7
Library of Congress Catalog Card Number 86-16798
Printed in the United States of America
*Librarians: Library of Congress cataloging information
appears on the last page of the book.*

*The paper in this book is acid-free and meets the guidelines
for permanence and durability of the Committee on Production
Guidelines for Book Longevity of the Council on Library Resources.*

CONTENTS

Preface   7
Abbreviations   9
Introduction: Variations on Odyssean Themes   13

I. MULTIFACETED DISGUISES

1. Sexual and Textual Jealousy   33
2. The Birth of a New Hero   44
3. Allusion and Misreading   50
4. Suffering and Trickery   56
5. Textual Disingenuousness in Portraying Odysseus'
     Suffering   63
6. Disguise   76
7. Disguise and Recognition   83
8. Disguising Truth: Fiction   98
9. More Light in the Epiphany, Less Light in the Text   110

II. RETURN TO THE SAME: DRIFTING AWAY

10. Return: No Return   127
11. Return, Death, and Immortality   139
12. Polemic Gestures between the *Iliad* and the *Odyssey:*
      Odysseus as a Champion   143
13. Return and Cheating Death   148

III. SYNONYMY

14. The Heart (*Thumos*) of the Iliadic Lion and the Belly
      (*Gastēr*) of the Odyssean Lion   157
15. Being Mindful of Food: Being Forgetful of Griefs   165

Contents

16. Pirates and Beggars   173
17. *Gastēr*: Eros and Thanatos   181

IV. READING: WRITING

18. *Gastēr* and *Thelgein*   191
19. The Song of the Sirens   209
20. Odysseus, Reader of the *Iliad*   214
21. Phemius and the Beginning of the *Odyssey*   228
22. Arte Allusiva   236

Bibliography   247
Index   257

PREFACE

Readers of this book will undertake a voyage into the pages of the *Odyssey* and the *Iliad*. The voyage metaphor is in keeping not only with the theme of the *Odyssey* but with the polytropic and drifting movements of Odysseus in his travels and of Odyssean writing. During these explorations, readers will be made aware of the possibility of an intertextual reading of the *Odyssey*. At the heart of this book lies the recognition that an intertextual approach can create exciting "sense" and reveal a powerful interaction between the two poems.

Of course intertextual confrontations occur everywhere in the texts, wherever a formula, a motif, or a scene in one poem evokes corresponding features in the other poem. In principle, therefore, I might have analyzed all the lines of the *Odyssey* or of the *Iliad*. Short of this, I had to choose passages; my choice has been determined by the epics' major thematic and rhetorical motifs. In part I, the theme of disguise develops simultaneously with the rhetoric of simulation and fiction. The theme of return in part II develops with the theme and the rhetoric of re-cognition and the *après coup*. The third part analyzes the troubling synonymity of *thumos* and *gastēr;* part IV illustrates the reading that the *Odyssey* enacts of its competitive texts.

These diverse yet converging lines of reading inevitably produce, I suggest, polytropic and multiple views. Therefore—by analogy with two famous novels—the book expands in the digressive, disseminating style of *Tristram Shandy* rather than in the cohesive fashion of *Middlemarch*. For this work emerges from the modern awareness—due to McLuhan, Barthes, and Derrida—that the book in its traditional form as an organic whole, a body fully harmonious and self-contained, is at an end, and writing is beginning. To some extent this must have been the *Odyssey*'s own sense of itself as a self-contained whole.

Preface

I quote Homer from *Homeri opera*, edited by David B. Monro and Thomas W. Allen (Oxford: Clarendon Press, 1902–12). Translations are mine unless I have indicated otherwise. I have transliterated all Greek words into Latin characters. At the same time, since one of the purposes of transliteration is to make the text intelligible to non-Hellenists, I have used the Latinate forms of Greek personal names with which English-language readers are familiar; accordingly, "Achilles," not "Akhilleus"; "Telemachus," not "Telemakhos"; "Charis," not "Kharis"; "Odysseus," not "Odusseus"; and so on. I have not been fully consistent, however; to preserve puns, for instance, I have reverted to the transliterations "Odusseus," "Telemakhos," and the like. The other exceptions—some geographical names—will be readily understandable to readers.

I owe assistance and help to many institutions and individuals. A fellowship from the John Simon Guggenheim Memorial Foundation (in 1980–81) allowed me to pursue research in the stimulating environment of the Centre de Recherches Comparées sur les Sociétés Anciennes in Paris.

Several grants from the College of Arts and Sciences of Cornell University and from the Townsend Fund of Cornell University's Department of Classics have helped with editing and typing.

The book would not have the form it has without this assistance and without the skillful editorial contributions of Martha Linke.

I am grateful to the friends who have read this book at various stages of its composition and have given generously of their time, advice, and insights. I mention here Robert Lamberton, Gordon Kirkwood, Gordon Messing, Frederick Ahl, and especially Andrew Ford, who in my seminar on the *Odyssey* and in reading this text has been a congenial and generous critic.

At the Centre in Paris, where I was invited to present some results of my research, I benefited from the illuminating responses of Marcel Detienne, Nicole Loraux, Pierre Vidal-Naquet, Jean-Pierre Vernant, and Heinz Wismann.

Gregory Nagy has supported this book with his powerful critical insights and his unending loyalty.

PIETRO PUCCI

Ithaca, New York

ABBREVIATIONS

A.H. Karl Friedrich Ameis and Carl Hentze, eds. *Homers Ilias*. With commentary. 2 vols. Leipzig: Teubner, 1884–87.

A.H.C. Karl Friedrich Ameis and Carl Hentze, eds. *Homers Odyssee*. Rev. Paul Cauer. 4 vols. (2 vols., each in two parts). Leipzig: Teubner, 1920–28.

AJP *American Journal of Philology*.

Allen Thomas W. Allen, ed. *Odyssey*. Vols. 3 and 4 of *Homeri opera*, ed. David B. Monro and Thomas W. Allen. 5 vols. Oxford: Clarendon Press, 1902–12.

BSL *Bulletin de la Société de Linguistique de Paris*.

Butcher and Lang S. H. Butcher and Andrew Lang, trans. *Homer's Odyssey*. London: Macmillan, 1879.

CP *Classical Philology*.

CQ *Classical Quarterly*.

CW *Classical World*.

DE Pierre Chantraine. *Dictionnaire étymologique de la langue grecque*. 4 vols. Paris: C. Klincksieck, 1968–80.

GH Pierre Chantraine. *Grammaire homérique*. 2 vols. Vol. 1, *Phonétique et morphologie*. Vol. 2, *Syntaxe*. Paris: C. Klincksieck, 1948–53. Reprint, vol. 1 only, Paris: C. Klincksieck, 1973.

GRBS *Greek, Roman, and Byzantine Studies*.

HSCP *Harvard Studies in Classical Philology*.

JHS *Journal of Hellenic Studies*.

Leaf Walter Leaf, ed. *Iliad*. 2d ed. 2 vols. London: Macmillan, 1900–1902.

LfrgE *Lexikon des frühgriechischen Epos*. General ed., Bruno Snell. 11 fascicles to date. Göttingen: Vandenhoeck & Ruprecht, 1955–.

LIMC *Lexicon Iconographicum Mythologiae Classicae*. Edited by Hans Christoph Ackermann and Jean-Robert Gisler. 2 vols., each in two parts. Zurich and Munich: Artemis, 1981–84.

Nitzsch Georg Wilhelm Nitzsch. *Erklärende Anmerkungen zu Homers Odyssee*. 3 vols. Hannover: Hahn, 1826–40.

Abbreviations

Odissea   Omero, *Odissea.* The Italian translation of G. Aurelio Privitera. General introduction by Alfred Heubeck and Stephanie West. 6 vols. Milan: Fondazione Lorenzo Valla, 1981–. Vol. 1, *Libri I–IV* (1981), ed. Stephanie West. Vol. 2, *Libri V–VIII* (1982), ed. J. B. Hainsworth. Vol. 3, *Libri IX–XII* (1983), ed. Alfred Heubeck. Vol. 4, *Libri XIII–XVI* (1984), ed. Arie Hoekstra. Vol. 5, *Libri XVII–XX* (1985), ed. Joseph Russo. Vol. 6, *Libri XXI–XXIV* (forthcoming), ed. Manuel Fernández-Galiano. (Citations include the editor and number of the relevant volume, e.g., *Odissea*–West, 1:25.)

Proclus   Proculi, *Chrestomathia.* In *Homeri opera,* ed. David B. Monro and Thomas W. Allen, vol. 5. Oxford: Clarendon Press, 1912.

Stanford   W. B. Stanford, ed. *The Odyssey of Homer.* With commentary. 2 vols. London: Macmillan, 1959.

TAPA   *Transactions of the American Philological Association.*

van Leeuwen1890   Jan van Leeuwen and M. B. Mendes da Costa, eds. *Odysseae Carmina.* Leiden, 1890.

van Leeuwen1917   Jan van Leeuwen, ed. *Odysseia.* Leiden, 1917.

Odysseus Polutropos

Had I unknown phrases
Sayings that are strange
Novel, untried words
Free of repetition
Not transmitted sayings
Spoken by the ancestors!
I wring out my body of what it holds
In releasing all my words;
For what was said is repetition
When what was said is said,
Ancestors' words are nothing to boast of,
They are found by those who came after.

The Complaints of Khakheperre-Sonb

Introduction:

Variations on Odyssean Themes

Critics have traditionally been fascinated by the representation of Odysseus at the beginning of the *Odyssey* and by the development of that initial image. But which is the initial image of Odysseus and how does it evolve in the course of the poem? To answer this question is to interpret Odysseus' traveling as the locus of experience through which he reaches his telos. Two major interpretations emerge from the critical literature: either Odysseus' traveling and return are viewed as the painful experience through which the hero transforms himself and reaches the full measure of his humanness, or these adventures are considered as episodes that endlessly repeat the same experience until Odysseus' return puts a temporary stop to his wanderings. In the former view the *Odyssey* becomes a sort of *Bildungsroman,* in the latter, a serialized novel that could go on practically forever.

In the former interpretation return—as an archetypal theme—means the long maturation of an experience, the crossing of borders, the recouping of a loss, the reappropriation of a lost self. According to this view, Odysseus would live with Calypso, in an *imaginary* world, himself half-conscious of his real self, since for some time he has been willing to live hidden with her. Only when he decides to come back and to accept his mortality does the hero begin to be himself and the *Odyssey* itself begin. Odysseus' return home, then, represents his return to humanity, consciousness, reality, and responsibility, and the episodes of this return constitute facets of those reappropriations. This interpretation therefore retrieves the "beginning" of the *Odyssey* from the metaphysical dynamics of the notion of return, for notions such as "reappropriation of the self" and "fulfillment of one's destiny" (*telos*) are metaphysical to the extent that they outline a perfect closure and a utopian sense of "humanness." It is from this end—

from this conclusion, from the closing up of the return—that a beginning, a point of departure at a lower level, is retrieved.

It is certain that the *Odyssey* allures and captivates the reader by precisely this trip and that most memorable critical pages on the *Odyssey* have capitalized on this metaphysical movement and on its handing down to us the edifying portrait of the noble, suffering hero, accepting his humanness and growing great in it.

Accordingly, critics have not hesitated to pursue allegorical or symbolic readings, for the fictional and fablelike episodes of the poem encourage this reading. In the symbolic readings of recent years Odysseus undergoes various births and is fostered by several mother figures as he ascends the difficult ladder to acceptance of his humanity and, with it, all its humiliating limitations.

The other reading—that which focuses on return as return to the same through analogous, repeated experiences—delivers no moral lessons, only inexhaustible pleasure. Odysseus is shown to cheat death at every corner, to compensate fully for each personal loss, and to retrieve his whole self after each sham and disguise. It is easy to understand the gratifying and alluring power such a character exercises over his readers: on the one hand, Odysseus satisfies our deepest and most uncontrollable desire, to outwit death; on the other, he is an imperishable "persona," an inerasable entity, forever self-identical. He is the supreme distillation of fiction that looks more real than reality.

But this interpretation too is metaphysical, for it is grounded in a utopian notion of sameness. Our critical reading cannot be blind to the incredible contradictions, gaps, and tricks that the text exhibits as it creates that sense of sameness; but in fact Odysseus does not return to the same, to begin with because his return does not stop his journeying. The man "of many turns" (*polutropos*) is engaged in a movement of *re-turn* (*hupotropos*, *Od.* 22.35) that will not end with his landing at Ithaca. He is conscious of having to journey again. Furthermore, his journey has already been a sort of centrifugal movement, endlessly drifting away from home. Rather than a return to the same, I see a multiplication of the same events, a sort of drifting repetition of analogous episodes.[1] This third reading also seems to suggest a

---

[1]See Pietro Pucci, "The Proem of the *Odyssey*," *Arethusa* 15 (1982): 39–62. The metaphor of the journey and its metaphysical premises have been perceptively analyzed in recent criticism. See, for instance, the rich and exhaustive analyses of Giuseppe Mazzotta in *Dante, Poet of the Desert* (Princeton: Princeton University Press, 1979), and the brilliant thesis of Georges Van Den Abbeele, "The Economy of Travel in French Philosophical Literature" (Ph.D. diss., Cornell University, 1981).

utopian, reassuring interpretation of the poem to the extent that the continuous drifting would never carry Odysseus to any fixed point, and therefore not even to death. And yet, as we pit the polytropic centrifugal movement against the movement back home (*hupotropos*), and as we focus on the fictional strategies that ensure his survival, the gratifying and domesticated movement of his return is jeopardized. The empire of necessity, of death, that he avoids by his shrewdness and cunning (*mētis*) presses on him and holds him in specific ways. On a few momentous occasions he appears to us between life and death, as when he goes down to Hades, returns to Ithaca on the Phaeacian ship, or spends seven years on Calypso's island. He returns on the Phaeacian ship without any awareness or consciousness, for he is immersed in a profound sleep "most similar to death" (*thanatōi ankhista eoikōs*, *Od.* 13.80): the hero dies to be reborn in Ithaca, where at first he will not recognize his fatherland. To the extent that on this and similar occasions Odysseus arrives in a new situation by passing through unconsciousness, or by himself being at the margin of the world of consciousness, his life as a character undergoes a crisis, remains suspended, or becomes irrelevant to the evolution of events. Death grasps him and coexists with his life, necessity with pleasure.

Analogously, as the hero passes through new situations and conditions, his previous self is deeply altered. Here too it is not mere chance that a physical change, a deep transformation in his body, momentarily takes place; for indeed when Odysseus, the beggar in his own house, is shown lying down like a dog before his dirty bag on which he has piled his food (*Od.* 17.356 ff.), he is a different man. Though his name and epithets are the same and his words are occasionally the same, something of the old hero is dead.

All this implies that as he cheats the necessity of death, death simultaneously cheats him, suspends his life, changes his physical appearance, constantly amputates or adds to his previous self. His cunning does not save him from becoming a sort of kaleidoscopic Odysseus that the sameness of the name and the many recognition scenes barely hold together. The edifying interpretation of the *Odyssey*, which focuses on the development of the hero toward his fulfillment (*telos*), obtains legitimation and power in these scenes. And yet, if my reading is correct, the text seems constantly tempted to deny any change in the inner nature of the hero.

The force of my inquiry consists in elucidating and bringing into the foreground the odd economy that holds Odysseus between these extremes: life and death, sameness and otherness, return to his house and turns away from home. It is the undecidable tension between these opposite terms that forces Odysseus to become the man of manyness and polytropy; to the extent to which these skills of the hero succeed, they domesticate (literally and figurally) all the issues that are implied in the unresolvable tension.

Polytropy is synonymous with *mētis*, "cunning," "shrewdness."[2] The theme of return and its drifting economy hinges on the notion of *mētis* itself. In the Odyssean epiphanies of Athena, *mētis* appears as the craft of disguise and illusion that can manipulate necessity and alter reality when there are people to deceive and obstacles to surmount. The power of this specific *mētis* (of which Athena's *mētis* represents the divine counterpart) is unbeatable, as the success of Odysseus' plan in his own house proves.

Yet through the constant manipulation of reality by calculated self-disguise and by reinvented biographies, Odysseus removes himself from his "real" self and falls into shadowy and intermediary postures in which he will at once be himself and not himself, true to his temper and disloyal to it. My contention is that Odysseus' "real" self can only be "presumed" to exist behind his disguises and his narratives and that therefore the disguising scenes are what create the illusion of his "real self."

The paradox here is that trickery should be astute enough to control and manipulate its own strategy of concealment, of shamming, without itself being taken in, but I suggest that these shadowy postures indicate rather that Odysseus and his *mētis* do not fully control the strategy they enact. Odysseus therefore sometimes appears both as manipulator of the ruse and as its dupe. To cite only one incident, his outward disguise as a beggar conceals him even when it is no longer necessary—for instance, in his first self-revelation to his wife (*Od.* 23.115–16).

Polymētis Odysseus, the man of many ruses, the man of many turns, appears, appropriately, in a text unsurpassed for rhetorical *mētis* and polytropy. If I choose to speak of Odysseus' polytropy rather than of his *mētis* it is because "polytropy" has the felicitous advantage of describing not only his character but the thematic and rhetorical qualities of his text, for the turns and re-turn of his wanderings, the turns and ruses of his mind, are mirrored in the turns (*tropoi*, rhetoric and rhetorical figures) of the *Odyssey* itself. Furthermore, whereas polytropy implies that the process of turns is open, *mētis* names the suc-

---

[2]The relations between the crafty turn of mind and *mētis* is one of the themes Marcel Detienne and Jean-Pierre Vernant trace in their book *Les Ruses de l'intelligence: La Mētis des grecs* (Paris: Flammarion, 1974).

cessfully accomplished ruse and trick. To this extent polytropy is a slightly more neutral word than *mētis*, which by evoking a successful, winning craft must be constantly demystified by the reader.

The dominant presence of notions such as polytropy, *mētis*, and *doloi*, "tricks," implies that the empire of necessity is harsh and inevitable. What I call here, generally, the empire of necessity receives more precise determinations in the various situations staged in the *Odyssey*. Essentially this empire of necessity includes death, self-forgetfulness, dissemination (drifting away forever), and loss of the self. As *mētis*, *doloi*, and polytropy succeed in controlling these threats, pleasure emerges for the character and for the reader as well. The text of the *Odyssey* applies endless variations to this same basic situation. My premise, which will become clearer further on in the book, is that necessity and pleasure are the terms of a supplementary structure that holds them together in a contiguous unstable tension.

Odysseus' return home and his turns (away from home) constitute a return of the hero to his literary tradition or lineage as well. The *Odyssey* narrates the final (or almost final) adventures of a hero whose previous deeds are, at the fictional time of his last journey, already known and sung throughout the Greek-speaking world. This "sequel" thus follows in a long tradition of songs, on both the thematic and the textual level. Yet, as I will emphasize, the relationship between the *Odyssey* and the tradition in which it takes shape is extremely ambivalent. The narrative tension that suspends Odysseus between his return home and his turns (away from home) is paralleled by the *Odyssey*'s intriguing textual economy, which simultaneously adheres to and diverges from its tradition.

Of the rest of the rich and vast epic tradition on the Trojan War we unfortunately know only the *Iliad*. Were we able to read the entire Trojan cycle, especially that part in which Odysseus played a prominent role, the view I am presenting here might be different; as it is, we must rely on the *Iliad* alone as the representative model of the epic tradition and the one term of comparison.

The most significant indication of the *Odyssey*'s ambivalent economy is its silence about the *Iliad*.[3] At several points the *Odyssey* indicates,

[3]See David Monro, ed., *Homer's Odyssey, Books XIII–XXIV* (Oxford: Clarendon Press, 1901), p. 325: "The *Odyssey* never repeats or refers to any incident related in the *Iliad*." This statement, soon raised to the absoluteness of "Monro's law," stimulated research such as that of Denys Page: see *The Homeric Odyssey* (Oxford: Clarendon Press, 1955), which tries to prove that the *Odyssey* was not aware of the *Iliad*. A sound position on the problem can be found in Gregory Nagy, *The Best of the Achaeans* (Baltimore: Johns Hopkins University Press, 1979): "if the avoidance was indeed deliberate, it would mean that the *Odyssey* displays an awareness of the *Iliad* by steering clear of it, or rather

blatantly, that it is ignoring the *Iliad* and its tradition.[4] Given this evidence, I favor the hypothesis that the *Odyssey* did in fact know the *Iliad*. The two texts probably evolved simultaneously, each aware of the other, before being fixed in the monumental compositions we now have, and it is likely that during the formative period some passages in each were intentionally revised to conform to corresponding passages in the other. Clearly, the *Iliad* and the *Odyssey* presume each other, border and limit each other, to such an extent that one, as it were, writes the other.

This thorough complementarity, however, does not mean the two poems constitute one consistent and harmonious unity. On the contrary, the *Odyssey*'s pretense of ignoring the *Iliad*—and vice versa— bespeaks a decidedly polemic, controversial relationship. For example, the heroes Achilles and Odysseus are represented in both poems in an intertextual dialogue in which one pretends to be deaf to the other, as each in his own poem represents an ontological mode opposing that of the other.

The *Odyssey*'s simultaneous dependence on and disengagement from the Iliadic tradition are highlighted in those passages of the poems that clearly seem to respond to each other and therefore to play with allusion. Line after line of the *Odyssey* adopts the epic diction and repeats its formulaic phrases, at times diverging from its model, at times renewing it with uncanny subtlety. The allusion would prove the dependence of one poem on the other and at the same time the desire of the alluding text to conceal, or at least to make enigmatic, such dependence.

---

it may be a matter of evolution. Perhaps it was a part of the Odyssean tradition to veer away from the Iliadic. Be that as it may, the traditions of the *Iliad* and of the *Odyssey* constitute a totality with the complementary distribution of their narratives" (pp. 20– 21).

[4]See, for example, *Od.* 23.310–41, where Odysseus recounts to Penelope his adventures since he left Ithaca twenty years before. He begins his narrative with the first adventure of the *Odyssey* and never even tells her about the capture of Troy! Monro's law was never intended to be a law. I will examine some passages of the *Odyssey* that clearly seem to refer to the *Iliad;* see, for instance, *Od.* 22.226–32. On my line of inquiry see, for instance, Götz Beck, "Beobachtungen zur Kirke-Episode in der Odyssee," *Philologus* 109 (1965): 1–29; and Walter Burkert, "Das Lied von Ares und Aphrodite zum Verhältnis von Odyssee und Ilias," *Rheinisches Museum* 103 (1960): 130–84. Recently Seth L. Schein, *The Mortal Hero: An Introduction to Homer's "Iliad"* (Berkeley and Los Angeles: University of California Press, 1984), p. x, has formulated well the approaches I generally find inspiring as "the most fruitful 'schools' of modern Homeric scholarship: the (chiefly Anglo-American) study of Homer as a traditional oral poet . . . and the 'Neo Analysis' originated by Johannes Th. Kakridis and exemplified by the works of . . . German students." Among the students he mentions is Karl Reinhardt, to whom I am particularly indebted.

Introduction

Allusion of course is always a tricky phenomenon, but it is especially so in our epic poems. Anyone who knows even the rudiments of Milman Parry's notion of oral tradition and its relation to formulaic diction will recognize the empirical difficulty of determining the "significance" of repetitions and variations in formulaic passages. Furthermore, even if we disregard the economic principles of Parry's theory, the question of how to grasp intentions and meanings in allusive texts is theoretically unresolvable. Repetition and differentiation, which constitute the processes of allusion, inevitably obscure the textual and authorial intentions: the recycling of formulaic expressions completely conceals their eventual allusive intention; the reworking of variations opens so many allusive possibilities that it dissipates the force of any single one.

The solutions I have offered are necessarily only working hypotheses and thus not wholly satisfactory. On the one hand, I have searched for empirical features that provide some evidence for an "allusion," that is, a repetition that in itself adds sense. On the other hand, I have presented some of the many possible meanings an allusion might offer. Generally I have avoided deciding what remains undecidable, and in only a few cases have I taken the risk of indicating what I consider the most forceful reading. In this way I have respected the notion that a text is finally the sum of its readings, that is, not a source of meaning, but an open re-source of meanings.

As the epic diction constantly repeats itself, the allusive, playful, meaningful "remakes" (or references) animate the repetition with a purpose. The ingenuity and the subtlety that the *Odyssey* shows in comprehending by its allusive style the whole epic tradition, and in transcending it, testify to the *mētis* and the polytropy of its writing.

Whether the *Odyssey* introduces a variant meaning in the same signifier, disguises old formulas by new touches, or arrays different signifiers to play synonymically with an old notion or idea, its rereading and rewriting give life and brilliance to the repeated diction and reanimate the diction's relative passivity. The only limit to the *Odyssey*'s success in this pleasurable practice resides in the inevitable economy of the "sign" that resists the full overcoming of repetition.

Repetition, as the matrix of epic poetry, shapes not only phrases but also poetic conceptions and ideology. For example, fame (*kleos*)—for which some heroes in the *Iliad* are ready to die—implies *repeated rumor*. Analogically, the notion of memory (*mnēmē*) is intrinsically connected with the process of repetition. The memory (*mnēmē*) of the Muses is unthinkable without the repetitive, fixed quality of epic diction.[5] As Berkley Peabody says, "The memory effect caused by the redundancy of the epic style" is "the epos's true Muse."[6]

The epic texts mention the *mnēmē* of the Muses as the origin and source of their song (see, for instance, *Il.* 2.484 ff.), thus raising the memory (repetition and recycling) of epic language to a metaphysical principle: the divine quality of the *mnēmē*. By locating the source of epic song in the original memory-voice of the Muses, the epic conception easily explains the long process of traditional poetic elaboration and reduces the endlessly complex phenomenon of poetry to a single and simple origin.[7] This way of explaining things is the quintessential process of myth.

This poetic ideology operates on many levels and in many episodes of the poems. A specific act of divine memory saves Odysseus from the concealment and the deathlike forgetfulness in which he lies in Calypso's (= the Concealer's) house. It is Athena's *mnēmē* that brings him back into visibility:

> Among them [the gods], Athena described [*lege*] the many toils of Odysseus for she remembered [him] [*mnēsamenē*].[8] It troubled her that he was in the house of the nymph. (*Od.* 5.5–6)

Just as Zeus, by an analogous act of *mnēmē* (see *Od.* 1.29), had raised the memory of Orestes and Aegisthus, so now Athena brings Odysseus back to life and light with a discourse that describes his toils. Our *Odyssey* is in part already contained in that discourse-memory of Athena. Now the *mnēmē* of Athena is that of the goddess of *mētis* (cunning, shrewdness), and accordingly the memory that snatched Odysseus from oblivion is appropriately the memory of *mētis*, whose craft consists in concealing and revealing, in manipulating necessity through the playful mingling of appearance and reality. The *Odyssey* names its own polytropic ruse as it mentions Athena's act of *mnēmē*.

[5]On these points see my analysis of *Il.* 2.884 ff.—where *kleos* and *mnēmē* of the Muses are correlated—in "The Language of the Muses," in *Classical Mythology in Twentieth-Century Thought and Literature*, ed. Wendell M. Aycock and Theodore M. Klein (Lubbock: Texas Tech Press, 1980), pp. 163–86.

[6]Berkley Peabody, *The Winged Word* (Albany: State University of New York Press, 1975), p. 113: "The thematically limited language of an oral tradition is a language of regular forms; for regularity is the symptom of limitation. The memory effect caused by the redundancy of the epic style was the epos's true Muse."

[7]See James Notopoulos, "Mnemosyne in Oral Literature," *TAPA* 69 (1938): 465–93, who tries to understand both the static and the creative sides of this oral memory; G. M. Calhoun, "The Poet and the Muses in Homer," *CP* 33 (1938): 157–66; and the quoted passage of Peabody, *Winged Word*, p. 113.

[8]The participle has no object: "by an act of remembrance."

The text, of course, attributes a divine, simple origin to the process that brings Odysseus out of concealment (= Calypso) and oblivion and makes him the character of a new poem; had this *mnēmē* not snatched him out of concealment, Odysseus would have terminated his literary career on Calypso's island, if not before.[9] His poem would have never been sung, for the text underscores, with singular consistency, that the people of whom he was the king have ceased *to remember him (ou tis memnētai Odussēos)*, as Athena says (*Od.* 5.11).[10]

Athena's *mnēmē* is only the noun for poetic, traditional memory. The text states that Athena, *mnēsamenē*, did recount (*lege*) the many toils of Odysseus (5.5–6), but since the text reports Athena's own words, it records only the conclusion, or the peroration, of her *mnēmē*, that is, of her recollection (5.5–20). Athena sounds indignant that nobody remembers Odysseus and that even his son is no longer safe (5.7–20). Do we hear then the outburst of the goddess in her own

[9]By Athena's act of *mnēmē*, Odysseus comes to life as a *literary* character. This is the only open issue: Odysseus is threatened by Calypso only to the extent that, by keeping him at the margin of the world of men and by wanting to make him immortal, she would prevent him from becoming the hero of the new poem, the *Odyssey*.

[10]At the risk of being accused of oversubtlety, I cannot refrain from calling attention to the first two lines of the *Odyssey's* fifth book: "Dawn rose from the bed by Tithonus in order / to bring light to immortals and to men" (*Od.* 5.1–2). These two lines recur exactly only once again in the whole epic tradition we know, in *Il.* 11.1–2, where after the coming of dawn Zeus sends Eris (Discord) to the Achaeans and she places herself upon the huge black ship of Odysseus (*Il.* 11.3–5). This precise repetition cannot be purposeless: it is true that parallel expressions appear elsewhere (*Od.* 19.1–2, 23.348) but with substantial differences. Here the Odyssean text seems designed to produce three effects. It forces the audience to remember the Odysseus of the *Iliad*, and to some extent therefore it points to the *Iliad;* it suggests that the light dawn is bringing to men will also snatch Odysseus from the remoteness of the Concealer (Calypso). This is an inspired way for the *Odyssey* to read the *Iliad*, especially in view of the literary jealousy that is exhibited in the fifth book. Finally, these opening lines foreshadow what occurs in that day. Tithonus was a mortal whom Dawn had taken and made her lover; she had given him immortality, though not immortal youth. One of their sons, Memnon, is the hero of the *Aethiopis*, a poem that describes the immortalization of Memnon and Achilles. These themes on the immortalization of a human being are evoked here at the beginning of the book where Odysseus refuses the immortality Calypso has promised him.

The relation between the beginning of a book and its content remains a problem to be studied. Here I offer some new hints. Commenting on the beginning of book 8, l. 3, Milman Parry notices that the noun-epithet *diogenes–ptoliporthos Odusseus* appears only once in the poem; see "The Traditional Epithet in Homer," in *The Making of Homeric Verse*, ed. Adam Parry (Oxford: Clarendon Press, 1971), p. 77. Parry explains this exceptional rarity by analogy with other formulaic patterns; yet this explanation does not prevent our adding that the text shows the will to have Odysseus named as *ptoliporthos*, "sacker of cities," and that this naming of course forecasts Demodocus' description of Odysseus as the destroyer of Troy in the same book (*Od.* 8.499 ff.).

improvised words? Not at all. The fourteen lines she utters are composed of repeated pieces and redundant phrases: lines 8–12 repeat what Mentor told the assembly in *Od.* 2.230–34; we have already heard lines 14–17 from the mouth of Menelaus, who repeats Proteus' words (*Od.* 4.557–60); we will hear them again as Telemachus gives his mother an account of his trip in *Od.* 17.143–46. The last three lines of Athena's outburst (18–20) are a redundant rendition of Medon's words in *Od.* 4.700–702. In addition, some of these lines (7, 13, etc.) are singularly formulaic. In short, the whole passage is such that it has been dismissed not only by the analysts of the old school, pre-Parryan in their approach, but also by Denys Page, who labels this "patchwork character" of Athena's outburst post-Homeric.[11]

Athena's recollection, this *mnēmē* that is the *original act* bringing Odysseus back to light and to the epic narrative, is itself an example of epic repetition and redundancy. The discourse that lies as the single and final source at the origin of this epic is itself composed of repeated epic phrases and is therefore already inscribed in what it supposedly sets in motion. Nothing could better illustrate the wishful and utopian character of the epic metaphysical convention that ascribes the inception of the epic song to an original *mnēmē*, lying outside the song itself.

It is no chance that the text chooses Athena's memory to bring Odysseus back to the narrative: Athena as goddess of *mētis* is the protective goddess of Odysseus. Accordingly, Athena names the specific epic destination of Odysseus and acts in the narrative, thematically, as his divine counterpart, the *representamen* of his strengths.[12]

---

[11] I quote from M. J. Apthorp, "The Language of the *Odyssey* 5.5–20," *CQ*, n.s. 27 (1977): 1–9. Apthorp shows that the passage is consistent with the familiar technique of composition, that some adaptations show felicity or "sensitivity," other phrases prove the poet's desire to play with allusions (p. 5), and other formulas are created by the poet of the *Odyssey* (pp. 7 ff.).

[12] The alliance of Athena and Odysseus is known also in the *Iliad:* on one occasion, *Il.* 2.166 ff., Athena asks Odysseus to stop the Achaeans' flight, and it seems that she chooses him because he is hero of *mētis;* see *Il.* 2.169: "she found Odysseus, equal to Zeus in ruses [*mētin*], standing." In fact, Odysseus has not rushed to flight (170–71a) and has remembered the words of Agamemnon during the council (see 2.75, 192 ff.). The formula "equal to Zeus in ruses" (*Dii mētin atalanton*) occurs again for Odysseus in *Il.* 2.406, 636, and 10.137, but it is not exclusive to him, since it is also used for Hector (*Il.* 7.47, 11.200). The *Odyssey* never uses this formula. It is of course meaningless to speculate on the reason for this, unless the speculation is consistent with the general critical discourse. We may think, for instance, that because the formula is not exclusive to Odysseus it is omitted by the *Odyssey*. A more forceful and intriguing explanation would be that in the *Odyssey* Athena's preeminence as goddess of *mētis* overshadows Zeus' as god of *mētis*. This might appear preposterous in view of the association of Zeus

Textually speaking—that is, at the level of the textual composition—
Athena also stands for the polytropic style of the *Odyssey*, for its intriguing, baffling ironies, its playful allusiveness, its many facets and
mirrors. An immense exercise of reading and misreading is couched
in this polytropy.

Another god, Hermes, defines more precisely the direction of
Odysseus' epic destination.[13] The figure and the role of Hermes as
they are described in the lines of the fifth book have been subjected to
endless criticism, and as scholars have questioned his role as messenger—in place of Iris, who is the messenger in the *Iliad*—they have
found some passages they judge infelicitous where the text repeats
the *Iliad*. But none of these objections is serious enough to throw
suspicion on the authority of Hermes' passage and role,[14] and valid
reasons may justify the god's intervention. Hermes is first of all a
familiar figure in Odysseus' clan: he is the patron god of Autolycus,
grandfather of Odysseus: "Autolycus . . . who surpassed men in theft
and oath: the god Hermes gave him this preeminence" (*Od.* 19.395–

---

with Mētis in Hesiod, a bond exemplified by Zeus' epithet *mētieta*. But the *Odyssey* does
not deny those relations; it simply emphasizes Athena's role as goddess of *mētis and*
patron of Odysseus and consequently discards a formula that would present Odysseus
in relation to Zeus' *mētis*. Athena's preeminence as goddess of *mētis* could be proved by
noting how rarely the epithet *mētieta* is used for Zeus—only three times—whereas the
Iliad uses it sixteen times and Hesiod (*Theogony* and *Works and Days*) five times.

[13]On Hermes, god of *mētis*, at once deceptive and technical intelligence, see Carlo
Diano, "La poetica dei Feaci," in *Saggezza e poetiche degli antichi* (Venice: N. Pozza, 1968),
pp. 199, 205.

[14]Whatever may be the grounds for the *Odyssey*'s choice of Hermes rather than Iris, it
is at least consistent throughout in excluding Iris. The *Odyssey* even introduces a mock
Iris in the person of Irus in book 17. On the supposedly improper description of
Hermes' iconographical *insignia* (5.43–49), which is repeated exactly as in *Il.* 24.339–
45, a convincing answer is possible. From antiquity it has been noticed that mention of
Hermes' staff in the *Iliad* is proper and apt, since Hermes actually uses the staff to put
the guards to sleep (*Il.* 24.445). But in the *Odyssey* this mention is useless. Supposedly
this would prove the mechanical nature of the repetition from the passage of the *Iliad*.
Yet it has not been remarked that, in this scene of the *Odyssey*, Hermes has the epithet
khrusorrapis, "with a golden staff" (5.87): this epithet shows that the staff is, at least for
the *Odyssey*, part of Hermes' permanent panoply. This epithet is missing in the *Iliad*
and, curiously, also in the *Hymn to Hermes*. In the *Odyssey* this epithet is a fixed element
of the iconography of the god: Odysseus sees Hermes in human disguise (*Od.*
10.277 ff.) and says, "Hermes of the golden staff [Hermeias *khrusorrapis*] met me." Thus
the *Odyssey* shows here its concern for the iconographic representation of the gods, and
in describing Hermes' insignia it could not bypass his staff.

L. 5.91 has been found an improper remnant from *Il.* 18.387, where the line is
properly placed. L. 91 does seem to contrast with l. 87, in which Calypso seats Hermes
in the chair, but as we cannot reach a sure sense of the inner topography of Calypso's
speos, "cave," we cannot be confident with any bracketing. Calypso may invite Hermes
to sit on the chair—a gesture corresponding to Charis' taking Thetis' hands in *Il.*
18.384—and then invite him to follow her (5.91) to another chair closer to the place
where she is preparing the food for him.

96). Now Autolycus is significant for the definition of Odysseus' epic destination, for he is the author of Odysseus' name (*Od.* 17.406 ff.). He names his grandson Odusseus because he himself is *odussamenos*, that is, hating or hated. The *Odyssey* traces a connection between the name Odysseus and his destiny and insists on it by punning.[15] The author of that name is Autolycus, the hero protected by Hermes.

But even more important is that Hermes shares with Odysseus the exclusive epithet *polutropos*, "of many turns," a word that qualifies the whole literal and literary essence of Odysseus, since it evokes or names at once his many travels, his many ruses, and his many rhetorical skills. It conjures up all these associations through the literal and metaphorical force of *tropos*, which itself is the word for metaphor. The word therefore also names the impossibility of separating the literal from the metaphorical meaning in the word itself and consequently points to the *Odyssey*'s Hermes-like irony and literary astuteness.[16]

The epithet *polutropos* occurs only twice in the *Odyssey*, in two significant passages. In *Od.* 1.1: "Sing me Muse of the man of many turns [*polutropos*]," the epithet names the quintessence of the hero and in a sort of riddling way takes the place of his name, which is left unmentioned until line 21. In *Od.* 10.330 ff., on the other hand, Circe realizes that her magic potion has no effect on the stranger and recalls a prophecy by Hermes that tells her who the stranger must be:

> Or are you Odysseus of many turns [*polutropos*]: the god with the golden staff [*khrusorrapis*], Argeiphontes, was always telling me that Odysseus would arrive, coming from Troy. (*Od.* 10.330–32)

Hermes' turn of mind is tricky and mocking. He warns Circe of the impotence of her magic against Odysseus; and when Odysseus arrives and naively moves toward Circe's house, Hermes comes to his rescue and gives him a magic counterpotion, the *molu*[17] (*Od.* 10.275–306) that makes Odysseus immune to Circe's potions. Hermes is authentically *polutropos* in this role, simultaneously warning Circe and cheat-

---

[15]For the etymology of Odysseus' name, see *DE*, s.v. "Odysseus" (with bibliography): "The true etymology is unknown."

[16]See Pucci, "Proem of the *Odyssey*," 39–62. Notice that as an epithet of Hermes in *Hymn to Hermes* 13 and 439, the word *polutropos* has no literal/metaphorical ambivalence, since it must mean "of many arts, resources"; thus it has only a metaphorical connotation. In *Od.* 1.1, however, the word could have literal or metaphorical meanings, or both at once.

[17]On the *molu*, see Hermann Güntert, *Von der Sprache der Götter und Geister* (Halle: M. Niemeyer, 1921); and Jenny Clay, "The Planktai and Moly: Divine Naming and Knowing in Homer," *Hermes* 100 (1972): 127–31.

ing her, letting her see light and blinding her. His magic is more powerful than hers, and she cannot predict his turns of mind.[18] Yet he deceives Circe through Odysseus so that the hero, not Hermes, appears to her as responsible for her humiliations and defeat. Accordingly, she calls Odysseus *polutropos*, an epithet that, as I noted, belongs exclusively to Hermes and Odysseus.

The exceptional occurrence of this epithet at this point (*Od.* 10.330)—when Hermes saves Odysseus from falling into Circe's trap—to characterize the essentially Hermes-like attributes of the hero, shows the sort of alliance between the hero and his patron god that is typical of the epic conception. But the hero remains a mortal human being, as the text makes clear, for instance in *Od.* 5.194 ff.:

> And he [Odysseus] sat there on the chair *from which Hermes had arisen* and the nymph placed by him all sorts of food to eat and drink such as mortal men eat. She sat facing divine [*theoio*] Odysseus and the maids placed by her nectar and ambrosia.

The text emphasizes the hero's privileged relationship with Hermes by explicitly mentioning the seat (*thronos*) on which the hero sits, taking the place of the god, and by repeating for Odysseus the same gestures of Calypso's offering and serving,[19] in what we know from the formulaic diction is a formal meal.[20]

The text, however, also underscores forcefully that, notwithstanding the divine patronage and divine attributes Odysseus receives, he is mortal. He eats bread. He is *theios*, not *theos*. The difference between adjective and noun opens up an immense gap: qualities are derivative, the thing itself is substantive. Even in this grammatical difference the specific relationship between the god and his hero is made evident.

The tension between divine qualities and the god himself is here limited to the realm of eating, in accordance with some deep-seated Odyssean and epic tenets. Since death will not touch Odysseus within the poem, the tension between the human and divine nature is here

---

[18]Hermes' magic is embodied in his golden staff, with which he opens and closes people's eyes: see *Od.* 5.47 and *Il.* 24.343.

[19]She served Hermes (*Od.* 5.85–94) but presumably she did not eat anything, and now she serves Odysseus while the maids serve her. Autolycus is mentioned in the *Iliad* as Odysseus' ancestor and as a thief (*Il.* 10.267), but no connection is drawn between him and Odysseus. Hermes too does not appear in any way connected with Odysseus. Even if the Iliadic Odysseus and the Odyssean Odysseus have many traits in common, Odysseus is not exactly the same character in both poems.

[20]By formal meal I mean a meal whose description includes the acts of setting the table and serving (see *Od.* 7.175 ff., 3.479–80, etc.), though the word *dais* and the implicit sacrifice do not occur.

momentarily reduced to the different menus Calypso offers her guests. It ignores the pathos that hangs over the entire *Iliad* and is made explicit in great Iliadic scenes.[21] This smiling difference, circumscribed by a table and a menu, is the best introduction one can imagine for Odysseus' travels, troubles, and tricks.

Writing: Orality

My *polutropos* Odysseus is now ready to appear after Athena's *mnēmē* has rescued him from concealment and Hermes' polytropy has indicated his epic destination. Yet before I present him in my critical pages, I wish to elaborate on the premises that underlie my critical discourse.

This book is a contribution to the textual (and aesthetic) understanding of the *Odyssey* and the *Iliad* from the point of view of the epic tradition and its formulaic diction. Contemporary critical and philosophical literature has shed some light on the nature of the linguistic sign and on the signifying processes that allow both oral and written signs to function. The complexity and the difficulty of these problems do not allow me to give here even a bare outline of the signifying process. Let me only indicate the points on which there is some consensus among critics of the Saussurian school. The chain of signifying differences that allow the spoken sign to communicate, the non-acoustic nature of these differences, and the homologous process that produces signification in the written sign are known today.[22] The alphabetically written signs, for instance, constitute a chain of differences: these differences are perceived only as different relationships.[23] These relational processes are the essential mechanism that produces signification in both the oral and the written sign. Nothing in the technical and contextual features that distinguish the oral from the written sign alters the full homology of these signifying processes and mechanisms. Consequently, the notion of and the potentiality for signification are homologous for both uses; the spoken

---

[21]See, for instance, *Il.* 22.393–94, 434–36.

[22]See, for instance, Jonathan Culler, *The Pursuit of Signs* (Ithaca: Cornell University Press, 1975), and *On Deconstruction* (Ithaca: Cornell University Press, 1982). These two books present a critical assessment of the achievements of the school of Geneva and its offspring, structuralism and semiotics, and of deconstruction.

[23]"The letter *t*, for example, can be written in various ways so long as it remains distinct from *l*, *f*, *i*, *d*, etc. There are no essential features that must be preserved; its identity is purely relational" (Culler, *On Deconstruction*, p. 101).

signs may deliver a signification that is as complex, rich, and intricate as the written ones.

If we transfer these definitions to oral and written poetry we realize that at the basic signifying level the two modes of poetry are capable of virtually the same achievements. Though the cultures that emerge through the oral techniques and those that develop through the written techniques may be very different because of the diversity and complexity of their communication networks, the process of signification itself does not disadvantage or cripple one of the two modes of signification. This realization should wreak havoc on the romantic views that even today identify *directly* written poetry with greater sophistication. The risk is that the notion of "primitivism," which has been successfully abolished by modern anthropology, may return under new and only apparently nobler labels such as "simplicity," "immediacy," or "myth." These qualifications of "orality," notwithstanding their apparent positive value, imply of course that only writing introduces critical thinking, rationality, and sophistication.

Some contemporary anthropologists have recently arued against this simplistic polarity: Ruth Finnegan, for example, has shown that there is no clear line between oral and written literature.[24] Her conclusion supports the theory on the nature of the sign that I have just touched upon and suggests that to assume a polarity between oral and written literature is to privilege deeply seated metaphysical assumptions.[25]

It is therefore with polemic intent and with a specific strategy in mind that in this book I speak of Homeric "writing." I use this expression to refer to the original oral mode of composition and performance of the lays that developed diachronically in the *Iliad* and the *Odyssey*. In this way I intend to provoke a rethinking on the nature of Homeric oral poetry as a phenomenon as technically complex and literarily sophisticated as written poetry.[26] This intent and this strategy, however, do not imply a denial or a neglect of the specific oral features of Homeric poetry. On the contrary, my research aims at

---

[24]Ruth Finnegan, *Oral Poetry* (Cambridge: Cambridge University Press, 1977), p. 2.

[25]On these assumptions, see Jacques Derrida, *De la grammatologie* (Paris: Minuit, 1967), published in English as *Of Grammatology*, trans. Gayatri Spivak (Baltimore: Johns Hopkins University Press, 1976); and "La Pharmacie de Platon," in *La Dissémination* (Paris: Seuil, 1972), published in English as *Dissemination*, trans. Barbara Johnson (Chicago: University of Chicago Press, 1981).

[26]I recognize that the term "writing" may introduce some ambiguity, as Paul Zumthor writes in *Introduction à la poésie orale* (Paris: Seuil, 1983), p. 27. Zumthor nevertheless acknowledges that "nos voix . . . portent la trace de quelque 'arch-écriture.'"

illustrating the specific literary aspects and awareness that Homeric oral diction exhibits with great force.

My book, therefore, goes against the grain of recent works that confuse the signifying homology of the signs and their different technology and by this confusion usually neglect what is specific to oral poetry. Jasper Griffin, for instance, has been able to justify the demise of the "oral theory" as unimportant for the aesthetic understanding of Homer.[27] Griffin's book, and its premises of course, arises from his teaching of undergraduates: the "intricacies of formulaic phraseology" and other technical questions "seemed almost to squeeze the poems out."[28] Yet the success of the book among the critics of the classical establishment proves that they too appreciate a return to the scholiasts' way of reading—that is, to a literary approach that generally looks for humanistic content from this as from any text. The cost of this sort of reading is the loss of discovering Homer's specific literary tone and sophistication in the very texture of his lines, in his unique diction and distinctive composition.

It would be foolish to say that the task of fully recouping these elements is easy. On the contrary, research on the distinctive features of an oral society and on the unique traits of oral poetry is full of traps and predicaments, and the conclusions must often be hypothetical for us modern readers immersed in writing. Yet our recognition of the homologous nature of the oral and written sign should not be a reason for ignoring the distinctive features of an oral society. The different economy and technology of the two signs deeply affect the ways of communicating. The demands made on the two signs are different. The mixture of written (painting, engraved signs, etc.) and oral communication is of an order that is difficult for us to reconstruct.[29]

These and other difficulties should not deter research, however. In the particular case of Homer, our ignorance of the specific modes of recitation and composition, of the diachronic formation of the poems, and of their monumental shape should not discourage us from fixing our attention on what is so uniquely Homeric—the diction—and from trying to unveil some of their secrets.

---

[27] Jasper Griffin, *Homer on Life and Death* (Oxford: Clarendon Press, 1980), pp. xiii–xv.

[28] Ibid., p. vii.

[29] The bibliography on the oral aspects of Greek society and culture is immense. I quote here Marcel Detienne, *L'Invention de la mythologie* (Paris: Gallimard, 1981). This book is exemplary of the arduousness of thinking seriously about myth and its oral means of expression. Bruno Gentili, *Poesia e pubblico nella Grecia antica* (Rome and Bari: Laterza, 1984), draws the highest profit possible from the "oral theory," especially in interpreting lyric poetry.

As I have already suggested, Homer's formulaic diction forces us to take seriously the question of intertextuality or allusion.[30] Because of the repetitive nature of Homer's diction, allusion is inevitable, and so is its significance. As Milman Parry observed, even the most mechanically repeated formula (or as he called it, "generic epithet") carries a *special* connotation.[31] Any formula belongs to the epic language and so to its special claims of being inspired and truthful. It is therefore a fragment of the epic language's extraordinary power to describe, interpret, and organize the world into a metaphysical construction of enormous rationality and coherence. Any formula endlessly repeats, in *different contexts,* the same claims to truthfulness, coherence, and identity. Yet because of the different contexts, no formula, even the most mechanical and the most indifferent to context, always "means" the same. An incessant play of sameness and difference animates the epic diction with connotational aspects of great literary significance.[32]

I grant that the study of the allusion along these lines tends to be subjective and demands careful, painstaking analysis. I grant too that my reading often becomes dense and difficult to follow, since it involves comparing several passages at once and assessing minute differences in texts and contexts. Yet the results are, I believe, rewarding. My contention is that formulaic diction has allowed its poets to weave an intricate texture of references, allusions, and quotations encompassing the entire epic cycle.

This extensive network of internal references adds to each passage a set of essential denotations and connotations. The precise repetition

[30]I use "intertextuality" to mean essentially "allusion." "Intertextuality," however, imparts a less forceful idea of authorial intentionality and of referentiality than does "allusion." The problem with "intertextuality" is that in its Barthian meaning it evokes the complete network of references that lies behind all the expressions of a text and consequently points to a utopian research; see Pietro Pucci, "Decostruzione e intertestualità," *Nuova Corrente* 93/94 (1984): 283–301. I use "allusion" and "intertextuality" interchangeably. I leave aside here the questions that, in the oral performance, concern the play of the shifters "you" (Muse) and "I" (me, the singer): the role of the "narrataire," that is, the Muse in relation to the singer, the "narrator"; the spatial and temporal shifters "here" and "now." The manifestation of those shifters cannot be considered as a distinctive feature of a transition from the oral to the written text. See Claude Calame, "Entre oralité et écriture: Enonciation et énoncé dans la poésie grecque archaïque," *Semiotica* 43 (1983): 245–73. In general I concentrate my attention only on one specific feature of oral diction: the formulaic repetition and the opportunities and difficulties it presents for the analysis of intertextuality.

[31]Parry defined a generic epithet as "one of the *ennobling* words of the language of poetry" (italics mine); see "Traditional Epithet in Homer," pp. 150–51.

[32]I call "connotation" the affective, stylistic, and practical values that are present in an expression. A word affects its listeners by what it does to them as well as by giving them a "meaning," a "denotation." Allusion adds a specific connotation since it evokes a comparison and therefore either a controversy or a gesture of admiration.

of an expression in determinate contexts creates a significant insistence and determination: the *specific* epithets of a hero, for instance, are essential denotations and connotations of his literary representation (*polutropos* points to the unique Hermes-like virtues of Odysseus); the difference between *timē* (honor) and *kleos* (glory) is essential in order to understand better the famous Sarpedon passage in the *Iliad* that is still read generically and without any focus.[33] Repetition, and the awareness of the repetition, is the matrix of important epic notions and conceptions such as *kleos* and *mnēmē*, which affect the whole idea of poetic activity and artistry, as we have already seen.

The network of internal references imparts to each line, scene, and episode the self-awareness of being part of a literary production in which one poet competes with another.[34] If we take this competition seriously, we must listen to the difference within the sameness of the repeated expression as to the artistic expression of the poets, their way of calling attention to their own texts. Retrieving such connotations is indispensable in order to understand the strategy of the text, its tendentious thinking, and its artistic force.

Now we can turn to Odysseus, as he appears in the Odyssean writing of book 5. Today we read it as a book, but at one time it was a song, a lay. Yet even as a song it was a kind of "writing," because it was always a *technically* complex form of orality and therefore an elaborate "text" composed through the differential systems of the "sign," words and gestures, through the gaps and lags of their movement, and through the allusion to other "texts."

---

[33]*Il.* 12.310–28; Griffin reads it just as Lord Granville did in 1763; see Pietro Pucci, "Banter and Banquets for Heroic Death," forthcoming in *Beyond Aporia?*

[34]Hesiod *Works and Days* 25–26: "and the potter is resentful of the potter, the carpenter of the carpenter, the beggar is jealous of the beggar, the poet of the poet." The statements that competition takes place among epic singers/poets and that one song (*aoidē*) is more praised than another (*Od.* 1.351–52) intimate what we would call "literary" awareness among professionals and audience. Even the necessary presence of the poet/singer among his listeners becomes an important literary theme in the *Odyssey*. The powerful effects of the poet's voice, the sudden entry of Penelope asking Phemius to cease from his wretched song, Phemius' final supplication of Odysseus are instances that testify to the physical and spiritual interaction between poet and audience and represent unforgettable scenes in the poem.

I

MULTIFACETED
DISGUISES

1

Sexual and Textual Jealousy

Tout reste à faire pour poser la question de ce qu'*il y a* dans un texte quand on prétend en délimiter le "corpus." Penser *à la trace,* ce devrait être, depuis assez longtemps, reconsidérer les evidences tranquilles du "il y a" et "il n'y a pas" "dans" un "corpus" en excédant, à la trace, l'opposition du présent et de l'absent, la simplicité *indivisible* du *limes* ou du trait marginal, le simplisme du "ceci a été pensé" ou "cela n'a pas été pensé," le signe en est présent ou absent, S est P. On serait alors tenu de réélaborer de fond en comble toutes les valeurs, elles-mêmes distinctes (jusqu'à un certain point) et souvent confondues de l'*impensé,* du *non-thématisé,* de l'*implicite,* de l'*exclu* sur le mode de la *forclusion* ou de la *dénégation,* de l'*introjection* ou de l'*incorporation,* etc., silences qui travaillent d'autant de traces un corpus dont elles paraissent "absentes."

Jacques Derrida, *La Carte postale*

Odysseus and Calypso enjoy food and drink with each other in what is their last *described* meal together.[1] After the enjoyment (*tarpēsan*) of the meal, Calypso turns to Odysseus with this expansive epithetic address (5.203):

> *Diogenes, Laertiadē, polumēchan' Odusseu*

> Descendant of Zeus, son of Laertes, resourceful Odysseus.

This is the first time we hear the formula in the *Odyssey,* since the vocative form of address can obviously be used only in the hero's presence. The use of this dignified expression of praise is not a matter of chance. In both the *Iliad* and the *Odyssey* this verse with its variant (found in *Od.* 24.192)[2] and the independent *polumēchanos*[3] occur in specific contexts and at specific moments. As Norman Austin re-

---

[1]See Stanford's commentary on 5.211 ff., 1:299.
[2]The line reads: *olbie Laertao pai, polumēchan' Odusseu.*
[3]See Athena's description of Odysseus as *polumēchanos* in *Od.* 1.205.

marks, "*Polymechanos* is no faded metaphor but one that proclaims that Odysseus is about to contrive or has just contrived some new stratagem, bordering on the magical."[4]

In our passage this dignified address can be taken seriously if we read it as glossing Odysseus' recent success in obtaining Calypso's oath, but it can be read as ironic and provocative if we assume Calypso implies that Odysseus, the hero of famous schemes, tricks, devices, and resources, now uncharacteristically behaves naively: he prefers to go home, heedless of the trouble he will have to face, simply to see a mortal woman, when if he remained with Calypso he could enjoy peace, the unparalleled beauty of the nymph, and immortality (203–313).

Read in this way, Calypso's words would be consonant with her jealousy, on which critics are quick to comment.[5] Yet I believe the sexual jealousy hinted at in her words coincides with other implications of a different nature. We can begin to perceive these implications when we listen to what the text has to say to us readers through its allusions, and therefore when we make sense of the precise repetition of the words with which Calypso opens her speech. Lines 203 and 204 repeat exactly the lines with which Athena, in the second book of the *Iliad*, addresses Odysseus when she asks him to stop the flight of the Achaeans. We recall that after Agamemnon's unhappy speech to the army a headlong flight ensues. At this point, upon Hera's suggestion, Athena appears to Odysseus and says (173–77):

Descendant of Zeus, son of Laertes, resourceful Odysseus, will you so flee home to the dear fatherland [*houtō dē oikonde philēn es patrida*

---

[4]Norman Austin, *Archery at the Dark of the Moon* (Berkeley: University of California Press, 1975), p. 53. This explanation applies only to the *Odyssey*. In the *Iliad*, although the epithet often does emphasize Odysseus' specific skills, not all uses of the formula can be glossed in this way. See in particular *Il.* 2.173, where Athena uses this line in asking Odysseus to stop the flight of the Achaeans; *Il.* 4.358, where Agamemnon uses the line as formal praise to offset the offensive statement he made earlier (4.399); *Il.* 9.308, where Achilles addresses Odysseus with this verse after listening to Odysseus' speech; and 23.723, where the epithet is in fact followed by Odysseus' *dolos*, "trick." Two other passages, *Il.* 8.93 and 9.624, are more difficult to gloss in accordance with Austin's explanation. The epithet *diogenes*, "descendant of Zeus," in both the vocative and the nominative, is used exclusively for Odysseus in the *Odyssey*, whereas in the *Iliad* it is used for other heroes (Achilles, Patroclus, Ajax) as well.

[5]Again, see Stanford's commentary on *Od.* 5.211 ff.: "These are Calypso's last recorded words. . . . They contain something of Juno's indignation at *spretae iniuria formae.*" The critics are led to this interpretation by Odysseus himself, who begins his reply to Calypso by saying, "Be not angry with me"; and of course, at the level of the characters' dialogue and self-perception, Calypso's words are an expression of resentment or jealousy. Readers, however, are allowed to see another aspect of her jealousy.

gaian/pheuxesth'] and fling yourself upon your benched ships? And would you leave to Priam and the Trojans their boast, Helen of Argos, for whose sake many Achaeans died in Troy, far from their dear homeland?

Calypso's words to Odysseus in 5.203–8 are:

Descendant of Zeus, son of Laertes, resourceful Odysseus, are you ready to go now at once back home to your dear fatherland [*houtō dē oikonde philēn es patrida gaian/autika nun etheleis ienai*]? May you fare well in spite of all. Yet if you knew in your mind the measure of pains that it is your destiny to fulfill you would remain here with me.

Because the allusion embraces one formulaic line and part of another it could easily be taken for a purely mechanical repetition. Nonetheless, the additional echoes we hear in both passages and the contextual, thematic connection between the two suggest that the texts read each other. To start with thematic similarities in both scenes: the central question is of a hasty, unconsidered flight home, of running away "in this way" (*houtō*) from a high and noble goal that has almost been achieved, and at great price. In the *Iliad* Odysseus is made sensitive to this situation and not only refuses to flee himself but also stops others from doing so. In the context of the passage in the *Iliad*, the *Odyssey* passage would read his decision to run away and flee homeward as foolish and hasty. Through the implication of this comparison, the reader is made aware that, in the *Odyssey*, "wily" Odysseus does not realize the foolishness of his rash departure and fails to persuade himself of his error.

In both situations the noble goal that Odysseus is asked to pursue is represented by a woman.[6] "Will you leave to Priam and the Trojans

---

[6]The *Odyssey* seems to allude to Odysseus' important role in book 2 of the *Iliad* two other times. In *Od.* 22.226 ff. Athena reproaches Odysseus, saying he lacks the *menos* and the *alkē*, "the fury" and "the force," that he had continuously while he fought nine years for Helen, until Troy was captured through his device. See below, p. 137. This Odyssean text clearly stresses Odysseus' fighting during the entire war at Troy, his *continuous, steadfast* contribution to its success, to the capture of Helen. It is reasonable to assume that Athena makes a general reference to the *Iliad*, and probably even to the specific passage we are concerned with in the *Iliad*, 2.173 ff. Note that in both passages (1) the speaker is Athena and (2) the goal of the war is Helen, and also that *Od.* 22.226 ff. makes the specific distinction between the nine years and the decisive tenth, a distinction Odysseus himself emphasizes so strongly in *Il.* 2.323 ff.

Furthermore, the two epithets for Helen, *leukōlenos* and *eupatereia*, also recall the *Iliad*, at least to the extent that the rarity of their usage is significant. *Leukōlenos*, "of white arms," occurs thirty-nine times in Homer, twenty-four times to form an epithet for Hera (which occurs only in the *Iliad*), three times for Andromache (in the *Iliad*), only four times for Nausicaa (*Odyssey* only), three times for Arete (*Odyssey* only), and their boast [*eukhōlē*], Helen of Argos?" Athena indignantly asks Odysseus. Similarly Calypso, echoing this Iliadic passage, suggests that if Odysseus returns home he will lose the love of an immortal nymph. Here the two texts resonate with echoing words: in the *Iliad*, Athena calls Helen "the boast" or the "shriek of triumph" (*eukhōlē*, *Il.* 2.176) that the Greeks, if they returned home, would allow Priam to raise; Calypso describes herself (*Od.* 5.211):

> Truly I boast [*eukhomai*] that I am not inferior to her [i.e., Penelope] in station and form.

That both women, Helen and Calypso, are described with a form of the idea of *eukhomai* ("I boast," "I strongly affirm," "I pray") is a striking coincidence. The different, though appropriate, meanings of the analogous words in the two texts seem to produce a sort of reciprocal echo. Helen is appropriately a glorious prize (the expression is formulaic) for which the Iliadic heroes fight, in accordance with the assessment of glory (*eukhos, kleos, kudos*) in that poem. Calypso's glory or boast, in contrast, concerns her sexual power over men. The two texts could not engage in dialogue through a more telling formal contact (the signifiers, *eukhōlē, eukhomai*) or, at the same time, on more opposite grounds.

The uncanny precision of these echoing words reinforces the allusive force of the initial repetition (see *Il.* 2.173–75; *Od.* 5.203–5) and supports the reader's feeling that the two contexts are tightly compared, but unfortunately it provides no decisive clue as to which text is the model for the other.

We can now return to the extensive contextual similarities between Athena's command to Odysseus (*Il.* 2.165 ff.) and Calypso's peroration to him (*Od.* 5.203 ff.). In both passages a similar moral censure stigmatizes the reprehensible action. In the *Iliad*, Agamemnon himself terms the failure to return without victory (that is, without Helen) "shameful for people in the future to know" (*Il.* 2.119), and later

---

twice for Helen (once in *Il.* 3.121 and once in *Od.* 22.226). Helen is therefore the *only* character for whom the *Odyssey* and the *Iliad* both use the epithet *leukōlenos. Eupatereia*, "from a noble father," for Helen, is distributed analogously: it occurs three times in Homer, twice for Helen (*Il.* 6.292; *Od.* 22.226) and once for Tiro (*Od.* 11.235). Another Odyssean passage that may refer to the episode of *Il.* 2.166 ff. is *Od.* 23.45 ff. (= 22.401). The lines "*heuron epeit' Odusēa meta ktamenoisi nekussi / estaoth'*" recall *Il.* 2.169–70: "*heuren epeit' Odusēa Dii mētin atalanton / hestaot'.*" Yet it is difficult to feel great confidence in this reference, since the two lines (*Od.* 23.45; *Il.* 2.169) have another echo in *Il.* 11.473.

Odysseus, having stopped the army's flight, agrees with that censure (*Il.* 2.298, *aiskhron*, and 285).[7] In the *Odyssey*, Calypso implies that Odysseus' desire to return home for the sake of Penelope is unbecoming because it is not proper to compare a mortal woman to a goddess.[8]

It is perhaps also important to notice that in both cases Odysseus' choice and action are essential to the continuation of the epic song. To put it bluntly, without that choice neither poem would exist. Let us see the reasons for this. When Agamemnon in *Il.* 2.119 declares that returning home is "shameful for people in the future to know," the text implies that no song of glory, no song of *kleos*, would be possible for the Greek expedition to Troy, but only a song of blame.[9] Accordingly, when Athena urges Odysseus to stop the fleeing army and when he succeeds in doing so, they become instrumental in saving the reputation (*kleos*) of the Greek army, and on the narrative level, therefore, also in ensuring the continuation of the *Iliad*. More explicitly, Odysseus collaborates with the modes and tenets of the epic song in the next scenes, first when he addresses the chieftains and extols Agamemnon's honor (*timē*) and then when, just as the praising epic poet would, he abuses Thersites, thus silencing the "blame poetry" that the most shameful of the Greeks represents in that scene.[10]

As for the *Odyssey*, obviously, without Odysseus' decision to return home there would be no *Odyssey*. Athena's memory (*mnēmē*) is a necessary condition for Odysseus' return, but perhaps not sufficient without Odysseus' own unwavering desire to see his home again.

These thematic correspondences between the *Iliad* and the *Odyssey* provide a context similar to that of the formal allusive repetitions. Before we assess the significance of this allusion, however, we should be aware that the Odyssean passage we have analyzed is surrounded by other repeated lines and itself refers to another Iliadic passage. Calypso's offer of immortality to Odysseus (*Od.* 5.209) may contain a glancing reference to and a rejection of other epic traditions, such as

[7]See A. W. H. Adkins, *Merit and Responsibility* (1960; reprinted Chicago: University of Chicago Press, 1975); and A. A. Long, "Morals and Values in Homer," *JHS* 90 (1970): 121–39, especially p. 129.

[8]Indeed, in the *Odyssey* the moral censure is malicious and frivolous, since the troubling theological question of the gods' superiority to humans is introduced in the specific context of whether gods or men are better *lovers* (see below, n. 11), and because Odysseus' unbecoming return home is a private, domestic act, unlike the public, historical one of the Greek army.

[9]I am of course using here the categories that Gregory Nagy has illustrated in *The Best of the Achaeans* (Baltimore: Johns Hopkins University Press, 1979), pp.222–42.

[10]Ibid., pp. 259–61. Let me add, however, that a specific appeal by Odysseus to glory (*kleos*) does not occur. The text sounds Odyssean in *Il.* 2.250–54, parodic of Odysseus in *Il.* 2.260 (see below, p. 42, n. 23), and again Odyssean in the speech in *Il.* 2.284 ff.

the *Aethiopis,* in which, we know, the most prominent heroes were immortalized.

Od. 5.105 contains another particularly telling literary allusion. Hermes, quoting Zeus, calls Odysseus "the most lamentable [*oizurōtatos*] beyond others, among the heroes who fought around Priam's city for nine years and who, on the tenth, went back home after destroying the city."[11] Thematically, the passage obviously refers to the epic cycle, the *Nostoi,* which chronicles the unfortunate return of heroes such as Ajax, Oileus, and Agamemnon. The text of the *Odyssey* is using the most knowledgeable critic of all, Zeus himself, to draw a comparison between the heroes of the *Nostoi* and the hero of the *Odyssey.* When Zeus declares that Odysseus is the "most lamentable" hero, he implies that the *Odyssey* is the more pathetic, forceful, pitiful poem of the two: in short, the better.

Formally, however, the text of the *Odyssey* refers to that of the *Iliad* and its tradition in its *literary* presentation of its hero.[12] The *Odyssey* contains for us, if not an allusion to the *Iliad,* at least a glance at it: in the *Iliad* only Achilles is defined as "lamentable" (*oizuros*), and he is so described in a comparative form, as is Odysseus in the *Odyssey.* Analogously, in his poem only Odysseus deserves the qualifying adjective *oizuros.*[13] This epithet, like the modifying phrase "the best of the Achaeans," is used only for Achilles in the *Iliad* and only for Odysseus in the *Odyssey.*

This evidence proves beyond doubt that the text of the *Odyssey,* in this first direct presentation of its hero in book 5, acknowledges and

[11]Note that in Zeus' reported words (*Od.* 5.21–42) such a statement does not occur. Hermes must have heard Zeus speaking of Odysseus in such a way on other occasions.

[12]Another allusion to the *Iliad*—or a reciprocal wink—occurs in Calypso's answer to Hermes. Calypso adapts an Iliadic line—or vice versa—(*Il.* 24.33): "You are hard, gods, and cruel" (*skhetlioi este theoi dēlēmones*), with which Apollo begins to indict the gods' insensitivity to Achilles' cruel treatment of Hector's body. Calypso, instead, says (118): "You are hard, gods, and jealous" (*skhetlioi este theoi zēlēmones*); and with this line she indicts the *male* gods who are jealous of the goddesses. The whole Olympian universe is suddenly viewed through the eyes of romance: Calypso's jealousy finds here a frivolous theological principle; the story of the love of Ares and Aphrodite is consistent with this view. On this point, see the illuminating remarks by Karl Reinhardt, *Die Ilias und ihr Dichter,* ed. Uvo Hölscher (Göttingen: Vandenhoeck & Ruprecht, 1961), pp. 471 ff. Even the concrete topography and reality of the Olympus that we behold in the *Iliad* lose precision in the first lines of *Odyssey,* book 5: see ll. 49–50 and Nitzsch 2:12–13.

[13]This adjective derives from *oizus,* "lamentation," "suffering"; *oizuō,* "to lament," "to suffer"; and ultimately from *oizō,* "to cry oi," "to cry alas." This adjective has the formulation in *-ros,* as in *anieros, almuros, arguros,* etc. The meaning can be either subjective ("lamenting," "suffering") or objective ("lamentable," "pitiful"). In Homer the adjective occurs fourteen times, and six of these times it qualifies a person: Achilles, once in the *Iliad,* and Odysseus, five times in the *Odyssey.*

limits its own literary territory by gestures of confrontation with the other poems and other heroic traditions from which it emerges, and by controversial acts of appropriation from those sources.

Calypso's offer implies for Odysseus the possibility of gaining immortality. Such a heroic ending is known in some epic and Hesiodic traditions,[14] in particular in the *Aethiopis* when Thetis snatches Achilles' body from the funeral pyre and carries it to the mythical land of Leuke,[15] which is, Gregory Nagy says, "an individualized variation on Achilles' other traditional abodes in the afterlife—either the Isles of the Blessed . . . or Elysium itself."[16] Indeed, Calypso's words, through their ironic innuendo, invite us to read a criticism of Odysseus' decision from the heroic perspective, like the one of the Cycle.[17] Resourceful Odysseus—the *Odyssey* suggests to readers, who alone can realize the force of the allusions—is really short on wits when he makes his fateful decision to return home, risking all the glory and renown he gained by destroying Troy. No glory (*kleos*) awaits him, only tribulation.[18] In this way the *Odyssey* makes clear to the reader that this new poem is not a *kleos* poem, that the vigorous encouragement with which the goddess Athena once inspired the hero now means nothing. There will be no new poem of glory—like the *Iliad*—to exalt Odysseus' name.

Finally, in Calypso's speech itself we find an allusion to a passage in the first book of the *Iliad*. Exclaiming

> Truly I say aloud [*eukhomai*, "I boast," "I affirm"] that I am not inferior to her [Penelope] in stature and form [*ou . . . keinēs . . . khereiōn eukhomai einai/ou demas oude phuēn*] for indeed it is unbecoming that a mortal woman rival goddesses in stature and beauty [*eidos*]. (5.211–14)

Calypso repeats some of the same words Agamemnon uses in comparing his wife, Clytemnestra, to Chryseis, the woman he lives with

---

[14]See Deborah Dickmann Boedeker, *Aphrodite's Entry into Greek Epic* (Leiden: Brill, 1974), pp. 64 ff.

[15]Proclus, *Aethiopis*, ed. Allen, p. 106, ll. 12–15.

[16]*Best of the Achaeans*, p. 167.

[17]To be sure, Calypso, speaking to Hermes earlier (5.118–28), intimates that male gods are jealous of the goddesses' affairs with mortals. The text suggests then that a permanent liaison between Calypso and Odysseus would not be normal (see Pierre Vidal-Naquet, "Valeurs religieuses et mythiques de la terre et du sacrifice dans l'Odyssée," in *Problèmes de la terre en Grèce ancienne*, ed. M. I. Finley [Paris: La Haye, 1973], pp. 269–92) and thus supports Odysseus' decision. For a more fully elaborated discussion on the question of the hero's immortality, see chap. 11, below.

[18]As I shall show later, the *Odyssey* mentions Odysseus' *kleos* only in connection with his past Trojan adventures. No *kleos* will come to him from his successful return home.

and prefers (*ou hethen esti khereiōn ou demas oude phuēn, Od.* 5.211–12; *Il.* 1.114–15).[19] The allusion is malicious: Calypso intimates for the reader that a hero in the Iliadic tradition would prefer his lover to his wife, as did Agamemnon, Odysseus' commander. In the absence of wars, therefore, and in view of Odysseus' past glory, he should terminate his human career there on the immortal bed of Calypso. He should be satisfied with the *kleos* he has reaped in the Iliadic tradition. In conclusion, Calypso delivers a message analogous to the one the Sirens give Odysseus: "stay here with us and listen to your past glories."

All these innuendos and intimations are stitched together by repetitions that weave a text of superior literary irony. An entire tradition is evoked, different heroic issues are presented and set against Odysseus' poor domestic pleasures: "Are you ready to go back home, now, at once?"

Yes, Odysseus is ready to return home because the heroic vision of the *Odyssey* agrees, on at least one point and to a significant degree, with that of the *Iliad:* the hero is mortal. Accordingly, the *Odyssey* cannot endorse Calypso's stance and offer. Odysseus must return and die as a mortal.[20]

Calypso already knows that Odysseus rejects her offer, and she graciously wishes him well.[21] Clearly, then, her jealous words aim at other purposes besides teasing (or provoking) Odysseus. They are, in fact, addressed to the reader, for whom they convey the force of literary jealousy that is concentrated in her name, her offer, and the

---

[19]Hans Ramersdorfer assumes the influence of *Od.* 5.211–12 upon the Iliadic passage: see his *Singuläre Iterata der Ilias,* Beiträge zur klassischen Philologie, vol. 137 (Königstein/Ts.: Hain, 1981), pp. 43–44. Of course he may be right, but the type of arguments he uses—and he uses them perceptively according to the methods of a time-honored school—shows the fragility of the foundation on which the conclusions are constructed. Ramersdorfer claims that Agamemnon's public comparison of his concubine with his wife (*Il.* 1.114–15) is "tasteless" and then quotes Pierre Chantraine to prove that the form *probeboula* (*Il.* 1.113) cannot be old (see *GH*). The subjective, arbitrary nature of the former claim and the tenuousness of the latter—a newer word can always enter an older text—are striking. Besides, the presumption underlying such arguments—that the borrower always contrives a less felicitous text than the original inventor—is romantic: it goes against the empirical fact that a later writer may improve upon an earlier one.

[20]On Odysseus' choice as the choice of humanity, see Charles Segal, "The Phaeacians and the Symbolism of Odysseus' Return," *Arion* 1 (1962): 17–63; and Vidal-Naquet, "Valeurs religieuses et mythiques," p. 283.

[21]Joachim Latacz defends the meaning "to fare well" for *chairō* here; see *Zum Wortfeld "Freude" in der Sprache Homers* (Heidelberg: C. Winter, 1966), p. 49. This meaning is psychologically correct, but in view of the joys Odysseus expects from his return, the text makes Calypso say also: "may you have joy, despite everything."

Iliadic repetitions. Jealousy must lie on both sides: on the side of the Iliadic tradition for which Odysseus' return implies a competitive epos, and on the side of the *Odyssey,* which displays its jealousy in the act of exposing the jealousy of Calypso, that is, of the Iliadic tradition.

Let us for the fun (and the seriousness) of it see how each text would read the other if we assume, for instance, that the *Odyssey* knew the Iliadic text or that the *Iliad* knew the Odyssean. In fact, it is most probable that both texts—as they now stand—were composed with knowledge of the tradition that precedes each of them and were therefore produced while they were, so to speak, simultaneously look-ing at each other. This assumption justifies both the effort of retriev-ing the reading each text gives of the other and the idea of consider-ing both readings as legitimate and necessary.

The *Odyssey's* remaking of *Il.* 2.172 ff.—and the allusion to that entire scene—could be interpreted as a smiling, ironic reading of the gloomy seriousness of the theme of return in that passage and in the *Iliad* in general. In contrast to the Iliadic Odysseus, who considers it base (*aiskhron*) to go home empty-handed (*Il.* 2.298), the Odyssean Odysseus wants to go home even on an empty raft, through all sorts of pain and toil. It is not necessary, of course, to legitimate the logic of survival—the yearning to complete the journey of life and to rest among domestic pleasures, whatever price must be paid—for this logic depends on the instinctive forces of man. This is the theme of the *Odyssey.*

Besides the thematic opposition—which is repeatedly spun and elaborated in the *Odyssey*—the text, by its parodic remaking, invites us to taste the pleasure and playfulness of Odyssean artistry. These aes-thetic qualities of the song, its playfulness and artistry, themselves constitute one aspect of the enticing pleasures in the sweetness of life.

If we see the *Iliad* as remaking the *Odyssey,* we find the *Iliad* insert-ing an Odyssean Odysseus (I mean the Odysseus of the Odyssean tradition) in its own atmosphere and style and changing him.[22] Throughout the entire *Iliad* Odysseus, unlike Achilles, Hector, Di-omedes, Priam, and even to some extent Ajax, never has a direct vision of a god. Whenever Athena reveals herself to Odysseus it is by her voice only (*Il.* 2.183). This aural sort of divine revelation to Odys-seus is almost exclusively Iliadic; it occurs rarely, if at all, in the *Odys-*

[22]Odysseus is called "equal to Zeus in ruses" (*Il.* 2.169); cf. above, note 12. He is made to allude to the *nostos,* "return," in terms that evoke the poetry of the returns (*Il.* 2.250 ff.); and other allusions are sprinkled throughout, for instance *Il.* 2.183 ff. and *Od.* 15.500 ff.

sey. In the *Odyssey*, however, Odysseus is almost the sole recipient of the divine visions apparently denied him by the *Iliad*. Accordingly, the *Iliad* signals to its readers that it refuses Odysseus the divine vision, whereas in the *Odyssey* he enjoys it *almost exclusively.*

This refusal is underscored by the contrast between Athena's full epiphany to Achilles in the first book of the *Iliad* (199 ff.) and her partial epiphany to Odysseus (in a similar situation) in book 2, where only her voice makes her presence known. This second passage, while implicitly comparing Odysseus with Achilles and contrasting Achilles' solitary brooding decision and plight with Odysseus' solidarity with the group, also reduces Odysseus' strengths merely to reasonableness and efficiency. His *mētis*, "shrewdness," would then consist of only these admirable but unheroic qualities.

Now if we try to read the innuendoes that the *Iliad* suggests by having Athena's words allude to Calypso's, we might read a more ironic text than the *Odyssey* has been able to contrive. Odysseus—the *Iliad* would suggest—applies his *mētis* to the proper deeds only when he is the modest but efficient character of the Iliadic narrative. In the *Odyssey*, his famous *mētis* leads him to foolish decisions and makes him pursue ridiculous, unheroic desires; even worse, at most his proverbial *mētis* is good for inventing entertaining tales to amuse people like Eumaeus.[23]

This particular interpretation of the two texts' mutual reading is of course only one of the many that could be proposed, and it claims only to be playful as the two texts *could* be when they are compared. Let us for the moment accept this interpretation and recognize then the *specular* reading each text would give of the other. One text would rewrite the other, but it would simultaneously be written by the other.

This point is of paramount importance for the readings I am retrieving in the course of my explorations in this book, and it needs another argument in its support: suppose, for instance, that we could determine for certain which of the two texts precedes the other. The certainty would be of extraordinary importance for all the historical questions that the two poems raise, but it would scarcely affect our specifically intertextual reading. The specularity of polemic gestures

---

[23]*Il.* 2.183 ff. evokes *Od.* 15.500 ff.: see Peter von der Mühll, *Kritisches Hypomnema zur Ilias* (Basel: F. Reinhardt, 1952), p. 40, and Hans Ramersdorfer, who believes in the priority of the Odyssean passage, *Singuläre Iterata*, pp. 49–51. In this Odyssean passage Odysseus makes up an amusing story about himself in order to get a cloak and also for the pleasure and edification of Eumaeus. If then the *Iliad* imitates and refers to that passage, the purpose could be, as I am suggesting, to make fun of the trivial expediency of the Odyssean Odysseus.

that we read in the two passages would remain untouched, even if we knew which of the two texts initiated the exchange, since by a sort of *après coup* the second text's reading would enforce this specularity on the earlier text.

2

The Birth of a New Hero

The most complicated mental achievements are possible without the collaboration of consciousness.

Sigmund Freud

therefore I forthwith put an end to the chapter,—though I was in the middle of my story.

Laurence Sterne,
The Life and Opinions of Tristram Shandy

Let us now return to our passage in *Od.* 5.203 ff. In the structure outlined above, Odysseus' rejection of Calypso (= the Concealer) intimates his return to his paternal house, to the world, *and to the epic song* (*aoidē*). The return home could signify all the meanings that "return," as a privileged metaphor, may hint at: return to oneself, to that which is "proper" to the self, and to death.[1] The return to the epic song means a *new* poem for Odysseus, and a new "heroic" substance, in accord with his new "pragma." All this is suggested through Odysseus' reply to Calypso. Tactfully, he first rephrases the aims of his return home and then, acknowledging the goddess's prediction of his future hardship and grief, says:

And if a god shall wreck the ship on the wine-dark sea, I'll endure it [*tlēsomai*], as I have within my breast a grief-enduring heart [*talapenthea*

---

[1]On the return of Odysseus—and especially on its symbolic meanings—the literature is immense, as might be expected. In chap. 10 I discuss the return that the text emphasizes in one crucial scene. For a recent interpretation of Odysseus' return as a "self-generated" rebirth to consciousness, see Ann Bergren, "Allegorizing Winged Words: Similes and Symbolization in *Odyssey* V," *CW* 74 (1980): 109–23. Her analysis gives a suggestive allegorical meaning to all the characters and events during Odysseus' travels from Calypso to the Phaeacians. On the metaphor of "travel" and its pertinence to the movement of philosophical and literary discourse, see Georges Van Den Abbeele, "Economy of Travel in French Philosophical Literature" (Ph.D. diss., Cornell University, 1981).

thumon]. For I have already suffered many times and toiled many times
in waves and war. Let this be added to the tale of those. (5.221 ff.)

This is Odysseus' answer: a text full of pathos and meditated suffering is set against the malicious, even frivolous text of Calypso. Here is
the epitome of the *Odyssey*'s programmatic responses to all other texts
that are quoted or alluded to or glanced at in the passages I have
cited.

Not one of the formal conditions that identifies a character as heroic and pathetic is missing: the mention of a god-sent necessity that
characterizes Odysseus as the target of a divine curse,[2] and implicitly
also of divine privileges; the solitary destination and experience of the
hero, alone in his experience and isolated from the whole world, so
that he acquires a second nature besides the ordinary one he shares
with common mortals; the courageous determination (*prohairesis*) to
risk his life, refusing or disdaining a more comfortable alternative;
the awareness that he is making some tale or history after all ("let this
be added to the tale of those").

Although all the formal conditions that shape an Iliadic hero are
present in this passage, no lines like these would ever surface in the
Iliad. What that poem would not accept in its text is a certain passivity
in Odysseus' sense of heroism, a somewhat vulgar pride in, as it were,
exhibiting the marks of his griefs, blows, humiliations, defeats, and
survivals and so great a tolerance for these injuries that his already
long record could be *indefinitely* lengthened. The hero is already
thinking of the length, of the excitement, of the adventurousness of
his own poem, not of the *kleos* of his death.[3]

All these new features are in large part contained in the two words
that are formed from the root *tle-*: *tlēsomai* and *talapenthēs*. These two
words compose line 222: "I'll *endure* it as I have in my breast a
grief-*enduring* heart." They also give the line a highly stylized tone, for
talapenthēs is a *hapax*, it constitutes an etymological figure with *tlēsomai*,
and it refers to the root *tle-*, which in the *Iliad* as well is applied solely to
Odysseus. This last fact is the most astonishing of all, for it implies that,
to put it bluntly, the *Odyssey* is able to express its fully un-Iliadic heroic
ideal by using Iliadic material. In fact, of the four examples of *tlēmōn*

[2]Poseidon is, in Gregory Nagy's terms, the ritual antagonist of Odysseus; see *The Best
of the Achaeans* (Baltimore: Johns Hopkins University Press, 1979), pp. 142–53.
[3]See the perceptive general remark by Tzvetan Todorov, *The Poetics of Prose*, trans.
Richard Howard (Ithaca: Cornell University Press, 1977), pp. 62–63: "If Odysseus
takes so long to return home, it is because home is not his deepest desire: his desire is
that of the narrator."

that occur in Homer, all appear in the *Iliad*, and in three of them *tlēmōn* is the exclusive epithet of Odysseus. In the fourth, *tlēmōn* is a generic designation for the supporters of the Trojans.[4] In the *Odyssey* the precise form *tlēmōn* never occurs, but of course several *tle-* compounds or *tle-, tla-, tala-* forms characterize Odysseus exclusively, as we have already seen in his statement (*Od.* 5.222, *tlēsomai en stethessin ekhōn talapenthea thumon*).

A more important question arises when we ask ourselves the meaning of *tlēmōn*, for like the verb itself, *tlēnai*, the adjective may mean either "daring" or "enduring."[5] As Pierre Chantraine explains in his *Dictionnaire étymologique*, the root *tla- tle-* means "to take upon oneself," whence, on the one hand, "to put up with [endure, support]" and on the other, "to take responsibility for,"[6] a meaning, similarly, of *tolmē, tolmao*. *Tlēmōn* too has a "split" and, though contiguous, opposite meaning (*enantiosema*): "enduring" or "daring." And because the epithet *tlēmōn* in each of the four passages of the *Iliad* can be understood to have one or the other meaning, an absolute interpretation is elusive. Analogously, the appropriate meaning of *tlēnai*—whose connotations range from "enduring" or "suffering" to "taking on the responsibility" and thus "resolving," "daring," or "feeling confident"—cannot always be ascertained in each passage.[7] Does context help us to distinguish one meaning from the other, at least in the three occurrences of *tlēmōn?* Yes and no. Yes, if we consider the meaning of the epithet to be adapted specifically to the context; no, if we assume that the meaning of the epithet is independent of the context. Because both conditions occur,[8] it would not be possible to reach any certain conclusion were it not for *Il.* 10.231, where the noun-epithet *tlēmōn Odusseus* is played upon etymologically and para-

---

[4]The three occurrences of *tlēmōn* as an epithet for Odysseus are *Il.* 5.670, 10.231, 10.498. The fourth example appears in *Il.* 21.430, "*Troessin arōgoi . . . tharsaleoi kai tlēmones.*"

[5]An analysis of words with this root can be found in Benedetto Marzullo, *Il problema omerico*, 2d ed. rev. (Milan and Naples: R. Ricciardi, 1970). See also Ernst Heitsch, "*Tlēmosynē*," *Hermes* 92 (1964): 257–64.

[6]"Prendre sur soi, d'ou d'une part 'supporter,' de l'autre prendre la responsabilité de" (*DE*, 4:1088–90).

[7]Most often critics, commentators, and translators do not account for their choices, and often they take upon themselves the responsibility for one meaning or the other, even when the most neutral connotation would be possible.

[8]*Polumēchanos*, for instance, is certainly not a dead epithet in the *Odyssey:* it is always used in relation to some contextual trickery or canny behavior of Odysseus, as Norman Austin has shown in *Archery at the Dark of the Moon* (Berkeley: University of California Press, 1975), p. 53.

phrased by "for his heart was always daring [*etolma*]."[9] Here, *tolmaō* must mean "to dare"—the meaning "to endure" is a rarer usage, one that does not seem to appear in the *Iliad*—so the causal clause *almost forces us* to interpret *tlēmōn* as "brave," "bold," "daring." The same interpretation is probable for at least one other passage, *Il.* 5.670.[10] Accordingly, the *Odyssey* would represent the un-Iliadic new heroism of Odysseus with the same root words that in the *Iliad* characterize Odysseus specifically. The *signifier* is the same, but the *signified* is possibly different.[11]

The evidence of the allusion, however, does not consist simply of the repetition, which is itself rare; it includes a significant variation and a specific and exclusive referent. In both *Il.* 5.670 and 10.231 Odysseus' specific epithet *tlēmōn*, "daring," is used to qualify his heart: he has *tlēmona thumon* (*Il.* 5.670), and he is "*tlēmōn* Odysseus . . . for his heart always *etolma*" (*Il.* 10.231). Turning to the *Odyssey* (5.222), we find "*tlēsomai . . . ekhōn talapenthea thumon*, "I'll endure as I have a

---

[9]It is true that here too Paul Mazon, for instance, disregards the context: see his *Homère, Iliade*, 4 vols. (Paris: Belles Lettres, 1937–38). In principle he may be correct, but he seems to neglect what is at the least a strong contextual suggestion in favor of the other meaning.

[10]In *Il.* 5.670 Odysseus is described as *tlēmona thumon ekhōn*, "having a *tlēmona* heart"; this heart (*ētor*) in turn "stirs him" to fight against Sarpedon. The meaning "enduring" would be anticlimactic, and some commentators translate it as "bold" (see A. H., for instance); others, however, do translate it as "enduring" (see, among others, Mazon). Comparison with *Il.* 22.251–53 may provide further evidence in support of "daring." In *Il.* 10.227 ff. the text lists the heroes who are ready to assail the camp of the Trojans: "also *tlēmōn* Odysseus was ready to plunge into the throngs of the Trojans, for his heart was always daring [*aiei . . . thumos etolma*] in him." Here the interpretation of *tlēmōn* as "daring" seems almost inevitable, since the epithet is explained by a word of the same root, *tolmaō*, which in the context most probably means "to take up responsibility," "to dare." See Marzullo, *Problema omerico*, pp. 64–65. No similarly precise interpretation is possible for the third *tlēmōn* passage, 10.498. Here *tlēmōn* could mean both "daring" and "enduring," although the connotation of bravery would be more appropriate to the context. Marzullo, pp. 24 ff., maintains also that *polutlas* in the *Iliad* and in the other tradition must signify "who dares all sorts of things" and finds confirmation of this in *Il.* 5.670, where *tlēmōn* must mean "daring," as we have seen above. He also notes the presence of the article *ho* in *Il.* 10.231, 498, which could be a mark of more recent composition.

[11]To appreciate the difference requires some effort. On the connotational level, the *tlēmōn* epithet in the *Iliad* implies active resolve, while the *tle-* forms in the *Odyssey* passage suggest passive acceptance of griefs. Because the denotation of the *tle-* root is "to take upon oneself," it is possible to see a drifting between the two usages and to formulate it as follows: in the *Iliad*, *tlēmōn* means "to take upon oneself" in the sense of an active, bold resolve, whereas in the *Odyssey* passage the analogous forms *tlēnai, talapenthēs*, etc., express the resolve to take upon oneself all sorts of grief. The contexts in which the word appears show up the contiguity and continuity of the meaning and also its difference.

grief-enduring heart." By formally remaking *Il.* 5.670 (*ekhōn tlēmona thumon*), the text characterizes Odysseus' heart and constructs an etymological figure analogous to *Il.* 10.231, *tlēmona-etolma*.

The formal precision of these repetitions and the unresolvable, contiguous difference in the meaning of the same root words suggest that the two texts are probably engaged with one another. Notice that while the *Odyssey's talapenthea thumon* absolutely excludes the meaning "daring"—one cannot "dare" griefs, only "endure" them—the *Iliad's* "for his heart always dared" (10.231) does not absolutely exclude the meaning of "enduring" for *tlēmōn* Odysseus. This fact makes the Iliadic text more baffling and consequently more ironic, as if it were aware that the *Odyssey* reduces the spectrum of the word's meanings.[12] On the other hand, the *Odyssey* seems to want to overdo, to exaggerate, for not only is *talapenthēs* a *hapax*, it is also a compound, that is, a form that sounds typical of the *old* epic diction.[13]

That two possibly different—and significantly so—signifieds are exhibited by the two texts under the aegis of the same or analogous signifiers implies a complex strategy of concealment and exposure, continuity and disruption, loyalty and betrayal.[14] Nothing is more scriptorial than this play acted out on the surface of the signifier: one text rewrites the other, *hiding* the possible rewriting beneath the sameness of the repeated signifier. The difference between the two signifieds of the analogous signifiers, if real, increases our perception

[12]One might be tempted to interpret the otherwise redundant *eni phresi*, "in his breast," in *eni phresi thumos etolma* (*Il.* 10.232) as a paraphrasis of the common epithet for Odysseus, *talasiphron*. Note that in *Od.* 5.222 a textual variant for *talapenthea* is *talasiphrona* in a manuscript, L4 (Allen).

[13]Antonino Pagliaro, "Origini liriche e formazione agonale dell'epica greca," in *La poesia epica e la sua formazione*, Problemi Attuali di Scienza e di Cultura, no. 139 (Rome: Accademia Nazionale dei Lincei, 1970), pp. 31–58, especially p. 46.

[14]The level of the poets' textual consciousness of this process does not come into question here. What I wish to stress is simply that the traditional epic diction, *because* traditional, is necessarily self-referential. Each specific usage refers to a previous one and acquires meaning, connotations, and force by referring to previous usages in a prior text. Accordingly, this traditional language could not avoid constant referentiality: as our analysis shows, the textual force of the *Odyssey* and of the *Iliad* lies in their linguistic relationships, differences, and similarities. This textual relationship is to some extent indifferent to the priority of one text over the other. When scholars read *tlēmōn* in the *Iliad* as "enduring," they are reading the *Iliad* after the *Odyssey*; but then why didn't the *Odyssey* use *tlēmōn*? To raise this question, however, is still a way of privileging one text and making it a model for the other. Better to realize that *tlēmōn Odysseus*, "daring" Odysseus in the *Iliad*, could be a singular variation on the *tlē-, tla-, tala-* theme that contributes the "insistence" of Odysseus' epithets. Just so, *talapenthēs* would be the *Odyssey's* singular and unique variation of the same theme. This theme (and its "insistence") does not exist as such but becomes perceived only in its "variations."

of the difference at work in the outlined strategy of exposure and concealment.

If we accept the difference between the two analogous signifiers as certain, we can see the two traditions as being engaged in a heroic confrontation. As *tlēmōn* Odysseus changes into *talapenthēs*, he would step out of the Iliadic text and its related traditions and, while seemingly remaining his prior self, would enter into the *Odyssey*. He must indeed be himself, the same Odysseus with his heoric pedigree, his formulaic epithetic traditions, and his thematic consistency, yet he must also be a new hero. This literary process occurs in the sliding of the signified of the *tle-* forms. As a result of this sliding, the "daring" man becomes "enduring"—that is, the man of many turns, travels, griefs—and thus implicitly "surviving."[15] This implicit idea of "survival" goes hand in hand with the notion of *nostos*, "return," whose etymology means "return to safety, to light," and with the polytropy of Odysseus (*Od.* 1.1). For *polutropos* indicates that Odysseus is the man of many travels and of many turns of mind and language. The etymological connection of *noos*, "mind," with *nostos*, "return," confirms the double meaning of *polutropos*. We find here a cluster of images that mutually support each other: *nostos*, "return," *noos*, "mind," *polutropos*, "of many travels and of many turns of mind," *tle-* forms, "enduring" (and implicitly "surviving").[16]

---

[15]This notion of survival not only is implicit in the connotation of *tle-* as "taking upon oneself" ("enduring" or "resisting") grief, but is also made explicit in the contexts where *tle-* forms with this connotation occur. In our passage, *Od.* 5.221 ff., Odysseus can display his readiness to *tlēnai*, "endure" grief, because he already knows that he finally will reach home (see Calypso's words in 206–7). Besides, Odysseus leaves undecided what specific blow he will receive from Poseidon. Literally all he says is, "If a god shall wreck on the wine-dark sea." He does not mention, and thus does not choose between, the two possible objects of "wreck": "me" or "the ship." He must mean the ship, but the verb *rhaiō* can also be used for a person, as in *Od.* 9.459. Were Poseidon to wreck him, he would "endure" death, not grief. This essential indecision is simultaneously emphasized by the ellipsis of the verb's object and glossed over by the implications of "enduring griefs." This indecision reveals the trickiness or deception that writing harbors even when exhibiting its supposedly clear-cut meanings: here this indecision reveals how difficult it is for the text to hide completely the idea that "enduring" necessarily implies survival, and so a questionable form of heroism.

[16]See Douglas Frame, *The Myth of Return in Early Greek Epic* (New Haven: Yale University Press, 1978), pp. ix ff.; and Pietro Pucci, "The Proem of the *Odyssey*," *Arethusa* 15 (1982): 39–62.

3

Allusion and Misreading

> The work can be seen in bookstores, in card catalogues, and/or
> course lists, while the text reveals itself, articulates itself according to
> or against certain rules. While the work is held in the hand, the text
> is held in language: it exists only as discourse.
>
> Roland Barthes, "From Work to Text"

The indetermination of the Iliadic *tlēmōn* and the defined meaning
of the Odyssean *tlēnai* can be endlessly construed to give an orientation, a pre-text, and a meaning to the repetition of their analogous
signifier. Whatever construction one erects, however, must always
crumble under the test of the indetermination of *tlēmōn*, for the Iliadic *tlēmōn* hides the difference, since it can mean exactly the same as
the Odyssean *tlēnai*, "patient," "to be patient"; and it simultaneously
enhances the difference, since it can, and possibly does, mean "daring," a meaning that *tlēnai* in *Od.* 5.222 cannot have. The *Odyssey*'s
expression can be taken as the writing that is provoked by the unreadability of the Iliadic epithet; vice versa, the Iliadic writing can be taken
as the ironic reading of the Odyssean misreading of the traditional
tlēnai, which is open to both of the contiguous meanings of "taking
upon oneself."

This difference does not sufficiently comment on itself to allow us
to resolve it. This difference lies as a limit, a contiguity between the
two texts, a limit that produces them as being inscribed on that line.[1]
Whether we call this line the place of allusion or of intertextuality, we
confront it as the realm of "implicitness," as Oswald Ducrot observes.[2]
The reading of the allusion in the realm of implicitness amounts to a

---

[1]The intertextuality (or the allusion) produces the text. For a recent evaluation of the
theoretical difficulties of intertextuality, see Jonathan Culler, *The Pursuit of Signs*
(Ithaca: Cornell University Press, 1975), pp. 80–118. See also my "Decostruzione e
intertestualità," in *Nuova Corrente* 93/94 (1984): 283–301.

[2]"Presupposizione e allusione," in *Enciclopedia Einaudi*, vol. 10 (Turin, 1980), pp.
1102 ff.

critical decision of the reader. Of course, choosing not to read the allusion is also a reader's critical decision.

There are, fortunately, several contextual conditions that suggest the presence of the allusion. It is clear that the formulaic repetitions I have singled out—for instance *Od.* 5.222 (*ekhōn talapenthea thumon*) and *Il.* 5.670 (*tlēmona thumon ekhōn*), with the addition of *Il.* 10.231— have at least three characteristics in common: they are unique or very rare, they contain a difference of form and perhaps of meaning, and they apply to a unique and exclusive theme, in this case, to Odysseus.[3]

Once the decision to read the allusion is reached, however, the meaning of the allusion still remains in the realm of implicitness. The allusion may uphold simultaneously all sorts of orientations, pre-texts, and intuitions: an undecidable spectrum of possible readings emerges. For instance—to begin with the most general question—the concealment of the signified in the sameness or similarity of the sig-nifiers could imply an extremely alert textual consciousness. But in this case it remains impossible to say whether this extreme con-sciousness testifies to the exceeding assuredness of the texts, their superb control of tradition, or their passivity before the tradition—in other words, to their author(s)' seigneurial control, or utter depen-dence and fear.[4] The punning, allusive, referential art of the *Odyssey* could testify either to a teasing, ironic amusement the text finds in subverting the epic tradition or to a mortal fear of abandoning the tradition and thus remaining speechless. We remember the serious warning the *Iliad* gives to the poets through the example of Thamyris:

> Here the Muses met Thamyris, the Thracian, and put an end to his singing . . . for he had declared in boast that he would prevail, even if the Muses themselves, the daughters of Aegis-bearing Zeus, were sing-ing against him; and they in their rage made him mute [*pēron*],[5] took away from him the holy song and made him forget the art of the lyre. (*Il.* 2.594–600)

The impossibility of pinning down the specific sense of an allusion and the temptation for the reader to use one sense of the allusion to

---

[3]Milman Parry implied that the epithet *tlēmōn* should have come to the *Iliad* from the *Odyssey*, but because the *Odyssey* never uses it, Parry argued, the reason never emerged for this use; see Parry's essay "The Traditional Epithet in Homer," in *The Making of Homeric Verse*, ed. Adam Parry (Oxford: Clarendon Press, 1971), p. 82. This assump-tion, which of course protects the mechanistic Parryan view, is improbable in view of the contextual conditions I am describing.

[4]See Paul de Man, "Hypogram and Inscription: Michael Riffaterre's Poetics of Read-ing," *Diacritics* 11, no. 4 (1981): 29.

[5]*Pēron* is a word of uncertain meaning: it has also been taken to mean "blind."

sustain and buttress his interpretation are complementary and inevitable features of allusion. I will try to escape both the paralysis of the former condition and the complacency of the latter by activating a whole spectrum of senses, thereby destabilizing all senses. My exercise will be an exercise in reading the readability/unreadability of the text. At other times, I will point to what seems to me the strongest reading the text produces, and I shall point to this sense even if I know that in doing so I am interpreting in some collusion with the reader's irrepressible desire to give a specific sense to the allusion. Thus, for instance, I have presented a reading that suggests a jealous posture in the *Odyssey,* and I have also sketched the outlines of a reciprocal jealousy.

The reason for starting from this textual paranoia is that despite the risks such reading presents to the critical operation, it certainly has an initial advantage: it involves us in textual "mirrorings" that demystify the traditional notions of textual "self-containedness" and "integrity." We may speak of the open, iridescent surface of the texts, of their containing other texts within themselves, and vice versa.[6] Furthermore, the emphasis on the allusive moment of the text helps us understand that any narrative is simultaneously an image of the text's self-awareness, since it is composed with the eye on other texts. The "textuality" of a text is precisely this reading::writing process through which a text takes shape.

In allusion, all textual intentions, even the textual intentions of showing or concealing the difference, or both—whether there are any or not—are fragmented, refracted, elusive. The fragmentation of the authorial or textual intentions as they are caught in the process of difference, or in repetition, creates that textual lack *and* excess of meanings, that iridescence of meanings, that prompts new writing. In other words the text—and not only the Homeric text—remains to be forever rewritten, because it always contains in itself a partial obscurity or refracts an excess of light. Writing, even the form of oral composition, always emerges from the dizziness provoked by this instability. With *ekhōn talapenthea thumon,* the *Odyssey*—if it is the *Odyssey* that concludes the long tradition—might aim at terminating the oscillating instability of *tle-* forms for Odysseus; but of course it opens

---

[6]For the general extension of such containing of other texts, see Culler, *Pursuit of Signs,* pp. 80–118. On the critical risks of a reading that capitalizes on the oedipal hostility of the texts, see Neil Hertz, "The Notion of Blockage in the Literature of the Sublime," in *Psychoanalysis and the Question of the Text,* ed. Geoffrey Hartman (Baltimore: Johns Hopkins University Press, 1978), pp. 62–85; reprinted in Hertz, *The End of the Line* (New York: Columbia University Press, 1985), pp. 40 ff.

up new instabilities, since the notion of "endurance" implies that of survival and beckons toward that of pleasure.

Playful Misreadings

The metaphor that turns the *tle-* form into meaning either "daring" or "enduring" is itself characterized by the two metaphorical meanings of *tlēnai*. Any expression becomes a metaphor when it *takes on* a different "meaning" while the signifier *withstands* the change and remains the same. In a certain sense, it dares to risk the death of its prior self in order to become a new expression encapsulated in the same signifier. The expression persists and survives by changing in this specific way.

But what does it survive for? The metaphorical process is vital to language, for the metaphorical polytropy allows it to extend, modify, and enrich its semantic range. Analogously, in passing from *tlēmōn*, "daring," to *talapenthēs*, "patient"—or vice versa—the character Odysseus enlarges and modifies his heroic possibilities and brings forth a new epic narrative. As endurance and polytropy go along together they outline a constant spinning of turns, and in fact they map the movement of Odysseus as a movement beyond and after his return to Ithaca.

Our text therefore seems to discourage the metaphysical interpretations that have so often been given of Odysseus' return as a return to humanity, or to himself (and accordingly as the acquisition of a "humanistic" self-knowledge).[7] From another perspective, however, the text is not without some complicity in these interpretations, for Odysseus' organic manyness and his endless turns are to some extent played down on many occasions. Take, for instance, Calypso's attitude toward Odysseus' return. How is it that she, who knows the future, does not tell him how vain or parenthetical his return home is to be? Is her jealousy blinding her? Does Odysseus' display of some "dissatisfaction" with her make her unable to see beyond her rival, for whom he longs all the time? Is Calypso so representative of the competition between texts that the *Odyssey* does not allow her to reveal the illusory goal around which Odysseus' return spins? Calypso, of course, levels some irony against his return: she alludes directly and indirectly, as I have suggested, to Odysseus' poor, wretched, unwise,

---

[7]See, for instance, W. B. Stanford, *The Ulysses Theme* (Oxford: Blackwell, 1954), pp. 39–41 and relevant notes.

and narrow-minded choice in relation to the alternatives he would embrace by remaining with her. She does not, however, remind him that the wife he yearns for so much will not engage his desire very long, and that he will abandon her again after his return (*Od.* 11.121 ff., 23. 248 ff.). She prefers to draw a comparison between herself and Penelope and a parallel between the possibility of his "guarding her house and being immortal"[8] (*sun moi tode dōma phulassois / athanatos t'eiēs, Od.* 5.208–9) and his choice of Penelope, for whom he longs (*eeldeai,*[9] 5.210), "always, and all the time." In this way Calypso misses the opportunity to give a thematic confirmation to the spinning and drifting of Odysseus' turns and implicitly sustains a metaphysical interpretation of his return as a movement pointing to self-recuperation, to the closing of experience and therefore to the process of reaching the fullest measure of humanity.

The irony in Calypso's words, however, is strong: against the privilege of immortality and against the noble task of protecting the house, tokens of lordly concerns, Calypso pits Odysseus' sexual desire[10] for Penelope, and by recalling the episode of Hera's offer to Hypnus she underlines for the reader a special example of the foolishness and rashness of Odysseus' desire.[11] If the text implicitly and on a surface reading opens itself up symbolically to all sorts of

---

[8]The notion of protecting the house points to his responsibility as a husband (*Od.* 23.151). In his absence, that responsibility falls to a friend of the husband (*Od.* 2.227) or, alternatively, to the wife (*Od.* 19.525 ff.). The protection Calypso asks for thus includes the reciprocal responsibilities of a faithful couple.

[9]The expression *tēs aien eeldeai ēmata panta,* "whom you always long for all the time" (*Od.* 5.210), returns almost literally in *Il.* 14.269, 276, when Hera offers Hypnus one of the Graces as a wife and comments upon her: *hēs aien himeireai ēmata panta,* "whom you always desire all the time" (*Il.* 14.269). When Hypnus accepts Hera's gift he says the words: *"hēs t'autos eeldomai ēmata panta,"* "whom I long for always all the time" (*Il.* 14.276). This is the only formulaic expression that is built around *eeldomai:* the repetition is therefore pointed, and the erotic force of the verb is obvious in both texts. The line in *Il.* 14.269, however, occurs only in a few manuscripts of the *Iliad* and is, besides, metrically wrong; *himeireai* must be a mistake for *eeldeai,* and editors accordingly reject the line. Nevertheless, it is important to recognize that this interpolation, if *Il.* 14.269 is one, probably has its source in the specular relationship between *Il.* 14.269 and *Od.* 5.209 ff. (See A. H. on *Il.* 14.268.) Note that the necessary *eeldeai* of *Il.* 14.269 corresponds to *Od.* 5.210 and that the faulty *himeireai* corresponds to the *himeiromenos* of *Od.* 5.209. *Himeireai* is probably a gloss for *eeldeai* and has entered into the text as glosses often do in later times of transmission.

[10]The verb *eeldomai* does not necessarily denote sexual desire, but in the formula of *Od.* 5.210 and *Il.* 14.269, 276 this denotation seems granted both by the context and by the hyperbolic adverbs: "always, all the time." The contexts in which this verb occurs show that it often expresses a desire *for what is one's own:* a wife, husband, son, home, fatherland, property (*Od.* 5.219, 15.66, 21.209, 24.200). Though the verb is a "survival" (*DE*) it occurs twelve times in the *Odyssey* and seven times in the *Iliad.* Our *Odyssey* is archaic or seems to archaize.

[11]Hera's offer is clearly intended as a bribe. Hypnus has resisted Hera's request by mentioning Zeus' anger at him for interfering with Zeus' plans on another occasion.

humanistic pieties, it also reveals that the immediate grounds for Odysseus' decision are sexual: he enjoyed sex with Calypso for some time, but now Calypso does not attract him any longer (*Od.* 1.151 ff.) and he desires to go home.[12] It is correct, then, that in Calypso's eyes Odysseus chooses to go back home on the urge of his sexual desire, but the *Odyssey* has a more positive view than the *Iliad* of this pleasure. By having Calypso quote the Iliadic Hera, the *Odyssey* suggests that sexual pleasure is also a divine pleasure; and we have only to await Demodocus' song on the loves of Ares and Aphrodite to have a full measure of the Odyssean flirtations with sex.

The scene unravels a marvelous play of ironies by making the reader witness to a series of misreadings. Odysseus is made to beg Calypso: "Do not feel angry at me [*khōes*] on this account" (*Od.* 5.215). Picking up the nymph's last words (on her superior beauty), Odysseus reads in them her jealousy. And of course she is jealous: her reference to Chryseis proves that she has sex on her mind. Yet her ironic allusions to the code that makes his decision unwise and narrow-minded are lost on him. His words ascribe to her a dangerous power while magnifying his own power of seduction. Odysseus' male confidence when dealing with women is made obvious in his first words. And these initiate a long history of critical commentary on the significance of Calypso's utterance.

On her turn the nymph misreads Odysseus when she teases him in accordance with his Iliadic past, since she should know that he is *talapenthēs* and no longer *tlēmōn*. The scene interweaves these misreadings as psychological misreadings while revealing, through the allusions, that they are also textual. In this frame of reference, that the frivolous nymph should be made to uphold heroic principles is amusing and consonant with the Odyssean tendency to reduce heroic themes to romance. This inclination simultaneously shows the Odyssean misreading of the *Iliad*'s tradition. The playful game of these tendentious interpretations constitutes the very texture of the scene: the *Odyssey* reveals here that its literary power and success lie in these readings and misreadings of its competitive texts.

Hera does not pay much attention to Hypnus' argument but bribes and seduces him with the offer of the Grace, "for whom you long always all the time" (*Il.* 14.269); "for whom," he agrees, "I long always all the time" (11.276). On this passage and on Hypnus' power to trap, see Laurence Kahn, "Ulysse, ou La Ruse et la mort," *Critique*, no. 393 (1980): 118.

[12]Odysseus acknowledges Calypso's beauty, but by using the epithet *periphrōn* (wise) for Penelope (*Od.* 5.216) he compliments her for a quality not ascribed to Calypso, one Calypso never mentions in relation to either herself or Penelope. This point was made long ago by Antisthenes (see *Odyssey Scholia* on this passage).

4

Suffering and Trickery

> The Text is plural. This does not mean just that it has several mean-
> ings, but rather that it achieves plurality of meaning, an irreducible
> plurality. . . . The Text's plurality does not depend on the ambiguity
> of its contents, but rather on what could be called the *stereographic
> plurality* of the signifiers that weave it (etymologically the text is a
> cloth; *textus*, from which text derives, means "woven").
>
> Roland Barthes, "From Work to Text"

Odysseus will tactfully agree that though Calypso has superior
beauty, he wishes and longs "all the time" for his home—he comprehends Penelope in the notion of home (*Od.* 5.215 ff.). Unmistaka-
bly, the text already had the opportunity to portray Odysseus' desire
for Penelope and for his home in most pathetic terms. Beginning with
Athena's earlier depiction of Odysseus' plight (*Od.* 1.55–59)[1] and
continuing until the narrative of *Od.* 5.151 ff., the tone is consonant
with Zeus' definition of Odysseus as "the most lamenting man." Odysseus' posture on the seashore is a case in point:

> [Calypso] found him sitting on the shore: his eyes were never dry from
> tears and his sweet life [*glukus aiōn*] was flowing away[2] in laments for his
> return, since the nymph pleased him no more. (5.151–53)

It is strongly reminiscent of Achilles' similar posture on the shore of
the sea and of his grief as he cries for the dead Patroclus.[3] Beneath his
heroic pathos and garb, however, Odysseus is a character of romance:
his desire for home is so strong that he wishes to die (*Od.* 1.57–59).

---

[1]See the justified irony Benedetto Marzullo levels at the heavy pathos of this passage:
Il problema omerico, 2d ed. rev. (Milan and Naples: R. Ricciardi, 1970).

[2]Tears and life are conceived of as ebbing away in a similar process: the verb *kateibeto*,
"flowed away," is often used for tears. Cf. *Il.* 24.794, for example.

[3]See *Il.* 23.59–61, 125–26. In this latter passage we find the only example of *ep'aktēs*
in the *Iliad*. Nitzsch's commentary suggests this comparison. See also Albin Lesky,
Thalatta: Der Weg der Griechen zum Meer (Vienna: R. M. Rohrer, 1947), pp. 182 ff. and
passim.

An idyllic idea of life is evident in that editorial comment "his sw~ life was flowing away," which suggests that Odysseus' life would be pleasurable if only he could return home. In the *Iliad* life is never sweet; on the contrary, "war is sweeter than return" (*Il.* 2.453–54 = 11.13–14).[4] But in the *Odyssey* life is desirable, for it is the source of countless pleasures, which the poem represents in detail.

Pleasure, however, appears only as a goal for which the hero must risk death: it appears therefore in the transparency of grief and pain. Sweet life and tears of pain are chiastically parallel (5.151–52): "From tears the eyes were never dry and flowed sweet life," and consubstantially similar in the phrase (152): "sweet life was flowing away."[5] Though I describe Odysseus' goal as pleasure, there is no doubt that the *Odyssey* presents Odysseus as the man who is continually ambushed by death, whose life is marked by lament, and who submits to a uniquely unfavorable fate.[6]

The features of Odysseus as a suffering man are well known: let it suffice to mention some of the formulaic expressions that become typical for him in the *Odyssey* and mark him as one persecuted by "fateful destiny." He is the man who *polla . . . algea pathen hon kata thumon*, "suffered many griefs in his heart" (*Od.* 1.4, 13.90); and whose *paskhōn*, "suffering," is mentioned innumerable times with *polla mogēsas*, "toiling through many hardships."[7] Some of these formulaic expressions again characterize him specifically in the *Odyssey* just as they characterize Achilles specifically in the *Iliad*, establishing a formal parallel between the two heroes.[8] In addition, just like Achilles, the hero of the *Odyssey* is the one character in his poem who deserves the specific epithet *oizuros*, "lamentable," "lamenting," as we have already observed. Two other expressions the *Odyssey* uses exclusively

---

[4]At one point (*Il.* 22.58) life is termed *philē*, "dear" or "own." Note that "sweet life" in the *Odyssey* passage receives a stronger evaluation than the immortality Calypso promises to Odysseus.

[5]This is one way for the *Odyssey* to represent the contiguity of pleasure and pain. Another, more original and powerful expression for this contiguity will be *gastēr*.

[6]Michael Nagler comments: "All adventures are thematically similar on one level, in that all of them are successful brushes with death that qualify Odysseus as a returning hero"; see his "Entretiens avec Tirésias," *CW* 74 (1980): 97.

[7]This formula occurs once in the *Iliad* (2.690, of Achilles) and eleven times in the *Odyssey*.

[8]In "The Proem of the *Odyssey*," *Arethusa* 15 (1982): 39–62, I have discussed how some of these formulas are shared by the two heroes. The parallelism is formally rigorous and unmistakable and thus emphasizes the opposite direction of their lives: Achilles' pain, grief, and labors in the work of war lead to his premature death; Odysseus' suffering and labors are the consequence of his attempts to preserve life—his companions' and his own. This opposition, enhanced by the formal parallelism, maps the essential difference between the two heroes: "The *Iliad* is the poem of total expenditure of life, and the *Odyssey* is the poem of a controlled economy of life," p. 42.

for Odysseus are *kammoros* (often in the vocative), meaning "marked by fate,"[9] and *dustēnos*, "wretched."[10]

These few hints show how ambitious the project of the *Odyssey* is in exhibiting its hero as the most anguished character of epos, in drawing parallels with Achilles' fateful dalliance with death, and in presenting him as a spiritual brother of Heracles. In *Od.* 11.617 ff. Heracles comments: "resourceful Odysseus O unhappy one, certainly you drag a life of evil fate such as I endured [*okheeskon*] beneath the rays of the sun." It is no wonder that Stoics and Cynics took this Odysseus as an emblem of Man who endures the human condition with stern steadfastness.

Yet our Odysseus is also "resourceful," as Heracles unwittingly calls him when he uses the standard formula of address to Odysseus (*polumēchane*):[11] he is a champion of *mētis*, "shrewdness," "practical intelligence," and the *Odyssey* has no trouble in rescuing Odysseus from the worst labors and perils.[12] This picture of Odysseus appears in the thirteenth book of the *Odyssey* when Athena confronts Odysseus, finally back home, and praises his cunning and tricks:

> He would be a smart one [*kerdaleos*] and a manipulator, the person who
> could outwit you in all your wiles [*doloisi*], even if he were a god who met

[9]*Kammoros*, by apocope from **katasmoros* (from the root **smer*); see *DE*, 3:378. The adjective occurs only in the *Odyssey*, and Telemachus uses it once, when speaking of Odysseus to the Nurse (2.351). It appears four other times, always in a direct address to Odysseus: first by Calypso (5.60); later by Ino (5.339), by Odysseus' mother (11.216), and by Athena (20.33). Note that the word expresses the speaker's pity for Odysseus and that all four speakers are female. Suffering pays off: on two of these occasions, the pitying female consoles or comes to aid Odysseus.

[10]*Dustēnos*, "wretched," is used fifteen times in the *Odyssey* by the poet and the compassionate characters to describe Odysseus (1.55, etc.), and twice (11.76, 80) for the dead Elpenor; in this latter case, *dustēnos* retrieves the main Iliadic use—in mourning speeches. Some pathetic Iliadic expressions are concentrated in books 5, 6, and 13, where we witness *directly* the last part of Odysseus' troubles in his voyage. For instance, the exclamation of sorrow: *o moi*, or *o moi ego*, "Ah, me!" is uttered by Odysseus only in these books (5.299, 356, 408, 465, 6.119, 13.200), while the other five occurrences of this pathetic expression are distributed among different characters. Analogously, the pathetic line with Iliadic tone that precedes the *o moi* utterance is used only in book 5 (298, 355, 407, 464): see chap. 5, n. 9.

[11]*Od.* 11.617. On the resourcefulness of Odysseus, see Marcel Detienne and Jean-Pierre Vernant, *Les Ruses de l'intelligence: La Mētis des grecs* (Paris: Flammarion, 1974), pp. 30–31, 47. On this characterization of Odysseus as a hero alien to the ideals of the "warrior aristocracy of the *Iliad*," and on the Aegean-Anatolian origin of his name and his themes, see the recent work by Marcello Durante, *Sulla preistoria della tradizione poetica greca*, 2 vols. (Rome: Ateneo, 1971–76), 1:149–50.

[12]On the connection between Odysseus' *mētis* and his ability to return home, see Douglas Frame, *The Myth of Return in Early Greek Epic* (New Haven: Yale University Press, 1978), who develops this theme around the etymology of *noos*, "mind," and *nostos*, "return."

you. Hard man, subtle and clever, insatiable of tricks! Even in your own country you were not going to cease from your deceits and manipulative stories [*muthōn . . . klopiōn*] that are fundamentally dear to your heart. Come on, let us no longer speak about these things, as both of us know deceit [*kerde(a)*][13] since you are the best [*aristos*] of all men in contrivances and speeches [*boulēi kai muthoisin*] and I, among all gods, am famous for my ruses [*mēti*] and deceits [*kerdesin*]. And you did not recognize Pallas Athena, daughter of Zeus. (*Od.* 13.291–300)

The Greek vocabulary of knavishness, simulation, and deceit is concentrated in these few lines, yet the interest lies in a certain formulaic quality of those expressions that are permanent characteristics of Odysseus in both poems. For instance, each part of the line:

skhetlie, poikilomēta, dolōn at'

hard man [*skhetlie*] elaborate and clever [*poikilomēta*] insatiable of tricks [*dolōn at'*]. (*Od.* 13.293)

is traditional. *Poikilomētēs,* "of various, elaborate cleverness,"[14] is a specialized epithet for Odysseus in the phrase

amph'
eis   *Odusēa daiphrona poikilomētēn*[15]

---

[13]In Homer the plural *kerdea* means "wiles," "cunning," "deceit" (*Il.* 23.515, etc.), but the singular, *kerdos,* means "gain," "advantage" (see *Il.* 10.225; *Od.* 16.311, 23.140). Therefore it is possible to understand *kerdaleos* as either "cunning" or "calculating." In *Od.* 6.148, for instance, Odysseus' *kerdaleon muthon* is understood as a "calculating" speech by A.H.C. In *Il.* 4.339, whether Agamemnon uses *kerdaleophron,* "calculating" or "cunning," cannot be decided. *Od.* 13.255 is the unique example in Homer of *polukerdes,* a word that insists on the manyness of Odysseus' ruses. *Polukerdiē,* "ruse of all sorts," is attributed twice to Odysseus (*Od.* 23.77) and once to Penelope (*Od.* 24.167). (Some of the typical epithets used for Odysseus—specifically those that characterize his craftiness—are also used for Penelope to indicate that they share the same virtues; on these mirroring facets ["like-mindedness"] of Odysseus and Penelope, see Helene Foley, "'Reverse Similes' and Sex Roles in the *Odyssey,*" *Arethusa* 11 [1978]: 7–26).

[14]Chantraine alleges that only in this epithet does Homer reveal the metaphorical sense of "cunning" in *poikilos* (*DE,* 4:923), but possibly this metaphorical meaning is already present in *Od.* 8.448. The concrete and the metaphorical seem to overlap in *Il.* 18.590, where *poikillō* means "to sculpt" and/or "to make [a scene] artistically, cleverly."

[15]"Around [to] intelligent and elaborately clever Odysseus." The meaning of *daiphrōn* is disputable, and its case is very interesting because the word could present a change of meaning fully analogous to the *tle-* forms. According to Chantraine (*DE*), *daiphrōn* means "courageous," "warlike" in all passages of the *Iliad*—even in *Il.* 11.482—for Odysseus, and in *Il.* 24.325, for the coachmen of Priam; yet in the *Odyssey* it seems to mean "intelligent." Durante, *Preistoria,* 2:40–41, denies the connection of *daiphrōn* with *daïs,* "battle," and asserts the connection with the Rig Veda's *dasra,* "endowed with great intelligence." Consequently the word should have the same meaning

59

in *Il.* 11.482; *Od.* 3.163, 7.168, 22.115, 202, 282. But *only* here in *Od.* 13.293 is the adjective found by itself, and in the vocative—in other words, as part of a noun-epithet vocative formula, it is the sole example in the *Odyssey* and the *Iliad.* This empirical feature could be explained in several ways: as an independent Odyssean development of an Iliadic formula or, what seems more probable, as a residue of a traditional epithet of Odysseus that in previous performances or compositions had wider use. This point can be better defined as we take into consideration the next formulaic part of line 293: *dolōn at(e),* "insatiable of tricks." This expression is found in *Il.* 11.430 where Sokus so addresses Odysseus:

> ō *Oduseu poluaine, dolōn at' ēde ponoio*

> O Odysseus, man of many stories, insatiable of tricks and of toil.

The line contains specific and specialized epithets of Odysseus. *Poluainos* implies that Odysseus knows and uses many stories for his own protection and success. He uses them just as "resources" or "tricks,"[16] and therefore the epithet elaborates the same notion of the next part of the line, "insatiable of tricks." The epithet *poluainos* appears in the *Odyssey* only once: in the invitation the Sirens address to Odysseus, a text that, as I have shown,[17] specifically mimes Iliadic formulaic diction.

The epithet *dolōn at' ēde ponoio*[18] appears more nearly complete, and appropriately so, than the fragment in *Od.* 13.292. Accordingly, since antiquity, *Il.* 11.430 has been taken as evidence of the unity of

---

in both the *Iliad* and the *Odyssey:* "intelligent." The poets, however, may have understood *daiphrōn* as "warlike," for the epithet appears in battle contexts in both the *Iliad* and the *Odyssey.* This noun-epithet attracted the attention of Milman Parry: see "The Traditional Epithet in Homer," in *The Making of Homeric Verse,* ed. Adam Parry (Oxford: Clarendon Press, 1971), pp. 106–7.

[16] For this meaning see Karl Meuli, "Herkunft und Wesen der Fabel," *Schweizerisches Archiv für Volkskunde* 50 (1954): 65–88 = *Gesammelte Schriften,* ed. Thomas Gelzer, 2 vols. (Basel: Schwabe, 1975), 2:742.

[17] See Pietro Pucci, "The Song of the Sirens," *Arethusa* 12 (1979): 121–32, and "La scrittura dell'*Odissea*," forthcoming.

[18] On this epithet, see *LfrgE,* s.v. "aatos." The adjective *aatos* (from privat. *a-* and *a-menai,* "to satiate") is used in Homer only with *polemoio* or *makhēs,* "war" or "battle," or *dolōn* and *dolōn ēde ponoio,* "tricks" and "tricks and toils." This last epithet is specific to Odysseus and occurs only in the passages we are analyzing, *Od.* 13.293 and *Il.* 11.430. On Odysseus' *ponos,* which is one of the many significations hinging on *tlēnai,* see Nicole Loraux, "*Ponos,*" in *Annali del Seminario di Studi del Mondo Classico: Sezione di Archeologia e Storia Antica,* no. 4. (Naples: Instituto Universitario Orientale, 1982), pp. 171–92.

the *Iliad* and the *Odyssey* and of their common author. And modern scholars tend to assume *Il.* 11.430 presupposes that Odysseus' portrait as we have it in the *Odyssey* must have already been in existence.[19] This assumption is strengthened by the empirical features of *poikilomētēs*. In this case the *Odyssey* either renews (and corrects) the data of the *Iliad*[20] or depends on a tradition that antedates the composition of both the *Iliad* and the *Odyssey*. This last hypothesis does not exclude the idea that at the moment the two poems were composed they glanced simultaneously at antecedents of their traditions and at themselves, reciprocally.

Because the word *aatos* belongs to the very restricted series *aatos polemoio* or *makhēs*, "insatiable of war" or "of battle," it suggests that Odysseus' tricks (*doloi*) are his specific military resources. As the epithet *aatos polemoio* in Homer qualifies exclusively Ares and Achilles and *makhēs aatos* only Hector, so the epithet *dolōn at' (ēde ponoio)* raises Odysseus to the level of the main heroes of the epic while specifying the exclusive field of his insatiability.

By itself the word *dolos* embraces many connotations, and it is therefore used in reference to many characters. The *dolos* is generally speaking "a trick," and to the extent that a trick is viewed as a weapon or as a resource for self-protection from, or self-enhancement amid, enemies it has in itself no derogatory meaning.[21] Odysseus uses *dolos* in a wrestling bout against Ajax (*Il.* 23.275);[22] he calls the wooden horse he helped to introduce into Troy a *dolos* (*Od.* 8.494); and he

---

[19]See *LfrgE*, s.v. "aatos." In fact, the whole epithetic line, *Il.* 11.430, characterizes Odysseus as we know him in the *Odyssey*, as a man of resources, stories, tricks, and endless endurance (*tlēnai*). Because *Il.* 11.430 has a more complete epithet (*dolōn at' ēde ponoio*) than *Od.* 13.293 (*dolōn at'*), it is possible to assume either that here the *Odyssey* abridges the epithet it knows *only* from the *Iliad* or that both the *Odyssey* and the *Iliad* draw freely on a tradition about Odysseus that antedates the monumental composition—as we have it—of both poems.

[20]In the *Iliad*, *poikilomētēs* appears in the context of military events, and unless the epithet denotes specifically *strategic* intelligence, the word would be used with some indifference to the context. In *Od.* 13.293, however, the epithet is used appropriately. See Marcel Detienne and Jean-Pierre Vernant, *Les Ruses de l'intelligence: La Mētis des grecs* (Paris: Flammarion, 1974), pp. 25–26, which describes the *poikilia* (elaboratedness or variegatedness) of *mētis* and the ambiguity that such a feature implies.

[21]See W. B. Stanford, *The Ulysses Theme* (Oxford: Blackwell, 1954), p. 13 and n. 17. When Zeus is tricked by Hera, he characterizes her *dolos* (Hypnus' trick, and her erotic seduction) negatively with the epithet *kakotekhnos*, "of evil craft" (*Il.* 15.14). Yet the use of any epithet with *dolos* is extremely rare in Homer: *pukinos*, "well connected," "shrewd," appears in *Il.* 6.187, and *kakos*, "evil," in *Il.* 4.229. In the *Odyssey* the epithets qualify exclusively the variety (*pantoios*) and the totality (*pas*) of Odysseus' tricks; see, for instance, *Od.* 3.119, 122 (in addition to *Il.* 3.202), and *Od.* 9.422.

[22]Antilochos too uses *dolos*, in the chariot racing against Menelaus: see *Il.* 23.515, 585; the actual cheating is described in 423 ff.

hides his tears by *dolos* in his first encounter with Penelope (*Od.* 19.212).[23] This is a remarkably scanty list of *doloi* among Odysseus' many wily dealings in the *Odyssey*. But in these other contexts another word is preferred, *mētis*, which indicates his intelligence and ruses.[24] When the text presents Odysseus in a formulaic sort of portrait, however, the *doloi* of the hero become his prominent characteristic; the word is used in the plural with *pantoioi* "of all sorts," or *pantes*, "all," as in *Il.* 3.202, *Od.* 3.119, 122, and possibly *Od.* 9.19.[25] In some passages (*Od.* 9.422, among others) *doloi* are attributed to Odysseus in a specific instance, and here too the meaning seems to go beyond the idea of military stratagem or ambush—which *dolos* often means—and suggests trickery and simulations of all sorts. This sense of *doloi* is also present at the moment when Athena praises Odysseus for trying to disguise his identity (*Od.* 13.291–92), just as in another passage, *Od.* 9.19, where Odysseus finally reveals himself to the Phaeacians.[26] In all these passages the plural, *doloi*, generically characterizes Odysseus as the man of trickery.

How this trickster can at the same time be represented as the most lamenting and troubled hero remains an intriguing and difficult problem for the *Odyssey*. Yet the *Odyssey* successfully attempts this feat: to make of the trickster and the sufferer one person. The result is an odd economy in which Odysseus' brushes with death and his familiarity with anguish and grief conspire, always, with his survival and his final pleasures. This paradoxical economy marks specifically Odysseus' posture of endurance (*tlēnai*), as I shall show. Instead of taking him into dalliance with death, *mētis* and *tlēnai* bring him into a frame in which the *Odyssey* first renews the textual occurrences and themes where that dalliance is represented and then cheats death itself. The spiritual brother of Heracles, the champion of future Stoics, has too many resources and expedients in his wallet to welcome a sacrifice on the mountain of Oeta.

---

[23]This is the only situation in which *dolos* has nothing to do with fighting, but it is fitting that by this *dolos* Odysseus covers and protects his disguise.

[24]See, for instance, *Od.* 9.414, 20.20, 2.279, and the epithets *poikilomētis, polumētis.*

[25]On *Od.* 9.19, see p. 217.

[26]In *Od.* 11.363 ff. there is an extremely tantalizing passage in praise of Odysseus' narrative ability. Alcinous praises the beauty of Odysseus' words and his noble mind but prefaces this praise by a series of negative definitions: "You do *not* look like a cheater and a simulator [*epiklopos*]." The word *epiklopos* and its synonym, *muthoi klopioi*, are used by Athena to praise Odysseus in *Od.* 13.291 and 295.

5

Textual Disingenuousness in
Portraying Odysseus' Suffering

The *Odyssey* is the epilogue of the *Iliad*.

"Longinus," *On the Sublime*

After a favorable sailing toward the Phaeacian land, Odysseus is suddenly threatened by a storm that the angry Poseidon raises against him. The hero recognizes the accuracy of Calypso's words (*Od.* 5.300), yet he unexpectedly—for the nymph had also assured him of his return home—fears for his life.[1] As he is stricken by this fear, he utters a pathetic lament (5.306 ff.) expressing the wish that he might have died

> the day the Trojans in great numbers hurled at me brazen spears over the body of the son of Peleus. Then I would have had burial and the Achaeans would have carried my glory [*kleos*] afar. Now it is my doom to be seized by a miserable death [*leugaleōi thanatōi*]. (*Od.* 5.309–12)

In these lines Odysseus reminisces about one of his heroic deeds—his rescue, with Ajax, of the body and the weapons of Achilles. Such an episode is not in the *Iliad* but was narrated in the *Aethiopis*.[2] The context, however, is reminiscent of Achilles' pathetic cry in *Il.* 21.273 ff., where he complains about what he imagines to be his imminent death by drowning under the rushing river's waters. One cannot

---

[1] He uses a pathetic phrase: *nun moi sōs aipus olethros*, "now hard death is sure on me," which occurs here (*Od.* 5.305) and later, in 22.28. The same phrase occurs only once in the *Iliad* (13.773), but the expression *aipus olethros*, "hard death," appears several other times and can therefore be considered to belong to the high pathos of the Iliadic tradition. The Odyssean passage seems to be thematically crafted in consonance with *Il.* 21.276, where Achilles, in danger of drowning—as is Odysseus in our passage—complains that he has been lured into danger by his mother's false promise: "She told me that I would die by the arrows of Apollo, after killing Hector, but now it is my destiny to be seized by a miserable death" (*Il.* 21.276–83).

[2] Proclus, p. 106, ll. 10–11.

fail to appreciate the similarity of the situations of the two heroes, and the texts underline this similarity by repeating the same line (*Il.* 21.281 = *Od.* 5.312): "Now it is my doom to be seized by a miserable death."

After Odysseus' heroic, Achillean pedigree is established[3]—while the text disguises, or exhibits, itself with ingenuity through a quotation—the description of his plight in the storm continues. A marine deity, Ino (Leukothea), takes pity on him, addresses him sympathetically, and offers him her divine *kredemnon*, the veil that covers her cheeks, which will function as a sort of life buoy for him. Even in the middle of the storm, near death, the titillating pleasure of sex surfaces in the form of a beautiful deity and her discreet gesture.[4] Death for Odysseus is merely a menace and, even if it comes from a powerful god, is to be warded off, as Ino says with a language that bespeaks— how properly!—the language of intrigue:

> Wretched man [*kammore*], why is earth-shaking Poseidon so violently enraged [*odusat'*] that he prepares [*phuteuei*] many evils for you? Well, he shall not destroy you [*kataphthusei*], however angry [or eager] he may be. (*Od.* 5.339–41)

[3]Complete appreciation of this one point would require the clarification of many other points, among them Odysseus' text in *Od.* 5.299–312, specifically his sudden certainty of dying, and the formulaic quality of *Il.* 21.281 = *Od.* 5.312, which returns almost literally in the description of Agamemnon's death—a real death this time—in *Od.* 24.34. Does this line belong to the theme of the "inglorious death of the hero"? It seems so, but the notion of "theme" raises more questions than it resolves. This difficulty is exemplified by Francis Cairns, *Generic Composition in Greek and Roman Poetry* (Edinburgh: Edinburgh University Press, 1972), which interprets *Od.* 5.299–312 not, as I have done, in relation to other epic texts and as a lament on inglorious death but as an "inverse epibaterion" (see pp. 61 ff.). At any rate, the distribution of *leugaleos*, "miserable," "deplorable," is interesting. In the *Iliad* it is an epithet—not a fixed one—of battle (*polemos*, 13.97; *daïs*, 14.387), mind (*phrenes*, 9.119), words (20.108), and death (21.281); in the *Odyssey* it functions as, among other things, a fixed epithet for the beggar (16.273, 17.202, 337, 24.157), since it belongs to a formulaic line. A third point: How should we understand and interpret the literary strategy that enables the *Odyssey* to reminisce about an episode from the *Aethiopis*—in a passage that alludes textually to a section of the *Iliad*? Here is the same kind of "double source" that lies behind *Od.* 5.105 ff. (see above, p. 38). For an analysis of a double source of allusion in Vergil see Giorgio Pasquali, "Arte allusiva," in his *Stravaganze quarte e supreme* (Venice: N. Pozza, 1951), pp. 11–20.

[4]Michael Nagler has analyzed the passages where *kredemnon* functions as what he calls "the chastity branch of the 'attendence motif.'" *Spontaneity and Tradition* (Berkeley: University of California Press, 1974), pp. 45 ff. And commenting on our passage he writes perceptively: "Leokothea actually hands over her *kredemnon* to Odysseus in book 5 of the *Odyssey*, and only the immediate interposition of a poetic substitute (i.e., an allomorph of the same token) saves her from the compromising situation" (p. 46). The author implies that the "wave" (*kyma*) that covers Ino (353) functions as a veil (*kalymma*). Even without this last implication the textual titillation is obvious.

Poseidon does not accomplish (*telein*) evils, but prepares them (*phu-teuei*), with a figural sense of *phuteuo*, a word that is used only once in the *Iliad* (15.134) but is common in the *Odyssey:* "to prepare," "to scheme," sometimes with an implicit notion of "ambush" (*Od.* 14.218, 17.82). Ino is there precisely to preempt that machination and scheming. No wonder Odysseus suspects that all the gods, even Ino, "weave snares": *huphaineisin dolon* (*Od.* 5.356).

The text, too, is scheming. Ino speaks of the violent rage of Poseidon and then reassures Odysseus that the god "shall not destroy" him. But the god himself, in previous lines, has said nothing about destroying Odysseus:

> he is close to the Phaeacians' land where it is his destiny to escape the great limit of woes which have come upon him. But I think that I will drive him still sufficiently into trouble [*haden . . . kakotētos*]. (*Od.* 5.288–90)

Poseidon does not speak lightly; knowing Odysseus' final destination, the god does not at all seek to destroy him. But the text, in accordance with its "gusto" for scheming, has Ino assuming that Poseidon really aims at Odysseus' destruction: "he shall not destroy you, however angry [or eager] he may be" (*Od.* 5.341). The textual indecision of *meneainōn*, "to be angry" or "to be eager," reveals its significance here: because of this indecision the text conspires—willingly or not—with the conspiratorial attitude of Ino, who tells Odysseus more than there is to be known, reassures him accordingly, and invites him, on account of his shrewdness (see line 342), to follow her orders precisely.

Moreover, the text schemes and plays by punning on Odysseus' name. Poseidon's rage (*odusato*) can be read in the name Odusseus, as though he carried his epic destiny in his name (*Od.* 19.406 ff.). We recall that Achilles (Akhilleus) also—according to Gregory Nagy's analysis[5]—has his epic destiny written in his name: *akhos* (woe) of the *laos* (army, people).

By this punning, theology, narrative, and *logos* combine in a marvelous unity producing textual pleasure for the audience as they are invited to contemplate this grand unity and note how well the text controls it. Epic language and being are identical, the one mirroring the other. The indissolubility of this mirroring is indeed most reassuring.

---

[5]Gregory Nagy, *The Best of the Achaeans* (Baltimore: Johns Hopkins University Press, 1979), pp. 69–83.

The text controls this grand unity so well that it shows this unity to be only a scriptorial ruse. After all, if the *odium* of Poseidon can be easily warded off, it is shown to be so ineffective that it ceases to be the real generator of Odysseus' troubles.[6] Consequently it functions as a mere mark in Odysseus' name, a scriptorial sign that only triggers further writing and textual scheming.

Troubling Scenes of Introspection

In this atmosphere of scheming and conspiracy, wily Odysseus, appropriately, does not at all trust the extraordinary help; he fears some god may "weave a new snare,"[7] and reasonably enough he resolves to use the *kredemnon* only as a last resort (361–64):

> So long as the timbers hold in the fastenings I'll remain here and endure [*meneō kai tlēsomai*] suffering pains [*algea paskhōn*], but when the wave shatters my raft, I'll swim.

Since we are prepared by the Achillean rhetoric of the few previous lines, by the commitment to *tlēnai* that Odysseus utters to Calypso, and by the sudden language of shrewdness and scheming, we find it difficult to assess the exact tone of these verses Odysseus exclaims, merely as a comment on the most reasonable alternative he faces. Yet at least there is no doubt of the heroic pedigree of his utterance,[8] for Odysseus' line 362 recalls a line he utters in the *Iliad* (2.299) when he invites his fellow soldiers to remain in Troy to endure the war rather than flee home: *tlēte philoi kai meinat'*, "endure, friends, and remain." More precisely, the phrase is used by heroes when they resolve to stand and persevere: so Diomedes in *Il.* 11.317 (*ego meneō kai tlēsomai*, and Achilles in *Il.* 19.308 (*meneō kai tlēsomai*), implying that he will persevere in his fast.

In using this expression—*meneō kai tlēsomai*—and using it within this context, the *Odyssey* comes close to presenting Odysseus in the tonal frame of the Iliadic passages I have quoted and in the ennobling aura of his answer to Calypso. Consider also the more Odyssean for-

---

[6]I introduce here the Latin word *odium*, "dislike," "hate," in order to pun on Odysseus' name.

[7]The question of deceiving gods in Homer is important but, as far as I know, yet to be studied. A few times heroes doubt the truth of the friendly god's message of advice (see *Il.* 21.275 ff., for example) and often antagonist gods lie to effect the ruin of their adversary heroes.

[8]For the *mermērizein* theme in which this utterance is couched, see below, pp. 69 ff.

mula, *algea paskhōn*, which emphasizes Odysseus' readiness to suffer pain.[9]

The situation in which Odysseus ponders his alternatives, however, has no reference to those in the *Iliad*. He utters the phrase that in the *Iliad* implies noble and risky resolve[10] only to account for the most reasonable course of action—that is, to remain on the raft as long as possible. He acts, just as he says, in accordance with what seems best for his survival: *dokeei . . . moi einai ariston*, "the best plan seems to me" (*Od.* 5.360), which is a variant of the phrase *kerdion doassato einai*, "it seemed more advantageous," often used in a type of the *mermērizein* scenes. The text therefore underlines his patient acceptance of troubles, his commonsense decision in the face of them.[11] In this way, of course, the text points to a "taking upon oneself" that comes close to describing a rapport with oneself: it intimates an inner quality of the hero, his thorough calmness and self-mastery.[12]

[9]This participial phrase occurs nine times in Homer, twice in the *Iliad* (once to describe Tlepolemos [2.667] and once for Philoctetes [2.721]). It appears seven times in the *Odyssey*, and three of those times the phrase concerns Odysseus (*Od.* 5.13, 362, 19.170). Note too that Odysseus utters his lament to his "great-spirited heart" (*megalētora thumon*). This line (355), *okhthēsas d'ara eipe pros hon megalētora thumon*, is formulaic and occurs seven times in the *Iliad* and four in the *Odyssey*. (All four occurrences are in book 5.) The formula shows neglect of the digamma and so is considered a recent addition to the epic's language; see *GH*, 1:146; Arie Hoekstra, *Homeric Modifications of Formulaic Prototypes* (Amsterdam: North-Holland, 1969), p. 69. The phrase is almost specialized for Achilles (*Il.* 17.90, 18.5, 20.343, 21.53) and his adversaries (Agenor, *Il.* 21.552; Hector, *Il.* 22.98). It is used once for Odysseus (*Il.* 11.403), its only appearance in the *Iliad* outside of the last books. In some of the passages in which this line occurs the hero is in an agonizing situation, and its presence is highly dramatic: Odysseus (*Il.* 11.404 ff.) ponders whether to flee the battle or to fight alone against the victorious Trojans and decides to stand (see the analogous cases of Agenor and Hector); Achilles is tortured by Patroclus' absence and the defeat of the Achaeans (*Il.* 17.90, 18.3 ff.). In other passages, however, its function is merely to introduce a speech that is bitterly ironic: *Il.* 20.343 ff., 21.53 ff.

[10]In *Il.* 2.299 Odysseus demands that his comrades remain at Troy to keep fighting; in *Il.* 11.317 Diomedes commits himself to staying and persevering in battle, helping Odysseus as long as he can; in *Il.* 19.308 Achilles, by continuing his fast, sympathetically mimes the death of Patroclus. See Pietro Pucci, *The Violence of Pity in Euripides' "Medea"* (Ithaca: Cornell University Press, 1980), pp. 50–51.

[11]To withstand the challenges of the sea is hardly considered courageous. When Socrates first asks Laches what he considers to be courage (*andreia*), Laches answers that courage consists in standing firm in battle (*La.* 190e.4–6); for him it is identical to endurance (*kartereia*). See also *Nicomachean Ethics* 1115a.28–31, where Aristotle states that situations of shipwreck or illness preclude acts of courage, because courage is possible only in the face of a *noble* death. (See Terence Irwin, *Plato's Moral Theory* [Oxford: Oxford University Press, 1977], p. 19.) Compare Achilles' resentment at the idea of drowning "like a farm boy," *Il.* 21.282, and Odysseus' agreement in *Od.* 5.306 ff.

[12]A parallel situation and a similar response occur in *Od.* 10.49 ff., when Odysseus narrates to the Phaeacians his bitter disappointment upon realizing that his companions have forfeited their return by opening the bag of winds. He describes himself as

What then? Do we hear the tone of a new dimension of man's "spiritual life"? Or rather the powerful cry of a character shown in conventionally heroic garb? Or a misplaced heroic disguise? All these at once, for the suggestion of Odysseus' reasonableness and of his shrewd self-control is made through "heroic" utterances as if he were facing imminent death (305). The text must therefore provoke the reader's admiration as he recognizes here the mark of heroic *prohairesis*, "decision" or "choice," and at the same time his pleasure, since he feels secure that his beloved hero will not abandon him as do so many heroes in the narratives of the Iliadic tradition. Here is a man of Achilles' temper who sees well the advantage of the raft and precisely measures the distance to the land, and who knows that this land is the place of his *rescue* (358–59). Nothing can be more pleasurable than this way of bordering and baffling death, that great unconquerable and uncheatable[13] power—until, of course, we realize that death here is conjured up only in its semblance, as a disguise. Odysseus, we realize, recites a theatrical piece, using conventional stage props. Then our pleasure is of a different sort, one that comes close to sheer textual pleasure. In fact, the *Odyssey* manipulates with skill the rules of heroic rhetoric, though denying it its proper reference.

Finally Odysseus reaches home. Yet he cannot throw himself into the arms of his wife, or those of his slave maidens—it has been noted how powerful is his desire to regain their devotion—nor can he take possession of his property. He first must kill all the suitors.[14] The pleasure for which he left Calypso is postponed, still deferred; and this postponement necessitates his disguise as an old beggar[15] and the endurance of all sorts of humiliation.

---

debating (*mermērixa*, 50) at that moment whether he should let himself fall into the sea and drown or endure in silence. He says: "Nevertheless I endured and I stood [*etlēn kai emeina*] and hiding myself I lay still in the ship." On the novelty of this experience to indicate a decision in an inward debate (*mermērizein*), see pp. 69 ff.

[13]On the representation of *thanatos*, "death," as being uncheatable, resisting all resources, *amēkhanos*, see Laurence Kahn, "Ulysse, ou La Ruse et la mort," *Critique*, no. 393 (1980): 116 ff.

[14]That this slaughter is necessary, and that it takes so absolute a form—no one is spared, not even the suitors' seer, Leodes—are difficult critical problems. See Fausto Codino, *Introduzione a Omero* (Turin: Einaudi, 1965), pp. 114–22.

[15]This is not the first time Odysseus has impersonated a commoner. Helen says that he disguised himself as a servant in order to penetrate the walls of Troy (*Od.* 4.244 ff.). Disguise is one of Odysseus' weapons, but a weapon that nevertheless harms him: "Marring himself with outrageous blows, casting a vile garment on his shoulders, he took the semblance of a servant" (*Od.* 4.244 ff.). Odysseus' ability and cunning in using words extend to the use of his body as another possible means of communication, another form of writing.

As Athena had foretold,[16] Odysseus is immediately assaulted and humiliated. First one of his old servants, Melanthius, kicks him brutally: Odysseus resists the temptation to kill him and the pleasure of doing so now; later he will take a much more gruesome revenge:

Odysseus pondered [*mermērixen*] whether he should rush on him and take away his life with the club or raise him and smash his head to the ground. Yet he endured and restrained himself [*epetolmēse, phresi t' eskheto*]. (*Od.* 17.235–38)

Odysseus' decision is couched in a *mermērizein* scene (scene of "introspection"). Such scenes—in which a character ponders alternative courses of action and finally chooses, or is led to choose, one alternative—are highly conventional and formulaic in Homer. For all their conventionality, however, they represent a deep tension in the innermost being of the character.[17] This scene follows various patterns: one (*a*) in which the character debates the alternatives and then chooses the one that seems best to him;[18] another (*b*) in which, after the mention of the alternative, the decision is imposed by an outside character—in the *Iliad* often by a god (*Il.* 1.188 ff., etc.); and a final one (*c*), irrelevant to our present purpose, in which the verb means simply "to think about, to devise" (*Od.* 2.93 = 24.128). The *Iliad* exploits this scene of tension and doubt in some of its most suspenseful moments. For instance, in *Il.* 1.188 ff., as Achilles ponders whether to kill Agamemnon or check his own rage, Athena suddenly comes down and induces him to spare Agamemnon's life. Achilles' entire destiny (and the narrative of the *Iliad*) depend on that divine

---

[16]See *Od.* 13.306–10: "And I will tell you how many troubles it is destined for you to bear up [*anaskhesthai*] in your well-built home. And you endure even under necessity [*tetlamenai kai anankēi*] and do not report to any man or woman of them that you have come back from wandering, but silently suffer [*paskhein*] many pains, bearing [*hupodegmenos*] the violence of men." The connotation of *tle-* forms is here defined by the addition of other expressions that emphasize bearing up under pain and violence without reacting, silently, with restraint (*anaskhesthai*), compelling oneself (*anankēi*). For *anankēi*, see A.H., *Il.* 15.199; A.H.C., *Od.* 13.307: "auch mit Zwang," i.e., even if you have to compel yourself.

[17]This type of scene has been studied by Walter Arend, *Die typischen Scenen bei Homer* (1933; reprinted Berlin: Weidmann, 1975), pp. 106–15; Christian Voigt, *Überlegung und Entscheidung* (1934; reprinted Meisenham am Glan: Hain, 1972); and *Odissea–Russo*, 5:170.

[18]The lines that describe the decision are *doassato kerdion einai*, "it seemed more advantageous," as in *Il.* 13.458, 16.652; *Od.* 6.145; *aristē phaineto boulē*, "the best plan seemed to be," as in *Il.* 2.5, 14.161; and *dokei moi einai ariston*, "the best plan seems to me," in *Od.* 5.360.

decision.[19] The *Odyssey* seems to take a bemused or skeptical view of pattern *b:* only humans ever intervene to resolve the anxious dilemma of a character. Gods never do. The companions of Odysseus deter him from punishing Eurylochus (*Od.* 10.438–42); Helen, more quick-witted than Menelaus, resolves his banal dilemma (*Od.* 4.116 ff.). One may easily suspect in the latter passage a parodical intention or, as always in an intertextual relationship, a superb disregard of the tradition, since the dramatic scenario of *mermērizein* is used for a silly alternative and since Helen—who is described as being similar to Artemis (chastity itself) (122)—intervenes in a role that in the *Iliad* would have been played by a god. Indeed, she intervenes as the goddess Helen-Artemis.

In the *Odyssey*, pattern *a* of this motif is more frequently used than pattern *b*. The *Iliad* exploits the dramatic force of this scene, its serious implication of inner tension, and presents Zeus himself in this dramatic posture. Once he deliberates whether Patroclus should die now over the corpse of Sarpedon or should go on slaughtering the Trojans (*Il.* 16.643 ff.); another time (2.1 ff.), Zeus is unable to sleep as he ponders how to honor Achilles. In this pattern (*a*) the characters by themselves reach the right, advantageous decision, so that as the theme is announced and the pattern develops through the verse (*doassato kerdion einai*, "it seemed more advantageous") the reader knows beforehand that the dilemma will be *successfully* resolved. Of course, this is the pattern in which the *Odyssey* situates Odysseus' frequent moments of introspection and deliberation, hesitation and doubt, and accordingly this is the pattern that announces that he always chooses well and advantageously. When he faces Nausicaa and debates how to petition her (*Od.* 6.141–47),[20] or when he faces Irus and ponders whether to kill him or simply beat him up badly (*Od.* 18.90–94), or when he hesitates between revealing himself to his father or testing him (*Od.* 24.235 ff.) he chooses what seems advantageous to him (*doassato kerdion einai*), and inevitably he obtains what he desires.

In four passages, however, this formula foretelling the hero's successful and advantageous choice is replaced by new, extraordinary

---

[19]With the exception of this episode, however, *mermērizein* scenes of pattern *b* in the *Iliad* do not intimate shattering, soul-breaking decisions; on the contrary, most often the dilemma the hero ponders is whether to continue fighting, and a protective god dissuades him (*Il.* 5.668 ff., 10.503 ff.).

[20]Notice how felicitously the text combines the formula of *Od.* 6.145: doassato *kerdion einai*, "it seemed more advantageous," with the expression of 148: *kerdaleon . . . muthon*, "he spoke a gaining word."

variations. In 5.353 ff. the pondering line (*autar ho mermērixe*, "he pondered then") is followed by a *direct speech* in which Odysseus ponders the alternatives—to stay on the raft or to leave—and asserts his will "to remain and endure" (*meneō kai tlēsomai*) (*Od.* 5.362).[21] In *Od.* 10.49 ff. Odysseus wakes up to find his companions have forfeited their return by opening the bag of winds. Recounting the story to the Phaeacians, he discloses to them the debate, the dilemma, that he entertained in himself:

> and I woke up and pondered in my noble heart [*kata thumon amunona mermērixa*] whether to throw myself from the ship and to die in the sea or to endure silently [*akeōn tlaiēn*] and remain alive. Yes, I endured and remained [*etlēn kai emeina*]: I covered my head and lay down. (*Od.* 10.49–53)

Here the decision comes without the line *doassato kerdion einai*, "it seemed more advantageous," for it might have sounded slightly ridiculous to say that it seemed to him more advantageous to live. Instead the inner debate is closed by Odysseus' stoic decision to endure the crisis, a decision that implicitly becomes—through the transference of the formulaic theme—the best solution.

By enduring, Odysseus chooses to live, but as he drops to the ground, silent and hidden, his condition mirrors, so to speak, the other course of action, death. The text disguises Odysseus' survival by presenting him in the stillness and silence of death. Despite or perhaps because of this, when he narrates that decisive moment to the Phaeacians, Odysseus recreates the scene's mood through powerful expressions that contrast with this mood. Using the by now often repeated expression "I endured and I stood," he amplifies what must have been, at the moment, a bitter gesture of silent resignation and gives vocal and ethical magnitude to a silence and a stillness that must then have been signs of utter defeat. He becomes a hero once again. This is the effect of epic: to monumentalize gestures and attitudes, to give voice to real silences, to grant visibility to the human being waning away. The *Odyssey* opens up the chasm between these opposites, thus enhancing not only the introspective power of its voice but also the mere vocal aspect of its introspective power.

The novelty of the development in the *mermērizein* theme is more

---

[21]See, above, pp. 66–67. The meaning of the formulaic line *doassato kerdion einai*, "it seemed more advantageous," is replaced by Odysseus' own l. 360: *dokeei de moi einai ariston*, "and it seems to me the best." In other words, Odysseus translates the *mermērizein* theme into direct speech.

extraordinary in *Od.* 20.10 ff. when Odysseus, at the sight of the slave girls' impudence, ponders whether to kill all of them or to let them go for the last time.[22] The dilemma rages furiously and vocally inside Odysseus: "his heart was barking inside" (13). A simile of an enraged she-dog growling in defense of her puppies intensifies this theme of the barking heart, and finally Odysseus talks to his heart:

> "Come on, endure my heart! [*tetlathi, kradiē*]. Once you endured [*etlēs*] something else more bestial [literally "more doggish," *kunteron*] in the day when the Cyclops, uncheckable in fury, was devouring your strong companions. You did endure [*etolmas*] until your cunning [*mētis*] led you out of the cave, you who thought to die." (*Od.* 20.18–21)

The description of the furiously vocal dilemma inside Odysseus is unique, but Odysseus' urging in the direct speech reminds us of the novelty of *Od.* 5.353 ff.[23] The *mermērizein* (introspection) theme has become the formal expression within which Odysseus' wisdom and hardened heart may be represented, and in which—as Walter Arend writes—the "decision is emphasized as a spiritual process. . . . Odysseus is not the 'patient' man but the one who can wait."[24] This judgment can be extended to all four *mermērizein* scenes we have analyzed.[25]

Yet we should realize that this "spiritual process" that unravels with the uttering of Odysseus' voice and stages the image of the growling heart is not a simple phenomenon. First, the text rehearses the utter-

[22]See Joseph Russo's precise description, *Odissea*, 5:262: the scene is unique in the Homeric corpus because it is closed not by a decisional act but by the odd metaphor of the growling dog. Odysseus' anxious introspection is not completely calmed by his warning to his heart (18–21); a second simile is introduced (25–30), and finally Athena intervenes and gives him the comfort of sleep. Actually, this scene *does* contain a decisional act after its introspective moments in ll. 10–13. Odysseus' appeal to his heart calms him enough so that he can decide to gain time.

[23]As Odysseus urges his own heart to endure, the scene takes on a resemblance to the *b* pattern in which an external intervention induces a decision. Ulrich von Wilamowitz-Moellendorf, *Die Heimkehr des Odysseus* (Berlin: Weidmann, 1927), p. 189, notices that Odysseus' heart is an agent acting by itself and not a "figure," as in several Euripidean contexts.

[24]Arend, *Typischen Scenen bei Homer*, p. 113. Max Horkheimer and Theodor W. Adorno, *Dialectic of Enlightenment*, trans. John Cumming (New York: Herder & Herder, 1972), interpret this confrontation between Odysseus' self and his "doggish" heart as a sort of allegory of a self that is split and must use violence against its inner nature, just as the self uses violence against the outward world of nature: from this confrontation Odysseus' self emerges united (cf. *autos* of 20.24).

[25]*Mermērizein* occurs thirty times in the *Odyssey* and only eleven times in the *Iliad*. Note, for instance in book 20 of the *Odyssey*, the use of *mermērizein* at ll. 10, 28, 38, 41, 93. On the untraditional intensity of the *mermērizein* scene in the opening part of *Od.* 20, see Joseph Russo, "Homer against His Tradition," *Arion* 7 (1968): 275–95, and also *Odissea*, 5:261 ff.

ance of Odysseus' voice as the voice of *mētis* and patience, while it does not articulate the voice of the growling heart. The text allows the effect of this voice to operate on Odysseus and on us, as if it were mere expression of Odysseus' spiritual essence and self. I will come to this point in the next chapter, but it is evident here too that Odysseus' voice of *mētis* is not fully accounted for and that far from *being* a guarantee of his psychological consistency, it *operates* only as a function of his epic topicality. It carries with itself all the gaps, lags, and predicaments of the sign. Thus, for instance, the privilege the text grants to the voice of *mētis* recalls, by contrast, the scene in *Od.* 14.29–34, where Odysseus, man of *mētis*, notwithstanding his *mētis*, fails to placate the enraged dogs. Besides, *mētis* appears in conjunction with a cluster of terms that can operate only if *mētis* has been either absent or unwise or self-deceiving. For it is clear that Odysseus must have been unwise in risking a visit to the Cyclops;[26] but without this unwise decision he would not be representable as a man of suffering, of resistance to suffering, and finally of *mētis*. Odysseus—that Stoic before the fact, that epic Heracles—holds the posture of *enduring* labors and troubles not because this is his spiritual quintessence and inevitable fate—in fact no necessity pushed Odysseus into the Cyclops' cave[27]—but because "enduring" is a premise and an accomplice of his cunning (*mētis*). But *mētis* sometimes must be not-*mētis* to produce the cycle.

As Odysseus calms the rage aroused by the sight of the unfaithful maids, what can his recollection mean? Of course, to endure, now as at that time, is the smart thing to do. If he kills the suitors, he will punish the maids; to gain time and to keep cool means for Odysseus only to postpone the growling of the she-hag, the murderous assault that he is so eager to initiate now (*Od.* 20.11). While he gains time we may look forward—with him—to the punishment of the maids.

"If he kills the suitors." Of course this is the condition. And although the recollection of the successful display of his *mētis* calms down the rage of Odysseus' heart,[28] he is now himself seized by

---

[26]On the arrogance of Odysseus in this fateful episode that determined Poseidon's hatred against him, see the rich, suggestive paper by Norman Austin, "Odysseus Polytropos: Man of Many Minds," *Arche* 6 (1981): 40–52, especially pp. 49 ff.

[27]See ibid., pp. 49–52.

[28]The tones and shades of the text are difficult to decipher. While there is no doubt that the text extols Odysseus' *endurance* and *mētis*—simply repeating these "virtues" of the hero emphasizes them—it also introduces disconcerting elements: the implicit comparison between the devouring of Odysseus' companions by the Cyclops and the seduction of the maids by the suitors; the characterization of both deeds, the Cyclops' and implicitly the suitors', as "doggish" (*kynteron*); and the sausage simile (20.24–30), which represents in a prosaic, almost comic image the perplexities and anxiety of the hero.

doubts whether he will be able to kill all the suitors alone. Another *mermērizein* scene ensues. This one, however, does not present any alternatives and is resolved by the intervention of Athena, who comes to Odysseus in a dreamlike fashion (line 32) and comforts him.[29] Here enduring and *mētis* mean nothing. Odysseus is humorously and sentimentally represented by the text as troubled and anxious.

The fourth passage in which the assertion of endurance is embedded in a *mermērizein* scene diverging from its "regular" development is *Od.* 17.235–38:

> Odysseus pondered [*mermērixen*] whether he should rush on him [Melanthius] and take away his life with the club or raise him and smash his head to the ground.[30] Yet he endured and restrained himself.

There is no formal novelty in the fact that the two given alternatives do not include the one Odysseus chooses (this happens other times; see, for example, *Il.* 10.503 ff.), but again in the fact that his choice— to do nothing—seems *implicitly* the best thing to do, without the expected *doassato kerdion einai,* "it seemed to him more advantageous," just as in *Od.* 10.49 ff. Here is a shortcut: The theme is closed by a sort of epigrammatic line that establishes endurance as the proper response to the situation, in disregard of the other alternatives that Odysseus, as himself, would have been more than eager to follow. But Odysseus is disguised as a beggar, and to protect himself he must maintain this disguise, as a matter of expediency, an act of his *mētis.*

I have deliberately lingered on this detour through the four passages in which Odysseus' posture of endurance partially renews the epic formulaic theme of pondering alternatives in order to illustrate

---

[29]Odysseus is shown *mermērizein hoppos* (20.28), "pondering how he alone could kill all the suitors." It is true that in the *Iliad* no god intervenes after *mermērizein hoppos* (see Russo, "Homer against His Tradition," pp. 292–93), and that here in *Od.* 20.28 we have the only example of a god's intervention after such a *mermērizein.* Since, however, Athena appears in a dreamlike fashion, the verb *mermērizein* in l. 28 corresponds to a verb depicting the stirring of the mind, after which a divine dream may follow. See, for instance, *Od.* 4.787 ff., where *hormainein* (789), *mermērizein* (791), and *hormainein* (793) correspond semantically and constitute the premise for Athena's sending of a dream to Penelope. This equivalence is also found in the absolute use of *mermērizein;* see, for instance, *Od.* 5.354, 365. See also M. W. Edwards, "Convention and Individuality in *Iliad* I," *HSCP* 84 (1980): 14, n. 32, who correctly shows how much less striking is Athena's arrival in *Od.* 20.30 than in *Il.* 1.194.

[30]I follow the most common translation; see also *Odissea*–Russo, l. 237. But the word *amphoudis* raises questions, and such scholars as Chantraine (*DE*) would like to understand it as "grasping him by the ears," which would be comic.

several features of the *Odyssey:* the dramatic suspense of some of the Iliadic passages is replaced by a more intimate, interior dialogue about issues; and the posture of endurance emerges repeatedly as the solution Odysseus embraces, it being the more advantageous for his survival and protection.

6

Disguise

> If the ego organizes itself through a process of narcissistic identification, then the formation of perceptual identities must be the first and indispensable step in that process. Stimuli, impressions, tensions are rendered recognizable, identifiable through a process of repetition in which that which is repeated comes increasingly to be apprehended as the same.
>
> Samuel Weber, *The Freud Legend*

The most intriguing formal novelty in the four passages discussed above is that the poet's narrative describing the character's alternative courses of action is replaced by Odysseus' direct speech, thus allowing Odysseus to pursue his inner debate in his own voice.[1] In this way a *repeated* trait of Odysseus' behavior is connected to his own voice, whereby the text builds and exhibits the notion of Odysseus' innermost self. That the hero is shown to weigh alternatives within himself *four times*—once, very graphically, within an innermost self that the speaking "I" of Odysseus can address (*Od.* 20.10 ff.)—and that the result of this inner debate (always in favor of endurance) repeatedly emerges in the voice of Odysseus himself suggest a new literary representation of man's identity. Something like the notion of man's "inner" voice must emerge from these repetitions. The self-identity of this voice, whatever disguise and situation a man is in, must intimate

---

[1] In *Od.* 5.355 ff. Odysseus ponders the alternatives and chooses to remain and endure; here the verb is used absolutely, in the sense of "pondering," and equals *hormainein*. In a few passages Odysseus' direct discourse follows the verb *hormainein*, for example, *Od.* 6.118 (in contrast to *Od.* 4.126). In 20.10 ff. he commands endurance to his growling heart—we must imagine his voice as coming from his *mētis* and as having authority over his heart; in 10.49 ff. Odysseus is the narrator of the story. However, 17.235 ff. are in indirect discourse, although a few lines afterward Odysseus repeats his determination in direct speech (*Od.* 17.273 ff.). When a god intervenes—as one often does in the *Iliad*—the will of the god is sometimes carried by direct speech: see *Il.* 1.188 ff., where Achilles answers. The inner monologue in the *mermērizein* scene I am illustrating is essentially Odyssean, but it is formally parallel to the monologues that heroes deliver when making some decision: *Il.* 11.401 ff., 17.91 ff., 21.551 ff., 22.98 ff.

that this voice "mirrors" or bespeaks what is immutable (essential) in man.[2] Let us listen to Odysseus' voice as he speaks to Eumaeus after Melanthius' attack

> I know, I understand: you say all this to one who is mindful. But go on ahead. I will stay here, behind, for I am not without experience of blows and hits. My heart is enduring [*tolmēeis moi thumos*] since I suffered many times in waves and war. Let this be added to the tale of those things. But it is impossible to disregard a ravening belly, accursed one, which causes many evils to men and because of which also the well-timbered ships are fitted out for the barren sea and carry evils to foemen. (*Od.* 17.281–89)

This passage presents two striking features: first, Odysseus repeats his decision to endure in almost the same words he used when he spoke to Calypso and uttered his heroic/human choice (*Od.* 5.223–24). This formal feature conspires with the thematic repetitions triggered by the very notion of *tlēnai*, at once the source and effect of Odysseus' manyness. Moreover, Odysseus repeats his own words while disguised as a beggar. While their ethos is—to say the least—excessive for the character he appears to be, it allows *us*, the readers, to recognize the same Odysseus. Finally, the repetition of the same words exposes the difference between the situations in which Odysseus utters them: with Calypso he asserted his will to return home at all cost; with Eumaeus he simply protects his disguise. To endure is, now more explicitly than ever, a response suggested by *mētis*.

The second startling feature of this passage is the connection of

---

[2]I do not intend this statement as an answer to the question whether there is an *individual* psychological characterization for each character in Homer. (For a vigorous denial of an "individual mark and character," see Fausto Codino, *Introduzione a Omero* [Turin: Einaudi, 1965], pp. 130 ff.) Rather, I wish to suggest the topicality of the epic voice, that is, that while certainly some speeches of, for instance, Diomedes and Achilles as paramount *promakhoi* could easily be interchangeable, Odysseus' voice in these passages seems recognizably his own, inasmuch as he is the man of *mētis* and endurance. Nestor too can be recognized by his specific language, that is, by his long-winded reminiscences. This peculiarity could be ascribed to Nestor's old age or it could be interpreted as Nestor's own inclination. Now the question is whether this epic voice mirrors a "self" or produces something like the establishment of a self. On the ways the *Odyssey* portrays and consolidates the self of Odysseus and makes it an enlightened master, see Max Horkheimer and Theodor W. Adorno, *Dialectic of Enlightenment*, trans. John Cumming (New York: Herder & Herder, 1972). I am trying to question this "consolidation of the self" by showing the complicity that the text entertains between "voice" and "being" as presence. The theoretical aspects of this complicity have been analyzed in Jacques Derrida, *La Voix et le phénomène* (Paris: Presses Universitaires de France, 1967), pp. 84 ff. Here, as in the previous chapter, I limit myself to activating some of the features of Odysseus' voice which, by functioning as "sign" ("signifier" and "signified"), efface the illusion of ideality and presence in the voice.

Odysseus' posture of endurance with his need for, and pleasure in, eating. Here the theme of *tlēnai* is accommodated in a realistic setting: the poor man must silently accept all sorts of insults if he wants to eat. But this is in no way a beggar's theme. Odysseus here repeats a point he made previously, when he was not disguised (*Od.* 7.215 ff.)[3] Eating and the pleasures of the belly are evoked, for an instant, as the powerhouse of man's life, activities, troubles. Man withstands all sorts of pains and troubles in order to satisfy his needs and his desires.

The various thematic strands I have been discussing appear here interwoven, and we must analyze them separately. The pomp and the high pitch of the passage are undeniable. From the epithet *polutlas* in line 280, through which the text dishes out the hero's pièce de résistance on *tolmē;* to the mention of his habitual hardships whose narrative we are now hearing in this poem: "Let this be added to the tale of those things"; to the short presentation of the belly's furiously destructive power, which formally repeats the Iliadic line defining Achilles' *mēnis,* "wrath," 1.2—all this is full of superior intemperance, or of incredible astuteness.

Let us examine the text point by point, and at length, beginning with the striking repetition of Odysseus' words. The verb *tolman* immediately repeats line 238, where Odysseus is shown to stiffen under Melanthius' kick ("he endured and restrained himself": *epetolmēse, phresi d' eskheto*), but of course the notion of Odysseus' enduring heart (*tolmēeis thumos*) goes back to *Od.* 5.223, *talapenthēs thumos,* and to the *Iliad*'s *tlēmōn thumos* (5.670).[4] Because lines 284–85 repeat almost verbatim *Od.* 5.223–24, when Odysseus speaks to Calypso, the repetition indeed aims at that passage and acquires force by evoking it.

Notice that here *tolmēeis* replaces *talapenthēs* of *Od.* 5.222, probably with the same meaning, "enduring," though this is no longer sure; in principle the translation "daring" would be possible here. This uncertainty, though a minimal detail, has some critical importance. First, it reveals how easily contiguous, opposite, metaphorical "signifieds" start sliding back and forth in these *tolma-, tle-, tala-* forms, making that difference uncontrollable, untraceable. Moreover, we may as-

---

[3]Note also the high tone of line 283, in which *ou . . . adaēmōn,* "not without experience," recalls the litotes—although not the formulaic position—of *Il.* 13.811 and *Od.* 12.208: "We are not without experience of pains."

[4]There is a form *thumōi tolmēenti* in *Il.* 10.205: "the daring heart." Nestor is the speaker, and the expression refers to the daring heart of the Greek heroes. This passage confirms the difference in meaning between *tolmaō* in the line from the *Iliad* and in *Od.* 17.284—the same difference in meaning that characterizes the *tle-* forms: "daring" for the *Iliad,* and "enduring" for the *Odyssey.*

sume that the text is here less self-conscious than in *Od.* 5.221 ff. with respect to the specific meaning of the word. There *talapenthēs* testifies to some formal intentionality, but here the text does not show any analogous intention. Here it is not the specific meaning of the word that is important, but the *repetition* of the whole motif.

The debased context—Odysseus is disguised as a beggar—in which the words are repeated does need illustration,[5] but the effects the repetition creates must be assessed on two levels. First, although he is concealed by the disguise, we the audience know that the speaker *is* the same Odysseus of the previous episode. That Eumaeus does not answer and that the dialogue between him and Odysseus the beggar terminates with this passage (289) strengthens our impression that Odysseus speaks to us. For while his immediate interlocutor is unable to connect lines 283–85 to anything, *we* on the contrary can hear the same voice, tone, and words; we can therefore *read them*, so to speak, *in depth*, as undercurrents expressing his spiritual identity. This means we are able to read these experiences at the place where the spiritual self-identity supposedly lies, at the depth of the self.

The text therefore sends forth a reassuring message, a comfortable notion, by inviting us to read the undercurrent identity in *Od.* 5.223–24 and 17.284–85. A world of reassuring certainties emerges from these deceptively innocent intimations: first, the voice becomes the gauge of spiritual self-identity, as if the "word" and "being" had some kind of organic connection; then this repetition of the same words on different occasions solicits and suggests the notion of its self-identity; finally, since this repetition emerges from introspection and inner debates, it proves the depth of its source.

My points entail the comforting conviction that the outward, surface appearances are only deceptive *semblances*, while the self's true *being* or *essence* is rooted in us as *logos*, "speech." Its "source" is probably what Homer calls *noos* and we call mind or consciousness. "Mind" and "consciousness" are what is postulated or presupposed by this "inner voice." When these observations are applied to Odysseus, it is obvious that the repetition of the passage, by allowing us to hear the same voice of Odysseus, constitutes one means through which the text generates our sense of the character's self-awareness and suggests his

---

[5]Odysseus' words are better integrated with the context at *Od.* 5.223–24: the reference to his experience of sea travel is more proper there (where he says he is able to survive shipwreck) than here, where the same phrase is used to illustrate his ability to endure kicks in the legs and similar offenses. The inappropriateness of these lines has raised the suspicion of an interpolation, at least for line 285; see Friedrich Blass, *Die Interpolationen in der Odyssee* (Halle: M. Niemeyer, 1904), pp. 173–74.

spiritual integrity and identity. The power of the *Odyssey* lies in the compelling and smooth presentation of these reassuring certainties.

In fact, the repetition makes almost no sense if one discards this comforting presentation. Of course Odysseus might have said something similar in meaning to what he says now—namely, that poor people must endure blows. But the exact repetition of his previous words is out of place here. Let us see why. There is here a new feature that cannot be suppressed by the audience, however much they might want to do so. Odysseus displays his will to endure while in disguise because he wants to protect his disguise, which is the trick (*mētis*) necessary for the success of his ambush.[6] Odysseus the beggar therefore cannot kill Melanthius on the spot *as Odysseus would.*[7] As a speaker, Odysseus is the same as in 5.221 ff., but as a "doer" he is a different man. The self-identity of the hero that the repeated words should sustain is broken: Odysseus' voice carries two personalities at once, that of heroic Odysseus and that of Odysseus who uses a "heroic" theme to simulate a faked weakness. Odysseus' voice thus sounds double, and therefore it cannot be selfsame; it cannot stem from a simple, original "innermost" place, and sound authentic.

One might indeed object that when Odysseus exclaims: "My heart is enduring since I suffered many times in waves and war. Let this be added to the tale of those things" (*Od.* 17.284–85) he asks his audience to understand that because of his experience of suffering he is capable of undertaking the necessary disguise of a beggar and enduring whatever blows this role entails. This is certainly what we understand. But another simulation is implicit here. Odysseus hides his real motivation for accepting suffering. He does not accept suffering *because* he is good at it; but because he is good at it he turns his adeptness into expediency. The repetition of his former heroic utterance, now for the sake of expediency, destroys the intended pathos and unity of the self.

By displaying the voice of Odysseus the text intimates an attempt to hide or gloss over Odysseus' disguising. Repetition, however, does not

---

[6]On Odysseus' skill in ambushing, see Anthony T. Edwards, *Odysseus against Achilles,* Beiträge zur klassichen Philologie, vol. 171 (Königstein/Ts.: Hain, 1985), pp. 15–41. The *Iliad* avoids developing stories on disguising and masking. For instance, even the strategic situation of Patroclus' wearing the arms of Achilles is hardly exploited by the text. See Karl Reinhardt, *Die Ilias und ihr Dichter* (Göttingen: Vandenhoeck & Ruprecht, 1961), p. 317.

[7]See *Od.* 17.235–38: "Odysseus pondered whether he should rush at him and take away his life with the club or raise him and smash his head to the ground. But he endured and restrained himself."

guarantee the certainty of identity; on the contrary, it hides the absence of identity while intimating the textual desire for it.

Now we have to listen to the repetition of Odysseus' voice as to the voice of a beggar speaking to a swineherd and commenting upon past and future kicks. We have to read the surface of his voice, since Eumaeus does not know who the beggar is:

> My heart is enduring [*tolemēeis moi thumos*] since I suffered many times in waves and war. Let this be added to the tale of those things. (*Od.* 17.284–85)

Even discounting our awareness of the royal pedigree of these words, we cannot fail to realize that they sound incongruous for such a speaker and for such a reference. To assimilate the pain of past and future insolence to the griefs of war and shipwrecks, and likewise to deem this fact worthy of glorious song,[8] is preposterous for a beggar, even for one who claims, as Odysseus the beggar does, a noble pedigree. This episode is recorded in the epic song that we are listening to only because the beggar *is* Odysseus, the king. If Eumaeus swallows Odysseus' awkward tone, we should nevertheless be aware of it, and that we are inclined not to take note of it constitutes a critical problem. The force of the repetition bewitches us as it induces us to read in depth, in accordance with the metaphysics of a voice identical to an inmost being. Consequently, we forget the surface level. We disregard the fact that Odysseus speaks as a beggar for whom no epic tale is ever possible,[9] for we are eager to recognize the self-identity of the character, especially when Odysseus' identity is threatened *by his foul disguise.*

The *Odyssey*, in this way, props up the notion of an identity between *logos* and *being* as presence, with smooth insistence; the *Odyssey* is perhaps the first text in the West to promote the scheme built around that *identity* and to play extensively with this scheme *in order to create a psychological portrait:* indeed, it dramatizes the voice of the inmost *being*

---

[8]I translate *meta kai tode toisi genestho*, of *Od.* 17.285 (= 5.224), following Butcher and Lang's translation. Of course the phrase literally means "let this one be added to those," but since each one of these episodes is sung in the text, the addition occurs in the tale that records them.

[9]See, on the contrary, the amusing scene in *Od.* 14.462–506, where Odysseus, disguised as a beggar, tells Eumaeus a story from the Trojan War—of which Odysseus himself is the protagonist.

h different *semblances,* and accordingly it displays sem-
mentary ways of disguising an immutable self.

tive to this interpretation implies taking seriously the
contexts and assuming that it is textually significant.
r the repetition would remain the same, but the relation
er to the text would change, for Odysseus would be
exposed as repeating himself, foolishly, in a situation that does not
justify and endorse that repetition. Odysseus would then appear to be
searching for his own identity through a purely rhetorical rehearsal
of his voice. The text would expose Odysseus' personality: his identity
would have only a (bari)tonal consistency. The *Odyssey* then would
show that no identity is ever reachable by an epic song, for whatever
means the song may use always functions as disguise.

In this case the difference introduced in the sameness of the repetition would be textually significant, and it would be fully controlled by
the text that uses it to mock Odysseus' pretense of rehearsing his own
identity. As we will see in the next pages, this interpretation would
find support in other passages of the *Odyssey* and therefore cannot be
simply dismissed here. The difficulty in this specific passage, however, is that the authorial presentation of Odysseus' endurance of
Melanthius' kicks (*Od.* 17.235–39) is spoken in the same repeated
heroic voice as Odysseus' own utterance. The text would then have
missed the force of the difference in this authorial passage or would
behave erratically.

7

Disguise and Recognition

Kyrnos, let a seal [*sphrēgis*] be placed by me, as I practice my wisdom [*sophizomenōi*], upon these utterances [*epē*, poetic utterances, verses]—they will never be stolen without detection and no one will replace the good thing that is there with something inferior; thus everyone shall say: These are the utterances [*epē*] of Theognis, the one from Megara, famous among all men.

Theognis, 19–23

Disguise is of such an uncanny nature that it is perceived as "disguise" only when it is detected and exposed—that is, precisely when it no longer functions successfully as a disguise. When it does appear as what it *is* (a disguise), it no longer obtains the effects for which it was adopted. In the *Odyssey*, Odysseus' disguises are always known to the readers, but they remain undetected by the characters who interact with him until the recognition scenes.

Sometimes the text allows us to perceive this double status of the disguise as it is subjectively experienced by Odysseus himself. In *Od.* 17.356 ff. Odysseus is described as eating the food that Telemachus sent him:

he took the food in his hands and placed it there in front of him at his feet on his miserable wallet[1] and began to eat while the singer sang in the hall. When he had eaten his meal and the divine singer had finished the

---

[1] *Aeikeliēs epi pērēs*. This Odyssean adjective (*aeikelios*) is used here, in the first description of Odysseus' begging, to describe the shabby, horrible wallet of a beggar. The adjective repeats the same notion as *aeikēs*, the epithet of the wallet in 13.437, 17.197, and 18.108. This wallet is a symbolic prop of Odysseus' new, reduced status. The adjectives *aeikēs, aeikelios* signify here and in several other passages both the objective "indecency" of the beggar, according to the viewpoint of the noble suitors, and his "unseemly" aspect, which instills pity in some characters, but especially in the reader. It is therefore futile to try to distinguish two meanings of the adjective without taking into account these two perspectives. This word expresses precisely the ambivalence of Odysseus' disguise: for the suitors, Odysseus' shabbiness is mere indecency, while for us who know his real identity and feel pity it is a measure of his misery. If these different points of view had been taken into consideration also in other contexts, much of the discussion

tors began noisily to chatter in the hall. Then Athena came
ear Odysseus, son of Laertes, prompting him[2] to collect
he suitors and to learn who were righteous and who lawless
, though even so she would not ward off ruin from any of
e went to beg from each in turn moving to the right, stretch-
and everywhere as if he had been a beggar for a long time.

(*Od.* 17.357–66)

In this unforgettable representation of dejection, Odysseus seems
to move as an actor (366).[3] The signs are all there—the miserable
wallet, the meager bread, the outstretched hand—but the "meaning,"
the set of the signifieds that go with *being* a beggar, is not; Odysseus is
actually spying on his enemies and, guided by the goddess, planning
revenge (363–64). However, when a confrontation between Odysseus
the beggar and Antinous occurs and Odysseus is humiliated by sneers
(*Od.* 17.448)[4] and is even hit, he suffers dishonor, pain, and mockery
not as an actor at all but as a victim, as a real beggar.

Athena's role underlines this distinction perfectly, for she *wants*
Odysseus to be humiliated (*Od.* 18.346–48 = 20.284–86):

Athena did not let the noble suitors refrain from heart-biting insults so
that pain [*akhos*] may sink even deeper into the heart of Odysseus, son of
Laertes.

Here Athena does not make her presence known to Odysseus, physically or vocally, to enhance his heroic stature. She does not prompt
him to *know* the attitude of the suitors; rather, she prompts the suitors
to insult Odysseus as if he were a real beggar. Her strategic reasons
are her own, no longer shared with Odysseus, who thus becomes an
unwitting victim of her designs. Though he knows, and we know, that

---

on this adjective would have been obviated: see, for instance, *aeikēs* in *Lessico politico
dell'epica greca arcaica*, ed. Lucio Bertelli and Italo Lana, vol. 2 (Turin: Bottega d'Erasmo, 1978), where Arthur W. H. Adkins' and A. A. Long's discussions are summarized.

[2]According to A.H.C., Athena becomes visible only to Odysseus. If this assumption is
correct, Odysseus would go through this experience clearly aware of her divine assistance. But it is not certain that Athena appears at all; she might inspire Odysseus
without manifesting herself. At any rate, her presence or inspiration validates him as
the hero he is and reminds us again that his attire and role are merely theatrical props.
Analogously, the epithet (361) underscores his "real" being.

[3]Joseph Russo pertinently describes Odysseus' skill in acting out his role; see *Odissea*,
5:180.

[4]"Antinous both threatens Odysseus and mocks his story." Stanford, 2:294. The text
cannot avoid representing Odysseus as ridiculous with his beggar's clothes and manner:
in addition to *Od.* 17.448, see 18.26–27.

he is still the "real" Odysseus—the hero of *mētis*, the same warrior who destroyed Troy—and that the beggar is a superficial disguise—a mere sign added to his "real" being—he is nonetheless presented as marked in his flesh and mind by this mere detachable sign.[5]

The uncanny nature of disguise depends on its seeming capability to meddle successfully with the system of "signs." Disguise seems to imply that the signs that "represent" an entity are, as it were, detachable from the entity: when the disguise is recognized for what it is, that is, a simulation, the disguising signs appear as "artificial," "added," and "controllable." In fact they are simply simulated, but simulation cannot be read in the signs, and therefore it does not become a constituent feature of the sign. The inference that disguising signs are "artificial," "added," and "controllable" intimates that when no disguise is intended the signs are "natural," "inherent" to the entity, and "necessary." Such an intimation is comforting and pleasurable.

Odysseus is made to use disguise as a convincing strategy to help ensure his survival and his victory. It is a weapon of his *mētis*. However, the constant disguises of Odysseus (and of other characters, such as Athena) play something other than a merely practical role. The possibility for the character to hide and simulate his "self" by means of "artificial," "added" signifiers intimates, as we have seen in *Od.* 17.283–85, the notion of his "real," "authentic" self, of which the voice in that instance is the "natural," "inherent" sign. Analogously Odysseus' scar is the natural and inherent sign through which Euryclea can detect and confront the "artificial," "added" signs of his disguise. The several scenes of disguise and recognition in the *Odyssey* place these two sets of signs in opposition, hold them neatly separated, and prompt the comforting notion that "natural," "inherent" signs exist and are therefore finally recognizable as such.

This strategy allows the text to create endless shams and simulations that deceive the characters. To the extent that disguise is undetected by the characters, the *disguising* signs appear to *truly* represent the character. Thus the signs operate as simulating, and independent, detachable tokens. From this perspective, signs of truth and of simulation are indistinguishable. That is why the text can say that Odysseus "while telling many lies was making them similar to real events" (*Od.* 17.203). And of course his lies are not detected. The *Odyssey*'s fiction is based on this premise. Consequently the text sug-

---

[5]Russo finely analyzes Athena's reasons for provoking the suitors against Odysseus: (1) Odysseus' pain helps to motivate his outrageous revenge, (2) the name Odysseus is understood by the poet as meaning "receiving (and giving) offense." *Odissea*, 5:216.

gests simultaneously the notions that signs are natural and artificial, inherent and added, truthful and false. Odysseus' "rags," for instance, are simultaneously natural, truthful signs for the characters who take him as a beggar and artificial and false signs for us readers. Whether the text displays one or the other notion depends, of course, upon its addressee at each particular moment; the only prescription it must follow is to try to keep the two notions under its control.

Notwithstanding the exceeding shrewdness (*mētis*) of the text, the two notions I have outlined cannot be controlled. In fact "disguise" as simulation implies that the sign has the *appearance* of truth though it is not true and that the simulating signs can be read as such only as an *après coup* or as retroactivation. Retroactivation (*Nachträglichkeit*, a Freudian concept) names the process through which some earlier experience becomes known, and significant, only when a later experience triggers a retroactivating reading of the earlier one. Analogously, a "disguise" is recognized as such only when the previous signs (the simulating ones) come to be perceived *as* simulating through the emergence of new signs that give new significance to the first ones. These new signs make known a difference in the referent, a difference that the previous signs had supposedly glossed over or successfully suspended. The two sets of signs now contend with one another about that supposition or that successful suspension of difference. As the "disguise" is detected, the early signs acquire a significance through signs *other* than themselves, and vice versa. This otherness that produces significance makes "disguise" a complex figure of difference and supplementarity in which it is impossible to separate the two sets of signs, since we cannot retrieve the significance of one set without the other, and often it is not possible to decide which set determines the significance of the other.[6] As a result, the two sets of signs, the artificial, added ones and the natural, inherent ones, appear only presumably and controversially so; in fact both tend to adhere to the character that has used them as at once added and inherent, artificial and natural. How this happens to Odysseus can be shown in several of the *Odyssey*'s disguise and recognition scenes. For the sake of clarity, it is useful to distinguish three moments in the interaction between the two sets of signs:

1. The "artificial" signs of the disguise still mark the character after his disguise is recognized, that is, when the disguise is known to be a simulation. This point is obvious in general—Odysseus, for instance,

---

[6]Detective novels and legal procedures show that comparing different pieces of evidence is often a difficult and unresolvable task.

would not be Odysseus were he not the man of disguises—but it is also clear in details. We can call this moment "the permanence of disguise" within the recognition.

2. The retroactivating reading is inevitable both for characters and for readers. The characters deal with a relatively simple set of disguising and undisguising signs—the rags of a beggar and a scar, for instance—and they know and see the referent. For us readers, it seems there is no need for a retroactivating reading, since we are always aware of the disguise a character has assumed. Yet we experience re-cognitions in the same way, either with the other characters or by ourselves, through the signs of the text. For instance, we re-cognize with Euryclea the Odysseus she recognizes—that is, the relative of Autolycus—and this new material gives a new focus to what we already know of Odysseus' cunning. On the other hand, the repetition of Odysseus' words in *Od.* 17.283–85 should, by a retroactivating reading, reveal to us alone the self-identity of the hero beneath the props of his disguise. For us readers, disguise and recognition always function as rhetorical devices through which the text tries to assure us of the self-identity of the hero.

3. Yet the process of recognition is what makes disguise disguise. Accordingly, the signs that, at their appearance, reveal the disguising (simulating) signs and allow the recognition are also those that simultaneously detect and constitute disguise as simulation. The process of re-cognition, true to its "re-" component, implies a knowing that simultaneously harks back to the early signs and moves forward toward new signs, through a constant movement of displacement and (dis)figuration.[7] This supplementary force of the disguise-recognition operation upsets the self-identity of the hero.

My specific analyses should expand and illuminate these definitions.

The force of the mark, of the signifier by itself, is the theme of "The Purloined Letter," Jacques Lacan's essay on Poe's story. Lacan shows how the signifier (the letter) takes possession of the person who happens to have it, although the nature of the signified is never once mentioned. One suspects, of course, that it is of an embarrassing nature, but no facts are provided. The entire story hinges on the

---

[7]On recognition as re-cognition see Samuel Weber, "*It.*," in *Glyph 4: Johns Hopkins Textual Studies* (Baltimore: Johns Hopkins University Press, 1978), pp. 1–31. On the signs (*sēmata*) and *anagignōskein*, "to recognize," see Gregory Nagy, "Sēma and Nóēsis: Some Illustrations," *Arethusa* 16 (1983): 36. Nagy shows with admirable precision that the recognition of the *sēma* "requires an act of interpretation."

possession of the letter and the power with which it endows the possessor.

The power and permanence of the disguise of Odysseus' travesties is analogous to this power of the letter as signifier. More precisely, the disguising props are somehow so possessive and masking that their force is never *fully* dispelled even when Odysseus reveals signs of his "real" self. For instance, when Euryclea recognizes Odysseus by the scar on his thigh, the text does not mention that any change occurs in Odysseus' looks and complexion. So when she recognizes him, exactly what aspect does she recognize? Certainly Odysseus himself, the real Odysseus, does not look like the old beggar Athena has made up, and yet Euryclea glances at this wrinkled, aged, miserable face and tells herself that this is Odysseus. *The disguise lasts and remains through the recognition* in an odd disfiguration of the identity. Odysseus' tender youth and old age are evoked by the signs of the disguise and by those of the recognition that stick simultaneously to his body. Analogously, the members of Odysseus' household, and those of the suitors who knew him before he left for Troy, probably retain the impression of the beggar even after Odysseus reveals his "real" self to them. Does he fight and kill all the suitors in the disguise of the old beggar or in that other one, only a little less unbecoming (*aeikēs*), in which he fought Irus?[8] Again, the persistence of the disguise in utterly improper situations risks upsetting and confusing the satisfaction and pleasure produced by the recognition.

The scar on Odysseus' thigh reveals for Euryclea the sham of the beggar. The scar *means* literally a wound, and Euryclea knows that Odysseus in his youth received a wound in his thigh from a boar. Her emotion, the fact that she accepts that old, miserable, wretched man to be—against all odds—Odysseus, tells us that her recognition is in every sense a re-discovery.[9]

We, too, learn something new about Odysseus, for the scar becomes the pretext for introducing the whole maternal side of Odysseus' family. It is at this point that we learn of Autolycus, his maternal grandfather, and of the ties between Odysseus and Autolycus, who in

---

[8]In *Od.* 22.1 we are told that Odysseus gets rid of his rags (*rhakea*). They would, of course, encumber the archer.

[9]On the relation of this crucial moment to the secrecy of Odysseus' identity, see Bernard Fenik, *Studies in the Odyssey* (Wiesbaden: F. Steiner, 1974), p. 39: "From the start of the poem [the poet] has played with the ironic and emotional potential of these scenes of secrecy and incognito. Here now is the climax to which they have been building. . . . The bare necessity for Odysseus to remain unrecognized does not account for the length of this meeting or the vehement passion that informs it. The poet's intent focuses on these ironies and emotional impact."

fact named Odysseus after the circumstances in which he (Autolycus) found himself (*Od.* 19.405 ff.). This connection between Odysseus and Autolycus is significant not only at the *literal* level of kinship; figuratively, it indicates their common patron god, Hermes, and their shared intellectual characterization. And so the scar assumes for us a *figurative* meaning both as the mark, left on Odysseus' body, of his relationship with Autolycus and as the mark, left in Odysseus' name, of his Hermes-like characterization. The portrait of Odysseus expands, becomes larger. However, the text here neither suspends the plot nor digresses, as a classic analysis of Odysseus' scar has accustomed us to believe.[10] On the contrary, it is grounding both the name and the destiny of the hero in a specific event and relationship.[11] Contradictorily, however, just when his intellectual powers are better identified, he seems to exhibit an odd weakness and indecision. It appears that only at the last moment does he remember the scar on his leg and realize the danger that Euryclea may recognize it. His last resource, to sit in the shadows, fails (*Od.* 19.388–93a). It seems that the disguise Odysseus wears so well has made him forgetful of his real self. Figuratively—and how can we avoid this sort of interpretation when the whole scene invites it?—the text suggests that Odysseus loses something of himself just when new features are added to his portrait. The signs of disguise and recognition spin together in an upsetting movement.

Penelope and Odysseus

In book 23 the text carries out the difficult and sensitive recognition of Odysseus by Penelope (23.1–230). First, Euryclea tries in vain to persuade Penelope that the old beggar has revealed himself as Odysseus and that he has killed the suitors. All the nurse's arguments and evidence fail to convince Penelope. That Telemachus knew the real identity of the old beggar (23.29) also does not impress Penelope; that Euryclea herself has seen the corpses of the suitors suggests to

[10]I refer to Erich Auerbach's essay, "Odysseus' Scar," in *Mimesis*, trans. Willard R. Trask (Princeton: Princeton University Press, 1953), pp. 3–23. In no way can we read the entire scar episode as an ekphrasis or as ornamentation. Odysseus' recognition by Euryclea correctly implies the clues of Odysseus' name and of his maternal family. See also Norman Austin, "The Function of Digressions in the *Iliad*," *GRBS* 7 (1966): 310; and Jenny Clay, *The Wrath of Athena* (Princeton: Princeton University Press, 1983), pp. 57 ff.

[11]Even the pathetic scene with Argus is a recognition scene: the dog recognizes the master notwithstanding the disguise. See also Aristotle *Poetics*, frag. 177 (Rose).

Odysseus' wife that a god accomplished the deed (63 ff.); that Euryclea has already recognized the famous scar of Odysseus means nothing to Penelope (*Od.* 23.80 ff.). The signs or clues of the recognitions are coded: they mean a different thing to each character. This feature proves the "artificiality" of the *revealing* signs and simultaneously confirms the figural meaning these signs of recognition have for the reader. Each clue therefore implies a personal, private access to Odysseus. Yet at the literal level this sign or clue has, generally speaking, a limited and uncertain significance. Granted, the nurse was present when the boy Odysseus came back from his grandfather's house with a fresh wound on his leg, but obviously a scar is too generic a sign to allow a plausible recognition many years after. It is at the figural level that the sign "scar" makes richer sense, evoking for us readers the relationship between the nurse and the boy, as against that of Penelope and Odysseus, for which an erotic "clue" is figuratively more fitting. Thus, for the audience's benefit, the text belittles the *literal* value of the sign as a clue of identity to emphasize the symbolic value of each sign.

This figurative process keeps on displacing Odysseus' traits for the reader, since each clue validates not his identity but his subjective and figural relationship to other characters.[12] It is for this reason that all those clues are coded to some extent in an arbitrary way, literally speaking, and in a deep symbolic way, figuratively speaking. This becomes evident as the Penelope-Odysseus recognition scene develops.

Penelope descends to the hall where Odysseus, still splashed with blood, sits facing the light of the fire (89). He is still in the garb of the beggar.[13] A mute encounter between the eyes of husband and wife does not convince Penelope. The text is cryptic in lines 93–95, and the suggested corrections seem to trivialize this sensitive point.[14] Telemachus becomes impatient (97–103), but Penelope answers that she is unable to speak and to look at Odysseus (106–7). She will test the "foreigner" through clues (*semata*) that only she and Odysseus know.

---

[12]Not only does each character, or group of characters, recognize a special clue, but the meaning and ramifications of the clues are presented only in relation to those specific recognitions. Accordingly, Autolycus is mentioned in the *Odyssey* only in connection with the scar, except once, when Odysseus' mother is defined by reference to her father (*Od.* 11.85).

[13]*Od.* 23.115–16, notwithstanding *Od.* 22.1.

[14]Most manuscripts read *esidesken* in l. 94, and some editors follow this reading, which makes a difficult sense. Other manuscripts and editors (A.H.C. and Stanford, for instance) read *eisken*, which makes good sense but trivializes the scene.

Odysseus understands, reassures Telemachus, and urges him to organize a dance in order to disguise the death of the suitors, which if not concealed could become the source of serious dangers for father and son. This new disguise that Odysseus' fertile mind concocts should have revealed Odysseus' identity to Penelope, but she needs— for the reader's benefit of course—clues more private than this one.

This odd, and in some way uncanny, concealment of the suitors' death is disturbing. On the one hand, it is devised simply to deflect the attention of people outside, who, hearing the merry music, will think Penelope has finally decided to marry one of the suitors (149 ff.). On the other hand, this sham also functions as the musical accompaniment to Odysseus' courtship of his wife and their new marriage; for it is indeed a new erotic scene and an exchange of witty clues (in which Penelope outdoes her husband) that finally establishes the recognition.[15] Yet the musical accompaniment to this marriage has an undertone of lament (see *peristenackizeto* of 23.146),[16] since it covers or disguises the death of the suitors who hoped to marry Penelope. Penelope's recognition occurs in a mystified—disguised—atmosphere of merriment.

Having proposed the dance, Odysseus is then washed by a slave and beautified by Athena (*Od.* 23.153 ff.). Most editors bracket the passage (157–62) that describes Odysseus' virile, erotic beauty in the exact words used to describe the same beautification that took place when Odysseus met Nausicaa (*Od.* 6.230–35). To our taste, of course, it seems improper that in this most serious moment, the goal of all Odysseus' journeying, we should be reminded of the erotic spell he worked upon the princess of the Phaeacians. But bracketing is only a puritanical reaction. The fact is that even if we dismiss lines 157–62, Athena's beautification of Odysseus remains (156). Odysseus is reconquering his wife, and if the appeal that aids his erotic reappropriation now is the same that attracted Nausicaa, it is equally proper to his role; in fact, in both cases it is Athena who is responsible for his beautification. Yet now, unexpectedly, Odysseus' power of seduction fails. Penelope still does not recognize him.

Where Athena fails, the text succeeds with a master stroke. To have Odysseus beautified and to have Penelope completely unmoved by those same divine looks that so impressed Nausicaa might indicate

[15]On this point, see Helene Foley's perceptive discussion in "'Reverse Similes' and Sex Roles in the *Odyssey*," *Arethusa* 11 (1978): 7–26.

[16]*Peristenakhizomai* here means "to resound all around," but one cannot forget its suggestion of "lament," since the verb is composed of (*stenō*), *stenakhō*, "to groan," "to lament," and *peri*.

that Penelope's and Odysseus' erotic recognition must occur through a different clue than that of his normal sexual attractiveness, a clue that instead bespeaks their conjugal relationship. Unknown to the characters, Penelope's unsuccessful recognition points toward the delicate and humorous intimacy that Penelope's private clue will create, metaphorically, for the reader.

The effect of the repeated lines could also be to invite readers to consider Odysseus' and Penelope's characterization. Does Odysseus think that once he has washed off his wretched aspect (115) Penelope will recognize him immediately? If he thinks so, he is either too cocky and sure of himself or simple of mind. He does not realize how mistrustful she is. Indeed, at the *literal* level of the recognition it is true that though Odysseus tries explicitly to make himself accepted as Odysseus, Penelope consistently fails to recognize his distinctive traits (*Od.* 23.94–95, 166–70, 174–76). If the repetition of the lines describing Odysseus' beauty (*Od.* 6.230–35 = 23.157–62) is meant to assure the reader of the sameness of Odysseus' traits, it also emphasizes the resistance of Penelope, who alone among the characters still does not recognize him. But are these "same" traits Odysseus' "real" traits, those of Odysseus himself? There is no certainty. He appears to be suddenly transformed from a beggar (a disguise) into a seductive man (a new mask). Odysseus' traits are constantly changing and continually being displaced. And what about Penelope's reaction? Does she think she has to deal with a god? Or, though beginning to suspect the truth, does she still require the evidence she would trust most? We cannot say. At any rate, only when she has obtained the evidence of the bed will she recognize the traits that Athena has beautified but that as yet mean nothing to her.

For the moment, then, Penelope resists recognizing Odysseus' beautiful, erotic traits. She either plays that hyperbolic, mistrustful role of the loyal wife we are accustomed to recognize in fairy or folk tales or she has serious reasons to avoid mistakes: on both accounts she renders the handsome portrait of Odysseus purposeless. His erotic power dies partially with the purposelessness of this portrait, and for the reader he undergoes a loss of his own previous identity.

Odysseus becomes impatient and repeats the words Telemachus impatiently addressed to his mother (168–70 = 100–102).[17] That Odysseus repeats the words used by his son implies that his offended reaction is generally "masculine" and that he does not put anything

---

[17]Some of this text belongs to Odysseus himself: see 102 = 170 and *Od.* 16.206, 19.484, 24.322.

personal or intimate in his reproach to Penelope. Ironically, Odysseus, who wants to be recognized, here does not present her with any specific traits or clues.

Now Penelope takes the lead and snares her resourceful husband, successfully. She provokes Odysseus by commanding Euryclea to displace Odysseus' immovable bed. Here literal and figural meanings converge. Odysseus is indeed the literal builder of the bed, but Penelope, by implying that the bed has become removable, leaves open the assumption that she has been unfaithful with a god (184–86). While Penelope's provocation compels Odysseus to reveal himself as the builder of the bed, and so as Odysseus, it also temporarily endangers his possession of the bed and of Penelope. Penelope's recognition therefore is thus effected by a representation of Odysseus as dispossessed of what determines his identity as husband and lord of the house.[18] Odysseus' "dispossession" lasts only a moment, however; he is immediately reassured that his bed has never been displaced. The delicate symbolic innuendoes of this scene do not need to be stressed; the mystery of the bed is the secret of their intimacy, its immovability the sign of her faithfulness.

But who has been recognized here? Certainly Penelope comes into the foreground, since she outdoes her husband in his own territory. We become aware of her rather than of him. And there are other delicate touches. For example, in facing his wife's "resistance" Odysseus loses the male self-assuredness and adroitness that the text has emphasized so many times. Here Odysseus is different from the seducer of Nausicaa, and for us this difference adds a new element to what it is now difficult to call "Odysseus' identity." The new clues do not *prove* the simulating significance of the old ones; they simply contradict the previous ones, and both old and new signs imprint on his image a displacing force.

These observations lead to two different conclusions. On the symbolic level, Odysseus' self-revelation as simultaneously a young, embarrassed seducer and the unique witness to Penelope's erotic and sexual experience is, as I am suggesting, a masterful representation; but on a more literal level, where no new courtship or marriage takes place and Penelope simply ascertains that the old beggar *is* Odysseus (*anagnorismos*), the recognition annuls many portraits of Odysseus and presents a new one, totally unknown to us.

And what about Penelope's feelings? She recognizes Odysseus as

---

[18]Note l. *Od.* 23.183, where Odysseus calls Penelope's pretense *thumalges epos*, "heart-biting word."

the builder of the bed, but is the simplicity of mind he now exhibits also one of his recognizable characteristics? The very possibility of posing such a question demonstrates how the recognition produces a sort of disfiguring representation of the character.[19]

Telemachus and Odysseus

Analogous features appear in the elaborate and stately recognition scene in which Odysseus is recognized by his son Telemachus (*Od.* 16.155 ff.). Let us recall that Athena appears to Odysseus alone in the same form as she appeared to him at his arrival in Ithaca (13.288–89 = 16.156–57) when, after her first deceptive epiphany (13.221 ff.), she appears as herself: "a beautiful, tall woman expert in splendid handiwork" (13.289 = 16.157). She appears (*phaneisa, Od.* 16.159) to Odysseus in a supernatural atmosphere that is heightened by her invisibility to Telemachus and by the nervous rushing of the dogs. She invites Odysseus to go out—Telemachus still does not react—and with her magic wand dispels or annuls Odysseus' prior disguise as the old beggar. One would imagine that as a result of this operation Odysseus would recover his natural complexion and aspect, but in fact he emerges in another disguise, one that is new even for the reader. The text here mentions his dark beard (16.176); elsewhere he is always described as red or fair (*xanthos, Od.* 13.299, 431).[20] Be that as it may, when Odysseus returns to the hut Telemachus cannot believe what he sees: the miraculous transformation of the old beggar into a young, imposing figure. And this transformation tells Telemachus that the figure he beholds is a god (*Od.* 16.179 ff.).

Ironically, Telemachus was unable to see a real god appearing (*phaneisa*), and now he is made to see a god when there is none. Of course, on a symbolic or figurative level this misapprehension makes

[19]The text forces Penelope to become aware of her daring in tricking Odysseus: in ll. 23, 209 ff. she is made to beg Odysseus not to be angry with her—for he is so smart (*pepnuso*)—and not to resent her long refusal to recognize him. She is aware that either God—as in the case of Helen—or men can easily confound the honest behavior of a wife: she has therefore shown that she is her husband's most loyal ally when she has applied all her ingenuity and mistrustfulness to escape the seeming danger of adultery—a danger and a dishonor of which Helen is again exemplary, since her husband moved all Greece to get her back. For a different emphasis, see Leslie L. Collins, "NEIKEOS APXH: Helen and Heroic Ethics" (Ph.D. diss., Cornell University, 1982), pp. 177 ff.

[20]In two other passages, *Od.* 6.231 = 23.158, Odysseus' hair is compared to the hyacinth. If this simile is taken as describing the color of his hair rather than its curliness—as it is more commonly taken—it would then be clear that these two passages support *Od.* 16.176.

sense. Odysseus is the hero and the father. As a hero, he has a privileged relation with the divine power, and Athena's appearance to him alone represents the conventional relationship of the hero and his protective god. Telemachus beholds the famous father as if he were a god: by this misapprehension the son is made to look at the father in the right or expected relationship with the divine, as though the presence of Athena, which eludes Telemachus, reverberates in the godlike figure of Odysseus. Here, as in the whole Telemachy, the young man is deprived of any direct and recognizable acquaintance with the divine power.

This is, of course, an edifying and gratifying interpretation of the scene. But a more troubling reading emerges from the text. Telemachus is utterly confused. Because he has no remembrance of his father, he cannot distinguish between Odysseus' "appearance" and his "being." And the appearances are bewildering. Odysseus must persuade Telemachus that the old and new signs of his appearance mean just what he says they mean, not what they *seem* to mean. An old beggar suddenly appears as a young, royal figure; all Telemachus can do is attribute this miracle to a god. And so Telemachus tells his father: "You *are* [*essi*] a god" (183). Odysseus protests (187): "*I am* [*eimi*] not a god. Why do you *liken* [*eiskeis*] me to a god?" Odysseus alone knows that he is *not* a god though he *resembles* one, and little by little he can persuade Telemachus, first, that he only *looks* like (*eoikas*, 200) a god, and then that only his *transformation* depends on a supernatural agent (207–13). This transformation and its cause are not simple propositions, for they imply that Telemachus accepts the uncanny fact that his father has an inconstant and changing form. As Odysseus himself declares, Athena does what she likes and makes him "sometimes similar to a beggar and sometimes to a young man with handsome clothes around my body" (16.209–10). No one can say that this amounts to an easily readable sign of his being. The suppression of one disguise does not reveal Odysseus' real, literal aspect under that disguise, but rather shows the permanent possibility of his being disguised. Like Athena in her epiphany in book 13 and the Odysseus in book 23, Odysseus is here revealed to his son as being changeable, disguisable. And this is the literal way of defining the retroactive effect of disguise: when the disguised entity is *recognized* as disguised, it becomes "disguisable." No self-identity is ever sure.

If Telemachus finally "recognizes" his father, it is because he lets himself be persuaded by Odysseus' voice. Confronted with conflicting outward signs—miraculous signs—and the voice of Odysseus, Telemachus chooses to believe the latter. If we transfer this confrontation of signs to the text and its author, we find an indication of where in the many folds of the text the truth is supposed to lie. We can read the scene allegorically, in the following way: the text (= Odysseus) tells us readers (= Telemachus who *anagignoskei* [reads] the signs of his father), "Do not read the signs in their reference to the external aspects of the story—miraculous transformations, journeys, and other marvelous tales—that the Muse (= tradition) knows and hands down to me; no, believe in the inner voice of the text (of Odysseus), for I am the voice of truth (I *am* Odysseus)."

This recognition of the Odyssean-textual voice has a threefold importance. First, it declares once more the decisive importance of the voice above all other signs in the epic tradition, then it reveals that hidden in the folds of the marvelous tales—as in the miraculous appearances of Odysseus—there is a sober truth, the allegorical voice of the text. And finally, it proves that the allegorical voice belittles the solid reality of the tales, since the allegory dissipates or even discredits the referent and brings into the foreground textuality itself. As the textual voice may present itself, it is caught in an undecidable track. It says either "I am the truth disjunct from the fiction (or even against the fiction)," or "I am the truth within the fiction." This amounts to delcaring that the voice saying "I am the truth" is itself a fiction.[21]

Like Odysseus himself who, Telemachus realizes, can be either a beggar or a young royal figure, the voice of the text is never one. When Odysseus in his final plea tells Telemachus:

ou men gar toi et' allos eleusetai enthade Odusseus, all'
hode egō toiosde.

No other Odysseus will come here for you again, but such as you see me.
(16.204–5)

he implies that somehow two or more Odysseuses could possibly come to Ithaca and claim, or seem, to be Odysseus. Odysseus' disguisability prepares us for Penelope's utter mistrustfulness and destroys forever our certainty about his real looks. For even now it is not clear which Odysseus is there for Telemachus—the royal young man or the old

[21]This reading focuses on a structure that shows the narrative as a discourse about narrative in which no reference is essential. Thus our reading illustrates exactly Paul de Man's statement in *Allegories of Reading* (New Haven: Yale University Press, 1979), p. 162: "But the necessary presence of the moment of utterance and of the interpretative moment of understanding has nothing to do with the empirical situation naively represented in [the] scene: the notions of audience and of narrator that are part of any narrative are only the misleading figuration of a linguistic structure."

beggar into which Athena will immediately change him again. Similarly, the voice of Odysseus telling Telemachus "I am the truth" does not tell us which truth it is, whether the allegorical one disjunct though emerging from the fiction or the truth within the fiction. The ambivalence between these statements of the narrative voice resounds forcefully in the last words of Odysseus' plea: "it is easy for the gods who hold the vast heaven to exalt [*kudēnai*] a man or to humiliate him [*kakōsai*]" (16.211–12). Since these words seal Odysseus' explanation, they presumably describe Odysseus' *literal* exaltation as a royal figure and his *literal* humiliation as a beggar. Yet it is obvious that the two verbs have a metaphorical use, and Hesiod's *Works and Days* 3–8 only strengthens our sense of their metaphorical force in this passage.

It is therefore in the space between a beggar and a hero, between the humiliated and exalted figures of his father, that Telemachus recognizes Odysseus. The son meets a constantly *self*-displacing figure. For us readers, however, an additional displacing element interferes: our inability to decide whether the entire scene has to be read metaphorically or literally. We cannot read it both ways because, as we have seen, the metaphorical meaning inevitably minimizes the referent, the literal story.

Analogously, Odysseus' own voice sounds different at different moments. In *Od.* 17.283–85 the text does not succeed in retrieving the authentic selfsame voice of Odysseus. But why would it repeat almost the very words of *Od.* 5.222–24 if this were not its intention? Instead of the authentic voice of the hero, we hear only the desire for this authenticity. The authorial voice that, from the midst of the fiction it establishes, promises to tell us the truth—this voice too can express only the desire for the authorial truth.

8

Disguising Truth: Fiction

The *Odyssey* . . . is a poem of the facets of intelligence, the poem of
many minds and many turns. Perspective in this poem shifts from
place to place, from person to person. Perspectives overlap, diverge,
converge, transect, subtend one another to give the poem a whole
configuration truly geometric.

> Norman Austin,"Odysseus Polytropos:
> Man of Many Minds"

No passage can better illustrate the nature of Odyssean fiction as a
"disguise of truth" than the line the poet uses to comment on Odysseus' lies as he narrates to Penelope an apocryphal story about himself
(*Od.* 19.165–203). At the end of this story, the narrative voice intrudes and pointedly comments: *Iske pseudea polla legōn etumoisin homo-
ia,* "While telling many lies he was making them similar to real events"
(*Od.* 19.203).[1]

In the preceding chapters I have pointed out that one of the effects
of "disguise" is to suggest that there are "natural," "real," "inherent"
signs of truth as opposed to the added and artificial ones of disguise.
Here the text produces just this effect: by defining Odysseus' own
story as a disguise of truth it suggests, of course, that the rest of the
story (of the *Odyssey*) is pure truth. That is, the *Odyssey* declares to its
readers that it contains some parts that are true (*etuma,* 203) and
others that are not (*pseudea,* 203). The text therefore exploits the
scenario staging the author, the narrative, and the reader, with the
goal of deluding the reader into assuming the truth of what he reads
(i.e., the reality of the referent) and consequently also into presuming

---

[1]This line has a long echo in archaic Greek texts, as it is "quoted" by Hesiod (*Theog.*
27) and Xenophanes (frag. 36). Obviously it declares in the most radical way the
shamming power of the word that can simulate the *etuma* (real things) so well that no
discriminating feature allows the listener to distinguish lies from truth. Men are pris-
oners of the delusive power of the *logos.* See Pietro Pucci, *Hesiod and the Language of
Poetry* (Baltimore: Johns Hopkins University Press, 1977), pp. 8 ff.

the author's control over the narrative. As we read the poet's statement at the level of the scenario in which author, text, and reader are involved, the deceptive power of the *logos* increases exponentially, for it deceives us in the very act of singling us out as those to whom truth is delivered.

The purposes of this type of deception are pleasure or self-interest. The suborner in this instance is Odysseus, and his purpose is to defend his disguise for the sake of his self-interest. On another occasion, Athena deceives Odysseus for the mere pleasure of deceiving and of seducing (*Od.* 13.221 ff.). And when Phemius sings of the Achaeans' homecoming (*Od.* 1.154, 227), he sings against his will, though he charms his audience: self-interest and pleasure are both at work in shaping his song. By incorporating Phemius' lies in its context, the *Odyssey* repeats the same gesture as in *Od.* 19.203, for it invites readers to distinguish truth from lie and, accordingly, deludes them into believing that they are privileged and granted the truth and that a responsible author lies behind the story. But of course Phemius' story simply makes up a different narrative, not a truer one. It is even a source of perfect pleasure and truth for Telemachus, as he firmly asserts in *Od.* 1.345–55. Telemachus on that occasion is in the same situation as Penelope before Odysseus in book 19, and both instances function as the *Odyssey*'s ironic denials of its own "fiction" (mingling truth and falsehood into a simulation of reality—*etuma*) and as evidence in favor of the *Odyssey*'s real truth.[2]

These denials are full of reckless irony, since the *Odyssey*'s displays of its own truth go hand in hand with its intimations that everything it narrates is fiction.[3] In this way the Odyssean narrative presents itself as double-faced, Janus-like, and thoroughly tongue-in-cheek.

A master stage manager of entertaining disguises is Athena when she appears before Odysseus in the thirteenth book of the *Odyssey*. Although we readers know all along who she is, Odysseus, here in a

[2]For what it is worth, it should be noted that "truth" (*alētheia*) is often used in the *Odyssey* with a slant or twist. For instance, in *Od.* 17.15 Telemachus assures Eumaeus that he likes to tell the truth (*alēthea muthēsasthai*)—just as he is knowingly painting a deceptive picture of the situation in order to bring the swineherd into Odysseus' plot. Eumaeus also tells lies, though unknowingly, when he repeats to Telemachus Odysseus' story and prefaces it with "I'll tell you the whole truth [*alēthea panta*]" (*Od.* 16.60 ff.). The formula *alētheien katalexa* and its other inflections seem to fare better as credible statements about the truth of truth.

[3]Readers who have difficulty accepting this statement or my commentary on Odysseus' lies (19.203) may refer to *Od.* 14.462–506, where Odysseus narrates a vintage Odyssean fiction, and in general to the illuminating paper of Ann Bergren, "Helen's Web: Time and Tableau in the *Iliad*," *Helios* 7, no. 1 (1980): 19–34.

alētheia – Truth itself is the act of revealing the logos, the act of revealing the hidden. the act of bringing non-being into being. truth is a verb. It is an active principle. not a static essence.

situation comparable to that of Penelope in book 19, does not. He, like Penelope, is fooled by an expert falsifier.

In this book, which significantly functions as the proem for the second part of the poem,[4] Odysseus has finally reached Ithaca, but he does not know it, for Athena has temporarily deprived him of the ability to recognize his own fatherland:

> And divine Odysseus woke up from his sleep and he did not recognize his fatherland since he had long been absent from it;[5] in fact the goddess Pallas Athena, the daughter of Zeus, had poured a mist around [him] in order to make himself unable to recognize [his country][6] and to tell him all the things necessary lest his wife and his countrymen should know him before he could punish the suitors for all their transgressions. Therefore everything appeared with a different aspect [*alloeidea*] to the king [*anakti*]. (*Od.* 13.187b–94)

The reasons for Odysseus' failure to recognize his homeland are his twenty years' absence and Athena's magical mist. This mist functions as the "artificial," added sign that transfigures the otherwise familiar traits of rocky Ithaca.

The first reason can be read at the literal and at the figural (allegorical) level. Literally, Odysseus has forgotten his own country, as

---

[4]The proem of the entire poem (*Od.* 1.1–10) does not refer to Odysseus' ambush of and victory over the suitors. Ll. 287–440 of book 13, on the other hand, do present Odysseus as hero of *mētis* and describe the plot that prepares the successful ambush. A large part of this commentary on Athena's epiphany appears in a first version in *MHTIS* 1 (1986).

[5]*Ēdē dēn apeōn:* Recent critics have tried to explain that this expression is not casual (see *Odissea*–Hoekstra, 4:175; and Stanford, 205, "after so long an absence"). The temporal clause, however, should still be attached to *oude nin egnō* and therefore explains why Odysseus did not recognize his fatherland. The reason for the critics' effort is that the text seems to attribute Odysseus' failure to recognize his fatherland to Athena's intervention (189): *peri gar theos* . . . "for the goddess . . . poured, etc." But it is futile to try to straighten out this illogicality by acrobatics: the text tells us that Odysseus did not recognize Ithaca both because he had been absent from it for so long and because Athena covered it with a mist. The theomagical explanation simply doubles the natural one.

[6]I read *agnōston* in its active meaning, "unrecognizing," and I construe the syntax with that meaning (*auton min*, "himself"). Yet one would expect the genitive of the place. See *LfrgE*, s.v. "agnōstos." The conventional translation takes *agnōston* in the passive sense of "unrecognized," "unrecognizable." Aristophanes wrote *autōi* instead of *auton* and understood *min*, "the country": "made the country unrecognizable for Odysseus." Others: "made himself unrecognizable"; but this latter view is more difficult because Athena makes Odysseus unable to recognize his country, not unrecognizable, and because she will make him unrecognizable later (13.397 ff., *all' age s' agnōston teuxō*). Even in my translation an illogical train of thought remains: it is not clear, for instance, why Athena should pour mist around Odysseus in order to tell him everything.

Alcinous, for instance, has forgotten the oracle;[7] allegorically this forgetfulness means—how exactly!—that everyone returns home to a different country, and always as a stranger, for return is a re-cognition, a retroactivation of one's former knowledge that becomes a rediscovery.

The second, explicitly magical, reason for Odysseus' failure to recognize his land can be read in the context of Athena's strategy. The goddess of *mētis* is preparing the stage on which she will be recognized by Odysseus and gives us a foretaste of her metamorphosizing powers.[8]

Meanwhile, the text itself is caught in this game of disguises. Its illogical train of thought seems to arise from conflicting goals: to describe Odysseus' failure to recognize his fatherland and the reasons for this failure, as well as Athena's desire to make him unrecognizable, the necessity for his being unrecognizable. The text, caught as it is in its multiple, literal, allegorical moves, is badly construed and can be read in different ways.

Though smart and resourceful, Odysseus cannot see Ithaca: to him everything appears foreign (*alloeidea*). He laments and curses the Phaeacians who did not take him to Ithaca: *Zeus spheas tisaito hiketēsios*, "May Zeus, the god of suppliants, requite them" (*Od.* 13.213). The text exposes Odysseus in a petty, mystified attitude. Though he is in Ithaca, he mistrusts the Phaeacians and begins the meaningless inventory of the possessions the Phaeacians gave him:

> After these words he began to count the exceedingly beautiful tripods and the cauldrons and the gold and the finely woven clothes. Of all these things nothing was missing. But he bewailed his fatherland, crawling along the shore of the resonant sea, weeping profusely. Athena came to him looking in form like a young man, shepherd of a flock, a *delicate figure* such as are the sons of the kings. . . . Seeing *her* Odysseus rejoiced. (*Od.* 13.217–23, 226)

---

[7]The narrative that immediately precedes Odysseus' awakening in Ithaca relates how Poseidon punishes the Phaeacians for giving Odysseus a safe return. As if in a nightmare, Alcinous forgot the ancient prophecy. Even the utopian world, then, when it comes into contact with the real world, cracks under the effects of deception, forgetfulness, and ignorance. Yet it is legitimate to ask: Why did Alcinous forget? Was it because of a divine will, or his foolish neglect, or because the narrative voice requires it? This last alternative reveals the trick of the narrative voice: it needs the magic of the Phaeacians' help for Odysseus but simultaneously punishes them and us, the audience, for believing in this magic.

[8]On *mētis* as power of metamorphosis and of autotransformation, see Marcel Detienne and Jean-Pierre Vernant, *Les Ruses de l'intelligence: La Mētis des grecs* (Paris: Flammarion, 1974).

As if in a bad dream, he counts these now useless objects, and of course the sum simply increases his sense of forlornness. Now, for the only time in the *Odyssey*, the text uses the long emphatic formula that describes Odysseus crawling "on the shore of the resonant sea." In so doing, it suddenly takes us away from this nightmarish scene to the pathetic scene at the beginning of the *Iliad* in which the priest Chryses is also described as "crawling along the shore of the resonant sea," weeping profusely as he supplicates Apollo (*Il.* 1.34).[9] The scene evoked by the repetition of this long formula establishes for the *Odyssey*'s audience both a conventional context for "epic" forlornness—the presence of a "sympathetic" setting (in this case, the sea)—and a conventional textual reference. Both these familiar conventions should reassure us, not only in themselves but also because the traditional epic "formula" prescribes that in such a situation a god will answer the wretched hero's prayer or cry. And in fact Athena does appear immediately. Her appearance, however, seems to turn the convention—and our expectations—upside down. This divine presence brings not comfort but confusion, for she has disfigured the reality of Ithaca.

When Athena appears Odysseus "rejoices," for he sees a young man he thinks can help him:

> a delicate figure such as are the sons of the kings with a well-wrought mantle that fell in two folds around his shoulders: at [his, or her] shining feet [he/she] had sandals and at [his/her] hand a spear. Seeing her [*tēn*] Odysseus rejoiced. (*Od.* 13.222–26)

Odysseus of course is fooled, for he cannot realize that the young man is actually the mysterious power that has concealed Ithaca from him. We, on the contrary, are able to recognize Athena in her disguise, and we confront the oddity of her mask: the stylish, sleek male attire vaguely insinuating some sexual appeal, like that of a young Paris. The pronoun "her" (*tēn*) allows us to see the delicate boy as a tall, beautiful woman. The purpose of this uncanny transformation is not at all easy to explain. Perhaps this seemingly gratuitous disguise constitutes the perfection of her magic trick (to disguise Ithaca), for in

---

[9]See Johannes Th. Kakridēs, *Homer Revisited* (Lund: Gleerup, 1971), p. 132: "The exquisitely worded picture (34) *bē d' akeōn para thina poluphloisboio thalassēs,* presents Chryses' isolation in nature, the vast ocean before him. Notice again what dimension the epithet takes as it is placed to qualify the element and how imposing its resounding movement (*poluphloisboio*) is in contrast to the insignificant monosyllable *bē* of the silent movement of the man."

accordance with epic convention Athena represents in this scene the aggrandized, divine image of the hero's force and destiny, of his *mētis*. *Mētis* is ruse, shrewdness, cunning, magic, transformation, changeability, unseizability. Accordingly, Athena, after frustrating Odysseus' attempt to recognize his homeland, tricks him with her false appearance in a seductive attire, thus mimicking and mocking *his* readiness (and his need) to disguise himself, to repeat endlessly his game of presenting himself always in the most favorable light, cajoling and seducing whomever he meets. In this way she anticipates and doubles his newest fiction and story (256 ff.),[10] when Odysseus in his turn presents a disguised version of himself and behaves as deceptively as Athena does in her disguise. The hero and his tutelary goddess complement each other perfectly.

Nevertheless, Athena's power of disguise diminishes that of Odysseus. She can assume any form she wants, adroitly uniting in herself male and female, different kinds of ruses and modes of seduction. Like the divinities of *mētis*, beginning with Metis herself, she can transform the appearance of the world. Odysseus' powers, however, are limited to creating lies about himself. He cannot seduce or play magic tricks as she does. He is shrewd, but he is not a god.

Nor is he a poet. We find ourselves constrained by the text to perceive an analogy between the gratuitous disguise of Athena and that of poetic fiction. Indeed, at the very moment it declares Odysseus' intention of disguising himself, the text itself puts on a literary disguise:

> and speaking to her, he uttered winged words; yet he did not say the truth but held back the words, since his mind was always wily [*polukerdea*] within his breast. (*Od.* 13.253–55)

Of the many interesting features of this text[11] I stress only the phrase "he held back the words" (*palin d' ho ge lazeto muthon*, 254b), which has

---

[10]On the quality of feigned speech, see Tzvetan Todorov, *The Poetics of Prose*, trans. Richard Howard (Ithaca: Cornell University Press, 1977), pp. 59 ff. Such speech is a discourse in which a discrepancy appears between reference and referent; feigned speech belongs to constative speech, and yet it is also performative, for speaking in order to lie is the same as speaking not in order to constate (truth or falsehood), but in order to act.

[11]Notice the maliciousness of the epithet *pteroenta*, "winged," which if it implies "straightness" (see Marcello Durante, *Sulla preistoria della tradizione poetica greca*, 2 vols. [Rome: Edizioni dell'Ateneo, 1971–76], 2:123 ff.), contests the lies Odysseus will state. The position of *alēthea eipe* is unparalleled in Homer, and it is also the only case in which the words appear in the poet's own voice. Otherwise they are spoken by some character.

the same "signifier" as in *Il.* 4.357 but a different meaning. The Iliadic passage describes Agamemnon, who has first insulted Odysseus but now, after Odysseus' protest, changes his mind and withdraws his accusations: *palin d' ho ge lazeto muthon,* "took back his words."[12] The expression is found only in these two passages in Homer, and so the two should be juxtaposed.

If the Iliadic text is taken as referring to the *Odyssey,* the *Iliad,* knowing from the *Odyssey* Odysseus' shrewdness in *holding back* improper words, would make it seem foolish of Agamemnon to launch accusations against him. The *Iliad* would then simply be conceding that Odysseus is smarter than Agamemnon, a compliment of no great value in the world of the *Iliad.* The *Odyssey*'s allusion to the *Iliad* would emphasize Odysseus' wiles (*polukerdes noos*)[13] as evidence of the superiority of his wit. It would suggest that because Odysseus is smart enough to *hold back* his words to begin with, he—unlike Agamemnon—will not need to take them back later. Furthermore, the allusion has pleasant associations, for it refers to festive occasions, banquets at which Odysseus once overcame Agamemnon in contests of wits.[14]

The playfulness of this allusion testifies how adept the text is in camouflaging plots and atmosphere. Even as it dramatizes the conversation between the two formidable characters, Odysseus and Athena—with all the attendant pleasures of ironic pathos and charming wit—the narrative voice mirrors their behavior by calling attention to itself and by hiding in itself a possible allusion or disguise. In other

---

[12]In the *scholia* (on *Od.* 13.254) the word *palin,* as it appears here, is understood to mean "against"; so Odysseus in the *Odyssey* would "grasp the word against the truth" and Agamemnon in the *Iliad* would "grasp the word in the opposite sense." There is one passage, *Il.* 9.56, in favor of this interpretation; here *palin* must mean "against." In support of this interpretation, see Hans Ramersdorfer, *Singuläre Iterata der Ilias,* Beiträge zur klassischen Philologie, vol. 137 (Königstein/Ts.: Hain, 1981), pp. 61–63. Yet surely *palin* means "against" only in that passage. Commentators and interpreters read *palin* in *Od.* 13.254 and *Il.* 4.357 with its meaning, "back," and as implying, in the *Odyssey,* "took back what he was about to say" and in the *Iliad,* "he took back what he said." See Leaf, A.H.C., Stanford, and *Odissea*–Hoekstra.

[13]On *polukerdēs,* see chap. 4, n. 13.

[14]Yet the *Iliad* pokes fun at Odysseus by having him call himself "father of Telemachus" (*Il.* 4.354)—father of him "who fights from afar." Since children are often named after some characteristic of their fathers, here the *Iliad* tricks Odysseus and makes him disclose that he is known as a man of the ambush just when he boasts of being a fighter in the first ranks. The *Iliad* turns out to be more powerfully ironic and amusing than the *Odyssey* in this playful mirroring of the texts. See Pietro Pucci, "Banter and Banquets for Heroic Death," forthcoming in *Beyond Aporia*? The rivalry between the two texts also hinges on the two different meanings of the word *kerdos*: "gain" and "ruse." In the *Iliad* Agamemnon calls Odysseus *kerdaleophron* (4.339) "calculating," "intent on gain," but the *Odyssey* praises Odysseus (13.255) as *noon polukerdea nōmōn,* "weighing smart ideas."

words, the narrative voice intrudes on its own dramatization and announces its own compositional patterns.

Another playful textual moment occurs when Odysseus turns to Athena in the disguise of a young man and tells him/her: "I supplicate you as a god" (13.231). This simile is of course a high compliment, used for ingratiating oneself to a savior, a superior person (*Od.* 8.467, 15.81; *Il.* 22.394), but here the text exposes Odysseus as being unaware that he uses the simile "as a god" for a god. The text smilingly shows the emptiness of the simile and intimates that one should know his referent very well before using a simile. A lesson, as we shall see, to be remembered.

The Unreadable Figure of Mētis

As Athena is expressing her appreciation for Odysseus' shrewdness in disguising himself, she smiles and appears to him as a "beautiful, tall woman, expert in splendid handiwork" (*Od.* 13.288–89).[15] At last this seems to be an epiphany of the authentic Athena: the artificial, added signs of her previous disguise vanish, and the new signs we and Odysseus see finally seem to provide trustworthy evidence of the real presence of the goddess. Indeed, Odysseus recognizes it as such. This epiphany does not produce the same certitude in us, however. In fact, this latest manifestation of Athena raises so many questions—textual, philosophical, and theological—that her initially clear image, or sign, in a sense dissipates before our eyes, leaving her unreadable and, ultimately, unrecognizable. But if we proceed slowly perhaps we can unravel the knotty problems this text presents: (1) the peculiar contradictions in Athena's appreciation of Odysseus' guile; (2) the ambiguous iconography of her figure; and (3) the theological implications of this recognition scene.

1. Just as the hero and his tutelary goddess vie with each other in feats of self-concealment and deception, so they contend in praising each other's shrewdness. Athena smiles at Odysseus' deceitful story about himself and compliments him on retaining his wit and guile even though he has reached his fatherland (*Od.* 13.293–95, 330 ff.). Forgetting that she herself has prevented Odysseus from recognizing his own land, Athena here seems to fall victim to her own wit: she

---

[15]See Franco Ferrucci, *The Poetics of Disguise,* trans. Ann Dunnigan (Ithaca: Cornell University Press, 1980), p. 53: "through the telling of his story the hero has won *the right to recognize Ithaca*" (italics in the text).

does not consider that Odysseus' deception is an instinctive act of self-protection, that he is acting as if he really has arrived in an unknown, probably hostile country. Later, Odysseus gives Athena a similarly inconsistent compliment when he attributes to her advice the fact that he did not blunder home openly, as Agamemnon did (383 ff.).

Of course, we cannot know whether Odysseus would have in fact acted as incautiously as Agamemnon did and is truly indebted to Athena or whether he simply attributes to her his own prudence. We reach here a blurred moment in which the shrewdest author leaves us unable to read exactly his shrewd characters—just when they recognize so glaringly their own cunning.

When *mētis*, even divine *mētis*, unwittingly traps itself, it reveals its own weakness and insufficiency. The goddess of *mētis* in this scene represents the divine embodiment of Odysseus' own strength and characterization. Therefore the fact that the goddess is trapped by her own *mētis* does not predicate anything about Athena's weakness but only illustrates *mētis*' own shortcuts and insufficiency.

Just as the shrewd disguises of Odysseus, products of his *mētis*, disfigure his image by an uncheckable displacement of his features, so Odysseus' *mētis* itself, wherever it produces a discourse or a strategy, obtains the effect of displacing the situation rather than resolving it. Notwithstanding the continuous display of his ingenuity and cunning, notwithstanding his famous ruses, Odysseus would be destroyed were it not for his destiny (*moira*) that decrees his return home (*Od.* 9.528–35). In this respect, Athena is both the goddess of *mētis* and the patron goddess who, in agreement with that destiny, favors Odysseus' return. Without a decision, a determination from a real power, Odysseus' *mētis* never would save him.

An analogous assignment, of course, is valid for the scriptorial *mētis:* in the present passage the text seems unable to control its own display of cunning, scheming characters. Later we shall see that even its textual ruses, allusions, and play on *tropoi* may be unwittingly trapped by their very scheming nature.

2. Athena's two appearances, as a young man and as a beautiful woman, are both described by the same verb, *eoika: demas d'ēikto gunaiki* (288: "she resembled in her stature a woman") and *andri demas eikuia* (222: "resembling in her stature a man"). When Odysseus answers Athena that it is difficult for a man to recognize her, since she makes herself similar to everything (*autēn panti eiskeis*, *Od.* 13.312–13), he again summons up the notion of resemblance and uses a verb related to *eoika* (*eiskō*—a present with a factitive sense). Even when she declares herself to be Athena, her figure *resembles* that of a tall woman.

The text's insistence on this word suggests that the phenomenology of the gods—their epiphanic forms—eludes all ontology. In this case, more than in others, identity of "language" and "being" cannot be successfully smuggled in by the text. When we realize that nothing distinguishes identity from semblance of identity, as Hesiod had already noticed (*Theogony* 26–28), we are at a loss: "You make yourself similar to everything" (*Od.* 13. 313).[16] Athena is whatever she wants to appear to be, and her multiple manifestations provide no certain mark to help us distinguish appearance from identity.

Athena's "pantotropy" explains well why scholarly opinion has long been divided in its assessment of (1) Athena's genuine figure as a beautiful and tall woman and (2) her specific iconographic form. As concerns the first point, Ulrich von Wilamowitz took this appearance to be her "natural form";[17] Friedrich Focke denied it, with good arguments.[18] Marion Müller decrees it is Athena's own real form, as does Benedetto Marzullo—although he assumes this scene was composed by an incompetent poet—and Jenny Clay argues that in this description of Athena's figure *demas* indicates a god disguised in human form.[19]

---

[16]Note that when Athena mocks Odysseus because he could not recognize her (*Od.* 13.299b–300: *oude su g'egnōs / Pallad' Athēnaiēn*), the text mimes or sounds like *Il.* 22.9b–10, where Apollo, who is Achilles' antagonist god, mocks the hero for not perceiving his disguise. (On Apollo as antagonist god of Achilles, see Gregory Nagy, *The Best of the Achaeans* [Baltimore: Johns Hopkins University Press, 1979], pp. 59 ff.) Does the text of the *Odyssey* disguise itself in sounding like the text of the *Iliad*? We will never know, though certain marks would make the juxtaposition of the two texts more significant for both. Because Athena is Odysseus' protective goddess, she does not need the benefits of disguise. Apollo, on the other hand, as the antagonist god of Achilles, exploits disguise to cheat him and uses mockery to humiliate him. This comparison both unites and distinguishes the two epiphanies: what unites them is that in each the god is presented as the alter ego of the hero, the *representamen* of his force or of his weakness (see Karl Reinhardt, *Die Ilias und ihr Dichter*, ed. Uvo Hölscher [Göttingen: Vandenhoeck & Ruprecht, 1961], p. 320); what distinguishes the two is that the divine deception carries a different weight of seriousness in each. In the *Odyssey* Athena's deception should duplicate Odysseus' own inclination toward wiles and tricks, and in fact hero and goddess both cheat one another. (Of course the goddess, like the poet, deceives also for her pleasure, while Odysseus—also like the poet—does so for self-defense.)

[17]"In ihrer natürlicher Gestalt," in *Die Heimkehr des Odysseus* (Berlin: Weidmann, 1927), p. 9.

[18]Focke states that because one of Athena's intentions is to inspire Odysseus with martial fury, her appearance in the form of Athena Ergane—expert in handiwork—is inappropriate: *Die Odyssee* (Stuttgart: W. Kohlhammer, 1943), pp. 275–76.

[19]Marion Müller, *Athene als göttliche Helferin in der Odyssee* (Heidelberg: C. Winter, 1966), p. 90; Benedetto Marzullo, *Il problema omerico*, 2d ed. rev. (Milan and Naples: R. Ricciardi, 1970), p. 161; Jenny Clay, "Demas and Aude: The Nature of Divine Transformation in Homer," *Hermes* 102 (1974): 130.

The structure of disguise favors the suggestion that "natural," "inherent" signs exist beside the "artificial" and added ones. Here the text has convinced the best philologists that by dropping her disguise Athena finally appears in her "natural" form. And yet the text clearly indicates that it knows and describes only the semblance, the appearance, the external form of the goddess. Its use of the same verb *eoika* to describe different figures of the goddess must mean that an appearance is all that can be predicated of her and that all the signs of herself point at a self-displacing figure.

As concerns the second point, we have to exclude the notion that Athena appears here as Athena Ergane, as Wilamowitz suggested,[20] since, as 13.298–99 make explicit, Athena wants to be recognized as goddess of *mētis* and not as a worker: "I have fame [*kleomai*] among the gods because of my ruses [*mēti*] and tricks [*kerdesin*]." Because there is no known iconographic figure of Athena as goddess of *mētis*, we should probably conclude that in this scene Athena is represented in the most "generic" and probably indistinguishable form a goddess could imaginably take.[21] It is even possible that Odysseus himself sees Athena for the first time in this attire.[22]

Our suspicion that here the goddess assumes an especially undistinguished figure is confirmed by the textual evidence. The same line (289) that describes Athena as similar to *kalēi te megalēi te aglaa erga iduiēi*, "a beautiful and tall woman, expert in splendid handiwork," also describes a Phoenician woman, the nurse of little Eumaeus in *Od.* 15.418. Eumaeus tells the story of his kidnapping: there was in his father's house a Phoenician woman *kalē te megalē te aglaa erga iduiē*, "beautiful and tall and expert in splendid handiwork" (15.418), and the sly Phoenicians seduced her and made her instrumental in the kidnapping.

Whether we should activate this textual repetition and assess this disrespectful comparison remains of course an undecidable question.

[20]*Die Heimkehr des Odysseus*, p. 9. Athena Ergane is of course known through several inscriptions but is rare in iconographic figures. *LIMC* has gathered about twenty iconographic examples of Athena Ergane (nos. 39–58): see vol. 2, pt. 1, s.v. "Athena," especially pp. 961–64.

[21]Any tall and beautiful woman specially attired could look like Athena to a naive audience. In Herodotus 1.60 a tall, beautiful woman with the proper attire fools the Athenians; similarly, in Homer an imposing figure of a hero is sometimes mistaken for a god (*Il.* 6.128–29; *Od.* 16.181 ff., etc.).

[22]In the iconographic illustrations of the *Odyssey* we find that Athena is always represented in the attire of a warlike goddess; see Odette Touchefeu-Meynier, *Thèmes odysséens dans l'art antique* (Paris: Editions de Boccard, 1968). See the following illustrations, where Athena is represented as Athena Promakhos (with helmet and/or spear): no. 5 (with Odysseus and the Cyclops); no. 364 (on the beach with Nausicaa); nos. 366, 367.

Yet the text might derive some profit from this indecision: it would leave the reader suspended between a possibly edifying figure of Athena (although a domestic nonentity) and a disrespectful image of her. It is certainly no blasphemy for the text to intimate, by the comparison between the two figures—that of Athena and that of the Phoenician nurse—the same sort of irony that Herodotus suggests in 1.60. For it could be an extreme form of edification to suggest the vanity of assigning a precise form to the goddess, since she *is* wherever she wants in whatever form she wants.

9

More Light in the Epiphany,
Less Light in the Text

The Text can be read without its father's guarantee: the restitution
of the intertext paradoxically abolishes the concept of filiation. It is
not that the author cannot "come back" into the Text, into his text:
however he can only do so as a "guest" so to speak. . . .

At the same time, the enunciation's sincerity, which has been a
veritable "cross" of literary morality, becomes a false problem: the *I*
that writes the text is never, itself, anything more than a paper *I*.

Roland Barthes, "From Work to Text"

In her next epiphany (*Od.* 16.155 ff.) Athena reappears in the same
figure as in book 13, and she is described with the same simile and
same lines (16.157b–58 = 13.288b–89). This time, however, the text
defines her appearance as a *phainesthai enargēs* (16.161).

A study of the expression *phainesthai enargēs*[1] shows that the etymological meaning of *enargēs*—"in full light" and thus "manifestly,"
"without any disguise," "truly"—pertains only in *Od.* 7.201[2] and is

---

[1]*Phainesthai* is used for gods only when they appear and become visible to men. The
expression is thus rarer than "divine epiphanies": see *Il.* 1.198; *Od.* 16.161. *Enargēs* is a
compound of *en* and the root of *argos*, "shine," of the Bahuvrihi form: "with *argos*,"
"surrounded by *argos*." In its five occurrences in Homer, the word always refers to a
divine presence (*Il.* 20.131; *Od.* 3.420, 7.201, 16.161) or to a divinely inspired and
transmitted dream (*Od.* 4.481).

[2]Here Alcinous denies that Odysseus may be a god, since he does not look like one:
"For always, up until now, the gods have appeared to us in their full forms [*phainontai
enargeis*] when we offer them most glorious hecatombs. . . . And even if one of our
people alone on the road encounters them, they use no disguise at all [*ou ti katakruptousin*, 7.206], for we are near kin to them as the Cyclops are and the savage tribes of the
Giants." In this text *phainesthai enargeis* and "without any disguise" must be synonymous, both meaning the true, authentic self-revelation of the gods. The careful
distinction between public and private appearances of the gods is also noteworthy.
Contrary to rule, among the Phaeacians the gods appear not only to individuals but also
at public gatherings.

probably what is meant in *Il.* 20.131;[3] while other meanings such as "visible" and "in the physical form" are suggested or made necessary by the contexts in *Od.* 3.420 and in *Od.* 16.161.[4] In these last two cases the adjective *enargēs* must be used simply for emphasis, since the notion of visibility is already expressed by *phainesthai*, "to appear," "to become visible." Furthermore, there is no intimation that the god appears in his or her undisguised figure; on the contrary, in *Od.* 3.420 Nestor says Athena appeared *enargēs*, and she was certainly in disguise (see 2.268, 3.371–72).

Accordingly, in *Od.* 16.161 the expression *phainesthai enargēs* must mean simply that the goddess is visible, but the question whether she is in disguise remains unsolvable. The expression lacks all diacritical, distinctive force, just like the figure of Athena it defines. Because the text uses *enargēs* with different, even contradictory, meanings (compare especially *Od.* 7.201 with 3.420), it provides no discriminating principles to help us ascertain whether the text does or does not count on its readers' ability to compare and read internal repetitions. The intricate grammar of epiphanies seems utterly confused.

At this point in my discussion I begin to doubt that the text is still holding our suspense and teasing our expectations. The text may be construed to suggest that it is cleverly in control of its ruses, but since it confuses its own protocols, it becomes unreadable. The result may be that the text, instead of contriving an undetectable, unreadable series of ruses, is caught by its own ruse and defeated by the ruse of unreadability.

As the preceding discussions suggest, the questions that the unreadable figure of Athena in book 13 raises, while specific to the text

---

[3]Here Hera fears that Apollo may come against Achilles and that consequently the hero may become frightened: "the gods are terrible in their appearing in their forms" (*khalepoi de theoi phainesthai enargeis*). Here too it is suggested that the gods appear in their recognizable divine figures.

[4]In *Od.* 3.420—after Athena, who had shared the dais disguised as Mentor, miraculously disappears—Nestor says "Athena came *enargēs* to me to the rich feast of the god." This text flatly contradicts *Od.* 7.201, for Athena was at the banquet in disguise and thus unrecognizable as a god. This contradiction has challenged critics and translators to accommodate *enargēs* to this context. Dietrich Mülder translates it as "physically, in corporeal shape": see his essay "Götteranrufungen in Ilias und Odyssee," *Rheinisches Museum* 79 (1930): 7–34, especially p. 29. *Odissea*–West has "visible," 1:105; Walter Shewring, *The Odyssey* (Oxford: Oxford University Press, 1980), p. 33, uses "in visible presence." In *Od.* 16.161 the context favors the less pregnant meaning of *enargēs*, since the word is almost synonymous with "visible": "Telemachus did not see or perceive her, for the gods do not appear to everybody visibly" (*phainontai enargeis*). The text seems to repeat and modify *Il.* 20.131 (see preceding note)—or vice versa. In either case, the two texts clearly react to each other.

of the *Odyssey,* indicate general philosophical and theological problems as well. Athena's epiphanies reveal that an essential difference separates the goddess's being from her possible appearances.[5] The sense of this difference constitutes the premise of a question that will be developed philosophically with Parmenides, under the terms *doxa,* "opinion," and *alētheia,* "truth."

The self-revelation of the goddess should contest the idea of the benevolent, domesticated nature of divine presence and support that seems to inform the *Odyssey* more than the *Iliad.* Although Athena eventually comes to Odysseus' aid and finally leads him to victory, the text seems to take pleasure in showing that the wily goddess has no scruples about mocking or deceiving even her favorite hero for her own amusement or sport. Her insistent duplicity makes him so wary that he continues to suspect her tricks. Accordingly, he must beg her to reveal whether he has really come to his own homeland (13.324–28), for despite Athena's assurance that he has (237 ff.), he still cannot recognize it. She has not yet dispelled the concealing mist.

A reader may well feel ambivalent about Athena, for it is clear that she could just as easily transform the world *in malam partem,* if she desired. (She effects this evil transformation for Ajax in the Sophoclean play.) Here, as in the Homeric religion generally, while the presence of a god enhances and illuminates all the important moments of heroic decision and deed with a dazzling light, the epiphany introduces a shade of incertitude about the divinity's will, purpose, and steadfastness.

But the question that remains the most unsettling—because the most resistant to answers—is, How much control does the text have over the readings it reveals? It is still impossible to say if Athena's epiphany suggests an ironic allusion to the stately epiphanies of other traditions and texts (for instance of the *Hymn to Demeter* 275–80 and the *Hymn to Aphrodite* 172–90) or if it is the pious representation of a religious event. Nor is it possible to say whether Athena or Odysseus wins this competition of wit and trickery; only because the two finally join forces against the suitors does the outcome of their competition seem insignificant. And of course, despite its insoluable questions, we continue to read the *Odyssey,* to write on it, and take pleasure in its fabulous stories, which, like fairy tales, permit us to take their literal

---

[5]We see Athena first as a young man, although the grammar still defines her as a female (*ekhousa,* 224); then as a stately woman, but one indistinguishable from any other stately woman; and finally Odysseus declares that she can make herself resemble anything.

meaning seriously or, if we wish, to invent all sorts of interpretations and symbolic readings of their uncanny, troubling elements.

For a text to invite this variety of responses, for it to unravel itself at the reader's wish, not only highlights the subjectivity of the reader's reading, it also exhibits the subjectivity of its author. That the *Odyssey* parades an authorial "I," a subjective master of the text, is evident: from the *moi* of *Od.* 1.1, *andra moi ennepe,* "tell *me* of the man," so marked by contrast with *Il.* 1.1, *mēnin aeide,* "sing of the wrath," to Phemius' assertion of being "self-taught" (*autodidaktos, Od.* 22.347), the text leaves no doubt of the intended presence of an author behind it.

Yet this subjectivity, as presence of the authorial intentions, is itself textual, that is, a moment of the textual code, this "I" being the "I" of endless literary performances. This "I" is an inscription in the text, rather than a single and unique agent creating the text *outside* it.[6] The textual appeals to the reader's understanding and collusion, which seem to be the signs of the author's presence and intentions, arise mainly from the textual interweaving of allusions and repetitions. These interweavings, while revealing the author's technique and cleverness, simultaneously drown these specific characteristics in the dazzling iridescence of intertextuality. Notwithstanding my efforts at outlining the rules or protocols that superintend the intertextual strategy, we reach spots where these rules cease to be operative. The excess of brightness blinds our reading, and simultaneously the author's control and intentions recede into darkness.

Figure and Literality

It is clear that in these scenes of disguise readers have more trouble than the characters at the moment of recognition. The characters recognize a familiar figure in what is oddly self-displacing or even fragmented, but they finally see it. Penelope may recognize her husband, paradoxically, in his being less quick than he was when he left, but still she recognizes him. The secret of their bed is a sufficient referent. Analogously, Odysseus may find it difficult to put together the pretty young boy and the stately figure of the goddess, but still he sees Athena. We readers, on the contrary, see only the linguistic sign,

---

[6]The *moi* of *Od.* 1.1 occurs, for instance, in *Il.* 2.484 in an apostrophe to the Muses: this *moi* thus points to another version of the invocation to the Muses. It is therefore a textually established subject, as the semioticians would say.

and this is a much more complex sign than the mere rags and wretched countenance that function as disguising signs for Odysseus. First, the linguistic sign fragments our recognition through the drifting chain of allusions; we have seen this drifting in the definition of Athena as "a beautiful, tall woman expert in splendid handiwork." Second, since we readers have no access to the referent, we are often unable to decide whether an image, a simile, a figure is to be understood literally or metaphorically. We now confront a scene in which this indecision affects our understanding of what happens and of the theology implicit in the event.

In Homeric studies there is a long-winded *querelle* about the nature of the gods in passages where the text describes them as "looking like" birds. Should we assume that they become real birds or that the descriptions are only metaphorical ("swift as")? There are six passages in Homer that have attracted critical attention in recent years,[7] and four are in the *Odyssey*. The most spectacular is *Od.* 3.371–72; here Athena, who, disguised as Mentor, has been sharing the sacrifice in honor of Poseidon at Nestor's palace, suddenly disappears looking like a seahawk before the eyes of Nestor and his guests, among them Telemachus.

Several hints in the text prepare us for Athena's self-revelation, in particular Nestor's recollection of how visible (*anaphanda*) Athena's love for and assistance to Odysseus were on all occasions (*Od.* 3.218–24).[8] The irony of the situation is underlined by Nestor's insistence on the visibility (*anaphanda*) of Athena's love and help: first because, throughout his wandering, her love and her assistance were not at all apparent to Odysseus, who a few times even complains of Athena's neglect;[9] and second because, even as Nestor is speaking, Athena is

---

[7]See Franz Dirlmeier, *Die Vogelgestalt homerischer Götter*, Sitzungsberichte der Heidelberger Akademie der Wissenschaften, Philos.-Hist. Klasse, no. 2 (Heidelberg: C. Winter, 1967), who maintains that all these similes are basically metaphors; Hans Bannert, "Zur Vogelgestalt der Götter bei Homer," *Wiener Studien*, n.s. 12 (1978): 29–42, who argues against Dirlmeier; and B. C. Dietrich, "Views of Homeric Gods and Religion," *Numen* 26 (1979): 148–49, who comes closer to Dirlmeier's than Bannert's position.

[8]*Anaphandon, -da* forms occur once in the *Iliad* (16.178) and three times in the *Odyssey* (3.221, 222, 11.455). In the three passages in the *Odyssey* it implies a sort of "public recognition," and in *Il.* 16.178 ff. it subtly intimates a public appearance that in fact is a lie (in this case, a nominal, putative paternity). It is debatable whether, in Nestor's speech, we should understand that Athena's love for Odysseus was simply "publicly recognized" or actually made visible by Athena's presence. The connection of *anaphandon* with *phainein, -esthai* may constitute an element in favor of the latter assumption.

[9]Odysseus complains bitterly of Athena's absence in *Od.* 6.324 ff., and directly to her in *Od.* 13.287 ff. The poet explains why Athena could not help Odysseus: "She felt respect for her father's brother [Poseidon] who furiously raged against godlike Odys-

demonstrating her love and care for Odysseus' son, but *in disguise*. Athena's visible love for Odysseus now manifests itself in *her disguise* and is apparent *only to the reader*, who knows that Mentor is in fact Athena. The troubling doubleness of an *enargēs* appearance *in disguise* occurs again, though under the different linguistic form (*anaphanda*).

The text exploits this dramatic duplicity with almost shameful insistence: just as the characters grieve for Telemachus' unhappy plight, the reader rejoices in his own certain and privileged knowledge that the characters' fears are unfounded. The reader knows that sooner or later Nestor's prayer will be answered: the suitors will be punished, Telemachus will live up to the noble example of his famous father.

The felicity of this performance of Odyssean fiction is undeniable. As Athena becomes disguised and unidentifiable by the characters, she acquires the freedom of playing on both sides, that of the characters and that of the reader.

Athena's split role as a secret persuader and mover of the characters and as an openly divine presence for us—and sometimes for Odysseus—parallels the split mode that every narrative necessarily employs. The knowledge of the narrative voice is always greater than that of the characters it presents; as long as the narrative voice—the speech act—controls the characters, it stands high in its own world where the characters cannot reach it.[10] Of course, readers are invited to share the knowledge of the narrative voice, but we are not full partners and cannot question the narrative voice on all the decisions this voice takes for the characters.[11]

In her split role Athena belongs simultaneously to the world dialogue of the characters and to the world dialogue of the narrator-reader and fulfills the specific narrative function of accounting for both worlds. While she still belongs to the world of the serious epic orthodoxy, she also belongs to the world of the specific fiction her role helps to create. By flaunting this role, the *Odyssey* exhibits that light, irreverent, teasing tone that convinced scholars of two genera-

---

seus till he reached his fatherland" (*Od.* 6.329–31). On Athena's assistance to Odysseus elsewhere in the epic tradition, see Marion Müller, *Athena als göttliche Helferin in der Odyssee* (Heidelberg: C. Winter, 1966), pp. 92 ff., and notes.

[10]Tzvetan Todorov distinguishes "utterance" from "speech act": "These two aspects give life to two realities each as linguistic as the other: the world of the characters and the world of the narrator-reader couple" (*The Poetics of Prose*, trans. Richard Howard [Ithaca: Cornell University Press, 1977], pp. 26–27).

[11]Ibid., pp. 60 ff.: "The narrator's dialogue with the reader is not isomorphic with that of the characters among themselves. . . . The narrator's dialogue with the reader, as all dialogues, leaves obscure forces, undecipherable parts and often disagreement."

tions ago that the poem was imbued with ironic and Ionic rationalism.[12] Are we then reading a Voltairean criticism of the old-fashioned conception of the gods, set in a delightful fable? Or are we listening to a story inspired by a religious desire for the return to the Golden Age when man and god were closer and friendlier than contemporary Epos represents? Although the *Odyssey* contains many elements that support the latter interpretation,[13] modern criticism prefers a version of the former and emphasizes the ironic effects of Athena's split role.

To return to our paradigmatic text for an example: as Nestor extols Athena's *visible* love for Odysseus, in her very presence (again, known to us but not to the character), the text reverberates with amusing innuendoes: the notion of divine presence is divorced from that of divine visibility; the will of the gods is made unreadable, their roles slightly frivolous. Other incidents yield other ironies. When Telemachus and Mentor-Athena are received by Peisistratus, the young man offers the golden cup, first, to Mentor-Athena, then to Telemachus. Athena receives the cup and "rejoices at the wise and fair man, for he had given first to her the golden cup" (*Od.* 3.52–53). Of course Peisistratus is well mannered and offers the cup first to the man who looks older, Mentor-Athena; but a reader cannot refrain from smiling at Athena's delight, which even in a human Mentor would seem a bit excessive and self-indulgent—unless Athena too is smiling at the very idea of her participating, as if she were a mortal, in this ceremony. When immediately afterward she prays to Poseidon, the roles of a divine participant in a feast (*dais*) and that of a human offerer of a sacrifice (*dais*) become hopelessly confused. Is this confusion intended to be humorous or serious? It is impossible to say.[14] When Athena finishes her prayer the text goes on to remark that she takes care to answer it herself (62), which causes W. B. Stanford to remark that this is "an example of what is dubiously called a 'pious fraud.'"[15] Indeed, the fraud is not only pious but double, since Athena certainly does not accomplish all that she has prayed to Poseidon

---

[12]See, for instance, Wilhelm Nestle, *Vom Mythos zum Logos* (Stuttgart: A. Kröner, 1942).

[13]For example, consider Alcinous' description of the undisguised presence of the gods both in the Phaeacian *daites*, "banquets," and in private encounters (*Od.* 7.199–206), or Odysseus' definition of the sacred functions of the king (*Od.* 19.109 ff.). On this mythical view of royalty, see Jean-Pierre Vernant, *The Origins of Greek Thought* (Ithaca: Cornell University Press, 1982), p. 30.

[14]Dietrich Mülder, "Götteranrufungen in Ilias und Odyssee," p. 25, n. 1, opts, hesitantly, for humor. The paradox is that Athena's double role allows the readers to believe they know more than the characters themselves.

[15]Stanford, 1:251.

for. She had asked Poseidon "that she and Telemachus might obtain that for which they came" (*Od.* 3.60–61), and, clearly, what Telemachus came to Nestor for was some specific news about his father's life and possible return (*Od.* 1.281–92, 3.85 ff.). But by the end of his sojourn Telemachus will have learned nothing new.

At the level of the characters' awareness, a serious religious ceremony is taking place, but meanwhile the text nods at us with all sorts of questionable and humorous theological implications. Again, is this Voltairean fiction or the fiction of pious simplicity? Whichever it is, it is certainly a pleasurable fiction, for it creates the perfect role and the ideal perspective for readers, keeping us enchanted in a (literally) spectacular position, from which—like a god—we can observe not only events, but Athena's extraordinary love for Odysseus, her equally extraordinary lack of scruples in dealing with both Odysseus and Telemachus,[16] and the troubling theological implications of her conduct.

But then, without any reason or explanation, the text suddenly deprives us of our pleasurable and privileged view of the spectacle. When the text tells us that Athena disappears "looking like a sea-hawk," the characters are supposed to see what happens, but we cannot penetrate this figure of speech. She vanishes in an unreadable simile:

> After these words, gray-eyed Athena left looking like a seahawk [*phenei eidomenē*]: amazement [*thambos*] seized all the Achaeans there. The old man marveled [*thaumasen*] at what he saw with his eyes; he took Telemachus' hands and spoke to him and addressed him: "My dear friend, I fancy that you will not be a coward and a weakling if gods escort you in this way while still so young. For truly of those who live in Olympus this was none other than the daughter of Zeus."[17] (*Od.* 3.371–78)

This is an impressive text full of amazing theological implications: Athena's disappearance, Nestor's accurate guess,[18] the reference to

---

[16]Odysseus will complain directly to Athena of having been neglected by her (*Od.* 13.314 ff.); Telemachus cannot complain, but he is to some extent baffled, since he does not receive those instructions for which he came to Pylos and which Athena could so easily have given him.

[17]On l. 378 and on Athena's epithets, see Benedetto Marzullo, *Il problema omerico*, 2d ed. rev. (Milan and Naples: R. Ricciardi, 1970), pp. 163–64.

[18]Nestor correctly derives the identity of Athena, but how does he know? Probably he guesses on the grounds of his own religious experience. Earlier he prayed, "Would that Athena were ready to love you [Telemachus]" (*Od.* 3.218 ff.); and now he must feel that the goddess has already answered his prayer. In this way he astonishes his young audience with the precision of his earlier prayer and with the miraculous response to it.

other epiphanies. But what is most arresting is the figure in which Athena disappears.

During the past century it has been generally assumed that Mentor-Athena transforms herself into a bird. Recently, however, Franz Dirlmeier[19] has joined the few dissenting voices and has strongly argued against the transformation interpretation. He starts from the fact that in Homer gods do not take animal forms:[20] Why should they occasionally be described only in a bird shape? Dirlmeier finds no reason for this exception and interprets all these descriptions as metaphors.[21] Taking a rather different angle, Hans Bannert[22] emphasizes the scene's religious atmosphere and the sacrificers' profound experience: they see that the guest close to Nestor has suddenly disappeared, and lo! high in the air a hawk is flying. This happens in a fraction of a second, and the miracle makes the god recognizable. This interpretation avoids the implication that a visible transformation of Mentor into a hawk occurs and eliminates an awkward moment in the scene. But Bannert's arguments are speculative and also inconclusive.[23]

Indeed, the arguments on both sides of the controversy always fail to produce decisive evidence, because that which could discriminate between the literal and metaphorical meanings of "looking like a seahawk" lies outside language, in the "referent." It is well known that any expression is taken in its literal meaning as long as it does not create any infelicity but is taken in a metaphorical meaning when the literal one does not make sense. In the case of a simile, what determines the literalness or the *tropos* is the referent: if I say, "he is like his brother," the simile is literal if the two brothers really look alike, but it is a mocking hyperbole if, for instance, one is a dwarf and the other a giant.[24] The *Odyssey* itself in 13.231 has shown that to use a simile well

---

[19]Dirlmeier, *Vogelgestalt*, pp. 5–36.

[20]This fact is debatable: Proteus, for instance, takes on animal forms, and so does Boreas (*Il.* 20.224).

[21]Dirlmeier also tries to demonstrate that the verbs expressing "similarity" do not imply transformation, but his evidence is inconclusive because the fact that *eidomai* is used to describe the transformation of Boreas into a horse (*Il.* 20.224) destroys all possibility of denying the meaning "transform" to *phenēi eidomenē*, *Od.* 3.372: see Jasper Griffin, *Homer on Life and Death* (Oxford: Clarendon Press, 1980), p. 151.

[22]Bannert, "Vogelgestalt der Götter bei Homer," pp. 29–42.

[23]It is impossible to make an absolute distinction between *eidomenos* and *eoikōs*, as Bannert does, for *eoikōs* too may imply identity. Twice Bannert appeals to the reader's impressions and reactions (pp. 38 and 42), a tactic that in itself proves the lack of discriminating evidence.

[24]See Jacques Dubois et al. (Groupe μ), *Rhétorique générale* (Paris: Larousse, 1970). On the undecidability of literal/tropic meaning see also Paul de Man, *Allegories of*

one must know the referent well. Otherwise one may, like Odysseus, turn to a god and tell him "I supplicate you as a god." In our present text no empirical referent can be valid, since the religious narrative suspends all empirical reality. Accordingly, the only valid referent might be the belief of Homer and his audience about the nature and the theriomorphic power of their gods. Since we do not know their belief, we have no way of deducing from the simile above how to interpret the passage. Finally, it is possible that their belief was shaped by passages like this one, and in this case they would be in our own position.[25]

It is an extraordinary feature that the text slips this indecision (i.e., whether to take the expression as figurative or literal) into the figure (the *tropos* of the simile) in which Athena disappears. While the text invites us to read, we have no way to read it. Here is another riddle like the one that has so long troubled the interpretation of *polutropos* in *Od.* 1.1: does the expression mean "who traveled a lot" or "with many turns of mind," or both, or more?[26]

The further question is: Is the text here embarrassingly incompetent or exceedingly shrewd? The rhetorization of grammar—to use Paul de Man's formula—makes all these questions unanswerable. Yet so disturbing is the fall from knowledge to ignorance that critics run blindly to seek some explanation. They either embrace the scholarly illusion that we can discriminate between letter and *tropos* and so arrive at definitive answers, or they define the text as ironic and pathetic. The incredible amount of scholarship produced in the service of the former illusion testifies to the power of the spell the text has cast over us. This spell lures us to read and to make sense of the story as though we were really present at the events. The illusion the text has given us—that we could follow each event with the text's own knowledge—has become our delusion, our blindness. Nothing is stronger than the reader's complicity in sustaining the fictional structure of the text and in obliterating the opacity of its indeterminacy and lack of referentiality.

Reading (New Haven: Yale University Press, 1979), pp. 3 ff. De Man analyzes analogous cases—a rhetorical question, for instance—under the general description of "rhetorization of grammar."

25Hermann Fränkel states that it is impossible to decide between the literal and tropic meanings and assumes that the poet himself was not clear on this point. See *Die homerischen Gleichnisse* (Göttingen: Vandenhoeck & Ruprecht, 1921).

26See my article "The Proem of the *Odyssey*," *Arethusa* 15 (1982): 53–57. Here I suggest another possible meaning for *polutropos*: "of many figures of speech." See also, Douglas Frame, *The Myth of Return in Early Greek Epic* (New Haven: Yale University Press, 1978), pp. ix ff.

The other common response of modern critics, when they do not try to master these baffling theological scenes, has been to emphasize the irony and pathos or even the soap-opera quality of the fiction. Even with the troubling epiphany of Athena in the thirteenth book, commentators prefer to focus on the ironic innuendoes in the charming competition between Odysseus and Athena rather than on its disquieting features.[27]

Of course, to speak of irony is a defensive response, for it assures us that we are not dupes: by recognizing the text's ruse and shrewdness (*mētis*), we grant ourselves the comfort of some lucidity. Yet an ironic reading still derives from the reader's complicity with the author's or the text's intentions and sustains the illusory scenario of an author who is master of his own text. To invoke "irony" does not explain or illuminate the several textual indecisions and indeterminations that, as I have shown, pervade the *Odyssey*. For these indeterminations depend not on intention but on two specific textual features: the drifting force of the sign that displaces, so to speak, the representation of the world of being and the disfiguring effects of disguise as it displaces the self-identity of the characters.

No simple notion of "irony" can take into account the effects I have described, for an ironic reading places the sense of the text in one of the several ambiguities that "irony" holds in its spectrum. But how can we determine the specific ambiguity that smiles at the reader in our text? Athena's odd disappearance from Nestor's banquet—whatever form it takes—reverberates with irreverent or edifying innuendoes that are complex and undecidable: for instance, that the divine is unreadable, yet makes itself known through the most surprising sign; that Athena has a theriomorphic form, after all, or a mere *rhetorical* similarity to an animal; that the poet knows exactly how the goddess chooses to transform herself or is teasing readers who are too curious about trivia. I could go on: Where do we stop the proliferating implications of contradictory readings? If this is "irony," then "irony" means "non-sense," the nonsense of textual indeterminacy.

The puzzle is endless. The text keeps piling up elements of indeci-

---

[27]In his commentary, W. B. Stanford speaks of pathos and irony specifically in the context of the recognition scene of book 13. In *The Ulysses Theme* (Oxford: Blackwell, 1954), p. 30, Stanford remarks on the "sophisticated charm" of this same scene (*Od.* 13.285 ff.) and continues: "It has been well compared . . . with the conversations of Benedict and Beatrice in *Much Ado About Nothing*. Nowhere in Classical literature can one find such a graceful portrait of two wits, male and female, exchanging banter and reproaches without malice and scorn in this free and easy style." The author of the more pejorative label "soap opera" is Jasper Griffin in *Homer on Life and Death*, pp. 57–61.

sion and of unreadability. I have already commented on the puzzle of Nestor's saying that Athena came "visibly" (*enargēs*) to the banquet of the gods (*Od.* 3.420) and shown that his use of *enargēs* contradicts that of *Od.* 7.201. We now have another reference with which to compare our passage. In *Il.* 13.43 ff., Poseidon first appears to the Ajaxes in the disguise of Calchas and speaks to them; he incites them to valor, then disappears as a hawk:

> he filled them with strong courage, made their knees light and their feet and their hands. Then as a swift-winged hawk sped forth to fly[28] . . . so Poseidon the Earthshaker rushed away from them. Of the two, the son of Oileus, the swift Ajax,[29] recognized [*egnō*] the god and immediately he spoke to the son of Telamon: "Ajax, since one of the gods who hold Olympus, in the semblance of the seer [*mantei eidomenos*], commands us now to fight by the ships—he is not Calchas the prophet and soothsayer, for easily I have recognized the traces of his feet and knees as he left: the gods are easy to recognize" [*arignōtoi de theoi per*]. (*Il.* 13.60–72)

The hero recognizes the god from the *ikhnia* of his feet and knees: the interpretation of the word is contested, but at any rate, the recognition ensues from something relating to this god's feet and knees, since he is still there in the semblance of Calchas.[30] Nothing of the theatrical event in Pylos occurs here: no amazement (*thambos, thauma*); no collective recognition of the god (the other Ajax recognizes after the first Ajax's recognition); no visible miracle, but a trace of the god's

---

[28]Twice in the *Iliad* gods are described as birds (7.59 ff., 14.290), but no human character *witnesses* this phenomenon. In *Il.* 7.59 ff., for instance, Apollo and Athena "sat looking like [*eoikotes*] vultures upon a tall oak sacred to their aegis-bearing father Zeus, rejoicing in their warriors." The text reveals to the audience (or readers) alone a *sacrum* that, because it is invisible to the characters, must belong to an ultramundane dimension.

[29]On the name of the two Ajaxes, see Hugo Mühlestein, "Le Nom des deux Ajax," *Studi Micenei* 2 (1967): 41–52.

[30]*Ikhnia* has been understood both as "movements" (see Leaf; Dirlmeier, *Die Vogelgestalt;* and Christoph Michel, *Erläuterungen zum N der Ilias* [Heidelberg: C. Winter, 1971], pp. 35 ff.), and as "traces"—which is the ordinary sense of the word—that is, the footprints of the god (see Fränkel, *Die homerischen Gleichnisse,* p. 81). What makes this latter interpretation difficult to accept is the violent zeugma with "knees" that it implies: otherwise it is convincing that the god may have left a larger footprint than a normal hero. Hans Bannert interprets *ikhnia* as "die (optischen) Bewegungen = Eindrücke," a graphic representation but unlikely to be in the Greek: "Zur Vogelgestalt der Götter," p. 41. In either case—whether Ajax recognizes the god by his swift movement or by a large footprint—it remains true that the hero sees only an extraordinary detail of the god still in the disguise of Calchas. The god disappears quickly, as a hawk does, but no transformation is intimated in this formal epic simile. In the end the hero, while boasting that it is easy to recognize a god, does not know which god was in the disguise of Calchas. The hero is made to look foolish, especially in relation to *Il.* 20.131.

past presence; no recognition of the individual god.[31] Thus Ajax's boast that the gods are easy to recognize sounds naive, for he cannot tell the name of the god who was there. But Nestor can. He even goes so far as to claim that "Athena came *enargēs* for me to the rich feast of the god" (*Od.* 3.420), a claim of despairing nonsense, as we have seen. She became *enargēs*, "visible," "recognizable as a god," perhaps because the *Odyssey*, competing with the *Iliad*, wants to name her physical presence with *enargēs* instead of *arignōtos* (*Il.* 13.72); or perhaps it is the other way around: the *Iliad* corrects the misuse of *enargēs* by the *Odyssey*.

We touch upon a bottomless play of references that have developed diachronically through the composition of the two poems. This new, possible reference is again exemplary of the abysmal process of intertextuality: through a simultaneous movement of retrieval and obliteration intertextuality "fabricates" the text. By this very process the notion of the "integrity" or "self-containedness" of a text finds itself destabilized. The text of the *Odyssey* here again seems to be produced by the text of other poems—for us, of the *Iliad*. It *is* therefore itself and not itself, for it contains the other—as other—as a constitutional part of itself.

Since here I conclude the part of my book on the process of disguising and recognition, I wish to underline the impact of the disguise and recognition process on the Odyssean fiction. The fictional frame derives from the act of disguising reality and from a constant invitation by the text to the reader to re-cognize this disguising. As readers succeed in re-cognizing it, and in viewing disguise as disguise, they are invited, tantalizingly of course, to confront the "truth" of the fiction. This occurs at the literal level when, for instance, we are invited to distinguish Odysseus' "real" adventures from the "simulated" ones, or when we are allowed to distinguish the level of "utterance" from that of "speech acts"; and at the figurative level as well, whenever "recognitions" deliver an allegorical meaning.[32]

---

[31]Here I recall Karl Reinhardt's brilliant remark that Poseidon—even though he is disguised as Calchas—betrays himself by his picky remarks against Zeus. "An undisguised Calchas," Reinhardt explains, "would have hardly given his advice in such a critical way." *Die Ilias und ihr Dichter*, ed. Uvo Hölscher (Göttingen: Vandenhoeck & Ruprecht, 1961), p. 280. It would be profitable to compare the Iliadic scene with *Od.* 1.319–20, as Bannert does in his essay "Zur Vogelgestalt der Götter bei Homer." Bannert observes, for example, that Poseidon's "flight" as a bird in *Il.* 13.62 ff. is expressed in a simile, as is Athena's "flight" in *Od.* 1.319–20.

[32]The notion of fiction I have outlined is different from other novelistic notions. For instance, according to the theory of novelistic fiction that prevailed in the eighteenth century, a fictional story gives an individual and particular representation of universal traits and events. See de Man, *Allegories of Reading*, p. 197.

The delightful shrewdness of this fictional process, its endlessly cunning resources, put in the foreground the textual scenario of an author who in narrating his tale constantly provokes the reader to become aware of his own control and artistry or, as we would say today, of the textuality of the text. The force of the Odyssean fiction lies in the risky challenge that it takes in exploiting the disguising, drifting power of the sign. In exploiting this power, the narrative of the *Odyssey* comes close, whether purposely or not, to destabilizing time-honored certainties and pious convictions. The confident use of the sign's polytropic nature, however, carries this text further away than it planned, perhaps. As polytropy becomes centerless and a sort of pantotropy, the text becomes unreadable. This is still a force of the text, for a certain mode of unreadability prompts new writing. Notwithstanding its fictional, delightful tone, the *Odyssey* is the text that the "first" Greek "philosophers" do not fail to dialogue with.

II

RETURN TO THE SAME: DRIFTING AWAY

10

Return: No Return

from the experience of the forgetting of Being it [i.e., the nearness of Being (the illumination of *Da-* of *Dasein*)] is called the "homeland." The word is thought here in an essential sense, not patriotically or nationalistically but in terms of the history of Being. The essence of the homeland, however, is also mentioned with the intention of thinking the homelessness of contemporary man from the essence of Being's history.

Martin Heidegger, *Letter on Humanism*

"Let us flee, then, to the beloved Fatherland"—this would be the truer counsel. But what is this flight? How are we to gain the open sea, as Odysseus ordered flight from the sorceress Circe or Calypso? For Odysseus, as it seems to me, stands for a parable—not content to stay though he have all the pleasures of the eyes and his days be filled with the abundance of the beauty of Sense.

Our Fatherland is There whence we have come, and There is the Father. What then is our course, what the manner of our flight? This is not a journey for the feet; ever the feet bring us from one spot of earth to another. Nor do you need to plan a journey by horse-and-chariot or over sea. All this order of things you must set aside. Nor do you need to see; you must close the eyes and call instead upon another vision which is to be waked within you, a vision which all possess, which few apply.

Plotinus *Enneads* 1.6.8

The theme of "re-cognition" leads easily to that of re-turn. In both themes/words the troubling "re-" activity manifests the connection with the process of re-petition in the modes of continuity and difference, sameness and otherness, reading and writing. Recognition (*anagignōskein*) presumes to establish the integrity and selfsameness of an object or entity while in fact, by trying to circumvent the displacing movement of the sign, it merely postulates that integrity and selfsameness. Analogously, "a return to the same" postulates a return to the source or origin, while in fact—as the text shows—it can be no more than a drifting back. Through its use of the epithet *polutropos*, which replaces the name of Odysseus in *Od.* 1.1 and suggests that the return of the hero is made up of *many* voyages (turns), and of the epithet *hupotropos*, "turning back," which is Odysseus' own description of his return (*Od.* 22.35), the text unambiguously undercuts the metaphysical myth of a "return to the same." This is a myth that the text may entertain but cannot achieve. Because it assumes the existence of a simple, identifiable origin and the possibility of repetition without difference, it contradicts the movement of the sign itself and of writing, even though, in their literary forms, signs and writing often seem to sustain the myth. Odysseus cannot return to the same, for the nature of return, no less than that of recognition, excludes the possibility of sameness.

Before we analyze the theme of return in the *Odyssey*, it is useful to examine the darker alternative presented in the *Iliad*: that of no return at all. This is the alternative chosen by Achilles, and it is the grounds of his immortal *kleos*, "glory." As we might expect, the *Odyssey* makes this radical difference in orientation the grounds for a deliberate confrontation with the *Iliad*. As in other cases, this confrontation exhibits the reciprocal readings that diachronically one text has effected on the other. The two texts confront each other as if their orientations on return and on *kleos* were the thematic key to their different metaphysics, and indeed the notion of return does involve a different economy of life/death in each poem. Furthermore, and not surprisingly, the thematic differences—between the expectation of return in the *Odyssey* and the choice of no return in the *Iliad*—are embodied in the very writing of the texts. The writing of the *Iliad* allies itself with the dark power of death; that of the *Odyssey* aims at cheating death. In the *Iliad* writing presents itself—ideally, of course—as the theological and historical record of a unique, unrepeatable *pragma* of luminous Being, while in the *Odyssey* writing presents itself as *polutropos*, circumscribing the multifarious appearances of being—hence the intense brightness of Achilles' life and the checkered somberness of Odysseus' alternations between life and death.

The *Iliad*'s and the *Odyssey*'s Views of Return

The most Iliadic part of the *Odyssey* is of course the twenty-second book, in which Odysseus, assisted only by three inexperienced aides (Telemachus and two servants), kills all the suitors. The episode is unique in both texts and so cannot be compared to any specific passage in the *Iliad*. It does contain one scene, however—the killing of the suppliant Leodes—that recalls exactly a scene in the *Iliad*: Achilles' murder of Lycaon (21.74 ff). The texts of *Od.* 22.297–312 and *Il.* 21.18–24, 71–74 strikingly evoke each other through quotational repetitions. This phenomenon would perhaps have only relative importance were it not that through the characters Achilles and Lycaon on the one hand, and Odysseus and Leodes on the other, the poems also bring into the foreground the theme of return. The two pairs in fact stand in an inverse relationship toward return: Lycaon returns from a safe place to be killed by Achilles, who will not return home; Odysseus returns home to kill Leodes, who prayed to the gods that Odysseus would not return.

The structural parallelism can be shown as follows:

Od. 22.297–98	
Intervention of Athena	
Od. 22.299–306	*Il.* 21.18
Heroic similes	Heroic simile
Od. 22.307–8	*Il.* 21.19–21
Odysseus massacres suitors	Achilles massacres Trojans
Od. 22.310–11	*Il.* 21.71–73
Leodes falls as a suppliant	Lycaon falls as a suppliant
at Odysseus' knees	at Achilles' knees
Od. 22.312	
Odusseu	
gounoumai s'	*su de m'aideo kai m'eleēson*
Akhileu	= *Il.* 21.74
Odysseus	
I clasp your knees	Respect me and have pity on me,
Achilles	

The frame of the Odyssean scene begins at *Od.* 22.307–9, where Odysseus is described massacring enemies just as Achilles is described in *Il.* 21.17–21, but it is preceded by an intervention of Athena that is uniquely Iliadic in tone and iconography. Let us begin with this intervention.

And now Athena from the height of the roof stretched forth her man-destroying aegis: their minds were panic-stricken. They scurried through the hall like a herd of cows. (*Od.* 22.297–99)

Athena is thought of as invisible, and yet present, in her iconographic figure, with the murderous *aegis*. This type of invisible intervention occurs frequently in the *Iliad* (e.g., 2.172–82), but in the *Odyssey* it is very rare: generally when Athena actually intervenes among men, she is almost always *visible* either in a disguise or in a described figure.[1] Furthermore, the iconographic figure of Athena *promakhos* ("warrior") is unique to this passage of the Odyssey, while in the *Iliad* it is a familiar form for Athena—as well as for other gods—to take (see, for example, *Il.* 5.733–47).

Another characteristic of this framing passage, though not exclusively Iliadic, has Iliadic echoes: the abundance of similes. Here, within a few lines, a simile with postponed *hos* (299–301)[2] is immediately followed by a new simile (302–9), a technique that is in the main Iliadic.

Finally the language is, as one might expect, Iliadic. With line 299,

> *hoi d'ephebonto kata* megaron *boes hōs* agelaiai,

one may compare *Il.* 11.172,

> *hoi d'eti kam' messon pedion phobeonto boes hōs,*

and notice that in the entire *Odyssey, phebesthai*, "to flee," occurs only here.[3]

The text of the similes, however, is not the product of a passive imitation of the *Iliad;* it clearly reveals its "independence." In fact the simile in 299–301:

> *hoi d'ephebonto kata megaron boes hōs agelaiai*
> *tas men aiolos oistros ephormētheis edonēsen*
> *hōrēi en eiarinēi, hote t' ēmata makra pelontai*

> They scurried through the hall like a herd of cows upon whom the fluttering [*aiolos*] gadfly rushes and drives them about in springtime when the days are long,

has no precise Iliadic references; the word *oistros*, "gadfly," is *hapax* in Homer, and the last line (301) is an Odyssean self-reference (= *Od.*

---

[1] A few cases are disputable—for instance, *Od.* 17.360 ff., where Athena may be visible only to Odysseus—but it is impossible to be absolutely sure. Another case, similar to 22.297–99, could be *Od.* 18.69 ff. Here Athena intervenes, probably invisibly, during the mock-heroic fight between Odysseus and Irus. See also *Od* 8.193–94.

[2] On the postponed *hōs*, see Marcello Durante, *Sulla preistoria della tradizione poetica greca*, 2 vols. (Rome: Edizioni dell'Ateneo, 1971–76), 1:82–83, 2:120. Durante maintains that this *hos* reveals a Mycenaean derivation.

[3] A.H.C., *Od.* 22.299.

18.367), and only the first part of it is reminiscent of the *Iliad* (2.471, 16.463).

This simile is followed by another that describes Odysseus and his men (*Od.* 22.302–9) in words almost identical to those that end the simile used of Achilles:

302   and they [Odysseus and his men] as the crook-clawed, hook-beaked vultures
303   coming from the mountains leap on [*thorōsi*] birds
304   that fly shrinking from the clouds on the plain,[4]
305   while the vultures jump over them and kill them: no defense
306   no escape remains for them and men rejoice at their capture;
307   so they were chasing the suitors down the hall
308   and hitting [*tupton*] them right and left [*epistrophadēn*]. Their unseemly moans went up
309   as the skulls were hit and the ground was seething with blood.

Compare *Il.* 21.18–21:

18   and he [Achilles] leaped [*esthore*] similar to a god [*daimoni isos*]
19   with his sword alone—he devised grim deeds in his heart—
20   and was hitting them [*tupte*] right and left [*epistrophadēn*]. Their unseemly moans went up
21   as they were struck by the sword, and the water was red with blood.

The lines of *Il.* 21.20–21 are also used for Diomedes in *Il.* 10.483–84, indicating that they constitute a heroic formula that even within the *Iliad* itself is not exclusive to Achilles.[5]

---

[4]On the textual details of the simile, see Stanford's commentary. Stanford rejects the idea that *nephea* means "nets" instead of "clouds."

[5]Although the *epistrophadēn* lines are not used exclusively for Achilles in the *Iliad*, there is sufficient evidence in the *Odyssey* passage that its allusions refer to Achilles' assault in *Il.* 21.20–21. For instance, *Il.* 10.483 (on Diomedes) reads *kteine* instead of *tupte* (for Achilles) in *Il.* 21.20 (= *Od.* 22.308): see Karl Sittl, *Die Wiederholungen der Odyssee* (Munich: Ackermann, 1882), pp. 48–49. And there are other details that confirm the interdependence of the Achilles and Odysseus passages.

Later, however, when Odysseus kills Leodes (*Od.* 22.326 ff.), the *Odyssey* repeats ll. 455–57 of book 10 of the *Iliad*, from the episode involving Odysseus and Diomedes. But because the *Odyssey* alludes first (ll.308–9) to Achilles, it enhances Odysseus and so contests his relatively passive role in *Il.* 10.490 ff., where he simply drags away the victims of Diomedes' *epistrophadēn* assault. By this rewriting, the *Odyssey* makes explicit an implied disagreement with the Iliadic representation of Odysseus in the joint adventure with Diomedes. The relationship between the two heroes has a long tradition; as Gregory Nagy writes, "there are numerous epic traditions featuring these two heroes on joint expedition. . . . Significantly, different epic traditions give more or less credit

In *Il.* 21.18, as in *Od.* 22.302 ff., a simile precedes the actual description of the hero's *epistrophadēn* assault ("all around," "right and left"); there the simile describes Achilles as *daimoni isos*.[6] The adonic formula *daimoni isos*, "equal to a god," always occurs in the nominative and appears nine times in the *Iliad*, never in the *Odyssey*, and once in the *Hymn to Demeter* 235. Of the nine Iliadic appearances, three qualify Diomedes (*Il.* 5.438, 459, 884; the distribution is limited to the fifth book, Diomedes' *aristeia*); four, Achilles (*Il.* 20.447, 493; 21.18, 227) and two, Patroclus (*Il.* 16.705, 786). Since Patroclus is the *therapōn* ("squire," "companion," "alter ego") of Achilles, the formula seems to indicate a hero in the moment of his *aristeia*, and particularly Diomedes or Achilles (Patroclus). These are also the only two heroes in the *Iliad* who fight *epistrophadēn*.

The Odyssean simile (22.302 ff.) introduces a new metaphor for the contending parties: Odysseus and the suitors have already been equated to a gadfly and a herd of cows (299–301); now they are likened to vultures and timid birds (302 ff.). This use of a double simile is not rare in the *Iliad* (see, for instance, *Il.* 16.751 ff., 2.455 ff.), but it is rare in the *Odyssey*.[7] The comparison of the heroes with *aigupioi gampsōnuches* ("vultures"—or "eagles"—"with crooked talons") is found in *Il.* 16.428–30 with a few verbal similarities to the *Odyssey* passage. A more interesting signal of allusion may lie in the formal similarity between *Od.* 22.305–6 and *Il.* 21.528–29, where a similar phrase describes the flight and confusion of the Trojans under Achilles' pressure:

> *oude tis alkē*
> *gignetai oude phugē*

no defense and no escape remains to them.

> *oude tis alkē*
> *gigneth'*

no defense remained.

---

to one or the other figure. In the *Little Iliad*, for instance, it is Diomedes, and not Odysseus, who brings back Philoktetes" (*The Best of the Achaeans* [Baltimore: Johns Hopkins University Press, 1979], p. 34, n. 4). The *Odyssey* here tells its audience that Odysseus, like Achilles, could also kill *epistrophadēn*, so there is no necessary reason for the *Iliad* to have given this role to Diomedes rather than to Odysseus.

[6]In the corresponding passage of *Il.* 10.483–84 no simile precedes the description of the *epistrophadēn* fighting.

[7]See Sittl, *Wiederholungen in der Odyssee*, pp. 48–49.

This formal equivalence—between the Trojans hard-driven by Achilles and the suitors/birds driven by Odysseus/vulture—stresses Odysseus' Achillean valor. The same effect is perhaps obtained by the formal similarity that the verb *throskō*, "to leap," activates in *Od.* 22.303:

> as the crooked-clawed . . . vultures . . . leap on [*thorōsi*],

and in *Il.* 21.18

> and he [Achilles] leaped on [*esthore*].[8]

Both Odysseus/vulture and Achilles are described as *leaping on* the enemy before the *epistrophadēn* assult.

Yet here the elements of similarity begin, at the same time, to orchestrate the first light tones of a profound contrast: these tones will burst forth later when the two texts start to sing, above the formal similarity, a song of tremendous contrasts.

For the present it is notable that Achilles, "equal to a god" (*daimoni isos*), is said to contrive evil deeds for his enemy (line 19), while the *Odyssey*'s simile, for all its truculence, ends with the image of men rejoicing (*khairousi de t'aneres agrēi*, 306) at the sight of the birds' massacre. It is difficult to determine whether this joy comes to the men from observing the vultures' prowess or from the hunt in which they participate;[9] but whatever its source, its presence is significant as a kind of announcement that Odysseus' revenge will bring joy to the people who see it.

Let us read again the lines that describe the fighting *epistrophadēn* and the moans of the falling victims (*Il.* 21.19–21):

> *phasganon oion ekhōn . . .*
> *tupte d'epistrophadēn. tōn de stonos ornut' aeikēs*
> *aori theinomenōn, eruthaineto d'haimati hudōr.*

with the sword alone . . . [he] was hitting them right and left. Their unseemly moans went up as they were struck by the sword, and the water was red with blood.

and *Od.* 22.308–9:

---

[8]The final position of *ethoron*, as here in *Od.* 22.303 is found in other Iliadic passages, e.g., 11.70 = 16.770.

[9]Both possibilities are considered in Stanford's commentary.

Return to the Same: Drifting Away

tupton d'epistrophadēn. tōn de stonos ornut' aeikēs[10]
kratōn tuptomenōn, dapedon d'apan haimati thue

[they were chasing the suitors down the hall] and hitting them right and
left. Their unseemly moans went up as the skulls were hit and the
ground was seething with blood.

Some of the differences between the two passages derive from the
differences between Odysseus' and Achilles' situations: the plural *tupton* is required because Odysseus fights with three companions; the
Iliadic "as they were struck by the sword" is inappropriate because
Odysseus and his men have no sword.[11] In addition, Achilles drives
the enemy into the river, while Odysseus and his party fight on the
floor of the main hall (*megaron*).

These differences create some infelicities in the text of the *Odyssey*,
which suggests that the *Odyssey* passage was composed with the intention of accommodating Odysseus and his party to the role of Achilles
in *Il.* 21.18 ff. The price of this accommodation is the infelicitous
repetition of *tuptō* in *Od.* 22.308, 309, and the odd description of
moans going up as the heads of the victims are struck, which replaces
the more natural expression of the *Iliad*: "the moans of those who
were struck by the sword went up." It is not necessary to take the
genitive *aori theinomenōn* of the Iliadic passage as a genitive absolute,
as we are forced to do for the Odyssean *kratōn tuptomenōn* (22.309).
Furthermore, why should only the skulls be crushed by Odysseus and
his men, or alternatively, why should only those who were hit in the
head raise moans or lamentations?

Finally, the notion of hitting *epistrophadēn* may be inappropriate to
the spears that Odysseus and his men use.[12] The last part of line 309:
dapedon d'apan haimati thue, "and the ground was seething with blood,"
replaces the Iliadic *eruthaineto d'haimati hudōr* (or *gaia*), "the water [the
ground] was red with blood" of 21.21 (and 10.484), though the latter
could probably have been used. The *Odyssey*, however, here prefers a
self-reference: the phrase Agamemnon uses in *Od.* 11.420 when he
describes his own death.[13]

---

[10]In the phrase *tōn de stonos ornut' aeikēs* the adjective *aeikēs* could imply the shameful
defeat of the victims.

[11]See David B. Monro, *Homer's Odyssey, Books XIII–XXIV* (Oxford: Clarendon Press,
1901), at 22.308.

[12]Sittl thought so (*Wiederholungen in der Odyssee*, pp. 48–49), and see also A.H.C. Sittl
suggests the bracketing of the passage.

[13]The blood of the suitors recalls, by contrast, that of Agamemnon, who was murdered by the suitor of his wife. Odysseus is simultaneously the anti-Agamemnon.

These observations may intimate the will of the *Odyssey* to compare Odysseus to Achilles. Indeed, Achilles' fight by the river and his near defeat have already been evoked in the *Odyssey*.[14] It is thus a passage, or an *oimē*, that the poem glances at several times as it develops its own themes and its own metaphysics. The martial, Achillean remaking in this passage of the *Odyssey* testifies to the technical ability of the poet: with only a few touches Odysseus and his inexperienced men become as ferocious and murderous as Achilles in that brutal dalliance with death on the shore of the river Scamander.[15]

In the *Iliad*, Achilles, carrying on the massacre, encounters the young Lycaon, unarmed and naked (*gumnos*) (*Il.* 21.50). Achilles comments sarcastically on Lycaon's bitter destiny, for Achilles had already captured him once before and sold him as a slave. Now, only a few days after his ransom and return home, Lycaon again meets Achilles. The young man runs to Achilles as a suppliant and begs him:

> *kai min phōnēsas epea pteroenta proseuda:*
> *"gounoumai s', Akhileu' su de m' aideo kai m'eleēson."*

and speaking to him, he said winged words: "I clasp your knees, Achilles. Respect me and have pity on me." (*Il.* 21.73–74)

In the text of the *Odyssey*, immediately following the description of Odysseus massacring the suitors *epistrophadēn*, Leodes, their seer, rushes to Odysseus' feet:

> *Lēōdēs d' Oduseos epessumenos labe gounōn*
> *kai min lissomenos epea pteroenta proseuda:*
> *"gounoumai s' Oduseu' su de m'aideo kai m'eleēson."*

Leodes, with a rush, clasped Odysseus' knees and, imploring, said winged words: "I clasp your knees, Odysseus. Respect me and have pity on me." (*Od.* 22.310–12)[16]

---

[14]See, for instance, *Od.* 5.312 and my commentary at chap. 5, pp. 63–64.

[15]To have Odysseus act with the heroic fury of Achilles perhaps allows the poet of the *Odyssey* to justify Odysseus' unnecessary cruelty in killing not only every suitor, but even the suppliant Leodes, who is found guilty only of having desired Odysseus' wife. Additionally, in the transference of the Iliadic text (*Il.* 22.328–29, 10.455–57) Leodes ceases to be an *Ithacan* suitor; he assumes the traits of a *public* enemy—as a Trojan would for an Achaean.

[16]The same formula, *Il.* 21.74 = *Od.* 22.312, is used by Phemius as he, immediately after Leodes, petitions Odysseus (*Od.* 22.344). Walter Burkert points out the difference between *aideo*, "respect me," durative present, and the aorist, *eleēson*, "have pity," that has no temporal duration (*Zum altgriechischen Mitleidsbegriff* [Inaugural Dissertation der

The formula of entreaty: "I clasp your knees [*gounoumai*]. Respect me and have pity on me [*su de m'aideo kai m'eleēson*]" is specific and exclusive: it occurs in three passages (*Il.* 21.74 = *Od.* 22.312, 344) and only when a man who is not a warrior, who is *unarmed*, entreats a warrior. What is the basis for this distinctive, precise repetition? Is it purely thematic? If so, how do poets know about a theme unless they meet it in other poems? And why should Lycaon not use the other pattern of entreaty, in which the suppliant begs to be taken as a hostage and recalls the parents of the threatening warrior?[17] Finally, the coincidental repetitions extend beyond the mere formula of one line: the whole frame of the scene is alluded to and recalled. Though of course I cannot speak with absolute confidence, the possibility that the two poems read each other in this scene is close to a certainty.[18]

Textual allusions continue in the next scene. Neither Lycaon nor Leodes is spared, and both are slain in a similar manner: they are struck in the neck. No *formal* repetition marks the similarity of the theme, however, and the *Iliad* indulges in longer descriptions of Lycaon's reaction (21.114–16a) and Achilles' murdering gestures (116a–20) and final address to the corpse (121 ff.). The *Odyssey* simply repeats two lines from the *Iliad*'s Dolon episode in book 10: *Il.* 10.455b = *Od.* 22.328b; *Il.* 10.457 = *Od.* 22.329. It is noteworthy that in *both* these passages the attacker is described as striking his victim with a sword. This similarity has particular significance for the *Odyssey* because until that moment Odysseus has fought only with the spear, and so it seems that here the text almost goes out of its way to provide him with a sword:

> [Odysseus] seized in his large hand a sword that lay nearby and that Agelaus had dropped on the ground as he was slain: with this he struck Leodes in the middle of the neck. (*Od.* 22.326–28)

With such repetitions, the *Odyssey* puts Odysseus himself in the foreground—Odysseus as a champion of the Trojan War, inferior neither to Achilles nor to Diomedes. The textual allusions and references I have pointed out are sure indicators that this comparison is intended. In fact, before Odysseus' encounter with Leodes begins,

---

Philos. Fakultät der Friedrich-Alexander Universtät zu Erlangen, Erlangen, 1955], p. 96).

[17]See, for example, *Il.* 11.131–35 = 6.46–50.

[18]The *Odyssey* has the Iliadic text in mind, but this fact does not necessarily mean that the reading occurred at the moment of the monumental composition of the two poems.

Athena, disguised as Mentor, appears to Odysseus and refers explicitly to Odysseus' valor in the Trojan War:

> You have no longer, Odysseus, the firm fury, no longer that force which you had when you fought constantly for nine years against the Trojans for the sake of white-armed Helen. (*Od.* 22.226–28)[19]

Here the *Odyssey* once again revises and corrects the *Iliad* in order to extol its hero and his *pragma*.

Even the theme of the supplication of the two victims has striking similarities: Lycaon is aware that Achilles is angry over the death of Patroclus, and accordingly he explains that Hector is responsible for that loss and that he, Lycaon, is blameless of the deed (*Il.* 22.316–18). Analogously, Leodes explains that he is innocent, that he even tried to stop the others' wickedness, though to no avail.

As these similarities increasingly enhance the general similarity of the two massacre scenes, the difference between Achilles and Odysseus becomes more evident in the answer each gives to his suppliant in denying him mercy. Achilles says that because of Patroclus' death he is unable to indulge in the pleasure of sparing men, as he once did, and then he adds:

> So, friend, die as well. Why do you lament in this way? Patroclus too is dead, who was much better than you. Don't you see what a man am I, how noble and powerful? I am the son of a noble father, and a goddess mother bore me. Yet death and mighty fate are upon me too. There shall be a dawn, a noon, or an evening when someone takes my life away in battle, whether by striking me with his spear or with an arrow from his bow. (*Il.* 21.106–13)

The paradox of the community of death,[20] elaborated in a variety of tones: sarcasm ("friend, die as well"), irony ("Don't you see what a man am I. . . . Yet death and mighty fate are upon me too"), pathos

---

[19]On the Iliadic references of this passage, see chap. 1, n. 6. Note the Iliadic coloring of *emarnao* (228), a word already "typically literary" in the *Iliad* (see Durante, *Preistoria*, 2:42), and of *en ainēi dēioteti* (229), which apart from this passage occurs only twice in the *Odyssey* (11.516, where Odysseus speaks of Achilles' son, Neoptolemus; and 12.251, in the Scylla and Charybdis episode). In fact, the whole line *Od.* 22.229 repeats *Od.* 11.516.

[20]Of this "community of death" Walter Burkert observes: "There is no irony in this word [*philos*, "friend"], but only an uncanny [*unheimlich*] amphiboly: the connection linking Achilles with Lycaon is a solidarity for death and in death . . . Lycaon with his *eleēson* [have pity] was appealing to the community and proximity of the living beings; Achilles' answer is the community of death" (*Altgriechischen Mitleidsbegriff*, p. 96).

("there shall be a dawn"), denies mercy to Lycaon. Achilles persists in his killing because Patroclus has been killed and he himself shall soon be killed. Life has become impossible: only death occupies all the hours of the day, and all the destructive tools are in its hands.

In contrast, there is Odysseus' voice:

> If you boast of being the sacrificing priest [*thuoskoos*] among them, certainly you must have prayed many times in these halls that the accomplishment of sweet return [*nostoio telos glukeroio*] might remain far away from me, and that my dear wife[21] might follow you and bear you children. Therefore you shall not escape grievous death. (*Od.* 22.321–25)

Odysseus denies Leodes mercy because Leodes hoped and desired[22] that Odysseus would never achieve his sweet return home. Sweet return! The epithet "sweet" (*glukus*) is unique for "return" in Homer, and this uniqueness shows that Odysseus' return, the theme of the poem, is also identical to the theme of pleasure.[23]

The contrast between Achilles' answer to Lycaon and Odysseus' to Leodes orchestrates, above the formal similarities of the scenes, their difference as a central theme. This theme, which begins with the proems of the poems,[24] is articulated over and over, unfolding parallel motives that now deserve careful attention.

---

[21]The text has *philē* for the possessive pronoun "my."

[22]It is true that this desire took the form of a prayer and that possibly Leodes prayed during sacrificial ceremonies for all the suitors. See Jesper Svenbro, *La Parole et le marbre* (Lund, 1976), pp. 19–20, and Pierre Vidal-Naquet, "Valeurs religieuses et mythiques de la terre et du sacrifice dans l'Odyssée," in *Problèmes de la terre en Grèce ancienne*, ed. M. I. Finley (Paris: La Haye, 1973), p. 285, n. 3.

[23]See, however, *meliēdēs nostos*, "honey-like return," in *Od.* 11.100.

[24]See Pietro Pucci, "The Proem of the *Odyssey*," *Arethusa* 15 (1982): 39–62.

11

Return, Death, and Immortality

After the *Returns* comes the *Odyssey* of Homer, and then the *Telegony* in two books by Eugammon of Cyrene which contain the following matters. The suitors of Penelope are buried by their kinsmen, and Odysseus, after sacrificing to the Nymphs, sails to Elis to inspect his herds. He is entertained there by Polyxenus and receives a mixing bowl as a gift. . . . He next sails back to Ithaca . . . and then goes to Thesprotis where he marries Callidice, queen of the Thesprotians.

Proclus, *Chrestomathy*

The pathos in the narrative of the *Iliad* and the sarcasm in Achilles' comments on Lycaon's return are what we expect from the *Iliad*, for Achilles knew that he could either return home to a long though inglorious life or stay in Troy and, dying young there, obtain immortal glory (*aphthiton kleos*).[1] The *Iliad* is not merely an instrument for proclaiming Achilles' glory; it is itself the embodiment of that glory (*kleos*).[2] Accordingly, it carries its whole force in favor of *kleos*, that is, in favor of the young hero's death and against the very notion of return. When Achilles arrives at his determination to fight against Hector and to die, he announces his resolve while predicting for his mother "endless pain for your dead son, whom you shall not welcome back home [*oikade nostēsant'*]" (*Il.* 18.88–90). The pathos of this line is certainly heavier than that of the famous "May I die immediately" of a few lines later (98).[3] In the great Lycaon scene, the narrative voice comments with teasing pathos on the absurdity of Lycaon's return:

---

[1] On this point, see Gregory Nagy's brilliant observations in *The Best of the Achaeans* (Baltimore: Johns Hopkins University Press, 1979), pp. 35 ff. On the *aphthiton kleos*, see also E. D. Floyd, "*Kleos Aphthiton*: An Indo-European Perspective on Early Greek Poetry," *Glotta* 58 (1980): 133–57, and Gregory Nagy's response: "Another Look at *Kleos Aphthiton*," *Würzburger Jahrbücher für die Altertumswissenschaft*, n.s. 7 (1981): 113–16.

[2] On *kleos*, see also Floyd, "*Kleos Aphthiton*," p. 134.

[3] Lucretius in *De rerum natura* 3.894 ff. levels heavy irony at the uncontrolled pathos of mourning for those who will not come home.

There he [Achilles] met the son of Dardanian Priam, in flight out of the river, Lycaon, whom once he himself had taken and brought unwilling out of his father's orchard, during a night assault. . . . And at that time he [Achilles] sold him into well-peopled Lemnos . . . and from there fleeing secretly he [Lycaon] came to his father's house. For eleven days he had rejoiced among his friends after he had come from Lemnos, but on the twelfth, once more god threw him into the hands of Achilles who was to send him to the house of Hades, though unwilling to go. (*Il.* 21.34–37, 40, 44–48)

Lycaon's return home after many toils (*polla pathōn, Il.* 21.82) is marked by eleven days of joyous celebration as though his return meant a *return to the same,* to the good life in his father's house. But no return is really a return to exactly the same. The paradox in this scene is bottomless, for Lycaon does return home to an almost uncannily exact sameness and repetition: on the twelfth day, the day after the celebration, he again falls into Achilles' hands, just as he had before. Clearly, the *Iliad* is cruelly mocking the notion of a return to the same and its domesticated, utopian quality.[4] The text embraces within this paradoxical, gruesome farce the tragedy of a "same" that is not exactly the same. By its mockery the *Iliad* both contests and enacts the famous Hegelian sequence in which the same episode is repeated first in a tragic mode and then in a comic one.

The pathos of the narrative voice is replaced by Achilles' sarcasm when he suddenly sees Lycaon:

Ah me! What a great miracle I behold with my eyes. For surely the high-minded Trojans whom I have slain shall rise up again from the murky gloom since this man has escaped his pitiless day, though sold into goodly Lemnos. (*Il.* 21.54–58)

Here the text produces a paradoxical equation between return and immortality: Achilles ponders whether Lycaon's return intimates that now the Trojans will come back from death, and in order to be sure that this is not the case, he makes certain that Lycaon will never come back again:

Let's go: he will taste the point of our spear so that I may see and learn in my mind whether he shall come back even from there, or life-giving

---

[4]The text emphasizes the naivete of Lycaon's desire to return home by contrasting it with the prudent attitude of his host, for the family friend who had freed Lycaon kept him in custody, possibly for his own safety. Lycaon, however, wanted to go back and "secretly escaped" (*hupekprophugōn,* 44).

earth [gē phusizoos] shall hold him down, that holds even the strong. (Il. 21.60–63)

Notice the calculated sarcasm in the pretense that it is possible to equate returning home and returning to life, and in the oxymoron of life-giving earth (gē phusizoos) that contains a corpse as a tomb does. This is one of the three Homeric uses of phusizoos and, just as in Il. 3.243, this use is an oxymoron—as the ancient scholiast already noticed.

The Iliad crudely rebukes the notion that life-giving earth may ever grant life to a dead man. When this text is read in connection with Od. 11.301, where the same expression phusizoos (aia) refers to the "grain-nourishing earth" that holds Castor and Poludeukes alive, we may hear an echo between the two texts.[5]

On the precise theme of return and homecoming the two texts clash in these scenes of Lycaon and Leodes, where the structural similarities and the specific remakings intimate a real confrontation.[6] Achilles first mocks and then murders Lycaon, who had wanted to come back home and after many toils had celebrated the joys of homecoming. But Odysseus murders the innocent Leodes because Leodes prayed that Odysseus might never return, nostoio telos glukeroio.[7] And that Odysseus, in punishing the suitors, is made to mimic Achilles emphasizes how complete is the Odyssey's revision of Achilles' sarcastic, pathetic attitude toward return. Odysseus, in the garb of Achilles, vindicates the value of homecoming, of life and its pleasures.[8]

Only the joy of return justifies Odysseus' massacre: the horror of the murder is hardly relieved by the pleasure it produces. On the contrary, when in the Iliad Achilles slays Lycaon while he himself is on the brink of death, he evokes the common destiny of death:

[5]For further comments on this line, see below, pp. 153–54.

[6]Nagy has already defined epigrammatically—because it is structurally engrained in the text—the difference between Achilles' and Odysseus' pragma as kleos, "glory," for one and nostos, "return," for the other; see his formulations in Best of the Achaeans, pp. 35 ff.

[7]The expression is made emphatic by telos and by the rhyme of nostoio . . . glukeroio, which is itself a repetition, a return to the same, one pleasurable to hear.

[8]The Odyssey's representation of Achilles in Hades goes hand in hand with these life-affirming premises. Achilles is made to say that he would "prefer to be the hireling of a stranger . . . rather than rule over all the dead and gone" (Od. 11.489 ff). On the Odyssey's extraordinary reinterpretation of Achilles, in which he is made to choose return rather than death and kleos, see Anthony T. Edwards, Odysseus against Achilles, Beiträge zur klassichen Philologie, vol. 171 (Königstein/Ts.: Hain, 1985), pp. 43–68.

Why do you lament in this way? Patroclus too is dead, who was much better than you. . . . Death and mighty fate are upon me too. (*Il.* 21.106 ff.)

Life and death, death and life are chiastically present in these two scenes, but the *Iliad* soars higher, reaching a sublime vastness. The text of the *Odyssey* capitalizes on explicit "literary" effects. If we allow each text to echo the polemic assault of the other, there is no doubt that the *Odyssey* is more fully capitalizing on allusive effects. The repetition of the scene, in other words, inasmuch as it is a revision of the other text, is more seriously and profoundly pertinent to the *Odyssey*.

12

Polemic Gestures between the *Iliad* and the *Odyssey:* Odysseus as a Champion

> The sun gives without ever receiving: men had a feeling of this before they measured the sun's ceaseless prodigality through astrophysics: they saw the ripening of harvests and connected the splendor that is proper to the sun with the gesture of him who gives without receiving.
>
> Georges Bataille, *La Part maudite*

When Athena in the disguise of Mentor comes to Odysseus and scolds him:

> You have no longer, Odysseus, the firm fury [*menos empedon*], no longer that force [*oude tis alkē*] that you had when you fought constantly, for nine years against the Trojans (*Od.* 22.226 ff.),

those who know the *Iliad* may ask themselves whether it really does contain such a portrait of Odysseus and realize that it does not. Consequently, Athena's words open up some serious questions: If the text alluded to here is that of the *Iliad,* the *Odyssey* would seem either to suggest an improbable reading of the *Iliad* or to present a polemic rebuke and correction of it. Of course the *Odyssey* may be alluding to texts other than the *Iliad,* but in the absence of the other texts of the Cycle all we can do is follow the former alternatives and investigate the *obvious* sense of Athena's statement: that Odysseus was indeed a major hero on the battlefield of Troy. Given Athena's statement and the *Odyssey*'s evident remakes of both the *epistrophadēn* scene and the supplication theme, we must choose between reading the scene as alluding to the *Iliad* and reading no allusion at all.

Yet I am aware that I am reading in accordance with a macroscopic gesture of intention of the text and that, in fact, though macroscopic, this intention could easily be contested and dismantled. For instance, when the *Odyssey* picks up the theme of fighting *epistrophadēn,* a theme that usually describes a single hero fighting against a mass of enemies, it applies it to four men, three of whom are novices in the business of fighting. The reader can construe this sometimes clumsy adaptation in several ways: as the foolish decision of an inexperienced poet, as a master stroke of a parodical genius, or as a powerful gesture of a disdainful poet changing tradition to suit his needs. But it is impossible to decide which among these readings is "correct," and so they invite any number of possible interpretations. The macroscopic intention dissolves, and the text parades, with its adaptation of the *epistrophadēn* theme, only the unreadability of the sense of its own allusion.[1]

Despite this unreadability, I nevertheless choose to pursue the one reading that the text seems to advocate most forcefully. The text, it appears to me, intimates both despair for the way its sets of intentions drift toward an indefinite number of meanings and pleasure in its polemic gesture as an assertion of its textual control. The *Odyssey*'s attack against the Iliadic representation of Odysseus thus gives a specific orientation to my reading.[2]

My earlier commentary on *Od.* 5.203 ff.[3] has already shown that if we juxtapose the Iliadic and Odyssean texts that seem to allude to each other, we are able to hear a significant echo from both the *Odyssey* and the *Iliad*. In the transparency of that Odyssean passage, the Iliadic passages could suggest that Odysseus uses his *mētis* profitably only within the *Iliad* and that in the *Odyssey* the hero's *mētis* amounts to nothing more than the cleverness of a good raconteur. The remaining parts of the *Iliad* do not offer a much more positive representation of Odysseus. Respected as Odysseus is by all the other great heroes, his accomplishments are actually rather minor and often marked by the shadow of trickery, so the portrait that emerges from the *Iliad* is in fact less splendid than it appears to be. I leave aside here Odysseus' manifest trickery during the games (*Il.* 23.725 ff.), his untimely and unsuc-

---

[1]Similarly, the specific forms I have analyzed suggest that the *Odyssey*'s references to Achilles, rather than to Diomedes, fighting *epistrophadēn* should not carry the weight they may seem to carry. Poets, even in literate traditions, often recite from memory, and in the oral tradition this must have been the rule. Accordingly, one cannot grant too much force of evidence to the choice of the verb *tupton* rather than its synonym *kteinon*.

[2]Great poetry often owes its force to this undecidable predicament: on the one hand, it knows that its own text is inevitably drifting toward a spectrum of indefiniteness; on the other, it is rigorously trying to say exactly what it wants. This predicament is clearly announced in the *Iliad*'s invocation to the Muses, 2.489 ff.: see my "The Language of the Muses," in *Classical Mythology in Twentieth-Century Thought and Literature*, ed. Wendell M. Aycock and Theodore M. Klein (Lubbock: Texas Tech Press, 1980), pp. 163–86.

[3]See above, chap. 1, pp. 33–43.

cessful intervention in *Il.* 9.222–24, and Achilles' rebuke in 9.305 ff.[4] Instead I will analyze the prosaic, if inoffensive, stance Odysseus takes in contrast to Achilles' ascetic mourning in *Iliad* 19 (see chap. 15), but first I will treat the military episodes in which Odysseus is involved. These amount essentially to his participation in Diomedes' massacre of the Thracians (book 10), and to his *aristeia* in book 11.

In book 10, notwithstanding the epic paraphernalia of lavish praise that makes Odysseus the equal of Diomedes (Diomedes' flattering choice of Odysseus, Athena's equal love for both heroes, the description of Odysseus' armor, etc.), it is undeniably Diomedes who accomplishes the grim deeds of battle, while Odysseus' contributions are those of his celebrated *noos* (10.147): he ensures the success of the expedition by noticing Dolon, making him speak, and keeping the road free for return. In book 11, however, Odysseus achieves his most glorious military success, and yet the image in which he disappears from the battlefield reverberates with all sorts of possibly amusing innuendoes. The epic paraphernalia of praise appears again—even Sokus, Odysseus' enemy, recognizes his virtues: "toils" and "trickery" (*Il.* 11.430). But these virtues are hardly Iliadic.

After Odysseus kills Sokus (11.441 ff.), he suddenly finds himself surrounded by the Trojans and must call for help (*Il.* 11.459 ff.). Menelaus and Ajax come to his rescue (*Il.* 11.473–88):

> They found Odysseus, dear to Zeus:[5] the Trojans were besetting him just as tawny jackals from the hills beset a wounded horned deer that a man has hit with an arrow from his bowstring; the deer has fled from him running on his feet as long as the blood is warm and the limbs are able to work. But when the quick arrow has overcome the deer, then the raw eating jackals rend it on the hill in the dark wood; a god leads there a murdering lion, and the jackals flee before him while he rends it [the

---

[4]The entire episode of Odysseus' participation in the embassy deserves to be studied from the perspective of the Odyssean revision or remaking of lines. Here I will mention only two such revisions. The first is found in *Odyssey* 16, where Telemachus' unexpected arrival at Eumaeus' hut allows the poet to represent Eumaeus' surprise (*Od.* 16.12) with a parodical remake of *Il.* 9.193, where Achilles is surprised by the arrival of the embassy. In the second example (*Od.* 11.507), the *Odyssey* seems to respond to Achilles' famous lines in *Il.* 9.312–13 by having Odysseus promise to tell Achilles the absolute truth ("I'll tell you the whole truth, *as you ask*"), when in fact, on that occasion, Achilles has not even asked for the truth. It is in the *Iliad* that he had asked for truth. I have already touched upon Agamemnon's insults against Odysseus, in chap. 8, p. 104.

[5]*Heuron epeit' Odusēa* (473) is formulaic (*Il.* 2.169; *Od.* 22.401, 23.45). The remainder epithet, "dear to Zeus," ennobles the hero in *Il.* 2.169 and *Il.* 11.473, though in the Odyssean text (22.401ff.) Odysseus is "found" more heroically, splashed with blood, like a lion, among the people he has killed. Here, on the contrary, Odysseus, dear to Zeus, is compared to a deer and is himself bleeding.

deer].[6] Just so, many and mighty Trojans were busy at Odysseus, wise and crafty in counsel,[7] but the hero rushing with his spear kept away his pitiless day. And Ajax came close with his towerlike shield and stood thereby, and the Trojans fled from him here and there. Then warlike Menelaus led Odysseus out of the throngs, holding him by the hand until the attendant drove the horses up.

The simile, of course, is a notoriously difficult literary mode to interpret, since the correspondence between the compared and comparing terms is often loose and uncertain, but in this passage it is clear that Odysseus is consistently compared to the deer. This in itself is an unflattering likeness, but its detractive quality is made even more emphatic by contrast with the simile used for Ajax—the god-sent lion, the royal animal[8]—that is, the usual image for the heroic warrior.[9] Odysseus seems even further disparaged when we realize that, in the simile, the lion (Ajax) begins to eat the deer (Odysseus). In fact, the deer is attacked by three different predators: the hunter who wounds it from afar with an arrow, the jackals that begin to rend it, and finally the lion who rescues it from the jackals, only to make a meal of it himself. Correlating the simile and the actual situation,[10] Ajax—the lion—consumes Odysseus only metaphorically, by taking his place and having him disappear from the battlefield—as it turns out, al-

[6]Though the object of *daptei*, "rends," "devours," is not mentioned, there is little doubt that what the lion begins to eat is the deer, not the jackals. On *autar* as "while," see *LfrgE*, col. 1573, ll. 52 ff. The verb *dapto*, which etymologically has a long and exciting history (see *dapanē*, Lat. *daps, damnum*, etc., and Emile Benveniste, *Le Vocabulaire des institutions indo-européennes*, 2 vols. [Paris: Minuit, 1969], 1:75–77, 2:226–29), is used in Homer essentially to denote animals' devouring.

[7]*Amph' Odusēa daiphrona poikilomētēn* is *hapax* in the *Iliad*; the combination of the two epithets makes the expression specific for Odysseus, while *daiphron* alone can be applied to other heroes, Ajax, Achilles, etc. On the meaning of the two adjectives, see pp. 59–60.

[8]See Pietro Pucci, "Banter and Banquets for Heroic Death," forthcoming in *Beyond Aporia?*

[9]For the unflattering use of the deer simile, cf. *Il.* 1.225, where Achilles uses it to insult Agamemnon. The bibliography on Homeric lion similes is so extensive that here I will cite only the latest works that I found stimulating: Annie Schnapp-Gourbeillon, *Lions, héros, masques: Les Représentations de l'animal chez Homère* (Paris: F. Maspero, 1981); Christian Wolff, "A Note on Lions and Sophocles' *Philoctetes*," in *Arktouros: Hellenic Studies Presented to B. M. W. Knox*, ed. Glen W. Bowersock et al. (Berlin: de Gruyter, 1979); Rainer Friedrich, "On the Compositional Use of Similes in the *Odyssey*," *AJP* 102 (1981): 120–37.

[10]The hunter corresponds to Sokus, who has wounded Odysseus, the jackals correspond to the Trojans (notice the similarity of sound between *Trōes* and *thōes*), and the god-sent lion corresponds to Ajax, who rescues Odysseus. Of course Odysseus, unlike the defenseless deer, has killed his attacker (Sokus) and resisted the onslaught of the Trojans.

most forever, since Odysseus does not again participate significantly in the battle.

When we realize that Ajax is essentially described as the second Achilles and that he will become a victim of Odysseus' victory in the game for the armor of Achilles—a victory to whose dubiousness the *Iliad* perhaps alludes in 23.725 ff.—there can be little doubt that the text presents Odysseus' predicament with a seigneurial amusement and superior irony. The god-sent lion arrives as a royal, towerlike, immense champion, and immediately all the Trojans run away, leaving the king alone to rescue Odysseus; and he, taken by the hand, disappears from the battle scene. It is probably not by chance that the *Odyssey*, in its Iliadic description of Odysseus' victory over the suitors, twice uses the simile of the lion to characterize its hero (22.401–5,[11] 23.45–46).

When the *Iliad* sings in this sort of double harmony, at once serious and comic, we suspect that, notwithstanding its marvelous aplomb, it does not take Odysseus' prowess and military contribution too seriously. Of course our reading is colored by Athena's emphatic statement that Odysseus showed "firm fury [and] force, when [he] fought constantly, for nine years" against the Trojans, a statement we read as the *Odyssey*'s correction of the Iliadic treatment of Odysseus.

Hero of return, trickster and raconteur, all this is well; but champion also of might, second to none: this is the marvelous story the *Odyssey* tells us by disguising its Odysseus as an Achilles and a Diomedes through textual allusions and through Athena's intimations. A marvelous story indeed to be appreciated as an exciting, pleasurable narrative, as a sort of *muthologeuein*, for notwithstanding his Achillean valor and *epistrophadēn* battling, Odysseus will not obtain "renown," "glory" (*kleos*) from his tremendous deed. He will return home, and this return deprives him of Achillean *kleos*.

---

[11]This simile is one of the best heroic similes in Homer, and though fully integrated into the Iliadic type of lion similes, it cannot be considered evidence of mere imitation of Iliadic passages. The type of lion simile in the Odyssean passage represents a lion who has slain his prey and eaten it; no mention is made of eventual pursuers. This type appears frequently in the *Iliad*: see, for instance, 5.161 ff., 11.113 ff., 15.323 ff., 16.887 ff., 17.541 ff. The Odyssean remakes of the *Iliad* are very few: cf. *Od.* 22.401a and *Il.* 11.473a. *Od.* 22.402 also recalls Hector splattered with blood (*Il.* 6.268), but not in a simile. *Od.* 22.403 (*Boos . . . agrauloio*) is formulaic in the *Iliad* and the *Odyssey*. *Od.* 22.404–5 corresponds in the *Iliad* to a few similes: see, for instance, the wolves simile (*Il.* 16.159) and the lion simile (17.541). On the other hand, *Od.* 22.801b, *meta ktamenoisi nekussi*, is not Iliadic; analogously, *Od.* 22.405b is not Iliadic. *Od.* 22.406 has no precise Iliadic correspondence (cf., for instance, *Il.* 11.169). The image of Odysseus who, as a lion, will conquer the suitors is anticipated by that of Menelaus in *Od.* 4.333 ff., and see also *Od.* 17.124 ff.

13

Return and Cheating Death

Question critique du savant: et si cette prétendue propriété, plus littéralement cette valeur d'immanence de la mort à la vie, si cette domesticité familière de la mort n'était qu'une croyance consolatrice? Et si c'était une illusion destinée à nous rendre, comme dit encore le Poète, "supportable le fardeau de l'existence" (*"um die Schwere des Daseins zu ertragen"*)? A le rendre plus supportable comme *Anankē* qu'il ne le serait comme accident ou hasard? Traduisons: et si l'authenticité propre au *Dasein* comme *Sein zum Tode*, son *Eigentlichkeit* n'était que le leurre d'une proximité, d'une présence à soi (*Da*) du propre, fût-ce dans une forme qui ne serait plus celle du sujet, de la conscience, de la personne, de l'homme, de la substance vivante? Et si c'était justement le *poème*, le poétique même, cette mort immanente et propre à la vie? Un grand poème narratif, la seule histoire qu'on se raconte toujours, qu'on s'adresse à soi-même, la poétique du propre comme réconciliation, consolation, sérénité? La seule "croyance" aussi, ou plutôt contre-croyance car cette croyance n'est pas originaire.

Jacques Derrida, La Carte postale

Odysseus' return home is no fairy-tale ending. As Charles Segal perceptively observes, in Odysseus' and Penelope's reunion "the joy of rediscovery is . . . mixed with the sadness of irreparable loss."[1] The recognition scene ends when Odysseus has been bitterly tricked by Penelope (23.183), and when, to justify her caution, she evokes "the danger of committing the *ergon aeikes* of adultery."[2] Neither the return nor the revenge unambiguously wins *kleos* for Odysseus.[3]

Furthermore, Odysseus' voyages are not over:

---

[1]"The Phaeacians and the Symbolism of Odysseus' Return," *Arion* 1(1962): 17–63. Segal comments specifically on *Od.* 23.212; see p. 30.

[2]See my remarks in chap. 7, n. 19, and Leslie L. Collins, "NEIKEOS APXH: Helen and Heroic Ethics" (Ph.D. diss., Cornell University, 1982), p. 118.

[3]See, below, chap. 20, pp. 216–19, for my analysis of Odysseus' *kleos*.

my wife, we have not yet reached the end of all the toils, but still there is before us the immeasurable labor [*ametrētos ponos*],[4] vast and terrible that I must accomplish entirely. (*Od.* 23.248–50)

This return is only one of the many turns of Odysseus. His next immeasurable labor is grounded not on *philotēs*, "friendship," but, apparently, on the arbitrary will of the gods. This arbitrariness makes the new voyage seem simply a necessity of Odysseus' polytropy or, what is equivalent, a requirement of the drifting Odyssean writing.

The comforting implication of this turning/returning movement is that through its constant displacement it defers the end; as long as Odysseus is *polutropos* he will cheat death. Here lie the text's irresistible ruse and temptation: to have Odysseus always drifting away to further adventures, to fascinate us again and again with his polytropy.[5] But the text cannot yield to this temptation completely, for if its drifting (a decentered polytropy, or a pantotropy) were not phased and controlled, however arbitrarily, toward a specific goal, it would completely explode the identity of the hero and the coherence of the narrative.

In fact this is in some odd way what does happen, for nothing can control the drifting movement of writing. The postponement of Odysseus' death means his partial death at each moment of crisis. His disguises, his moments of unconsciousness, are the figures of this ambivalence. And paradoxical as it may seem, his frequently assumed anonymity (so strongly emphasized in, among other passages, the beginning of the poem) points to the manyness that forever threatens to annul the singularity of his identity as it is embodied in his proper name.[6] In fact, this bare figure of the wandering hero will be revived in the pages of later fictions, as Aeneas, as Jason, as Dante's Ulisse, and as Joyce's Ulysses.

This Odyssean strategy, which posits "return" as both a circular

[4]On *ponos*, "labor," as characteristic of Odysseus' life, see Nicole Loraux, "*Ponos*," in *Annali del seminario di studi del mondo classico.* Sezione di Archeologia e Storia Antica, no. 4 (Naples: Istituto Universitario Orientale, 1982), p. 182.

[5]On Teiresias' prophecy (*Od.* 11.134 ff.), see John Peradotto, "Prophecy Degree Zero: Teiresias and the End of the *Odyssey*," in *Oralità, cultura, litteratura, discorso* (Rome: Ateneo, 1986), pp. 429–59).

[6]It is within this dynamics that one may explain Odysseus' total renunciation of a "personality," as happens in the cave of the Cyclops, when Odysseus calls himself *Outis,* "Nobody." The text intimates that Odysseus' strategy here is a product of his *mētis.* Analogously, when Odysseus is disguised in Ithaca, he assumes a new name, Aithōn (*Od.* 19.183). On the relation between Odysseus' anonymity and his manyness, see Pietro Pucci, "The Proem of the *Odyssey*," *Arethusa* 15 (1982): 39–62, especially pp. 55 ff.

movement and the ceaseless drifting away of its hero, produces the constant menace of death and the temptation to tease death. On the one hand, return as a circle implies the end of the rotation, and therefore death; on the other hand, the ceaseless drifting tricks death by constantly putting off an end. I maintain that these aspects of return operate deeply in the text of the *Odyssey* and that they are responsible for, among other things, the *Odyssey*'s indulgence toward immortalizing some heroes and for its presentation of a magic world.

These are complex problems that I cannot examine fully here and for which I can only begin to provide some suggestions. In the *Odyssey* the notions of *nostos*, "return" (and re-turn), *noos*, "mind" or "intelligence," *tlēnai*, "[to] take upon oneself," and *polutropos* become so intimately connected that they form a cluster of powerful images whose underlying metaphysical premises all bespeak survival and defeat of death. In addition, the *doloi*, *mētis*, and the *muthoi* or *ainoi* (stories) that Odysseus possesses in abundance and uses as weapons for his survival reveal that the whole conceptual frame that sustains him on his journey is constantly preempting the possibility of death. The complicity between the conceptual frame of Odysseus' journey and the textual teasing of death invites us to regard the magic world of the *Odyssey* as a figural embodiment of this frame. The structural premises of Odysseus' journey (away from darkness and death), Odysseus' tricky intelligence (*mētis*, *doloi*), his experience of survival, and his manyness—all of which function as forces able to cheat death—are, so to speak, translated and magnified into extraordinary entities (sorceresses, concealers). Correspondingly, Odysseus' brushes with death metamorphose into concrete monstrous menaces.

Consider, for instance, Calypso and her island: from this perspective the nymph and her hospitable house are concrete, real entities that assure Odysseus' survival and ensure his return. They are *explicit* figures of the same comforting metaphysics that operates, but more *discretely*, in what critics call the "real world" of the *Odyssey*. Once we have understood the full complicity between the world of magic and the comforting conceptual frames of Odysseus' journey of return, the distinction between the supernatural world of magic and the "real" world of Ithaca becomes merely a matter of their *degree* of fictionality. That is, the distinction affects *our perception* of what is empirically imaginary and real, but not the comforting premises of the *Odyssey*'s narrative. This point is enforced by Odysseus' own perception and perspective; for example, he lost his companions, really and forever, in the cave of the Cyclops and in passing between Scylla and Charybdis, but through those very same adventures *he saved himself*. For him, the magical world of his journey was no less real than the world of Ithaca to which he returns.[7]

These observations should suffice to confirm that the domesticated premises of Odysseus' journey go hand in hand with the *Odyssey*'s explicitly miraculous and metaphysical statements. Among these statements are the assertions that some heroes have become, or will become, immortal. While the *Iliad* rejects absolutely the possibility of immortality for all its heroes, the *Odyssey* has a less rigid attitude.[8] Not that the *Odyssey* betrays the Iliadic ideal—indeed, it confirms the death of the Iliadic heroes and announces the death of its own hero. Nevertheless, the *Odyssey* likes to play with the idea of immortality, teasing the reader and raising provocative suggestions. Of those heroes who actually appear in the *Odyssey*, it is said that Menelaus will obtain immortality in the Elysian plain (*Od.* 4.563),[9] and the obvious assumption is that Helen will be with him. The text explains that Menelaus obtains this favor by virtue of being "consort of Helen and son-in-law of Zeus" (*Od.* 4.569). If this premise—whose flippancy seems evident—were operating in the *Iliad*, it would grant immortality to many heroes of that poem, for there are many heroes who are sons of gods, among them Sarpedon and Heracles, sons of Zeus himself, and Achilles, son of Thetis, nursed by Hera herself. But the *Iliad* denies immortality to them all. In the case of Sarpedon, the *Iliad*'s denial of immortality is emphasized by Zeus' anguished acceptance of his son's death (*Il.* 16.439–57).[10] And the different fates the two poems assign Heracles

---

[7]Of course the language of the *Odyssey*'s magic world should be carefully analyzed if we are to fully appreciate the text's bemused use of epic diction, with its tragic realism, to describe miraculous happenings. For example, earlier I analyzed the textual plotting in the passage describing Ino's sudden emergence to save Odysseus from the sea. Elsewhere I have shown the strikingly Iliadic diction of the Sirens, when they ask Odysseus to stop and to listen to them: see Pietro Pucci, "The Song of the Sirens," *Arethusa* 12 (1979): 121–32, and see below, chap. 19, pp. 209–13.

[8]See Gregory Nagy, *The Best of the Achaeans* (Baltimore: Johns Hopkins University Press, 1979), pp. 151–210. Although the epic cycle as a whole confirms the immortal destination of the hero—as is proper for heroes who are simultaneously cult figures—the *Iliad* and the *Odyssey* demonstrate their poetic sophistication, and their independence from the cults, in denying this destination. The two poems inquire into the stern law of the human condition ruled by the necessity of death. Nagy reconstructs a possible allusion to Achilles' immortal destination, using as evidence the golden amphora made by Hephaestus, in which Achilles' bones, together with those of Patroclus, will be placed: see *Best of the Achaeans*, p. 209 and n. 50.

[9]For the etymology of Elysion (*en-elusios*, adj.: "place made sacred by virtue of being struck by the thunderbolt"), see Nagy, *Best of the Achaeans*, pp. 167, 190.

[10]In l. 456 the expression *tarkhusousi* implies the use of techniques for preserving the body, as in Egyptian mummification. See Gregory Nagy, "On the Death of Sarpedon," in *Approaches to Homer*, ed. Carl A. Rubin and Cynthia W. Shelmerdine (Austin: University of Texas Press, 1983), pp. 187–217.

show how deeply the *Iliad* and the *Odyssey* are divided in this matter. The *Iliad* absolutely denies Heracles immortality (*Il.* 18.117), whereas the *Odyssey* states that he is among the immortals (*Od.* 11.602).[11] This marked difference between the two poems explains the immortal destiny of Helen[12] and Menelaus, but it surfaces as well in provocative suggestions or winks at the reader in regard to Odysseus' destiny. For example, the reader is tempted to assume that Heracles' praise of Odysseus as a spiritual brother evokes the possibility that an immortal destination awaits Odysseus too. Calypso's offer of immortality to Odysseus is even more suggestive, for here the text implies that it is possible for heroes to be immortalized—in fact, an ongoing process in the narrative time of the *Odyssey* (5.209)—and if Odysseus is not an immortal, it is only because he refuses to become one.[13]

That Odysseus alone may be responsible for his not attaining immortality shows that the *Odyssey* implies it is easy to cross the border of death to immortality as if, for the heroes, the two realms were contiguous. Whether this conception of heroic destination predates the *Iliad*, or was simply more popular than the Iliadic one, or must be read as an ironic interpretation of the heroic ideology cannot be said. What can be said is that such an assumption is unthinkable in the *Iliad*. In fact we have a passage in which the two poems, through the emphasis of a repetition that is probably a quotation, openly diverge on this matter. Their point of contention is the Dioskouroi's destiny.

In *Il.* 3.243–44 the poet comments on the destiny of Castor and Poludeukes, after Helen has pondered where they might live. The poet knows that they are dead:

> *Hōs phato tous d'ēdē katekhen phusizoos aia*
> *En Lakedaimoni authi, philēi en patridi gaiēi*

[11]See Nagy, *Best of the Achaeans*, p. 208, for the interpretation of the double figure of Heracles, who is present in Hades and yet lives among the gods.

[12]The *Iliad* does not know anything about the future destiny of Helen. There is also some ambiguity about her father: in *Il.* 3.140 her father is Tyndarus, but in 3.199 and 426 (just as in *Od.* 4.184) her epithet *Dios engegauia* could mean she is "daughter of Zeus."

[13]Calypso offers a different reason: male gods are jealous of mortals who accede to the goddess's bed. At least this is Calypso's interpretation of Zeus' order to let Odysseus go, and she cites the destinies of Orion and Iasion, who were destroyed by the jealousy of gods. However, we know well that Zeus' order is not prompted by jealousy. The examples of Orion and Iasion are interesting in themselves, for they are referred to as recent cases that set a precedent. Their relation to *muthos* is felicitously discussed by Ann Bergren, "Allegorizing Winged Words: Similes and Symbolization in *Odyssey* V," *CW* 74 (1980): 109–23, especially pp. 116–17. For another example of an immortalized human, see *Od.* 5.333 ff., where we are told that Ino, the mortal daughter of Cadmus, has received divine honors. The *Iliad*, too, occasionally refers to mortals who were abducted and immortalized, for example, Ganymedes, *Il.* 20.232–33.

So she spoke, but the grain-nourishing earth already held them fast
there, in Lacedamon, in their fatherland.

In the *Odyssey*, the hero narrates to the Phaeacians how in Hades he
saw Leda, the wife of Tyndarus, the mother of Castor and Poludeukes, "whom the grain-nourishing earth holds alive" (*Od.* 11.301):

> *tous amphō zōous katekhei phusizoos aia.*

The repetition is marked by the rare *phusizoos aia* (which appears only
three times in Homer)[14] and by the diction of *zōous katekhei phusizoos
aia*, with the etymological pun—as the ancient Greeks thought—between *zōous* and phus*izoos*, emphasizing that the "life-giving earth
holds" them "alive," in contrast with the Iliadic line in which the
callida iunctura lies in the oxymoron of the life-giving earth holding
them fast, that is, dead.[15] Because the repetition is doubly marked, it
clearly seems intentional. Furthermore, the line defining the twins
with their epithets—*Il.* 3.237 and *Od.* 11.300—is repeated exactly.[16]

The form of immortality the Dioskouroi enjoy in the *Odyssey* is
worth noting:

> [they] whom life-producing [I translate in accordance with the intended
> etymology] earth holds alive: even under earth they have honor from
> Zeus and live one day while they die the other; they have honor just like
> gods.[17] (*Od.* 11.301–4)

[14]*Il.* 3.243, 21.63; *Od.* 11.301. It appears once in *Hymn to Aphrodite* 125.

[15]Pierre Chantraine defines *phusizoos* as "producing grains" (see *DE*, s.v. "phyomai")
and "producing grain, fertile" (*DE*, s.v. "zeiai"). The ending -*zoos* is the same as the first
part of *zeidoros*, "that gives grains," an epithet of *aroura*, "plowed land." Etymologically,
there is some relation to Skr. *yava*- "grain." Chantraine adds that in both *phusizoos* and
zeidoros the ancients recognized—by popular etymology—themes connected to *zēn*, "to
live," and to *zoē*, "life." In this case, as in others, it is difficult to decide whether we
should translate according to our linguistic judgment or according to the meaning the
text suggests. The case of *meilikhios* is analogous: the Homeric text often uses it in
connection with *meli*, "honey," but we know that this is a false etymology. See Pierre
Chantraine, "Grec MEILICHIOS," in *Mélanges Emile Boisacq*, 2 vols.; Annuaire de l'Institut
de Philologie et d'Histoire Orientales et Slaves, vols. 5 and 6 (1937–38; reprinted
Brussels: Kraus, 1969), 5:169–74.

[16]The third occurrence of *phusizoos* is in the scornful words of Achilles in *Il.* 21.63:
"so that I may see . . . whether he shall come back even from there, or life-giving earth
[*ge phusizoos*] shall hold him down." Here the intended oxymoron heightens Achilles'
sarcastic comments. However, the *Iliad* may simultaneously be responding, in a rather
blunt manner, to the *Odyssey*'s fablelike intimations that it is possible to cross the border
between life and death. Conversely, the *Odyssey* perhaps smiles at the crude oxymoron
of the *Iliad*, simultaneously hinting at the immortal destination of heroes that cult
sustained and the epic cycle *as a whole* granted.

[17]One can interpret this obscure passage as meaning that the twins have the privilege
of *being alive* in Hades and of returning up into the light (*zōousi*) one day out of two. But

This is indeed an odd form of immortality, one that seems to suggest that the border between life and death can be crossed without any decisive loss, as if the realms of life and death were equivalent and return from the one to the other always possible. It is another instance of the ruse through which the *Odyssey* suggests that the wish to evade and deceive death is in fact a possibility. This possibility is what gives force and persuasiveness to all the magical moments of the poem, most obviously to Odysseus' descent to Hades and his *return* to life, but also to his concealed life with Calypso and his decision to return home; his loss of identity (a figurative death) in all his disguises (particularly as "Nobody" in the cave of the Cyclops) and his *return* to himself and presumably to his identity; his transport to Ithaca, asleep and unconscious, in a state like that of death; his failure, at decisive moments, to awake in time to prevent disasters, as when his companions slaughter the cattle of the Sun. In all these and analogous situations Odysseus has a kind of double existence, as both alive and dead.[18]

---

it could be understood to mean that the Dioskouroi are alive in the sense that even in Hades they continue to live, changing constantly from life to death and vice versa. Or finally, the twins have "the privilege of being alive in turn on every second day while the other [lies] in his grave" (Stanford, 1:392). The first interpretation seems the most convincing to me.

[18]See Laurence Kahn, "Ulysse," in *Dictionnaire des mythologies et des religions des sociétés traditionelles et du monde antique,* Yves Bonnefoy, 2 vols. (Paris: Flammarion, 1981), 2:517–20.

III

SYNONYMY

14

The Heart (*Thumos*) of the Iliadic Lion and the Belly (*Gastēr*) of the Odyssean Lion

What is old repeats itself with new tones. Evidently it belongs to the inventions of the *Iliad*'s poet to effect iridescent transfers of tragic turns into untragic, ironic ones, while these transfers succeed less well for the *Odyssey*'s poet, though he too is not alien to irony.

Karl Reinhardt, *Die Ilias und ihr Dichter*

The undecidable line in whose wake the "writings" of the *Iliad* and the *Odyssey* emerge as simultaneously similar and opposite passes through all sorts of figures and grammatical features. The signifiers *tlē-*, *tolma-*, and so forth, with their different metaphorical meanings, and the repetition of lines, similes, *topoi*, and scenes with different intent and implications are some of these figures and features. The two texts seem to recall each other by some sorts of disguise, and the *Odyssey* in particular, which seems to exhibit its textuality more openly, plays recklessly or humorously, or both, with these intertextual features.

We come now to an interplay of two words that seem not at all related to each other in the fashion of a "figure," and yet on some occasions the *Odyssey* uses one of these words as "synonymous" with the other. I am referring to the notions contained in *thumos* (approximately "heart") and *gastēr* ("belly," metaphorically "hunger"). I would not elaborate so pointedly the allusive interplay between these words in the two poems were it not that *gastēr* in the *Odyssey* assumes a significant role as the notion that points to the principles of death and life, of instinct and culture, of deprivation and fullness, necessity (death) and pleasure. Let us begin by tracing the parallelism between the Iliadic *thumos* and the Odyssean *gastēr*.

Sarpedon, who is ready to attack the Achaeans' wall, is compared to a lion that approaches a flock of sheep even though they are protected in a stable (*Il.* 12.299 ff.):

He went as a mountain-nurtured lion that for a long time has lacked meat and his *bold heart* commands him [*keletai de he thumos agēnōr*] to try for the sheep even by going against a well-fenced dwelling.

Like King Sarpedon, the lion feeds on (fat) meat, but unlike him, the lion must risk his life to obtain this food. The ideal portrait of the king (in *Il.* 12.310–28), however, shows that for Sarpedon the rich banquets are one of his prerogatives, just as risking his life is one aspect of his high-mindedness.

When the *Odyssey* uses this same lion simile to portray Odysseus, it is in a much different context. Odysseus, who is naked and hungry, is about to present himself to Nausicaa and her maids (*Od.* 6.130–36):

He went as a mountain-nurtured lion, confident in his power, that goes through the rain and wind, with his eyes shining: he comes on cattle or sheep or among wild deer; *and his belly* commands him [*keletai de he gastēr*] to try for the sheep even by going against a well-fenced dwelling.

In this passage the *Odyssey* clearly appropriates both the language and themes of the Iliadic tradition, and again, though nothing definitive can be said about when this occurred, there can be no doubt that the passage from the *Odyssey* adapts what *for us* is a passage of the *Iliad* and rewrites it.[1]

The most telling point of the *Odyssey*'s reading of these lines concerns the presentation of the lion's motives: though the lion in the *Iliad* has long been deprived of meat, it is still his *bold heart* that

---

[1]Although the lion simile is common in the *Iliad*, it is rare in the *Odyssey*, occurring only five times (4.333–40 = 17.126–31, 6.130–36, 22.402–6, 23.48). In all these passages, with the exception of 6.130–36, the simile is used as an image for Odysseus' battle against the suitors. In our passage, 6.130–36, the text adopts the Iliadic simile with several changes, the most telling of which I will analyze in the following pages. Here I note that: (*a*) the *Odyssey* simile follows the *Iliad* only to 12.301, thus leaving aside the description of the lion's heroic determination to continue, even if he should fall in the first ranks; (*b*) the *Odyssey* adds the shining eyes, a detail we find in the boar simile of *Il.* 13.474 (see also *Od.* 19.446) and the lion simile of *Il.* 20.172 and that is a feature of the heroic code (see *Il.* 19.16 ff., a description of Achilles, whose eyes shine when he looks at weapons); (*c*) the *Odyssey* simile describes the lion as *huomenos* and *aēmenos,* "through the rain and wind," which is both more appropriate and more relevant to Odysseus' situation than it is to that of a lion, especially a mountain-nurtured lion that obviously can be exposed to bad weather without pathos; (*d*) the *Odyssey* simile implies that the lion has various choices: he joins (*meterkhetai*) cattle, or sheep, or deer; he is thus shown to hunt animals grazing freely before he tries the well-protected stable. Here the simile intimates that Odysseus is compelled to face the women, who are far from their city, and that he is so desperate that he would even present himself naked to them.

compels him (*keletai de he thumos agēnōr*)[2] to attack the flock, while the lion of the *Odyssey* simile is driven solely by his *belly's* urgings (*keletai de he gastēr*).

The replacement of *thumos* (heart) with *gastēr* (belly) reveals several intentions and purposes. In the *Iliad* the gesture of defying the stable remains a matter of heroism. We are told that, despite his hunger, the lion is motivated by his *thumos agēnōr*, and thus he is assimilated into the *objective* code of the high-minded heroes. In the *Odyssey*, however, the same gesture of defiance is dictated by hunger, a bodily need, a subjective and ephemeral concern. This shift is emphasized by the parallel in lines 135–36:

> In the same way, Odysseus, though naked, was about to mingle with the fair-haired girls, for need had befallen him [*khreiō gar hikane*].

Khreiō means simply "need" in the sense of a "subjective and occasional tendency to appropriate something."[3]

With this use of *gastēr* and *khreiō*, which reduces the lion's high-minded Iliadic aspect to more prosaic but also more natural dimensions, the *Odyssey* bemusedly frames the heroic code. The text of the *Odyssey* juxtaposes itself to the *Iliad* and retains its general contours, thus creating the tension that gives the simile its ironic force.[4] In both poems the lion remains an image or symbol of the king (*basileus*), but whereas in the *Iliad* it is a symbol of heroic behavior and so a cultural representation of the king, in the *Odyssey* it is naturalized, its savagery exposed. The text smiles ironically as it uses the Iliadic tradition for its own purpose, namely to hide the embarrassingly elegiac situation of the hero who must *present himself naked* to the young and noble girls. The image of the hungry lion conveys how savage a breach of civility Odysseus is compelled to commit.[5]

---

[2]On the formula *thumos agēnōr* see *LfrgE*, s.v. "agēnōr." The word *agēnōr* implies the notion "leader of men" from the verbal theme *age-*, but other etymological explanations have been proposed by both ancient and modern scholars. The word is interpreted as meaning "courageous," "audacious," and this sense enters frequently into the formula *thumos agēnōr*.

[3]See Georges Redard, *Recherches sur* ΧΡΗ, ΧΡΗΣΘΑΙ: *Etude sémantique* (Paris: H. Champion, 1953), p. 67. See also p. 68.

[4]See Benedetto Marzullo, *Il problema omerico*, 2d ed. rev. (Milan and Naples: R. Ricciardi, 1970), pp. 281 ff. While attributing the Odyssean simile to an epic epigone, Marzullo correctly emphasizes this point: "persino i leoni si immeseriscono . . . hanno da fare anch'essi con le petulanti necessità della quotidiana esistenza" (even lions become miserable . . . and must cope with the mean necessities of everyday life).

[5]The simile functions as the poet's editorial comment and is meant to protect his hero from scorn. In this way the simile is a gesture analogous in intent to Odysseus covering

Though prompted by the subjective and passing demands of his belly, the Odyssean lion does not lack all nobility, for he "trusts his own power" (*alki pepoithōs,* 130). This formula *integrates* the Odyssean lion into the heroic code of the *Iliad,* which uses the expression once for Hector (*Il.* 18.158) and several times for animals in heroic similes.[6] In other words, we are encouraged to recognize the *same* animal in both passages, as if the divergence in the two descriptions was dictated by nothing more than their different contexts.[7] We can thus read the *Odyssey's* own readings as a form of disguise (its needy lion wears the trappings of its synonymic Iliadic counterpart), taking pleasure in this ruse (synonym) as one of the novelties of the text.[8]

---

himself with a branch. This simile presents Odysseus as still a king, and it lends his nakedness the quality of an awful obstacle or predicament. Indeed his nakedness is, subjectively speaking, what Odysseus finds difficult to expose, and he does so only under the compulsion of his belly and vital needs. Objectively, however, Odysseus' nakedness also enables the women to take him for a wild beast, as Nitzsch has already noted (2:106–7) and as Rainer Friedrich develops in "On the Compositional Use of Similes in the *Odyssey,*" *AJP* 102 (1981): 123. In the end, all the girls except Nausicaa run away. Thus the simile dramatizes Odysseus' necessary violation of civility and of his own culture's mores. The lion simile simultaneously conveys a wholly different sense. By likening Odysseus to a lion amid the flocks, the simile intimates the ease of his task, the likelihood of his victory, and also reminds the reader of Odysseus' characteristic success with women. The "well-fenced stable," in Odysseus' case, does not correspond to a wall he must overcome, as in the case of Sarpedon; rather, it refers to the "prudery," civility, and societal codes that Nausicaa and her friends represent. It is a barrier that Odysseus faces and overcomes with ease, again thanks to the simile. By giving Odysseus the traits of a ferociously hungry lion, the bemused commentary of the *Odyssey* defends him from what might otherwise be an embarrassingly elegiac situation, and it protects him through the humor of this amusing perversion of Iliadic formulas.

[6]In four of the five Iliadic examples where *alki pepoithōs,* "trusting his power," qualifies an animal (either a lion or a boar) in a heroic simile, the animal is described in a defensive and resistant posture: *Il.* 5.299, 13.471, 17.61, 18.158 (although in this last example Hector receives the qualification, and the simile that follows compares him to an animal in a defensive posture). Only in *Il.* 17.728 is the situation ambivalent, for though the boar is described as wounded and pursued by dogs, he still, *alki pepoithōs,* turns here and there among the dogs and puts them to flight. If *alki pepoithōs* evokes—in the formulaic code—the theme of a resistant, wounded animal, then it would seem to have been used in the Odyssean passage to tone down Odysseus' aggressive attitude or to emphasize his vulnerability—or it might have simply been used improperly.

[7]Even the lion to whom Achilles is disparagingly compared by Apollo (*Il.* 24.41–43) "goes after the sheep of men in order to get a feast [*daita*]"—notwithstanding his *thumos.* See Gregory Nagy, *The Best of the Achaeans* (Baltimore: Johns Hopkins University Press, 1979), pp. 135 ff.

[8]Analysts' critical assessments have attributed this simile to an epigone or a later poet; see Marzullo, *Problema omerico.* In addition to the analysts, W. C. Scott emphasizes the untraditional character of this simile: *The Oral Nature of the Homeric Simile, Mnemosyne,* suppl. 28 (Leiden: Brill, 1974), p. 62. See also Carroll Moulton, *Similes in the Homeric Poems* (Göttingen: Vandenhoeck & Ruprecht, 1977), p. 140; and Hermann Fränkel, *Die homerischen Gleichnisse* (Göttingen: Vandenhoeck & Ruprecht, 1921), p. 70. Finally, as

The Heart (*Thumos*) and the Belly (*Gastēr*)

And yet this reading faces an impenetrable opacity. Certainly the allusion is there and lets itself be read, but what sense should we grant it? Should we attribute to the *Odyssey* a humorous intent and imply that the *Odyssey* smiles at the high-minded lions of the *Iliad*? Or should we assume the timidity of the text and say that for its tradition a king is always comparable to a lion? Probably both answers are correct in the sense that the Odyssean "allusion" can mean at the same time the need for the poet to follow the traditional patterns and also his need to get out of them.

Thumos and *Gastēr* of Fighters

The synonymy of "heart" and "belly" is curiously presented in a passage of the *Odyssey*. In *Od.* 18.1 ff., the arrogant Irus forces Odysseus to fight with him. The suitors suddenly intervene to referee the fight and propose a ridiculous prize of sausages for the winner. Odysseus the beggar then justifies his seemingly foolish acceptance of Irus' challenge:

> Among them resourceful [*polumētis*] Odysseus said cleverly [*dolophroneōn*],[9] "Friends, it is not possible for an old man, worn out by misery, to fight against a younger one. Yet the reckless belly compels me [*alla me gastēr / otrunei kakoergos*] to be conquered by his [Irus'] blows. (*Od.* 18.51–54)

Odysseus goes on to ask the suitors to swear to remain impartial during the fight, and after they do so, Telemachus addresses him with the following words:

> Stranger, if your spirit and your bold heart compel you [*ei s'otrunei kradiē kai thumos agēnōr*] to ward off this man, do not fear any of the other Achaeans. (*Od.* 18.61–63)

---

already noted, Nitzsch, 2:106–7, emphasizes the uneasiness of old and new interpreters and quotes, disapprovingly, Lessing's view—analogous to that of Themistius—that the lion portrays Odysseus' trust in his intelligence and suggests that Odysseus feels shame before the young girls. Nitzsch goes on to suggest that the audience cannot but think that Odysseus must come before the girls as *smerdaleos* as a lion. Friedrich, "On the Compositional Use of Similes," p. 123, develops this point with sensitivity.

[9] This line repeats *Od.* 21.274, which puzzles scholars because they do not see what Odysseus' cleverness and trickery consist in throughout this passage. See, for instance, Karl Sittl, *Die Wiederholungen in der Odyssee* (Munich: Ackermann, 1882), p. 132.

Telemachus seems to have picked up his father's words almost as if he were quoting him: "if—as you say—your *kradiē* and *thumos agēnōr* compel you" but in fact he has changed the subject. Odysseus had spoken of his "reckless belly," not his "spirit and bold heart."[10]

In this exchange the text artfully suggests the multiplicity of its purposes by producing a multiplicity of effects. Basically, these lines serve to mask and unmask Odysseus, confirming and reminding us of his double persona as he plays the beggar. That is, when Odysseus himself speaks it is as a beggar, someone who justifies his boldness by adducing his hunger. (His adversary Irus is himself known and conspicuous for his hunger and "voracious belly" [*gasteri margēi, Od.* 18.2].) But when Telemachus speaks, only *apparently* quoting his father, it is to intimate that Odysseus actually fights as an Iliadic hero, someone compelled by his "spirit and bold heart." Thus the text seems to illustrate a sort of nodding, or sotto voce communication between son and father that eludes all the suitors, though not, presumably, the reader. Or is Telemachus' remark supposed to sound synonymous with Odysseus'? But this alternative seems untenable inasmuch as the substitution, with its rare and formulaic expression, is so pointed that it might justify D. B. Monro's generalization that "in the story of Irus the language of the *Iliad* is borrowed and parodied."[11]

Parody would explain how "belly" and "heart" can be equated in the passage as if they were synonyms, despite the fact that they belong to different codes, for through parody the *Odyssey* perhaps ridicules the high-mindedness of the Iliadic hero. The *Odyssey* smilingly intimates that although the Iliadic heroes are well aware of the enormous privileges associated with fighting (in particular the great quantity of good food),[12] heroes nevertheless often seem to forget those benefits and so appeal to their fierceness (*menos*), their bold hearts. By drawing a parallel between the belly and the Iliadic heart, the *Odyssey* appears to remind its audience of the totally practical and mundane fact that great banquets, with their abundance of meat and wine, must figure even in the Iliadic heroes' determination to fight. This is, in a nutshell, Aristophanic humor. The parody may be heavy-handed, but

---

[10]*Thumos agēnōr* is also the lion's heart in the simile of *Il.* 12.299 ff. The entire expression, *otrunei kradiē kai thumos agēnōr*, in *Od.* 18.61 shows fully the original meaning of *agēnōr* (*LfrgE*, s.v. "agēnōr"). This whole expression occurs three times in Homer: *Il.* 10.220 (of Diomedes), 10.319 (of Dolon), and *Od.* 18.61.

[11]David B. Monro, *Homer's Odyssey, Books XIII–XXIV* (Oxford: Clarendon Press, 1901), appendix, p. 331.

[12]Cf. *Il.* 12.312 ff., 4.261 ff., 4.341 ff., 8.161 ff.

that is in keeping with the battle Odysseus is engaged in: when the epic stage is occupied by voracious bellies, nothing too subtle can be expected.

These conclusions, however, must be reconciled with and substantiated by Gregory Nagy's brilliant suggestions about the story of Irus and its significance. Starting from Marcel Detienne's findings,[13] Nagy has elaborated and described the features of the language of praise (epic poetry, *kleos*, etc.) that distinguish it from its antagonist, the language of blame (*phthonos, eris, gastēr,* etc.).[14] The poet of blame, when unrighteously castigating noble people, is described by the poets of praise as "fattening himself on envy," and his language is indicated as a "means for getting a meal" or, even more radically, as devouring its victim. Applying his findings to the Irus episode in the *Odyssey,* Nagy shows that Irus' fight can be read as a parody of the language of blame: "Like the unrighteous blamers who are righteously blamed by praise poetry, Irus has *eris* 'strife' with a good man (18.13, 38–39) and initiates 'quarrelling' against him (18.9). Like the blamers he is *margos* 'gluttonous' (18.2) and has *phthonos* 'greed' for the *olbos* 'prosperity' that the good man gets from the gods (*Od.* 18.17–19). . . . Now we also see that Odysseus himself is generous even with the provocative Irus (18.16)."[15]

From Nagy's characterization it appears that Irus' gluttonous belly is a distinctive feature he shares with unrighteous blame poetry and its authors, and so it follows that Irus and Odysseus occupy reciprocal stances, reflected in their antagonistic and opposing use of language.

When we apply these observations to the repartee between Odysseus and Telemachus (*Od.* 18.53, 61), we are led to conclude that Telemachus corrects Odysseus' expression in a manner both tactful and pertinent for the poem's audience. When Odysseus is forced to fight against the beggar/blamer Irus, his language resembles Irus'. The suitors arrange the conflict in such a way that even Odysseus is eager to win the sausages: when a good man becomes the mirror image of his antagonist, differences collapse. We would not even be able to distinguish Odysseus' voice were it not for Telemachus' remarks.

The *Odyssey* therefore uses Irus as a foil for Odysseus the beggar, and they both function—though Telemachus' repartee invites us to see Odysseus at the same time in a different light—as blamers (par-

---

[13]Marcel Detienne, *Les Maîtres de vérité dans la Grèce archaïque,* 2d ed. (Paris: F. Maspero, 1973).

[14]*Best of the Achaeans,* pp. 222 ff., specifically pp. 225–26.

[15]Ibid., p. 231.

odic blamers) of the high-minded Iliadic heroes. For a moment, then, the *Odyssey* itself speaks from the point of view of blame poetry: Telemachus saves the day for the hero, his father, with his timely intervention. Or perhaps his "rescue" is only partial, for the adaptation of the heroic *thumos* pattern to the *gastēr* pattern inevitably diminishes the former. Consequently, the neat distinction between the terms that define and separate blame poetry and praise poetry collapses. The one can always revert to the other and vice versa. For it is obvious that this is the case: praise poetry, by depicting blame with abusive terms, finds itself in the analogous posture of the poetry it blames.

The foregoing analysis indicates that the contrast between the belly and the heart produces the same tensions as the Odyssean modification of the *Iliad*'s lion simile. In both cases a tantalizingly ironic synonymy is presented, suggested, almost imposed, at the same time that the rhetorical operation, in the form of a pointedly tropic substitution, intimates their traditional difference.

15

Being Mindful of Food:
Being Forgetful of Griefs

In Homer, the matter of food is never treated lightly.
                                    Fausto Codino, *Introduzione a Omero*

The heart (*thumos*) and the belly (*gastēr*) are not synonymous, though both may be used figuratively in Homer for man's "desire" or "impulse." *Thumos* may even be the "appetite," as in the phrases: "satisfying the *thumos* with food and drink" (*Od.* 17.603) or "when the *thumos* commands to drink" (*Il.* 4.263). But the two words cannot be literally, figuratively, and stylistically synonymous, for *thumos* has a more abstract meaning—"heart as vital principle"—and it habitually occurs in martial contexts, while *gastēr* means the "belly" and its physiological need, "hunger." Moreover, *gastēr* in the sense of human "appetite" or "hunger" does not seem to conform to the heroic style, for it is used only *once* in the *Iliad*—and then, it should be no surprise to learn, by Odysseus (*Il.* 19.225).[1] This occurs in the reconciliation

---

[1] The word *gastēr*, which is probably connected with the verb *graō*, "devour" (see *DE*, pp. 211–12), occurs thirty times in Homer, eleven times to indicate the belly as an anatomical part of the body, especially as a place where heroes are wounded. It is used once of the uterus (*Il.* 6.58), three times to mean "sausages," and fifteen times to refer to the stomach as the seat of hunger and thus, metaphorically, to hunger. Of these fifteen examples, thirteen occur in the *Odyssey* and only two in the *Iliad*: at 16.163, for the stomach of wolves in a heroic simile, and at 19.225, where Odysseus uses *gastēr* to refer to the Achaeans' hunger. On *gastēr* as a kind of synecdoche for the "human condition," see Jean-Pierre Vernant, "A la table des hommes," in Marcel Detienne and Jean-Pierre Vernant, *La Cuisine du sacrifice en pays grec* (Paris: Gallimard, 1979); and Marylin B. Arthur, "Cultural Strategies in Hesiod's *Theogony*: Law, Family, Society," *Arethusa* 15 (1982): 75. In addition, the word *limos*, "hunger," occurs once in Odysseus' speech in the *Iliad* (19.166) and twice during the episode in which Zeus and Athena aid Achilles, also in book 19 (348, 354). The word occurs five times in the *Odyssey*. Curiously, in some instances *limos*, "hunger," wears out the *gastēr*, "belly" (*Od.* 4.369). In these cases *gastēr* is used almost literally.

scene (*Il.* 19.40 ff.)[2] in a sharp and pointed confrontation with Achilles.

The context for this confrontation is the assembly Achilles has summoned to resolve his quarrel with Agamemnon (*Il.* 19.56 ff.) and to urge the Achaeans to launch an immediate assault against the Trojans. Amid the general delight, Agamemnon too puts an end to the quarrel, declaring himself ready to give Achilles the gifts that—as we know—he had already promised through Odysseus in book 9. Achilles answers with few words:

> "for the gifts, if you want, give them, as it is befitting, or keep them.[3] It is up to you. Now let us be mindful of the battle, immediately [*mnēsōmetha kharmēs*]. . . . For a great work remains to be done." (*Il.* 19.147–49a, 150)

Everything seems to be finally agreed upon when, unexpectedly, Odysseus intervenes to try and cool Achilles' eagerness to fight with the argument that men must first eat:

> Do not, for all your valor, godlike[4] Achilles, push the sons of the Achaeans to Ilion on an empty stomach,[5] to fight against the Trojans: the battle shall not be short when the ranks of men first meet and god inspires fury on both sides. Command instead that the Achaeans eat

[2]Philologists consider the reconciliation scene a "recent" part of the *Iliad* and therefore already conscious of the *Odyssey*. See Leaf's cautious remarks, as well as Jacob Wackernagel's specific remarks on the recent forms in this scene, in *Akzentstudien* 2 (1914): 35, n. 1 (= *Kleine Schriften*, 2 vols. [Göttingen: Vandenhoeck & Ruprecht, 1953], 2:1137, n. 1); Emile Benveniste, "Renouvellement lexical et dérivation en grec ancien," *BSL* 59 (1964): 36. On other features, see Denys Page, *History and the Homeric Iliad* (Berkeley: University of California Press, 1959), pp. 332–34; and G. P. Shipp, *Studies in the Language of Homer*, 2d ed. (Cambridge: Cambridge University Press, 1972), pp. 300–301. Fausto Codino offers a historically suggestive commentary on this scene in his *Introduzione a Omero* (Turin: Einaudi, 1965), pp. 98, 114. I have no difficulty accepting that this scene is already conscious of the *Odyssey*. In fact, all my analyses presume that the two texts have looked at and listened to one another all along, before and during the monumental composition. In speculating about a tradition, however, it is highly questionable to define specific passages that contain linguistic novelties as "recent," for this way of thinking risks denying the continuity of themes within the tradition and takes what could be a recent reformulation of an older theme as entirely new.

[3]Achilles' spiritual distance from Agamemnon's gifts intimates no disrespect; his neglect of material goods is stressed in order to emphasize his urgent desire for war—indeed, his mother had already determined his inclinations (*Il.* 19.34–37)—his total commitment to killing Hector. Achilles is on the side of an economy of total expenditure, of total waste.

[4]*Theoeikel' Achileu.* Although l. 155 repeats *Il.* 1.131, the epithet itself is used only in these two passages in the *Iliad* but is used three times in the *Odyssey*; there is one example in *Hymn* 28.15.

[5]*Nēstias,* "without eating," is a compound of the negative prefix *nē* and the root of the verb *edō,* "to eat" (*Il.* 19.156, 207; *Od.* 18.370).

food and wine[6] by the swift ships. Fury and power come from these.[7] For no man fasting from food can fight the whole day until the sun sets:[8] his heart [*thumos*] longs for the battle, his knees, however, unaware grow weary, and thirst and hunger come upon him and his knees fail him as he goes.[9] But when a man has satisfied himself with food and drink,[10] then he fights the whole day against enemies with a confident heart [*ētor*], nor do his knees tire[11] until the battle is over. Come, disperse the men and tell them to prepare the meal. (*Il.* 19.155–72)

The message and the tone are clear enough: Odysseus offers practical advice (within an almost Hesiodean frame, notes Fausto Codino):[12] the *thumos* and the *ētor* alone do not suffice to sustain the effort of the battle; food too is needed. In contrast with Achilles' "let us immediately be mindful of the battle," Odysseus is made to recall the trivial necessities of the body. And he has still other practical points to make: the gifts should be carried in the assembly to be seen by everybody; Agamemnon should make an oath that he has never had sexual relations with the girl and should offer a banquet (*dais*) to the *basileis* (172–83).

Agamemnon is happy to comply with Odysseus' requests, but Achilles returns to his impelling desire for slaughter. He ignores Odysseus[13] and asks Agamemnon to dismiss, for now, all these concerns about gifts and food, adding (19.205–14):

---

[6]*Pasasthai . . . / sitou kai oinoio.* The verb *pateomai*, "to eat" (etymol.: Got. *fodjan* "to nurse," modern Engl. "food," Lat. *pasco*, etc.) is used here by zeugma with both "food" and "wine," but the addition of "wine" (*oinoio*) is unprecedented, as when it is a question of drinks, the usual expression is *potētos*, *Od.* 9.87 = 10.58; see n. 7 below. Here the verb refers to the common meal of the soldiers. The *basileis* will have a *dais*, "banquet" (179).

[7]This line (161) repeats *Il.* 9.706, where Diomedes expresses the same concerns that occupy Odysseus in this passage. Note that lions and wolves in heroic similes are often described as hungry or feeding on prey.

[8]L. 162 is typically Odyssean: it is used five times by Odysseus himself in the narrative of his travels (*Od.* 9.161, 556, 10.183, 476, 12.29), and once by the narrative voice in *Od.* 19.424. In the *Iliad* the whole phrase appears only in 1.601 and here in 19.162 (see the same distribution of lines in *Il.* 19.155 = 1.131); otherwise only bits of the whole phrase occur.

[9]This phrase, *blabetai de te gounat' ionti* (166), occurs in *Od.* 13.34 in a simile.

[10]For the phrase *oinoio koressamenos*, see *Od.* 14.46. *Edōdē* and its declined forms occur eight times in the *Odyssey* and four times in the *Iliad*, always at the end of the line; it is indiscriminately used by various heroes.

[11]The phrase of l. 169–70, *oude ti guia / prin kamnei*, corresponds to *Od.* 12.279–80, *oude ti guia / kamneis.*

[12]Codino, *Introduzione a Omero*, p. 112. In the notes to the passage I have pointed out some consonances with the Odyssean style.

[13]Achilles ignores Odysseus during this entire scene. He does not answer him, not even after l. 237, although his remarks in ll. 199 ff. clearly include Odysseus.

Now I will lead the sons of the Achaeans to fight, on an empty stomach
[*nēstias*], without eating, and when the sun is setting, prepare a mighty
meal, when we will have avenged the shame. Until then, neither food
nor drink shall go down my throat, since my friend is dead, who lies in
the hut mangled by the sharp bronze, his feet toward the door; around
him friends mourn. Therefore in my heart I do not care for those
things, but for slaying, blood, and the grievous lament of men.

His desire for food replaced by a desire for blood, Achilles here
reveals the same anthropophagous desire expressed in *Il.* 22.346–47,
where he wishes his fury would impel him to slice up and eat Hector's
raw flesh.[14]

Against this bloodthirsty attitude the text sets a down-to-earth
Odysseus, a tough, no-nonsense man of better judgment than
Achilles (216–19)[15] who proposes:

It is not by hunger [*gasteri*] that the Achaeans can mourn a dead man
[225]. For too many and thick they fall each day: when then there should
be rest from toil [i.e., from this mourning you advocated]? It is, on the
contrary, necessary to bury him who dies, with impassive heart, after we
have wept one day. And those who survive the hateful war must be
mindful of drink and food [*memnēsthai posios kai edētuos*] so that we may
fight even more. . . . (225–31)

Nothing could be more opposed in tone and content to Achilles'
ascetic bloodthirstiness than these lines. *Gastēr* in line 225—the
unique Iliadic example of this word for human "hunger"—used in
the context of the somber theme of mourning, sounds snappy, irreverent, vulgar;[16] the mention of the "too many" who die each day
(226 ff.) directly offends the sensitivity of Achilles and the decorum of
the situation: Patroclus cannot be compared to the anonymous crowd
of dead soldiers. Finally, it is clear that Odysseus has no patience with
or understanding of Achilles' deathlike asceticism; in the name of the
common needs of the army he simply dismisses Achilles' grieving
rejection of food and, with it, all heroic etiquette. Of course Achilles,

[14]Apollo emphasizes Achilles' bestial fury in the lion simile of *Il.* 24.41–43, where the
lion/Achilles goes after the sheep of men in order to get a feast—here properly called a
dais; see Gregory Nagy, *The Best of the Achaeans* (Baltimore: Johns Hopkins University
Press, 1979), pp. 135–37.

[15]For these lines, see my commentary in "The Song of the Sirens," *Arethusa* 12
(1979): 122. They are perfectly Iliadic lines.

[16]Leaf's comment on *gasteri* is telling: "*gasteri* is evidently used to make the idea
ridiculous." Johannes Th. Kakridēs notices that "Odysseus speaks in a similar spirit to
Alcinous in *Od.* 7.215 ff." *Homeric Researches* (Lund: Gleerup, 1949), p. 104, n. 16. For
my comments on that passage, see chap. 16, pp. 173–75.

mourning Patroclus, cannot eat, for he is totally overwhelmed by grief. And his reaction is in full accord with the epic convention that the person who grieves and mourns rejects the idea of food. Obliviousness to eating goes hand in hand with the presence of death, whatever form it announces itself in—mourning, the wish to kill, or utter despair. Mourning, for instance, mimes death and its effects; accordingly the mourner refuses food, the source and support of life. Thus Achilles will refuse to touch any food until he has killed Hector. Only at *Il.* 23.48 will he comply with the "hateful *dais*" (*stugerēi peithōmetha daiti*), though even then he continues to carry out some of the other rituals of mourning (23.43–47). When, against his heart, he finally agrees to the hateful *dais,* he is overcome by sleep; all the organic needs take possession of him again. And yet this collapse of his mourning does not pass unnoticed or uncensored. Patroclus' *psuchē* appears to Achilles and gently reproaches him for being unmindful of his slain friend (*Il.* 23.69–70). Achilles' radical mourning demands such a miming of death, such a communion with death, that food must be banished, and it is only because he is human that he must eventually yield to the hateful *dais.*

In this confrontation between the man of *gastēr* and the man of *thumos* the *Iliad,* with devilish accuracy, depicts Odysseus' character as it is drawn in the *Odyssey.* Here the *Iliad* answers the *Odyssey* directly. Achilles mimes the death of his friend Patroclus and carries death to the enemies, while Odysseus grieves only a few hours—even after the loss of all his friends—then eats and faces life again. Achilles knows that because Patroclus is dead, he himself cannot remain among the living; in Patroclus' death he discovers his own, and with desperate lucidity he hurries toward it. Odysseus can take upon himself everything (*tlēnai*), deferring death until after the next trip or adventure, staging all sorts of *doloi* to circumvent the pitfalls he encounters, and forgetting the inevitable outcome of life. But of course Odysseus cares for his men, here (*Il.* 19.226 ff.) as in the *Odyssey* (*Od.* 1.5–6), and he cares also for Achilles, for whose sake he has the gifts carried into the assembly, the oath sworn by Agamemnon, and the food distributed to the men. Achilles, however, has taken no notice of him. With this ferocious confrontation between the two heroes, the *Iliad* and the *Odyssey* are clearly, and fiercely, opposing their views: the *Iliad* enhances Achilles' sublime asceticism while implicitly debasing the mean concerns of Odysseus, as well as his—and the *Odyssey*'s—inability to understand the heroic poem of *kleos* and death.[17]

---

[17]See Pucci, "Song of the Sirens," pp. 121–32; and "The Proem of the *Odyssey,*" *Arethusa* 15 (1982): 39–62.

Although Odysseus' tone offends the desperate asceticism of Achilles and his words show a special insensitivity, his advice to abstain from excessive grief is correct from another point of view of epic etiquette. When a hero indulges excessively in death-miming mourning he is regularly advised to remember the necessities and pleasures of life. The mourning asceticism should perform what Freud calls the work of mourning and then allow the return to normality. Achilles himself makes this precise plea to Priam in book 24 of the *Iliad*. Yet how elegantly and sensitively can Achilles speak to the old king with whom he shares the same experience of desperate pain and ascetic mourning, for Priam too has not eaten or drunk since Achilles killed Hector:

> "For never did my eyes close beneath the lids since my son lost his life at your hands, but I continuously mourn and nurse my countless griefs [*kēdea muria pessō*, 639], always rolling in the courtyard amid the dung."
> (24.535 ff.)

Mourning for Hector, Priam cannot eat, but by a sort of figurative inversion his mind "feeds" on its pain and despair.[18] Analogously, when Achilles loses Patroclus he performs a rigorous fasting and mourning until he has slain Hector. Then he yields to the need for food, but even in the beginning of book 24 Achilles' mother, Thetis, is still begging him to relent:

> *sēn edeai kradiēn, memnēmenos oute te sitou*
> *out' eunēs?*

> My son, until when, amid laments and griefs, will you eat your heart, without being mindful either of food or sleep? (24.128–30)

Achilles, like Priam, consumes himself in pain and lets his heart be devoured by grief, instead of concerning himself with the needs of his body.

After Achilles lifts the dead body of Hector and lays it on Priam's wagon, he tells Priam:

> Your son, old man, is given back, as you urged, and lies on a bier and with the break of day [*eoi phainomenēphin*] you shall see him yourself as

---

[18]When pain forbids eating, eating attacks the heart itself: see the compound *thumoboros*, "devouring the heart," which occurs five times in the *Iliad* only. The *Odyssey* has *thumodakēs*, "heart biting" (8.185).

you carry him.[19] But now let us be mindful of food [*nun de mnēsōmetha dorpou*, 601]. For even fair-haired Niobe was mindful of food [*emnēsato sitou*], she whose twelve children perished in her home, six daughters and six lusty sons. (*Il.* 24.599 ff.)

Achilles can now urge Priam to eat because Hector's body has been returned: the convention teaches that Priam can finally relent. After all, Niobe ate even after the gods buried her twelve children.[20]

According to the heroic code, the return to food after mourning represents the need to stop miming the death of the dear deceased, to forgo the desperate communion with the dead.[21] In general, the return to food means the return to the controlled economy of life, to sex, to pleasures (see *Il.* 24.128–32), and to the acceptance of one's mortality.[22]

To this extent the *Iliad*'s presentation of Achilles' and Priam's mourning asceticism—with its ceremonial gestures, its rolling in the dung, its abstinence—intimates that their heroic etiquette, sublime as it is, dangerously oversteps the human condition. This intimation suggests the hero's contiguity with death on the one hand and on the

---

[19]The return of light and the return of Hector's body to Ilion are emphasized as parallel events. With the appearance of light, Priam will see Hector with his eyes; the return of the dead body is conceived also as the last vision of it, the last sight of the flesh and features.

[20]On the exemplary function of the myth of Niobe in the Iliadic context, see Kakridēs, *Homeric Researches*, pp. 96–105, and Malcolm M. Willcock, "Mythological Paradeigma in the *Iliad*," *CQ*, n.s. 14 (1964): 141–54.

[21]Mourning is not the only occasion on which a return to food means a return to the concern for life and merriment: Menelaus, in the *Odyssey*, bids his guests to cease crying (when an especially saddening conversation has evoked their tears) and adds, "Let us remember to eat" (*Od.* 4.212–13). In the tenth book of the *Odyssey* Odysseus carries a big deer to his companions, who for two days "have eaten their hearts for weariness and pain" (143), and says, "For all our sorrow we shall not enter into Hades' house . . . let us remember about food" (*Od.* 10.177). When the suitors are plotting to kill Telemachus, an omen discourages them and Amphinomus says, "Friends, this plot, the killing of Telemachus, will not go smoothly for us. Let us remember about food" (*Od.* 20.245–46). Finally, in *Il.* 24.129, Thetis asks Achilles how long he will mourn, "not remembering about food and sleep." Notice the pointed paradox: in pain one eats one's heart and not bread; to eat bread is to be human (see, for example, *Il.* 6.142, 13.322). Of all the examples above, *Od.* 20.245–46 is the most aberrant; yet even here "remembering about food" signals the mind's return from death (albeit a plotted death) and the return to normal, quotidian existence.

[22]The *Odyssey* teaches us that the bards used to sing epic stories during and after the meal of the *basileus* and his retainers: Achilles' or Priam's ascetic rejection of food is therefore evoked and represented while the listeners eat abundantly and drink full cups of wine in seats of honor. And when the hero in the epic song finally eats, the listeners are also satiated with food. Symbolically, then, when the royal listeners hear these imaginary celebrations of death, they are themselves asserting the power of life over death, in accordance with the tenets of the epic song itself.

other with the divine. The contiguity with death, manifested by the suspension of bodily needs, parches the human body and makes it mime death itself. Both heroes receive divine assistance. Zeus sends Athena to sustain Achilles with nectar and ambrosia (*Il.* 19.342 ff.) in order that hunger may not take him. This divine intervention shows that in carrying his mourning asceticism to an extreme Achilles exceeds human capabilities. Zeus allows Achilles to satisfy his ascetic urge, but only temporarily, since that fulfillment brings Achilles into contact with the divine. He cannot continue to eat divine food, the privilege of the gods (*Il.* 5.341; *Od.* 5.196–99), for men, by definition, are "bread eaters" in relation to beasts and gods.[23]

[23]See *Il.* 6.142, 13.322, 21.465; *Od.* 8.222, 9.89, 191.

16

Pirates and Beggars

> Marring himself with outrageous blows he [Odysseus] took the semblance of a servant.
>
> Helen in the *Odyssey*

There are no light or humorous touches in the words Odysseus is made to say about the violent tyranny of bodily needs. The opposition between the grieving asceticism of Achilles and the tough practicality of Odysseus is treated seriously in the *Iliad,* notwithstanding Odysseus' breach of the "decorum" of high-minded heroism. As the great confrontation between Achilles and Odysseus in the nineteenth book of the *Iliad* announces, Odysseus in the *Odyssey* will meditate on, and sometimes suffer from, the implacable needs of *gastēr*. Again, there is no doubt of the seriousness of Odysseus' position in the *Odyssey,* though there the unsuitability of his concern, within the context of the heroic code, has shocked ancient and modern critics.[1]

I have avoided comparing Achilles and Odysseus on psychological or moral grounds; their positions simply represent two opposite economies of life, two exemplary extremes in conceiving our relationship with life and death and accordingly two different ways of writing and circumventing our anxiety about death.

Thus it is possible to consider, without indulging in ironic or indignant comments, Odysseus' meditations on the implacable needs of the *gastēr* that force us to *be mindful only of food.* The first such meditation occurs in Odysseus' response to Alcinous in the seventh book of the *Odyssey.* Odysseus has appeared, almost miraculously, to Arete, Al-

---

[1]For a decided contrast, see W. B. Stanford's indignant defense of Odysseus against the "armchair critics who censure the conduct of a ravenous shipwrecked mariner for not conforming with the etiquette of Alexandria or Versailles" and against "the moralists who demand the scruples of the confessional in the speeches of the banqueting-hall" (*The Ulysses Theme* [Oxford: Blackwell, 1954], pp. 69–70). Among the ancient critics who criticized Odysseus for his gluttony, or indulgence of the belly's needs, are Plato *Rep.* 390b; Athenaeus *Deipnosophistai* 412b–d and 513a–d; and Lucian *Tragodopodagra* 5.261–62.

cinous, and their retainers, and he begs them for a safe return. The
king grants his petition and then addresses his still anonymous guest
with a cryptic and complimentary question, asking whether he is a
disguised god or a man. Here the *Odyssey* titillates (and teases) the
audience with the intimation that gods may appear to men easily, in
full light (*enargeis*), just as in the golden age.

This wishful and utopian ideology frames Odysseus' down-to-earth
response and creates a violent contrast. Of course, Odysseus' resemblance to a god has already been emphasized by the text, and his
miraculous appearance was accomplished through divine assistance.
Accordingly Alcinous' assumption that Odysseus may be a god in
disguise raises the audience's expectation of a truly "heroic," high-
minded, sublime spectacle. But Odysseus denies his resemblance to a
god; he assures Alcinous that he has nothing of the gods' features (*Od.*
7.208–12) and says he is a man who has suffered immensely. Then,
unexpectedly, he adds:

> Come, let me now, though I am distressed, take my meal. For there is
> nothing more bestial[2] [*kunteron*] than the hateful[3] belly [*gasteri*] which
> perforce commands a man to be mindful of it, however worn he may be
> and grieving in his mind. Thus I too have grief in my mind, but the belly
> commands me all the time to eat and drink, and it makes me forget all
> the pains I suffered and demands to be filled up.[4]

The *gastēr* is portrayed as a lower *thumos*, a vital principle that forces
upon men its irresistible needs; it *lives* as an *entity*, let us say as a beast,
inside man and needs to be taken care of, fed, and listened to.[5] It
forces upon man forgetfulness of his griefs and makes him mindful
only of eating and drinking.

The thematic and even verbal contrast with the ascetic mourning of

----

[2]It is difficult to translate *kunteron*. It is possible that the ancient scholiasts' rendition,
"shameful," is marred by a moral concern that should not be present here. "Brutal" or
"ghastly" might be a better translation. Notice that in *Od.* 20.18 (see chap. 5., n. 28) the
same adjective qualifies the ghostly anthropophagy of the Cyclops and implicitly the
maids' debauchery.

[3]Cf. *Il.* 23.48, where Achilles speaks of the *stugerē dais,* "the hateful banquet" that he
is sharing. The banquet is hateful to him because he has not yet accepted Patroclus'
death.

[4]This passage has, of course, been condemned by several philologists purely on the
grounds of "decorum" (see van Leeuwen 1890, but the change of mind in van Leeuwen
1917); or it has been considered recent, as it is, for instance, by Pierre Chantraine (*GH,*
1:315).

[5]As far as I know, the first critic who has tried to produce a significant structure of
the terms governed by *gastēr* is Jesper Svenbro, *La Parole et le marbre* (Lund, 1976), pp.
54 ff. My own scheme differs from his in some important aspects, but I acknowledge
here the suggestive power of his system. Marylin B. Arthur, "The Dream of a World

Achilles or Priam is explicit.[6] Grief makes them forget food and forces them to nurse their *hearts* with grief itself; the *belly* makes Odysseus forget grief and forces him to feed the belly itself. In fact, Odysseus does remember and narrate his *kēdea, algea, penthos*—the names of his "suffering"—but only after a good dinner whose rich food and drink he praises at length before beginning his story (*Od.* 9.3 ff.). Of course, it is an epic convention that the guest be invited to eat before he is questioned, but Odysseus' praise of the plentiful table functions as a punctuation mark indicating that, within the coordinates of *gastēr*, one can remember his suffering only when he has fully satisfied his hunger.

Two poetics are contrasted: that of hearts that remember griefs, since *thumos* is the powerhouse that pushes heroes to their glorious death, and so to the immortalization of their lives in the *Iliad*; and the poetics of bellies that forget griefs, for the belly is the powerhouse of endless adventure. Or, as Odysseus says in *Od.* 17.286–89, after first acknowledging his enduring heart:

> But it is impossible to disregard the furious [*memauian*] belly, accursed one, which causes many evils to men, and because of which also the well-timbered ships are fitted out for the barren sea and carry evils to foemen.

It is significant that lines 286–87 repeat the syntax and the leading words of *Il.* 1.1–2:

> *mēnin . . . / oulomenēn, hē muria . . . alge' ethēke*

the wrath / accursed, which caused countless griefs

and

> *gastera . . . / oulomenēn, hē polla kak' . . . didōsi*[7]

the belly . . . / accursed, which gives many evils.

Without Women: Poetics and the Circles of Order in the *Theogony* Prooemium," *Arethusa* 16 (1983): 97–116, offers a revision of Svenbro's scheme. Arthur correctly sees that the *gastēr* theme "is not exhausted by a consideration of its application within the social order" (p. 103), and she argues, against Svenbro, that *gastēr* does not simply connote marginal people, outside the social structure (pp. 103–4).

[6]See Arthur, "Dream of a World without Women," p. 103: "As evidence of his mortal nature and by contrast with Achilles . . . Odysseus instances the pressures of *gastēr*."

[7]This line returns in *Od.* 17.474.

The "remake" is certain. Through this allusion the *Odyssey* quotes the *Iliad* and names the secret force behind Odysseus' adventures, his *gastēr memauia*,[8] indicating that, like the *mēnis* (wrath) of Achilles, it is accursed and the origin of evil for men.

The text opens up a series of uncanny connections: *gastēr* pushes men to fight far away from their fatherland and, in particular, sends them to ravage far-off shores as pirates.[9] The text seems to refer to the pirates' raids, but the Trojan expedition as a whole might not be excluded. *Gastēr,* therefore, spurs activity and sharpens the courage of men and thus leads them to ruin. Many of Odysseus' companions perished in Troy and many more in the raids that the *Odyssey* describes in book 9, and the rest died because, unlike Odysseus, they could not endure ravenous hunger and ate the cattle of the Sun.

Suddenly the *Odyssey* offers a new perspective from which to interpret the bloody adventures of the *Iliad* and the *Odyssey*: the restlessness that lies at the root of those deeds is named *gastēr*. The *Iliad,* in contrast, names as the origin of its own story the *mēnis* of Achilles, the wrath of the hero.[10] In *Od.* 17.288–89:

> because [of *gastēr*] the well-timbered ships are fitted out for the barren sea and carry evils to foemen,

the text leaves room for thinking that *gastēr* is at the origin of navigation itself. A parallel passage occurs in *Od.* 15.343–45. As Odysseus tells Eumaeus:

> There is no worse evil for men than endless roaming [*planktosunē*]: Yet it is for the sake of the accursed belly that men get evils, wandering, pain [*pēma*], and grief [*algos*].

It is interesting that here Odysseus attributes to the effects of *gastēr* the specific evils he is so good at enduring: the endless wanderings and the *algos*, the griefs he suffers so often in those wanderings. Yet the same *gastēr* forces men to forget these pains (*ek . . . lēthanei oss' epathon, Od.* 7.220–21) and move on to a new enterprise in order

---

[8]This epithet occurs four times in the *Odyssey*. The three other times it appears it is as the epithet of Athena (13.389, 16.171, 24.487) and names her furious eagerness to fight. I also retain the meaning "furious" in respect to *gastēr*.

[9]In *Od.* 3.103, Nestor distinguishes the raids on the coasts from the war against Troy. On piracy as a customary activity, see, for example, *Od.* 3.71 ff., 9.252–55, 17.425 ff.

[10]On wrath as a conventional attitude of the Homeric warrior, see Fausto Codino, *Introduzione a Omero* (Turin: Einaudi, 1965), pp. 136 ff. On *mēnis*, see Pietro Pucci, "The Proem of the Odyssey," *Arethusa* 15 (1982): 39–62.

again to fill up the stomach, which, in a continuous cycle, soon is empty and again making known its demands (*Od.* 7.217).

For pirates, a *thumos agēnōr*, a "bold, commanding heart," is always accomplice to and indistinguishable from their *gastēr*. Those who are deprived of a *thumos agēnōr*, however, listen only to the constant dictates of their *gastēr*. These are the beggars or, generally, the parasites on the active society,[11] those who are unable to do anything else but be mindful of the *gastēr* and satisfy it by eating what *other people* produce or gather. The beggar, for instance, begs in town to feed (*boskei*) his insatiable (*analton*) *gastēr* (*Od.* 17.228, and analogously 18.364). To express this feeding the text uses the verb *boskō*, which denotes specifically the sustenance that the earth's vegetation provides for grazing animals.[12] This specific analogy suggests that the *gastēr* is a living, devouring creature just like a grazing cow or sheep.[13] Thus the *gastēr* produces forgetfulness not only of griefs but also of work and of any other activity.[14]

Just such a beggar is Irus, who was known all too well for his "greedy belly" (*gasteri margēi*, *Od.* 18.2) and his incessant eating (*phagemen*) and drinking (18.3).[15] He had no strength (18.15) and no might (*biē*);[16] moreover, his "*thumos* was badly troubled" at the sight of mighty Odysseus, and he kept trembling (18.75, 88). He is the antithesis of the heroic Iliadic being.

[11]The Hesiodean analogue of the beggar who constantly feeds his *gastēr* is the drone, which in the simile in *Theog.* 594–602 designates the woman. In this Hesiodean passage notice the use of the verb *boskō* (595), the repetition of the Odyssean line 596 (= *Od.* 9.161, 556, 10.183, etc.; *Il.* 19.162), and the animal simile. Those who simply keep on feeding their bellies with food that other people produce are in some way like animals.

[12]*Boskō* corresponds to the Latin *pascere* (Jacob Wackernagel, *Sprachliche Untersuchungen zu Homer* [Göttingen: Vandenhoeck & Ruprecht, 1916], p. 245); cf. also Gregory Nagy, *The Best of the Achaeans* (Baltimore: Johns Hopkins University Press, 1979), p. 185.

[13]There is an additional connection between *gastēr* and the grazing of animals: Greek *grastis*—which is derived from *graō*, "to devour"—means "grass," "green fodder," as does the Latin correspondent, *gramen*. (See *DE*, s.v. "grao.")

[14]The verbs of which *gastēr* is here the subject are the same verbs of which *thumos* is often the subject: for the *thumos keleuei* "commands" (*Il.* 7.68; *Od.* 7.187, etc.), *keletai* "commands" (*Il.* 12.300), and *anōgei* "orders" (*Il.* 4.263, etc.) just as the *gastēr* does (*Od.* 6.133, 7.217, 221).

[15]Just as in *Od.* 17.404, *phagein* (aor. of *esthiō*) implies the glutton's pleasure and his greed for eating. *Esthiō* is the verb that is frequently used for inviting friends or guests to eat amicably and to enjoy the meal: *Od.* 14.80, 443, 10.460, 12.23, 302, 17.479. For the qualifying *azekhēs*, "incessant," see analogous adverbs in *Il.* 3.25, *mala*, "a lot," in a lion's simile; *Il.* 21.26 in a dolphin simile; and *Od.* 14.109, where three adverbs (*endukeōs*, *harpaleōs*, *akeōn*) qualify Odysseus' eating.

[16]On *biē* as the heroic attribute of Achilles, see Nagy, *Best of the Achaeans*, pp. 48–49 and 89–90, where Nagy shows that *is* is synonymous with *biē* (317 ff.). On Irus himself, see pp. 229–30.

The suitors, too, fit the description of a man whose *gastēr* feeds incessantly on food that others produce, though the text never calls them *gasteres* or connects them *directly* to *gastēr*. Of course, noblesse oblige and the aristocratic youth of Ithaca cannot be identified with *gastēr*, for that would empty Odysseus' fight against them of all value. However, there is an affinity between the beggar (*ptokhos*) and the suitors (*mnēsteres*) inasmuch as both are eating up the goods of the house. This affinity is reinforced by the similarity of the language that describes the beggars (*Od.* 17.378–79) and the suitors (*Od.* 1.160, 11.116, etc.).[17] The suitors are not characterized by a lack of *thumos* or by the label *gastēr*, but the text suggests indirectly that they are ruled more by the dictates of *gastēr* than by those of the *thumos agēnōr*.

Finally, Odysseus himself exemplifies the *gastēr* of the beggar. He is at once the hero of the enduring heart (*thumos*), of *mētis*, and the man of the active and (in disguise) of the passive *gastēr*. We see him motivated both by his *thumos* and by his *gastēr* in the scene with Irus (*Od.* 17.50–68). In all his "heroic" adventures he is the exemplar of the active *gastēr*—that which pushes men to sail and ravage foreign shores—and of the enduring heart. For instance, when he attacks the Ciconians (*Od.* 9.45–56), or when he wishes to meet the Cyclops, he is impelled and defined by the concerns of the active *gastēr* (plundering, eating and drinking, procuring gifts) and, at the same time, possessed with a *talapenthēs thumos* or even *thumos agēnōr*.[18] As Odysseus comes to meet Nausicaa he is represented like a lion that *gastēr* forces to look for food, since "necessity" (*khreiō*) has overtaken him (*Od.* 6.130 ff.). Necessity (*khreiō, anankē*) forces Odysseus into adventures (cf. 10.273, 490; 11.164, etc.). And what are we to say about Odysseus when he

---

[17]The suitors' incessant action of eating up Odysseus' livelihood and house is represented by a series of formulaic expressions: to eat up the livelihood (*bioton [kat] edō*), *Od.* 1.160, 11.116, 13.396 = 428, 419, 14.377, 15.32, 17.378, 18.280, 19.159; to eat up the house (*oikon esthiō, edō*), 1.250, 2.237, 16.127, 431, 21.332 (see *doma* in 21.69 and the passive form of *esthiō* in 4.318); to eat up the possessions (*ktēmata edō*), 1.375 = 2.140, 19.534 (*ktēsis*), 23.9, also (*ktēmata phagein*), 3.315 = 15.12; to eat up livelihood and possession (*bioton kai ktēmata*), 2.123; to eat up (*keimelia te probasin te*), 2.75–76; to eat up (*chrēmata*), 16.389; to eat up (*kamaton*), 14.417; to eat up (*siton*), 16.110; to eat up pigs, cattle, 14.17, 41, 81, 20.214; finally, see *Od.* 22.56: *ossa ekpepotai kai edēdotai*. Such a slightly figurative use of *edō esthiō* with such objects as house and substances is never found in the *Iliad*. This does not mean that these verbs are not used metaphorically in other ways, for as we have seen, one may eat one's own heart in pain: *Il.* 24.129; *Od.* 9.75.

[18]As Odysseus is initially motivated by *gastēr*, he often acts unwisely, contrary to his proverbial *mētis*: see chap. 5, p. 72. See also *Od.* 18.375–80, where Odysseus first speaks like an Iliadic hero (see especially 18.379 and compare it with *Il.* 4.354) and then utters an Odyssean statement about *gastēr*.

enchants the Phaeacians for the sake of greater possessions and is ready to prolong his stories and his stay for the same purpose?

As a beggar in his house, he is also marked by the humiliating stance of the passive *gastēr*,[19] for instance, when he speaks to Antinous after the latter has hit him:

> There is no grief [*akhos*] in the mind [*en phresi*], nor weeping [*penthos*] when a man is hurt while fighting for his own possessions, either his cattle or his white sheep; but the blow that Antinous gave me was all because of my wretched belly, accursed! which gives many evils to men.
> (17.470–74)

Odysseus is now literally fighting for his possessions, and as a fighter he must have *thumos* and be resistant to, or even untouched by, *akhos* and *penthos*; but before Antinous he plays the role of a beggar and fittingly he suffers just like a man who obeys *gastēr*. Were he a real beggar, conspicuous for his *gastēr*, he would quickly forget suffering and turn his mind to food. But he is Odysseus, not Irus.

Readers may be surprised that I see Odysseus as being characterized by *gastēr*, a word that has so many negative connotations in the *Odyssey*. Indeed, *gastēr* is consistently labeled by epithets of blame: "evildoer" (*kakoergos*), "accursed" (*oulomenē*), "insatiable" (*analtos*), "wretched" (*lugrē*), "greedy" (*margē*). These epithets of blame mark the word and distinguish it from the unmarked word *limos* that names "hunger."

Precisely because the *Odyssey* views *gastēr* in such a negative way, it never uses this word to define directly Odysseus' craving for knowledge and for larger possessions; it is applicable only when Odysseus speaks of human restlessness in general and especially when he is disguised as a beggar and can reasonably borrow a term from a cultural realm far removed from the epic decorum. Thus the *Odyssey* presents an odd strategy: on the one hand, *gastēr* names the instinctual source of all the human activity the poem presents; on the other, the text uses this word cautiously and restrictedly. I can impute this caution only to the *Odyssey*'s moralistic stance—more specifically, to the *Odyssey*'s metaphysical representation of man's attempt to satisfy his desires in an ideal way, through wisdom, shrewdness, and endurance so that the crudest features of *gastēr* are controlled and subli-

---

[19]For the question whether Odysseus simply *acts* the part of a beggar, bearing the humiliation and suffering without being affected, or whether he *experiences* and *feels* the humiliation, see above, pp. 83–89.

mated. Throughout his endless wanderings Odysseus is constantly driven by the desire of increasing his possessions, or he is forced to fight or beg for food and other material goods. It is through his *mētis* that he escapes from troubles and because of his enduring heart (*talapenthēs thumos*) that he stands and resists the disastrous or suicidal dictates of *gastēr*.

17

Gastēr: Eros and Thanatos

> Narration therefore emerges as theater in which the dream is both situated and dislocated. In this sense the synchronic aspect of the dream—which taken by itself would like all synchrony imply the reference to a transcendent standpoint—is caught up and displaced by the narrative that retells it.
>
> Samuel Weber, *The Legend of Freud*

The moralistic stance is also responsible for the fact that the *Odyssey* uses other, more decorous terms than *gastēr* to describe the urge to action—terms like *thumos*, which in the epic tradition mean the same urge. Consequently, *gastēr* appears as a negative, evil *thumos*. And yet it is *gastēr* that strikes as the new, provocative term. Despite, or perhaps because of, its negative connotations, the *Odyssey* chooses it to name man's instincts and presents it with enormous emphasis in the remaking of *Il.* 1.1, as the instinctual source of all that happens in its narrative. It is therefore a courageous gesture the *Odyssey* makes, notwithstanding its ambivalence, in using this provocative and feared metonymy to define man's basic instincts and needs. Yet this incisive and realistic naming and definition are combined simultaneously with a certain distortion and disfiguration. For *gastēr* is, in the text, "stomach," "beast," "biological need," "rhetorical figure," and more, and all of these determinations are together defining man's needs. It remains therefore undecidable whether *gastēr* is, to adopt Paul de Man's phrasing, a "referential name for an extra-linguistic entity or a mere phantom of language."[1] Or to view it from another perspective, *gastēr* names not only the belly but, after it, both hunger and satiety, lack and fullness, sexual need and suicidal risk, or, as it were, Eros and Thanatos.[2] Since these meanings form a supplementary structure, the whole semantic field of *gastēr* is troubled. Hunger and satiety, pain

---

[1] Paul de Man, *Allegories of Reading* (New Haven: Yale University Press, 1979), p. 161.
[2] On the contiguity of Eros and Thanatos, see Jacques Derrida, *La Carte postale* (Paris: Flammarion, 1980).

and pleasure emerge as opposite terms only through a collusion and a will of the reader to domesticate and consolidate what in fact is connected or contiguous in a drifting movement. Consequently, the idea of "man's needs" also drifts away unless the reader intervenes with excisions, simplifications, and domestications. Short of this intervention, the reader may glimpse "man's needs" in the *Odyssey* only through the phantasmatic semantic field and/or displacing, supplementary movement of *gastēr*.[3]

The Odyssean "man" lives under the empire of necessity and accordingly under the phantasmatic, upsetting effects of *gastēr*: he endlessly returns to familiar pleasures; he never ceases to disguise his kaleidoscopic self; he fights constantly to fill his belly and lose everything, for he obeys a master whose orders are incompatible, vicarious, and without reference.

The warriors and pirates who raid neighboring shores to satisfy their needs and indulge their luxurious cultural cravings and the parasites who, like drones, steal or beg the gathering of others are all men obeying the dictates of *gastēr;* the former court death together with their pleasures, while the latter court exile together with their survival.

It is perhaps because the *Odyssey* knows that the undecidable force of *gastēr* informs the motives for all human actions that it adopts the odd strategy I have described. Through its textual *mētis*, the *Odyssey* perceives the pitfalls of this undecidability and attempts to separate the opposite but contiguous terms that constitute the force of *gastēr*. Thus, while asserting the all-encompassing power of *gastēr*, the text simultaneously assumes a discriminating and moralistic stance, rejecting this label for the motivations of *noble* characters (the suitors, for instance) and attributing its qualities to Odysseus only or especially when he is disguised as a beggar.

Does the *Odyssey's* scriptorial *mētis* succeed in controlling the upsetting force of *gastēr?* The question is appropriate, since *mētis* is the strategy that saves Odysseus from all situations of necessity into which *gastēr* casts him. For instance, Odysseus attributes to his own *mētis* his escape from death in the Cyclops' cave.[4] If Odysseus' *mētis* can rescue him from the troubles into which *gastēr* casts him, should not the scriptorial *mētis* give the author an analogous power over *gastēr?*

---

[3]On the notion of "supplement," see Jacques Derrida, *De la grammatologie* (Paris: Minuit, 1967), pp. 207–18, 219, 237–38, 306–8. See also below, chap. 18, pp. 194–95, for a more elaborate analysis of "supplement."

[4]"You," Odysseus says, apostrophizing his *thumos*, "did endure until cunning [*mētis*] rescued you from the cave, you who thought to die" (*Od.* 20.20–21). See also *Od.* 9.414.

My answer is no. To begin with, not even Odysseus' *mētis* can completely save him from death in the Cyclops' cave. After all, one of his tricks (*mētis*) is to call himself Outis, "Nobody,"[5] and so to sacrifice or deny himself as an entity, a person, a hero.

Through this extraordinary disguise Odysseus dies symbolically as "Odysseus," hero of a specific *kleos,* only to be reborn again as the "Odysseus" whose name now signifies "hated by" Poseidon (see *Od.* 5.339–40 and above, p. 65).[6] The name disguise permanently disfigures the characteristics of Odysseus: it fully annuls his previous self-identity, and it asserts even more precisely his new identity as the antagonist hero of Poseidon.

Thus Odysseus' *mētis* would have *unwittingly* only deferred his own death were it not his destiny (*moira*) to obtain return (*Od.* 5.288–89, 9.532–35). His *mētis* saves him from the irrational, monstrous force of nature (the Cyclops) and submits him to the rational hatred of a god. Of course there is an advantage in this switch, because Poseidon is part of a constellation of gods superintending a certain design in the universe. Now, since the inscrutable *moira* decrees Odysseus' return, Poseidon spares Odysseus.

Mētis acts unwittingly: we have already seen how, in Athena's and Odysseus' display of their *mētis,* their own cunning traps them. *Mētis'* strategy unravels a movement of displacements, of procrastinations, of differences (simulations) within which *mētis* itself gets lost and acts unwittingly and naively. The man of cunning and trickery can achieve real results against the urges and the forces of necessity only when a real power, as here, Moira, sustains the trickster. But then if Moira decrees that Odysseus should survive and return, what need is there for *mētis?* None, of course.

The scriptorial *mētis* draws the highest profits from the display of Odysseus' cunning, for the text hides (another disguise), its own deci-

---

[5]*Od.* 9.364–412. The text in *Od.* 9.410 also puns on the name Outis, "Nobody," and on *mētis,* "cunning"; cf. *Odissea*–Heubeck, 3:209. Heubeck summarizes the scholarly literature that illustrates the pun. See also Ann Bergren's remarks in "Odyssean Temporality," in *Approaches to Homer,* ed. Carl A. Rubino and Cynthia W. Shelmerdine (Austin: University of Texas Press, 1983), pp. 66–67.

[6]Odysseus in this trick shows that he attaches no magical power to his own name and that he recognizes the arbitrariness of the signifier. Nothing in his person tells that he is *odussamenos,* "hated," and he can easily produce a different name. At the end of the episode, however, Odysseus does not resist the temptation to reestablish his identity and to cry out that his name is Odysseus, not Nobody. In this way Odysseus heedlessly grants the Cyclops the condition to call down a curse on him. In accordance with the magic practice, the name of the cursed person must be spelled out, and the Cyclops now names Odysseus, son of Laertes (*Od.* 9.528–35): the Cyclops' father, Poseidon, can now take care of Odysseus.

sion to assure Odysseus' return by attributing its success to the hero's *mētis*. Thus the *mētis* of the hero disguises the a priori of the textual decision and functions as a machine to produce more writing and more textual schemes. The reader, however, is no dupe and realizes the a priori of the textual decision.

Analogously, the scriptorial *mētis* simply disguises the urges that are operating in the supplementary structure of *gastēr*, by attributing them to *thumos*, for instance, or by attributing these urges only to some specific characters. But in fact the disguise reveals that *gastēr* affects all men and that pleasure and freedom in the human rush to life contain, as their constituent otherness, pain, compulsion, and the rush to death. No textual disguising succeeds in concealing the phantasmatic nature, the upsetting contiguity, of *gastēr*'s urges. Thus in *Od.* 17.50–65 the text, through the retorts of Telemachus, suggests that while the lusty desires of the beggar come from his *gastēr*, the same desires may be viewed as noble when they are prompted by the *thumos*.

The ethical and social premises attached to *gastēr* and to *thumos*, "appetite," are occasionally different, but the goals, the satisfaction of instinctual drives, the pleasures (*kharis, terpsis*, etc.)[7] are just the same. Even in the Phaeacian land that functions as the utopia of the *Odyssey*[8] the pleasure of the *daites* might still proceed from the dangerous and self-enhancing orders of *gastēr*. Odysseus gives a serene and spiritual picture of these banquets:

> Mighty Alcinous, illustrious among all, truly it is a beauty [*kalon*] to listen to such a bard as this whose voice is like a god's. For I think that there is

[7]On all these words, see Joachim Latacz, *Zum Wortfeld "Freude" in der Sprache Homers* (Heidelberg: C. Winter, 1966). The author's analyses are valuable also for our points: the *tarp-* forms of *terpomai* imply the sense of "take satisfaction" (*sich befriedigen*) and are used for physical as well as nonphysical pleasures such as the contemplation of beautiful objects. The *terp-* forms of *terpomai*, in particular, when used for pleasure at the banquets, are connected with *dais, daites*, but not with *edō* (*Zum Wortfeld "Freude,"* p. 202). The pleasure is found in all the festive forms of the *daites*, not simply in eating and drinking.

[8]One of the most eloquent, and critically elaborated, statements on this subject has been written by Carlo Diano, "La poetica dei Feaci," in *Saggezza e poetiche degli antichi* (Venice: N. Pozza, 1968), pp. 185–214. Diano begins with the Odyssean sphere of *tekhnē, dolos*, and shows how it is connected to "pleasure." Note, in particular, these points: "Is it the mere whim of an extravagant poet that here [book 8 of the *Odyssey*] Hephaistos has Aphrodite as his wife? The *Iliad* knows nothing of this marriage and gives him one of the Charites"; and on art: "Art that is grounded on *pseudos* has pleasure as its goal" (p. 210). I have very little to add to this except to make clear one should understand "Art that declares itself grounded on *pseudos* has pleasure as its goal."

nothing more pleasurable in life [*khariesteron*][9] than when a whole people engage in festivity, and the banqueters in the hall are seated one next to the other and pay attention to the poet, while beside them the tables are laden with bread and meat, and the cupbearer draws wine from the mixing bowl and pours it around into the cups. That, I think [*en phresi*], is the most beautiful thing [*kalliston*].[10]

But your mind [*thumos*] is inclined to question me on my bitter suffering so that I'll lament and weep even more. What, then, shall I tell you first, what shall I leave for last? For many are the griefs that the gods of heaven have sent to me.

First I shall tell you my name so that you may know it henceforth, and if I escape the day of evil I shall remain your guest-friend, though I live far from here.

I am Odysseus, son of Laertes: among all men I am known because of my wiles, and my glory [*kleos*] reaches heaven. (*Od.* 9.2–21)

All this is merry, festive, and exciting, and yet one cannot forget that this description of the urbane and civilized banquets of the Phaeacians is prefaced by Odysseus' graphic description of the savage demands of *gastēr* (*Od.* 7.215–21).

Nor can we forget that Odysseus reveals himself only now, as if it were literally true that he could not think of his pains and griefs until his *gastēr* was filled and his hunger satisfied.[11] Failing to satisfy the

---

[9]The words for pleasure in the *Odyssey* are *kharis* and the verb *terpein*. *Hedus*, "sweet," may also be used.

[10]There is a revealing line in *Od.* 4.193 ff. that seems an apt commentary on Odysseus' speech here. When Menelaus has brought all his listeners to tears by his recollections of Odysseus, Peisistratus, who has meanwhile thought of his dead brother Antilochus, cries out: "I do not find any pleasure in weeping after dinner: but soon dawn will be with us." Peisistratus adjourns the mourning to the morrow, which is an Odyssean way to turn things around. Perhaps Menelaus, unlike Odysseus, is not a good poet and spoils the pleasures Peisistratus expects from the joyous occasion of the *dais*. On this meaning of *terpomai* (i.e., to "feel pleasure") in this passage, see Latacz, *Zum Wortfeld "Freude,"* p. 202.

[11]On Odysseus' refusal to reveal himself, see Uvo Hölscher, "Das Schweigen der Arete," *Hermes* 88 (1960): 259. Hölscher correctly defends the passage (7.215–21) with sound arguments and suggests that just when we expect the mention of Odysseus' name, the theme of hunger intervenes. See also Jesper Svenbro, *La Parole et le marbre* (Lund, 1976), p. 54, who believes Odysseus would not be able to speak the truth unless he were fed. He compares Odysseus' situation to *Hymn to Hermes* 560–63, where the three virgins tell the truth after having eaten honey. Regarding the words Odysseus uses in this passage, it is noteworthy that he picks the typical expressions that name the griefs and pain of his wandering—the verb *paskho* and its noun *penthos, algea,* and *oizus,* for of course he is the *oizurōtatos* man. Some of these words form the most frequent or specific formulas for naming Odysseus' suffering: *polla . . . paskhen algea* (*Od.* 1.4, etc.), *algea paskhōn* (*Od.* 5.13, etc.), *polla pathōn* (*Od.* 5.377, etc.), *penthos ekhonta* (*Od.* 10.376, etc.).

needs of *gastēr* would entail his symbolic death, but now that he is indulging in the pleasure of the banquet, he identifies himself and presents his *kleos*, his fame and reputation as a man of tricks (*doloi*).

The song of the poets is the normal accompaniment of the *dais*, and here Odysseus himself becomes the poet, replacing Demodocus and entertaining the Phaeacians—an odd transformation under the sign of *gastēr,* since the bitter stories he tells, for *others'* pleasure, are of those adventures into which *gastēr* plunged him and from which his *mētis* rescued him. But even in telling his stories Odysseus is still prey to the outrageously ambivalent dictates of *gastēr,* for as he gives pleasure he receives more gifts but, simultaneously, defers his "return." Not only does he claim that he would consent if the Phaeacians were to ask him to stay a whole year with them and give him gifts, he plunges symbolically into the realm of death as he, like the Sirens, bewitches and fascinates his listeners by his narrative of loss and death. The economy that promises pleasures and gain out of a somber relationship with death is called, in the *Odyssey,* that of *gastēr.*

In Ithaca, when Odysseus is the beggar of the house, his participation in the banquets is said to be forced upon him by *gastēr.* This comment is especially interesting because the text links *gastēr* to poetry, or at least to praise. Odysseus makes an odd promise to Antinous:

> Give, my friend! You seem to me not the vilest of the Achaeans, but the best: you look like a king. Therefore you ought to give and give more food than the others. And I will glorify you [*se kleiō*] over the whole world. (17.415 ff.)

When Antinous refuses and then hits Odysseus, Odysseus the beggar complains:

> the blow that Antinous gave me was all because of my wretched belly, accursed! which gives many evils to men. (17.473–74)

In the service of his wretched belly, Odysseus is ready to sing the praise of Antinous, to act as a poet whose songs confer *kleos* on his master. The "gain seeking" discourse (*kerdaleon*) is always affected by the pressures of *gastēr.*[12] What is telling here is that the text has disguised Odysseus as a poet of the Iliadic tradition—line 474 is a remaking of *Il.* 1.1—one who confers *kleos* on his hero, unlike the

---

[12]See *Od.* 6.148, and Pietro Pucci, *Hesiod and the Language of Poetry* (Baltimore: Johns Hopkins University Press, 1977), p. 20.

poet of the *Nostoi,* "Returns," on whom the listeners confer *kleos* when he charms them (*Od.* 1.338, 351–52). Through Odysseus, the *Odyssey* pokes fun at the Iliadic tradition, or at least seriously destabilizes one of its premises, by suggesting that although the Iliadic tradition grants *kleos* to the masters, its songs of *kleos* derive ultimately not only from the need of the poet but also from the narcissistic pleasure of the masters—and both bespeak the presence and effects of *gastēr.* Here again the text of the *Odyssey* clearly shows the dangerous contiguity between the song of praise and the song of blame. The song of praise is quick to insult the song of blame as having but one aim—to fill the belly of its poets—but Odysseus, in the Odyssean scene, is shown striving for that same end by singing a song of praise.

I V

READING: WRITING

18

Gastēr and Thelgein

Every text, being itself the intertext of another text, belongs to the intertextual, which must not be confused with a text's origins: to search for the "sources of" and "influence upon" a work is to satisfy the myth of filiation. The quotations from which a text is constructed are anonymous, irrecoverable and yet *already read:* they are quotations without quotation marks.

Roland Barthes, "From Work to Text"

According to epic tradition, the inspiration provided by *gastēr* does not lead straight to truth but, rather, follows the meandering, labyrinthine ways of gain-seeking discourse, "sweetened" talk, and adulatory and ingratiating speech. This relation between *gastēr* and epic is illuminated by the attitude *kleos* (praise) poetry takes toward *gastēr:* that it is a master of deviousness, ingenuity, wiles, and lies.[1] The most elaborate examples of this attitude appear in Hesiod, where the woman Pandora is both emblematic of *gastēr* and representative of a devious mind. In *Works and Days* 77–78 Hermes bestows on Pandora "lies, crafty talk, and a deceptive attitude"; in *Theogony* 589 she is called *dolos aipus*, "utter deception,"[2] and a few lines later the woman is compared to the drones who fill up their *gastēr* with the harvest of the bees (*Theogony* 594 ff.).[3]

---

[1]Jesper Svenbro, *La Parole et le marbre* (Lund, 1976), pp. 50–70; Gregory Nagy, *The Best of the Achaeans* (Baltimore: Johns Hopkins University Press, 1979); and Marylin B. Arthur, "The Dream of a World without Women: Poetics and the Circles of Order in the *Theogony* Prooemium," *Arethusa* 16 (1983): 102, show that on the level of discourse, *gastēr* produces lies. See also Jean-Pierre Vernant, "A la table des hommes," in Marcel Detienne and Jean-Pierre Vernant, *La Cuisine du sacrifice en pays grec* (Paris: Gallimard, 1979), pp. 92–98.

[2]The text continues with *amēchanon anthropoisin*, an "aporia" for men. On the "aporia" in Greek territory, see the illuminating comments by Sarah Kofman, *Comment s'en sortir* (Paris: Galilée, 1983).

[3]Vernant notes that in the Hesiodean woman, the appetite for food goes hand in hand with sexual appetite; see "A la tables des hommes," p. 96. This observation allows us to integrate Hesiod's texts and to suggest that the woman is also a source of pleasure—in accordance with the logic of *gastēr*.

Reading: Writing

The strongest statement on the connection between the poets and the psychological world of *gastēr,* however, is *Theogony* 26–28, where the Muses tell Hesiod, who is tending the flock on Helikon:

> Shepherds of the fields, poor fools, mere bellies [*gasteres oion*]
> We know how to say many lies similar or identical to true things
> but, if we want, we know how to sing the truth.[4]

To whom the derogatory apostrophe is addressed is open to speculation: critics have thought the Muses may be referring to Hesiod himself, who "has hitherto been preoccupied with false things,"[5] or to the class of epic poets distinct from Hesiod's didactic-theological poetry, or to poets in general, all too human in their limited powers and thus in need of the Muses' inspiration.[6]

Speculations, of course, are difficult to dispute, and their force of persuasion depends solely on their coherence with the whole critical discourse that produces them. In keeping with my preceding discussions, I favor the second alternative: that line 26 refers specifically to the poets of the epic tradition, and in particular to those poets of the *Odyssey*'s tradition. After all, it is in the *Odyssey* that the *gastēr* theme is developed into a complex category, embracing precise social and psychological features.

Equally significant is line 27:

> *idmen pseudea polla legein etumoisin homoia*
>
> We know how to say many lies similar [or identical]
> to true things,

which echoes *Od.* 19.203, where, as we have seen,[7] the text comments on Odysseus' ability to tell many lies about himself, similar (or identical) to truths:

> *Iske pseudea polla legōn etumoisin homoia.*

[4]These lines have received much critical attention since the appearance of Marcel Detienne's *Les Maîtres de vérité dans la Grèce archaïque,* 2d ed. (Paris: F. Maspero, 1973). See, more recently, Pietro Pucci, *Hesiod and the Language of Poetry* (Baltimore: Johns Hopkins University Press, 1977); Ann Bergren, "Language and the Female in Early Greek Thought," *Arethusa* 16 (1983): 69; and Arthur, "Dream of a World without Women," 97–112. Arthur has carefully studied the epic use of each of the three forms of abuse in l. 26: *poimenes agrauloi, kak' elenkhea, gasteres oion.* See also Francesco De Martino, "Eraclito e gli efesi 'sempre ottusi,'" *L'Antiquité Classique* 52 (1983): 221–27.
[5]Hesiod, *Theogony,* ed. M. L. West (Oxford: Clarendon Press, 1966), p. 162.
[6]Arthur, "Dream of a World without Women," pp. 97 ff.
[7]See, above, pp. 98–99.

Now the analysis I have presented has shown that such a pointed repetition, marked by a purposeful change (the Hesiodean text is less repetitious and is finely connected with *idmen* of the next line)[8] could be a sort of quotation—a deliberate, and critical, allusion to the *Odyssey* or of the *Odyssey* to the *Theogony*. In the former case, the Hesiodic text, through the Muses' "revelation," condemns the poems that are so loosely connected with the language of truth and chides the poets representative of that tradition, poets who must be dependent on others and who, like Odysseus the beggar, are ready "to celebrate" the king "all over the world" (*Od.* 17.415–18) in order to fill up their *gastēr* with good meat.[9] And on another level, the Hesiodic text censures the song of *gastēr* as one that induces forgetfulness of truth (*etuma*) (*Theogony* 26–28) and of justice.[10] Thus the human—all too human—concerns emblematized by *gastēr* interfere in the ideology of epic poetry and destabilize the neat separation and distinction that the ideology wishes to draw between the terms of praise poetry and those of blame poetry. True to its supplementary force, *gastēr* produces a poetic discourse of praise that is itself blamable.

The organic and generic urges and needs represented by *gastēr* are, however, too encompassing to account specifically for the pleasurable and painful effects of poetry. A more accurate word for these effects appears in the context of Odyssean poetics: *thelgein*. *Thelgein* points to the psychological effects of poetry and defines them as "pleasurable enchantment" and "ruinous fascination." The use of *thelgein* (to designate aesthetic effects) is exclusively Odyssean and gives a special twist to the other epic terms—such as *kharis, terpsis*, "joy," "pleasure"—that traditionally describe the pleasurable effects of poetry, for *thelgein* describes a supplementary structure whereby the "pleasure" produced by poetry contains simultaneously the "loss of oneself."[11]

In the *Iliad*, *thelgein* is used to describe either the beguiling effects of Eros/Aphrodite (*Il.* 14.215) or the psychological paralysis that a god produces in a hero in order to destroy him (*Il.* 12.255, 15.322, etc.). It

---

[8]For a discussion of these two lines (*Od.* 19.203 and Hesiod *Theog.* 27), see Pucci, *Hesiod and the Language of Poetry*, p. 35, n. 6.

[9]"*Kak' elenkhea* is a standard term of abuse in the *Iliad*, where it means 'cowardly' (5.787, 8.228)" (Arthur, "Dream of a World without Women," p. 101). Does Hesiod use an Iliadic term of abuse for the *Odyssey*? Or does he refer to another poem? I cannot say.

[10]As we shall see, Hesiod and the *Odyssey* agree only on the power of poetry to dispel man's sorrows.

[11]In both the *Iliad* and the Hesiodic tradition the song of poetry gives pleasure, *terpein* (*Il.* 9.186, *Theog.* 37, etc.), but this pleasure is not connected with *thelgein*. For *terpein* in relation to song and dance, see Joachim Latacz, *Zum Wortfeld "Freude" in der Sprache Homers* (Heidelberg: C. Winter, 1966), pp. 208–9.

is often associated with deception and magic, as in *Il.* 21.276, 604, for example. Emblematic of *thelgein*'s magical and possessive powers is Hermes' rod (*rhabdos*) that lulls men when they are awake or awakens them when they sleep (*Il.* 24.343–44 = *Od.* 5.47–48, 24.3–4).[12] The pleasurable/ruinous effects of *thelgein* are evident in the *Iliad* as well as in the *Odyssey*, but only in the *Odyssey* are they attributed to poetry and to speech in general (*Od.* 1.57, 3.264, 17.514, 521, etc.). The range of *thelgein*'s extreme, polarized meanings extends from Penelope's innocent (or almost innocent) enticement of the suitors (*Od.* 18.212) to the dangerous, even lethal, effects produced by the song of the Sirens, which so to speak paralyzes men's mind with pleasure and leads them to self-forgetfulness and therefore to self-destruction. The former use implies no magical power and produces a certain amount of pleasure; the latter evokes an irresistible magic and a mind-beclouding pleasure.[13]

Such incompatible meanings of the word evoke the structure of the "supplement," as in the case of *gastēr*. The "supplement" does not correspond to a rhetorical figure like the "paradox" or the "oxymoron." To begin with, the incompatible effects or meanings spin together in the supplementary structure and surface as neatly opposite *only* through a domesticated and self-serving reading. Thus, for instance, when Penelope calls all poetic performance *thelktēria* (*Od.* 1.337), we decide to read in this word "enticement" and not, let us say, "intoxication." We do so because the text invites us to this complicity both by a kind, even positive, representation of Phemius' poetry and by an implicitly favorable assessment of poetry in general. Later Circe defines the Sirens' *thelgein* as destructive: with her we read in the

---

[12]This is the only formulaic expression that the epic tradition has built with *thelgein*.

[13]There are also intermediate states of self-forgetfulness and psychological paralysis. Athena denounces Calypso's attempt to constantly beguile (*thelgei*) Odysseus with tender and coaxing words, so that he may *forget* Ithaca (*Ithakēs epilēsetai, Od.* 1.56–57). Here the tender words have an erotic, not a poetic intention, although, as I have shown, there is some poetic jealousy in Calypso's words. Odysseus escapes the power of Calypso's *thelgein* by assuming the posture, indeed the life, of a mourner (*Od.* 1.57–58; 5.151–58). Circe's *pharmaka*, "drugs," are said to *thelgein* (*Od.* 10.213, 218, 291, 326): they transform men into beasts and of course make them forgetful of themselves and of their fatherland. Notice that *thelgein*, in producing forgetfulness, acts just like *gastēr*. On the function of drugs, *pharmakon*, see again Jacques Derrida, "La Pharmacie de Platon," in *La Dissémination* (Paris: Seuil, 1972), pp. 71–197. On the function of Helen's drug (*pharmakon*) in *Od.* 4.219 ff., see Roselyne Dupont-Roc and Alain Le Boulluec, "Le Charme du récit," in *Ecriture et théorie poétiques: Lectures d'Homère, Eschyle, Platon, Aristote,* ed. Jean Lallot and Alain Le Boulluec (Paris: Presses de l'Ecole Normale Supérieure, 1976); and Ann Bergren, "Helen's Good 'Drug,'" in *Contemporary Literary Hermeneutics and Interpretation of Classical Texts,* ed. Stéphane Krésic (Ottawa: University of Ottawa Press, 1981).

thelgein only its negative aspect. In the "supplement," however, this separation of the opposite meanings is illegitimate, since they spin (however incompatibly) together.

Furthermore, the "supplement" evokes a linguistic addition that *simultaneously* detracts from or removes what this addition describes. When Penelope calls all poetic performances *thelktēria,* she in effect uses a metonymic definition of "poetry," defining it by its promised effects.

The incompatible and even phantasmatic effects of poetry "supplement" poetry in the sense that they give an account of, and re-present poetry; in the act of representing poetry the effects also put themselves in the foreground. The entity called "poetry" is supplemented, that is, *replaced* and *displaced,* by its figure—the metonymy. In the *Odyssey* we glimpse poetry through this replacement and displacement, and therefore we glimpse poetry itself through what is not exactly itself. In this glimpse the notions of "itself," "not itself," presence and absence (of poetry) appear inextricably intertwined so that no act of separation and distinction would be legitimate.

When we add that the terms contained in *thelgein* constitute a contradictory and phantasmatic semantic field, we realize more fully the distressing nature of the "supplement." For the meanings/effects of *thelgein* operate not only in literature but also in love and sex; they have not only a more or less known referent as the "enchantment" produced by love, but also no referent at all, as in the case of the magic wand's *thelgein.* The semantic field that replaces and simultaneously displaces "poetry" is itself a linguistic product that defines "enchantment" through a cryptic and self-displacing movement.

As a consequence, the terms that spin in the "supplement" are never isolated, self-contained, and fully retrievable. In the case of *gastēr,* the text of the *Odyssey* reveals some strategic moves designed to control the daedalic force of the supplement. But in the case of *thelgein,* the text seems less anxious about the displacing power of the supplement.

Beguiling Poetry: Penelope, a Sober Reader

We encounter a sober and an intoxicated reader in the scene in which Phemius is singing about "the wretched return of the Achaeans" (*Od.* 1.325–59). Penelope, the sober reader, censures the poet; but Telemachus, the intoxicated reader, praises the poet.

I use the word "reader" and "reading" with a specific intention, since this scene evokes by a play of mirrors—that is, of mimetic substitutions—our position as readers of Homer's *Odyssey*. This play of mimetic substitutions triggers a first exciting question about the very authority of the reader. Telemachus dismisses his mother's criticism of Phemius, not merely by rejecting her arguments, but also by inviting her to leave. This authority of one reader over other readers, and finally over the by now silent poet, outlines an unfair but inevitable situation of all acts of reading.

Phemius seems to be a locus for both the *gastēr* and *thelgein* themes. Socially, he is a man of *gastēr*, since he is dependent upon others for food and sings under compulsion of necessity (*anankē*).[14] Singing under these conditions, and for the listeners' pleasure, Phemius, who is Terpiades, the "son of Terpios" or "Giving Pleasure," forgets truth, enchants the suitors, and paralyzes their minds.[15]

His name, Phemius, on the contrary, could make him a voice or an embodiment of "poetic, divine utterance" (*phēmē*). He sings at the *daites*, "banquets," of (and for) the princes of Ithaca, the suitors of Penelope, in Odysseus' palace, in the absence of Odysseus. He sings to the lyre (*phorminx*), the musical instrument "that the gods have made the companion to the banquet" (*Od.* 17.271).[16] Although the banquets

[14]In Homer the poet is never given the label *gastēr* or any feature specifically related to *gastēr;* on the contrary, the *Odyssey* tries, in some passages, to draw a separating line between the poet (*aoidos*) and the beggar (*ptōkhos*), who is characterized by the world of *gastēr*. Thus, for instance, in *Od.* 17.381 ff. Eumaeus draws a neat distinction between the craftsmen—among whom he places the *aoidos*—and the beggars. Furthermore, as we have seen, to depend on strangers' food and to take advantage of it is not (contrary to some recent assertions) a *necessary* feature of people marked by *gastēr*'s qualities. But Hesiod labels the poets *gasteres* and does not draw any distinction between craftsmen, poets, and beggars (*Works and Days* 24–26; see also West's commentary: "It is noticeable that the singer is coupled with the beggar" [*Works and Days*, p. 147]). In addition, the examples of Odysseus the beggar promising to give *kleos* to Antinous (*Od.* 17.415–18), speaking as an *aoidos* at the Phaeacians' banquet (see especially *Od.* 11.363 ff.), and compared by Eumaeus to an *aoidos* (*Od.* 17.517–21) suggest that the line of demarcation between the *gastēr*'s attributes of *ptōkhos* (beggar) and *aoidos* are not always neatly drawn by the epic tradition itself.

[15]The form Terpiades of *Od.* 22.330 could be a patronymic form—thus naming Phemius' father, Terpios—or an adjective qualifying *aoidos*. See. W. H. Roscher, *Ausführliches Lexikon der griechischen und römischen Mythologie*, 6 vols. (Leipzig: Teubner, 1884–1937), s.v. "Terpiades." The name Phemius, on the other hand, is connected with *phēmē*, which can be either an unmarked "speech" or a marked "speech about the future," or with "divine" power. See the illuminating note by Ann Bergren, "Odyssean Temporality," in *Approaches to Homer*, ed. Carl A. Rubino and Cynthia W. Shelmerdine (Austin: University of Texas Press, 1983), p. 69.

[16]See also *Il.* 1.602 ff., where *dais* and *phorminx* are coupled, and *Od.* 8.99, where the *phorminx* is termed *sunēoros*, "linked to," "wedded to" the *dais*. A careful and lucid analysis of the formal expressions that connect the song (*aoidē*) to the banquet (*dais*), and of the ceremonial, substantial relations between the two, can be found in *Lessico*

of the suitors lack the religious quality that marks so profoundly the *daites* sacrifices described in some famous Homeric passages,[17] the suitors' *daites* cannot be considered as profanations of religious rituals. Leodes, a sacrificing priest (*thuoskoos*), is among them, and besides, one thing the suitors are never accused of is sacrilege. Neither profane nor devotional, the *daites* of the suitors are represented as essentially merry occasions on which the lighthearted youth of Ithaca enjoy themselves, ultimately sinking into a sort of brutish condition, oblivious of everything but their own pleasure.

He, "the very famous" (*periklutos*) poet (*Od.* 1.325), sings *often* (*aiei*, *Od.* 1.341)[18] a song that the suitors must find wonderful, the song on the "wretched homecoming of the Achaeans, that Pallas Athena ordained, as they came from Troy" (*Od.* 1.326–27). Already the epithet *periklutos*, "very famous," with its relationship to *-klu-* and *kleos*, tells us some of the novelty that the *Odyssey* will find in the poetry of the *Nostoi*. The epithet *periklutos* for the poet (*aoidos*) is exclusive to the *Odyssey*, while it is a common epithet for Hephaestus in both poems. It seems to be a specific epithet of craftsmen, since with only two exceptions it is used for Hephaestus and for the poet. This epithet therefore characterizes the poet as a man of *tekhnē*, and it is understandable that *tekhnē* and *mētis* should be connected with pleasures (*gastēr*).[19]

---

politico dell'epica greca arcaica, ed. Lucio Bertelli and Italo Lana (Turin: Bottega d'Erasmo, 1978), pp. 190 ff. On the latter point, the authors conclude that the song cannot be considered an *institutionalized* part of the banquet, but rather is a social custom characteristic of the courtly life, a cultural aspiration of the aristocratic paideia. See also Massimo Vetta, *Poesia e simposio nella Grecia antica* (Rome and Bari: Laterza, 1983).

[17]See the masterly analysis of these descriptions in Karl Reinhardt, *Die Ilias und ihr Dichter*, ed. Uvo Hölscher (Göttingen: Vandenhoeck & Ruprecht, 1961), pp. 88 ff. See *Il.* 1.458–74, 2.421–33; *Od.* 3.447 ff., etc.), where the cult elements and the eating features combine in a highly elaborated formulaic block of expressions.

[18]This *aiei* is important both because it helps to incriminate Phemius in his constant complicity with the suitors' wishes and because it helps explain the practice of the historical singer who would often perform the same song again once he found that the audience liked it. This repetition must have produced special effects in different aspects of his song, for it is likely that the singer constantly improved details of his song by responding to more specific requests while repeating the same basic version. Judging that he had found the perfect version, he would then try to repeat it. But of course, in the absence of writing, his repetitions would not be absolutely identical. Within this historical perspective my metaphors "reading" and "writing" show all their pregnancy and force if they are understood with the specificity of the conditions I have outlined: the bard perceives immediately the way his audience likes or dislikes [reads] him. He composes, therefore, in view of a reading reaction that is immediate and final. His readers do not put the book aside, they remove or silence the bard himself.

[19]Pleasure, as we have seen, arises from a cunning strategy (*mētis*) that interferes with the supplementary force of *gastēr*. By displacements, simulation (producing difference), deferral, etc., the dangerous urges of *gastēr* are *somehow* and to some extent held in check to allow the pleasurable urge its satisfaction. Odysseus claims to have the "famous name of Aithon" (*onoma kluton Aithōn*, *Od.* 19.183). Since he is called *kluton* only

Simultaneously, however, this epithet looks forward to Telemachus' later speech, when the prince will say that the audience gives *kleos* (praise) to the poets.

The text does not in fact tell us whether Phemius includes Odysseus among the wretched homecomers, but the theme itself sounds dismal enough in the house of Odysseus to provoke Penelope's anguished reaction:[20]

> "Phemius, since you know many other lays to beguile [*thelktēria*] men's hearts, deeds [*erg'*] of men and gods that the singers celebrate [*kleiousin*], sing one of these as you sit among the suitors while they drink their wine in silence, but cease from this wretched lay that *always* wrings my heart in my breast, since an unforgettable grief holds me, so dear a head I long for, and so mindful am I always of a man whose glory [*kleos*] is large in Greece and Argos." (*Od.* 1.337–44)

Penelope does not deny that Phemius' current song is a beguiling one, but she asks him to select from among the other beguiling songs (*thelktēria*) he knows one of a different sort, presumably one of Iliadic or Hesiodic tradition; for the *erg' andrōn ta te kleiousin aoidoi*, "the deeds of men that the singers celebrate" and (*erga*) *theōn* are certainly equivalents of *klea andrōn* and *theōn* and intimate respectively the Iliadic and the Theogonic tradition.[21] The relative *ta te kleiousin aoidoi*, "that the singers celebrate," qualify these *erga* as objects of *kleos*, and so as *klea*. Penelope therefore requests either a song in which Odys-

---

once (*Od.* 24.409), this epithet *klutos*, attached to the obscure name Aithon, must be considered another of those ironic uses of *kleos* on which Charles Segal has written so eloquently in "*Kleos* and Its Ironies in the *Odyssey*," *L'Antiquité Classique* 52 (1983): 22–47.

[20]Both Penelope and Telemachus in their comments bring up Odysseus (*Od.* 1.343–44, 354), which means that Phemius' song has forced them to think of him. Svenbro takes Phemius' song to be about the death of Odysseus (*La Parole et le marbre*, pp. 20–21), and before him, some of the scholiasts arrived at the same conclusion; see the Scolion on *Od.* 1.340. Telemachus considers that Odysseus has lost the day of return (354), and in 350 he paraphrases what has been the gist of Phemius' song, using the expression *kakos oitos* (of the Danaans), which usually means "death" (see *Il.* 8.34 = 354 = 465, etc.; *Od.* 3.134, 13.384, etc.). In the *Iliad* the expression *kakos oitos* never means "glorious death"; on the contrary, it hints at a wretched death, since it is used only by gods to speak of mortals' wretched death ("woman," *Il.* 3.417; generically "men's"). In the *Odyssey*, the expression is used here in book 1 and in 3.134, where it again refers to the return of the Achaeans.

[21]For *ergon* as an epic, military deed see *ergon Achaiōn* in, for example, *Il.* 7.444. For the identification of *klea andrōn* with the Homeric tradition, and of the *klea theōn* with the Theogonic tradition, see Nagy, *Best of the Achaeans*, p. 96. Of course for this, as for many other themes, I draw a distinction between the *Iliad* and the *Odyssey*. In the *Odyssey*, *klea* are exclusively the deeds of the Iliadic, Trojan tradition.

seus' *kleos* shines in the manly "works of Ares" or a song about the immortal gods. In either case she is rejecting the Odyssean theme in general, and Phemius' version of it in particular. In other words, she rejects any song that does not celebrate her husband and whose poetic principle is exclusively that of beguiling.[22]

But note the *callida junctura:* The text introduces the mention of Phemius' lay on the return of the Achaeans *that Athena ordained* (lines 326–27) the moment Athena departs from Odysseus' house, leaving Telemachus in wonder and thinking he has been visited by a god (*Od.* 1.319–23). If lines 326–27 constitute, so to speak, the "title" of Phemius' song, the text *preempts* (for the readers) the truth of the song, insofar as it concerns Odysseus, by demonstrating Athena's care for Odysseus' family. On this point, at least, the text confirms Penelope's rejection of Phemius' wretched lay or its intimations. That Telemachus fails to connect Athena's visit to any divine design, however, perhaps confirms the beguiling power of Phemius' song.

Penelope rejects Phemius' song on the grounds that it pains her because of her unforgettable grief (*penthos alaston*), her unshakeable memory of Odysseus. A *penthos alaston* is a "grief that is unforgettable" because it cannot transform itself into "mourning" and into the appeasing work of mourning conducive to acceptance and resignation.[23] Presumably Penelope fears that Odysseus is dead, but she has no absolute knowledge of his death: because of her fear she is in a posture of mourning, but because of her uncertainty the work of mourning cannot properly begin. Accordingly, Penelope (or the text) simultaneously tells two things to the poet Phemius, who knows well the use of the formulas: "there is no certainty that Odysseus is dead" and "thus my grief for his absence is unappeasable, and so I want to hear a song that celebrates him, not one that charms and lulls me at the expense of his *kleos*." Because Penelope lives mindful of griefs, unable to eat and to sleep, in an attitude of frustrated mourning, her relation to Phemius' song is similar to Achilles' relation to Odysseus in

---

[22]To this extent Penelope's reaction is unconsciously correct and also politically shrewd. Whatever may have happened to Odysseus, her psychological—and political—interests require that his memory be enhanced as glorious, his stature as godlike. Only in this way can she maintain all her privileges as queen, as well as her emotional equilibrium. Note that Phemius never sings that song of glory that Penelope requests, for even the most famous poet is a slave of necessity/pleasure (*gastēr*).

[23]*Alaston*, "unforgettable," is often used to qualify a pain (*penthos*) that one character feels, fearing for another whose fate is unknown but probably unfortunate (see *Od.* 4.108–9, 14.174; *Il.* 24.105; *Hymn to Aphrodite* 207). The only exception (*Od.* 24.423) does not contradict the other cases, since here we read *alaston penthos* with the adjective in attributive position, and thus as a pure intensive adjective.

book 19 of the *Iliad*. There Odysseus tries to mitigate Achilles' asceticism when Achilles can still find no solace in mourning because he has yet to kill Hector and bury his dead friend Patroclus. Analogously, Phemius offers Penelope a beguiling performance whose purpose is to please (*terpein*) when she cannot properly begin the comforting "work" of mourning because Odysseus' fate is still unknown.[24]

The Iliadic (and Hesiodic) premises of Penelope's wish, however, seem to be contradicted by her omission of any reference to the Muses and by her use of the word *thelktēria* (*Od.* 1.337): she terms all songs— whether those on "Return" or those other, heroic and theogonic ones—"enchantments," a uniquely Odyssean label. And yet if Penelope's speech here really does refer to the Hesiodic poetics, her text may read the Hesiodic passage (*Theogony* 98–103) with greater accuracy than it would seem:

> When a man feels a new anguish in his grieving heart and he is dried up inside from grief, if the poet, servant of the Muses, sings about the glory [*kleia*] of the old generations of men and about the blessed gods on Olympus, then man soon forgets [*epilēthetai*] his great thoughts and he does not remember his griefs at all. And quickly the gifts of the goddesses turn him away [*paretrape*] from them.[25]

The last line seems to refer to something like a magic power of the Muses, a certain inherent *thelktērion* in the effect of their song. And although the word *thelktērion* does not appear, the supplementary logic is the same. The *Odyssey*, then, shows Penelope interpreting the power of poetry "correctly." But at the same time the *Odyssey* mis-

---

[24]On *Il.* 19, see above, pp. 168–72. This analogy is emphasized, structurally, by the ending of the episode. Penelope withdraws to her upper rooms and begins to "weep for Odysseus, her dear husband, until blue-eyed Athena poured sweet sleep upon her eyelids" (*Od.* 1.363–64). This divine intervention parallels that in *Il.* 19.340 ff., where Athena refreshes Achilles with nectar and ambrosia. There are, in addition, several tantalizing "remakes" in Penelope's words that recall Achilles' *penthos* for Patroclus; see especially *Il.* 23.16 and *Od.* 1.343, and also *Il.* 18.81–82; and see *Il.* 24.105, where *penthos alaston* is used to express Thetis' grief for Achilles.

[25]On this passage, see among the most recent works Gregory Nagy, *Comparative Studies in Greek and Indic Meter* (Cambridge: Harvard University Press, 1974), pp. 257–58; Pucci, *Hesiod and the Language of Poetry*; and of course Detienne, *Maîtres de vérité*. The passage defines all the mythical features of the poetic song, the inspiration of the Muses, the poet as alter ego of the Muses, the effect of honey (96), the contradictory play of memory (of the past) and forgetfulness (of the present), the contradictory play of straight and devious discourse (see here *paretrape*, 103) and, accordingly, of truth and lies.

chievously attributes to the poet himself the power of enchantment that Hesiod attributes to the Muses.[26]

The text has yet another twist, however. In making Penelope resist the enchantment of Phemius' song, Homer could merely be emphasizing her consciousness that Odysseus is still alive, or he may insinuate that Phemius' powers of enchantment are simply not great enough to conquer the extremely shrewd Penelope. Phemius would then be presented as a weak poet, far inferior to Odysseus (who beguiles and fascinates the Phaeacians) and, of course, to Homer himself.

An Intoxicated Reader

The *Odyssey*'s reading of Phemius' song must be to some extent polemic and to some extent congenial. On the one hand, the poet of the *Odyssey* must reject a song that by narrating, or even merely hinting at, Odysseus' inglorious death has no claim to being inspired and truthful. The poet of the *Odyssey* has made this point clear by clever editing, placing Phemius' song immediately after Athena's departure. On the other hand, the poet of the *Odyssey* wants the theme of the *Nostoi* and the poetics of pleasure to be defended, and to be defended by someone who has the same ties to Odysseus as Penelope has. Accordingly, Telemachus intervenes to legitimize the principle that the poet, whatever his theme, charms and gives pleasure with his song:

> My mother, why grudge the faithful poet the right to please us [*terpein*] in any path his mind takes? The poets are not responsible but Zeus, who allots to bread-eating [*alphēstēisin*] men whatever it pleases him for each. He is not to be blamed if he sings the evil destiny [*kakon oiton*] of the Danaans. For men praise more [*epikleiousin*] the song that comes newest to the ears of the listeners. Let your heart and mind endure [*epitolmato kradiē kai thumos*] the hearing of these things, for Odysseus is not the only hero whose day of return was lost in Troy, as many other men perished also. (*Od.* 1.346–55)

[26]In accordance with the data of epic poetry, Penelope might expect to be relieved by a song evoking the heroic *kleos*, death, and immortalization of the *basileis*. In this case she would, in accordance with the Hesiodic principle, forget her "unforgettable" grief and herself: a paradox, of course. See Pucci, *Hesiod and the Language of Poetry*, pp. 16 ff.

The power of *thelgein*, which failed to charm Penelope, completely enchants the son of Odysseus. He hears the song on his father's death and praises it as truthful and pleasing. Nothing in this candid directness (and, generally, in Telemachus' characterization) raises suspicion of oedipal perversion. But if his pleased reaction *were* an oedipal reaction it would be so candid because it is expressed under the intoxication (*thelgein*) produced by the poetic song. Oedipal reaction apart, however, Telemachus' political candor, amid the Ithacan youth eager to take his place as Odysseus' successor, alone testifies to the intoxicating power of Phemius' song. Furthermore, Telemachus too quickly takes it for granted that Zeus is responsible for what he assumes has happened. He forgets Athena's recent visit and her reassurance. The enchantment created by Phemius' song annuls all memory and self-awareness. This striking point is underlined by a statement that shakes the foundations of the Iliadic poetics. In accordance with this poetics, Penelope had asked Phemius to sing one of the heroic deeds "which the singers celebrate"—literally, "to which the singers give *kleos*" (*Od.* 1.338)—but Telemachus defends Phemius' newest song by responding that to this song the listeners "add more glory" (*mallon epikleiousin*) (*Od.* 1.351–52). This means an entire reversal: the center of the song is no longer the hero and his *kleos*, "glory," but the poet and the fascination he exercises over his listeners, who consequently praise and celebrate (*epikleiousin*) him. This new, provocative representation that the poet of the *Odyssey* stages at the very beginning of his work stresses the importance of the subjective relationship between poet and listener, the univocal force of the performance, and the beguiling power of the song. Given this frame, we understand the diminished importance of *kleos* and the appearance of a different, partly novel principle: that of incantation and charm (*thelgein*). This is the exciting view the *Odyssey* parades: the glorious deeds (*kleos/klea*) of the heroes, "their beautiful death," are no longer the force that attracts the listeners; instead it is the singer's power of seducing his listeners that makes his song glorious. Glory belongs to the singer, not to his hero.

Everything here contributes to the "romantic" portrait of the poet as an "original" voice that enchants his listeners. Reading the song of Phemius through its readers, Homer emphasizes the poet's authority and mastery ("in any path his mind takes") and his sublime independence (as if Telemachus had forgotten that Phemius sings an old traditional theme—the wretched return of the heroes—and that he sings under "compulsion"). As the text extols the originality and independence of Phemius' song, it effaces the Muses and, with them, the entire tradition, that is, the system of epic intertextuality. The poet sings this same song many times (*aiei*, 341), and this song belongs to the same tradition as the *Odyssey;* yet Telemachus, under the spell of the authorial voice, perceives that voice as unique and original. This spell is the marvelous effect of art that the poet of the *Odyssey* at once reveals and *exposes* through the song of his fellow poet Phemius. For the *Odyssey* maliciously also exposes this portrait of the poet as the result of Telemachus' infatuation.

The anonymous poet of our *Odyssey*, faithful to the bardic tradition, withholds his own name while identifying by both name and patronymic the poet Phemius.[27] This contradictory gesture resonates with deep implications, for it grants fictional identity to the poet whom Homer quotes and whose song he refers to but retains the force of truth as the property of his own anonymous song. For "naming" means for the *Odyssey* not truth but the entrance of the named entity into the world of signs and so into the world of fiction and enchantment. I recall here the three names of Odysseus—Outis, Aithon, and Odysseus—as evidence of the potential fictionality of the name and of its function as a prop of disguise.

There is no doubt that the *Odyssey* reads Phemius' song from the privileged perspective of the truth. Accordingly, it reads Phemius' false report of the events with amused impertinence, elegance, and ironic innuendoes. No direct reproach is leveled against the veracity of his narrative, only the reticent hint that Phemius may not even know what happens beneath the roof under which he sings. The *Odyssey*'s sublime touches of calling him by name and having Telemachus bring in Zeus to defend Phemius' story add grace and wit to its implicit claim of truth. For the *Odyssey* not only knows that Odysseus is alive: the *Odyssey* can also sing it.

Nothing can be more comforting than this scene, where the *Odyssey*'s author gracefully invites us to read his truth through his reading of Phemius. Reticently he resurrects the hero whom the other text had lost somewhere!

The pleasurable effects of Homer's reading seem to have raised no suspicion about the fairness and the truth of this reading. Scholars and critics read this scene hardly conscious that they are being charmed by the drug of Homer's poetry or perhaps dazzled by the poetry's play of mirrors and mimetic effects. For they are invited to

---

[27]On the naming of the poet as a *sphragis*, see Onofrio Vox, *Solone autoritratto* (Padua: Antenore, 1984), who shows that the *sphragis* also contains the ethnic adjective. In Phemius' case the absence of this ethnic determination may suggest the fictional quality of this naming.

feel at least the same admiration for the Homeric song that Telemachus feels for Phemius', since Telemachus' response is the one Homer proposes as the ideal response of the reader. But is it possible to escape this powerful mimetic fascination?

The mimetic relationship between Telemachus and the reader, however, also encompasses Telemachus' blindness. It is difficult at this point to say whether the poet of the *Odyssey*, our sublime master of enchantment, takes his pleasure in gently fooling his readers—just as Phemius might do with Telemachus in Homer's interpretation—or himself becomes blinded by his own charm and enchantment. In the latter case he would be subject to the same effect of *mētis* as when the strategy of *mētis* becomes self-trapping.

But let us first try to point out Homer's unfairness. First, he presents to us two readings of Phemius' songs but no text of Phemius himself. He proposes to us the ideal model of a passionately appreciative reader but does not give us any way to judge the correctness of Telemachus' reading response. The *Odyssey* whets our appetite and then leaves us without enough food for comparison, as if this were not necessary. Consequently, the *Odyssey* leaves us attached to Telemachus' reading and to this reading as a model for us: the reading that praises and also substitutes for the text.

While the *Odyssey* invites us to realize the inappropriateness of Phemius' song for Penelope's unforgettable grief, we are not even sure of the terms in which Phemius speaks of Odysseus. If here the questions of truth should be seriously raised, why is Penelope speaking of "enchantments" rather than of the Muses' inspiration? And why should Telemachus introduce Zeus as responsible for the events Phemius narrates? How can he know? As we shall immediately see, the text bungles his theological elaboration.

Furthermore, Homer—deliberately or not—seems to confuse the issue of Phemius' freedom. In *Od.* 1.154 he states unambiguously that Phemius "was singing among the suitors by constraint" (*anankēi*), a statement that in book 22 is repeated with the approval of Telemachus himself (see 22.353, 356). Yet here Homer presents Telemachus as saying: "Why grudge the faithful poet the right to please us in any path his mind takes?" (1.346–47). In other words, Telemachus is made to attribute to Phemius a freedom of choice the poet does not really enjoy. Is Homer then intentionally, and maliciously, emphasizing Telemachus' total blindness, his thorough infatuation? If so, he would also be pointing to the blindness of *his* readers, their inability to see his maliciousness or his own constraints. In his desire to present the ideal portrait of the poet and of the reader, does

Homer himself fall into an unconscious contradiction? Or does he know that whenever the poet sings, even if he sings under the constraint of his audience, he still enjoys some freedom, since within the bounds of the imposed theme he is the one who chooses the paths his mind prefers?

It is not easy to decide between these alternatives; all of them are appealing and strong. Yet to the extent that we remain unable to prefer and justify one of these interpretations, we remain unable to read. The excess of meanings in this text obscures our reading of Homer reading Phemius.

The whole passage (346–50) dealing with the relationship between the poet, his theme, and the god is murky and ambivalent. When Homer first introduces the song of Phemius, he seems to imply that Phemius attributes to Athena the Achaeans' inglorious death (326–27), in accordance with the tradition that made Athena the Achaeans' pursuer.[28] A few lines later, however, Telemachus, presumably summarizing Phemius' song, points to Zeus as the agent of their "wretched return": "The poets are not responsible but Zeus, who allots to bread-eating men whatever it pleases him for each. He [the poet] is not to be blamed if he sings the evil destiny of the Danaans" (347–50). Because the *Odyssey* itself sings a variation on this plot, and an important one, it as much as Phemius' song has a stake in identifying the agent of the Danaans' misery. This agent explains the specific cause of the narrated events and, as a divinity, inscribes the plot in a theological plan, thus intimating poetry's familiarity with divine matters. Though elsewhere in the *Odyssey* Athena is mentioned as a pursuer of the Achaeans, she is in fact patron goddess of Odysseus at least from the time he is with Calypso.[29] No doubt Telemachus is right when he concludes that the poet is not to be blamed for what he sings (*ou nemesis*), and his conclusion about Phemius can be extrapolated and applied to the plot of the *Odyssey* itself.[30]

---

[28]The name of Athena is part of the "title" or "content" of Phemius' song, and her role agrees with other statements in the *Odyssey* that Athena persecuted the Greeks on their return home from Troy: see, for example, *Od.* 5.108 ff. By having Telemachus suggest that Zeus is responsible for whatever happens to men, the text implies either a theology in which Zeus is ultimately responsible for everything—even for other gods' intentions—or that Phemius, or possibly only Telemachus, is wrong in attributing the wretched return of the Achaeans to Zeus.

[29]See Jenny Clay, *The Wrath of Athena* (Princeton: Princeton University Press, 1983), pp. 50 ff.

[30]The expression *ou nemesis*—I emphasize *ou nemesis* and not, for instance, *nemesis esti* or *oude tis nemesis*—occurs only once again in all Homer, in the passage of the third book of the *Iliad* (156–57), where the old men say: "there is no blame [*ou nemesis*] that the Trojans and the well-greaved Achaeans have been suffering griefs for a long time for

The *Odyssey*'s reading of Phemius' song becomes murkier or bright-er depending on our interpretation of the divergence between the two statements that Athena ordained the wretched return of the Achaeans and that Zeus was responsible for it. Is it an indication of Homer's malicious reading? Or should we infer that in Telemachus' statement "Zeus" stands for all gods, even Athena? This is not always the case in Homer, as the autonomy often granted Poseidon, Ares, and even Athena shows. Furthermore, the verb *epeteilato (epitellō)*, "ordain," seems to require a real agent, not a vicarious or substitute one, and in the condensed proemium of Phemius' song (326–27) Athena is certainly the real agent. In general in the *Odyssey* each mention of the trials encountered during the *Nostoi* is accompanied by the naming of a specific agent, Athena or Poseidon.

Although we cannot make a sure choice among these readings, this indecision marks only the *Odyssey*'s reading of Phemius' song, which might properly be perceived as mocking Phemius' (?) or Telemachus' (?) hasty theology (or both). In other words, the *Odyssey* itself might be playfully pointing up the contradiction I am describing and thus "deconstructing" Phemius' song with its authoritative and masterful reading. The contradiction is, after all, still contained within the text that displays it.

And yet there is one undecidable reading that exceeds the text that contains this reading and makes it irremediably murky and indeterminate. Lines 347–49 have been rendered: "The poets are not responsible but Zeus, who allots to bread-eating men whatever it pleases him for each," but they can be translated differently: "The poets are

---

the sake of this woman." Here too the statement prefaced by *ou nemesis* announces the subject or the generic plot of the *Iliad*, the war for the sake of Helen, just as in the Odyssean passage the statement prefaced by *ou nemesis* evokes the generic subject of the *Odyssey*, the wretched return. Nicole Loraux (to whom I am indebted for noticing and for communicating personally to me this extraordinary piece of intertextuality) observes that in both statements the subject is formulated in accordance with the generic and traditional theme within which both poems are couched, and from which the *Iliad* distinguishes itself as the specific poem of the wrath of Achilles and from which the *Odyssey* detaches itself as a variant. She would like therefore to call this *ou nemesis* a reading indicator that would recall the traditional subject matter while the two poems invite the readers to see their own novelty.

The precision and force with which the two poems reflect each other, in the very act of reflecting their difference from the generic themes out of which they emerge, indicate to us their literary awareness, their consciousness of being part of a traditional narrative, of emerging as a new story from that narrative. To that extent the names of the gods who are presumably the causes of the events amount to mere fictional labels to sustain the fable of the truth and historicity of those events. No wonder that these names can be changed ad libitum, that in the *Odyssey* Athena has become a patron goddess, while for Phemius she is still the pursuer of the Danaans.

not responsible but Zeus, who allots to bread-eating men [i.e., the poets] whatever [song] it pleases him for each."[31] This interpretation is made possible by the generic meaning of the expression *hos te didōsin . . . hopōs etheleisin hekastōi.* In these lines the traditional diction interferes with the thought and makes it so vague that, contrary to the statement that Zeus inspires poets, we should say that it is grammar and rhetoric that inspire—and dull—them. For here the traditional diction dulls the reading of the sharpest reader of all, our anonymous poet of the *Odyssey*, who stages Phemius' song so as to anticipate some of his own themes—those of his new poetics and of his divergence from generic and traditional treatments of his theme. But this sharp and original poet, reading the tradition of the *Nostoi*, is unable to make clear his own reading on the responsibility of the poets. The necessity that the poet use the epic grammar inevitably marks the text and restricts the pleasurable freedom that he otherwise grants to himself and even to Phemius: "to sing in any path his mind takes." The *anankē* presents itself in the form of grammar, tradition, and inescapable textuality. Consequently Homer vanishes as a powerful author, and in his place intertextuality enters. For a moment the clarity, the freedom, and the joy of reading are clouded.

This exercise in reading stops here, with a few concluding remarks. I have destabilized both the "romantic" portrait of the poet and the implication that such a poet is a superb reader. With this exercise the scenario of reading becomes opaque, and thus the poetics of the *Odyssey* becomes difficult to grasp. Unfortunate as this is in some respects, it is stimulating in others. At first, by underlining the good and bad aspects of Phemius' song, the *Odyssey* seems to make explicit the poetic perspective from which it judges him. But because of the displacements, the ironies, the unsettled questions, and the murky spots, what remains of the *Odyssey*'s poetics is simply the series of its central issues: truth, pleasure, enchantment, fame, freedom. Yet how these terms coalesce, and what their precise outline is, remains difficult to determine.

To take only two examples: it is impossible to know what degree of intoxication the *Odyssey* approves of. Although Penelope defines all

---

[31]On these two interpretations, see Nitzsch, 1:56–57, who produces convincing but not definitive arguments in favor of the former. As concerns their claims to truth, the two interpretations do not differ greatly: whether the wretched return is a song inspired by Zeus or an event promoted by Zeus, it remains defined by Zeus' authority. The difference in the two interpretations consists mainly in the fact that the latter implies a truthful relation between song and reality, a relation for which the poets themselves are responsible.

Phemius' "songs" as "enchantments," it is clear she is not "charmed" at all, while Telemachus, the favorable reader, is fully charmed by the poet. Is there then a proper measure of enchantment that the *Odyssey* would recognize as its own golden mean? By refusing to answer this question, the *Odyssey* provides perhaps evidence of its profound understanding of the enchantment of poetry, for its very reticence acknowledges the impossibility of prescribing a golden mean for the poetic drug.

Analogously, it is impossible to say whether the poet's dependence on the will of a master interferes with his freedom to sing "in any path nis mind takes." Probably the poet boasts of this last claim especially when he has to serve his master's will—and I do not mean only the will of another man, but also that of his *gastēr*, for the poet also desires to please the audience and to receive gifts. The text opens up serious and upsetting questions about the freedom of the singer in his society, within his own self, and within the established pattern of the poetic genre.[32]

[32]The noun *gastēr* enters unexpectedly in one of its synonymous forms to declare its supplementary activity in Telemachus' statement referring to "bread-eating men." In l. 349 the expression *andres alphēstai*, if it was taken to mean "bread-eating men," functions as a label for *gastēr*, since *alphēstai* is an Odyssean epithet that the *Iliad* absolutely ignores and that Hesiod uses in two texts referring to the appearance of Pandora and her effects on men (*Theog.* 512; *Works and Days* 82). A third Hesiodean example occurs in *Scutum* 29. In *Od.* 6.8 the epithet defines men in general (as distinguished from the Phaeacians specifically), and in *Od.* 13.261 it defines men in the games. It is exciting to consider that, in the interpretation that makes Zeus responsible for the song because he gives to the *andres alphēstai* whatever pleases him, the *andres alphē stai* would be the poets! According to this same interpretation, the necessity that the song be what it is shifts from the poet to Zeus, while the poet himself gives pleasure "in any path his mind takes him."

19

The Song of the Sirens

Youth of delight, come hither
And see the opening morn
Image of truth new born.
Doubt is fled and clouds of reason
Dark disputes and artful teazing.
Folly is an endless maze,
Tangled roots perplex her ways
How many have fallen there!
They stumble all night over bones of the dead
And feel they know not what but care,
And wish to lead others when they should be led.

William Blake,"The Voice of the Ancient Bard"

Another song, another reading scene in which we find one of the characters in the *Odyssey* miming, or acting out, our own role as readers of the *Odyssey*. The song here is that of the Sirens, the paradigmatic reader Odysseus, who in listening to the Sirens' invitation becomes mesmerized, ready to fling himself recklessly into their arms. For three thousand years readers of the *Odyssey* have, with Odysseus, yearned for and dreamed of this song.

Actually, the first reader of the Sirens' song might have been Circe, herself a mistress of erotic *thelgein* and a magician adept in administering intoxicating potions (*Od.* 10.213, 291, 318, 326). Yet we do not know how familiar she is with the Sirens' song. It seems reasonable to question the extent of her knowledge, since not all the details of her description of the Sirens agree with those Odysseus later provides. For example, when Circe tells Odysseus about the Sirens, she emphasizes the danger of their songs:

First you will come to the Sirens who beguile [*thelgousi*] all men, whoever comes to them. Whoever is inexperienced and comes close to them and listens to the Sirens' voice, he will not return home, and his wife and

209

children will not be by him for him to enjoy them: for the Sirens beguile him [*thelgousi*] with their clear song [*aoidē*] to sit on the meadow. And a large heap of bones is around them, of rotten men and the flesh is wasting away.[1] (*Od.* 12.39–46)

However, when the Sirens appear to Odysseus and invite him to stop and listen to their song of the Trojan War and "all that happens on the bountiful earth," the text presents quite a different scene: Odysseus sees no heap of bones, no evidence of any enchantment or curse; there is no mention of the beguiling power of the Sirens' song (*thelgein*). In fact, their version of the song they sing amounts to a rational reassurance that it offers knowledge (or truth) and produces pleasure:

Come hither, Odysseus, famous for your stories, great glory of the Achaeans. Pause with your ship, listen to our voices. Never has any man passed by in his black ship without hearing the honey-sweet voice from our lips, but he has taken his pleasure and has gone on with greater wisdom. For we know all the pains Argives and Trojans suffered in the wide land of Troy because of the gods' will, and we know whatever happens on the bountiful earth.[2] (*Od.* 12.184–91)

These words alone are powerful enough to overwhelm Odysseus with an uncontrollable desire to stop and to continue listening forever to the Sirens' beautiful voices (*opa kallimon, Od.* 12.192). Nothing declares like this passage the subjective collusion into which poet and listener enter, to the exclusion of everything else. Nowhere in literature have the enchantment and the curse of "reading" been so forcefully represented. Perhaps only Plato provides a comparable moment: in his portrayal of Alcibiades' cursed subjugation to Socrates' beguiling discourse, a possession similar to that which the *Odyssey* here evokes in sublime terms. Odysseus is willing to sit and remain with the Sirens, forever reading and rereading (rehearing) the great texts (songs) of the Trojan War, and thus to end his life, as a reader. Death is the price of the reader's sublime subjugation. However, he is saved by the greatest reader of all, by the poet(s) of the *Odyssey*, preventing him from following the Sirens. A sense of vastness and a proximity to death—that is, of experience beyond discourse and rational control—

---

[1]On the disputed interpretation of the last two lines see A.H.; *GH*, 1:237–39; and Stanford, 1:407.

[2]On the possible translations of l. 12.191: "all that all the time happens" or "we know each time all that has happened," see Pietro Pucci, "The Song of the Sirens," *Arethusa* 12 (1979): 131, n. 10.

pervades the scene. Indeed, at least three features in this passage (*Od.* 12.184–91) create that wondrous, uncanny feeling that, following the Kantian definition, we generally call "sublime":

First, as Odysseus' ship approaches the Sirens' island, a sudden stillness descends upon the sea as though all the natural elements had fallen into a deathlike sleep (see *koimaō*, *Od.* 12.167 ff.). Through this deathlike atmosphere Odysseus' companions, deafened by wax ear-plugs, row like unconscious automatons while Odysseus is transported to the reach of the Sirens' voices.

Second, Odysseus is conquered by their invitation and strives to respond. He commands his men, through signs, to loosen the ropes that bind him to the mast; instead they tighten his bonds, as he had earlier directed them to do. Interpreted figuratively, Odysseus' striving to loosen the ropes seems to represent a conflict between the bewildering force that invades and occupies his mind and the natural order—that is, the comforting reassurance of the bonds. A leap toward the fascination of an endless song and a restraining prudence are graphically contrasted: perhaps here we may read the notion of blockage of the Kantian sublime.[3]

Finally, the nature of the Sirens' promised song contributes to the sublimity of the scene. It is infinite in scope: the Sirens tell Odysseus that he will learn not only all that happened in Troy but also all that happens in the world. The vastness of this poetic journey is left forever in the realm of a promise; the text's reticence in leaving the Sirens' song forever unsung, forever unknowable, is precisely what endows it with the force of sublimity.

Thus this scene suggests that, for its first reader and mimetically for us, the Sirens' poetry produces an uncanny tension between, and a mingling of, opposites. Delight is contiguous with awe, voice with silence, life with death.

Now, this contiguity can be read both in the spectrum of the effects of *thelgein* and in the reticence whereby the *Odyssey* leaves untouched the contradictory statements of Circe and of the Sirens.[4] The redundancy of this undecidability echoes forcefully throughout the scene.

---

[3]On the economy of the sublime, see Neil Hertz, "The Notion of Blockage in the Literature of the Sublime," in *Psychoanalysis and the Question of the Text*, ed. Geoffrey Hartman (Baltimore: Johns Hopkins University Press, 1978), pp. 62–85; reprinted in Hertz, *The End of the Line* (New York: Columbia University Press, 1985), pp. 40 ff.

[4]Circe, in *Od.* 12.29 ff., emphasizes only the destructive effects of *thelgein;* because of her polemic bias, she interprets the undecidable force of *thelgein* reductively. In 12.184–91 the Sirens underline only the pleasurable effects of their song: whoever listens to it not only returns home but takes his pleasure first and then goes on much wiser. In focusing only on pleasure, the Sirens, too, interpret the force of *thelgein* reductively.

The power of the undecidable puts poetry in a disturbing light. The Sirens, Muses of Hades,[5] have the same power of *thelgein*[6] as the Iliadic, epic Muses, and the pleasure they create can never reach a stable moment but oscillates between (innocent) titillation and destructive intoxication. Even their poetic themes become contiguous: because the Sirens are Muses of Hades, their promise to sing of all that happens in Troy sounds like a polemic intimation by the *Odyssey* that the epic cycle on the Trojan War is obsessionally involved with what today we would call the "beautiful death" of the heroes.[7] Yet the power of the undecidable that we are tracing forces us to confront the fact that the *Odyssey*, through its detours, makes Odysseus simply avert death, but never fully escape it. The song of survival holds the "beautiful death" at the center of its concerns as the center that must be avoided.

In the text of the Sirens' song, the *Odyssey* demonstrates the full force of its critical and literary awareness, for this passage tantalizingly suggests that the *Odyssey*'s own sublime poetry cannot be inferior to that of the Sirens. No text can incorporate the titillating promise of a song as sublime as the Sirens' without implying that this same sublimity resides in the incorporating text itself. Furthermore, the *Odyssey* clearly fulfills the thematic goal of the Sirens' song, since it records Odysseus' long journey from Troy to the last horizons of the bountiful earth, to Hades, and even to the land of the Sirens themselves. By incorporating in its own song the Sirens' unsung poem, the *Odyssey* becomes a substitute for that poem. The Sirens' song is thus the negative, absent song that enables its replacement—the *Odyssey*—to become what it is.

That the Iliadic hero, Odysseus, can feel so strongly the desire to

---

[5]See Ernst Buschor, *Die Musen des Jenseits* (Munich: F. Bruckmann, 1944); John R. T. Pollard, *Seers, Shrines, and Sirens* (London: Allen & Unwin, 1965), pp. 137–45; Charles Segal, "*Kleos* and Its Ironies in the *Odyssey*," *L'Antiquité Classique* 52 (1983): 38; Pucci, "Song of the Sirens," pp. 126 ff.

[6]Remember that Penelope defines as "enticements" the lays of poetry that Phemius knows as *thelktēria* (*Od.* 1.337).

[7]In "Song of the Sirens" I prove that the text of the Sirens' invitation and promise (*Od.* 12.184–91) is "written" in strictly Iliadic diction, and I suggest that the *Odyssey* presents the Sirens as the embodiment of the paralyzing effects of the Iliadic poetics because their song binds its listeners obsessively to the fascination of death. What I am adding here presents a more complex and cryptic view of the episode's relationship to the *Iliad*, but it does not contradict my previous analysis. Although it is impossible to establish the full range of meanings the Iliadic allusion triggers, I suggest one of the possible meanings. The Iliadic diction, which frames the Sirens' diction, reveals the seductive power that the Iliadic song and its severe Muses still exercise over the text of the *Odyssey*. Odysseus, too, is seduced by the power of the Iliadic poetry.

exchange his destiny as a doer for that of a reader should make us wary of accepting the Nietzschean view that it was Socrates who taught the Greeks the superiority of the life of knowledge and contemplation. Odysseus is already virtually a student of Socrates, since he is ready to forgo his homecoming and end his journey in order to learn "whatever happens in the bountiful earth."

20

Odysseus, Reader of the *Iliad*

> One is interested in conventions which govern the production and
> interpretation of character, of plot structure, of thematic synthesis,
> of symbolic condensation and displacement. In all these cases there
> are no moments of authority and points of origin except those which
> are retrospectively designated as origins and which, therefore, can
> be shown to derive from the series for which they are constituted as
> origin.
>
> Jonathan Culler, *The Pursuit of Signs*

The Odyssean poetics of pleasure constantly confronts the risks
emblematized by the Sirens' and Phemius' songs: those of frustrating
men's will in a total paralysis of pleasure and even of making the false
death of a father a pleasurable theme for the son. At the same time,
however, it celebrates the hypnotizing, seducing poet who receives
fame and gifts.

The *Odyssey*'s answer to these opposite urges is not consistent and
one dimensional. Even when it censures the deadly *thelgein* of the
Sirens, the *Odyssey* leaves some indeterminacy. For the *Odyssey* recognizes the difficulty of containing within precise borders enchantment
and intoxication, fictional truth and truth in fiction, personal freedom and the desire to please the powerful and the rich. The *Odyssey*
also recognizes that a song intended to cheat the strongest power of
all—death—inevitably creates with the greatest pleasure the greatest
forgetfulness of the self, of man's essence, and conjures up an elegiac,
fabulous world. But of course the *Odyssey* knows also that such a song
can only camouflage the risks of death, since death is unbeatable in
the *Odyssey* itself. Furthermore, the *Odyssey* is aware that not only the
Iliad but even Phemius' song can make the theme of death produce
delight. The critical wisdom and distance that the *Odyssey* seems able
to take in relation to the traps of the poetic intoxication derive certainly from the poem's constant exercise of reading, that is, from

producing its writing in the act itself of reading different literary modes. Its most challenging confrontation—and the one most difficult for us to understand—occurs when the poem reads directly the epic tradition on the Trojan War and has Odysseus as the "reader" of that tradition. In this confrontation the *Odyssey* again realizes the intoxicating power of the epic texts upon the reader and fully illuminates the precise rhetorical stance of the readers in general.

Odysseus listens to the songs that describe his participation in the Trojan War in the utopian setting of the Phaeacian island. Demodocus sings three narratives: on the strife between Odysseus and Achilles (8.73–82), on Aphrodite's and Ares' love (8.266–369), and on the Trojan Horse and the defeat of the Trojans (8.477–532). None of these songs is said to be a charm or an enchantment (*thelgein*) for the listeners, and on the occasion of the two songs on heroic themes (8.73–82, 477–532) the Muse is explicitly mentioned as Demodocus' inspiration. No mention of the Muse precedes the song on the love of Ares and Aphrodite, however.

Both features—the absence of *thelgein* and the emphasis on the Muses—help us assess how the *Odyssey* evaluates Demodocus' poetics. The absence of *thelgein* is emphatic[1] and suggests here—as in the Sirens' statement about their song (*Od.* 12.184–91)—that the *Odyssey* is not unaware of the disquieting, uncontrollable effects of *thelgein*.

We must pit the emphatic and sustained mention of the Muses' inspiration and teaching in 8.72 ff. and 477 ff.—just before Demodocus sings the heroic themes—against 8.277 ff., and against the faint presence of the Muses' inspiration throughout the entire *Odyssey*. For—as we shall see better in the next chapter—the *Odyssey* invokes the Muses only at its inception (1.1) and asks them to tell the stories that cover roughly only books 5–12 of the poem. If we consider that books 9–12 contain Odysseus' own remembrances, we realize the scarce influence of the Muses' inspiration on the matter of the poem. Therefore the emphatic evocation of the Muses in 8.72 ff. and 477 and the absence of any mention of the Muses in 8.277 ff. must be labeled *marked*. Demodocus is presented as an Iliadic poet and therefore as a truthful and inspired one on the first two occasions, but as a self-taught singer on the last occasion. Here he begins by playing music for dance (256 ff.), then suddenly he begins to play *and* sing the

---

[1]The emphasis, of course, is determined by how frequently the beguiling effect of poetry is mentioned in the *Odyssey*. See 1.337 (of Phemius' song), 11.334 (of Odysseus' narrative), 12.40–44 (of the Sirens' song), 17.514–21 (of the poet's song), and *Hymn to Apollo* 161.

on the divine love (277) without any clear interruption, as
h the latter were a mere continuation of the entertainment.[2]
narrative voice introduces Demodocus' first epic song by an
allusion to the Iliadic tradition when it mentions the Muse in relation
to the *klea andrōn* ("the glorious deeds of men"):

> Mous' ar' aoidon anēken aeidemenai klea andrōn
> oimēs tēs tot' ara kleos ouranon eurun hikane,
> neikos Odussēos kai Pēleideō Akhilēos.

The Muse launched [*anēken*][3] the poet to sing the glorious deeds [*klea*]
of men, to start from the lay [*oimēs*] whose fame [*kleos*] at that time
reached wide heaven, the strife between Odysseus and Achilles, son of
Peleus. (*Od.* 8.73–75)

The expression *klea andrōn* defines heroic Iliadic poetry, not the sort
of poetry the *Odyssey* is.[4] In fact, as we have seen, Penelope explicitly
pits the *erg' andrōn te (theōn te)* against Phemius' song on the return of
the heroes, since this theme is not glorious and heroic. The *Odyssey*'s
domestic theme of homecoming, while celebrating the traditional
mētis and *doloi* that enable Odysseus to reach home, does not unambiguously grant him *kleos* for his successful return.[5]
    The only *kleos* of Odysseus the *Odyssey* celebrates unequivocally is
the one that is traditionally associated with his name and that has

---

[2]Walter Marg, *Homer über die Dichtung*, 2d ed. rev. (Münster: Aschendorff, 1971), p.
16, thinks that the song on Ares and Aphrodite still accompanies the dance. More
correctly, I believe, Antonino Pagliaro, *Saggi di critica semantica* (Messina and Florence:
G. d'Anna, 1953), p. 10, distinguishes the music for dance from the music with song,
which the Phaeacians listen to without dancing.

[3]The precise realm of the metaphor *anēken*, "launched," is probably that of "launch-
ing" a horse, letting a horse have its head; Marcello Durante, *Sulla preistoria della
tradizione poetica greca*, 2 vols. (Rome: Ateneo, 1971–76), 2:129, quotes, among others,
Plato *Protag.* 338a, *epheinai kai khalasai tas henias tois logois*, "slacken and loosen the reins
of speeches," and Ovid *Fasti* 1, 25, *rege vatis habenas.*

[4]On the expression, see Durante, *Sulla preistoria*, 2:51, who asserts that it is impossible
to establish whether this locution labels any sort of heroic poetry or a particular genre;
Gregory Nagy, *The Best of the Achaeans* (Baltimore: Johns Hopkins University Press,
1979); and Charles Segal, "*Kleos* and Its Ironies in the *Odyssey*," *L'Antiquité Classique* 52
(1983): 22–47.

[5]Anthony T. Edwards provides a lucid and informative survey on *kleos* in *Odysseus
against Achilles*, Beiträge zur klassischen Philologie, vol. 171 (Königstein/Ts.: Hain,
1985), pp. 71–93. Edwards lists (p. 74) the various grounds on which *kleos* is attributed
to characters in both poems. For instance, generous hospitality earns *kleos*, and Odysseus is quick to promise *kleos* to Alcinous if he sees to Odysseus' return (*Od.* 7.331–33). I
have shown that Odysseus promises *kleos* to Antinous on the same grounds, that is, if he
gives generously (*Od.* 17.417). In *Od.* 1.298–300, Orestes wins *kleos* for killing Aegisthus, and his deed is presented as exemplary for Telemachus.

become part of his royal portrait, the *kleos* of his *mētis* and
through which he contributed to the capture and destruction of
In *Od.* 9.19–20 Odysseus claims such *kleos* for himself: earlier h
asked Demodocus to sing of the wooden horse "that Odysseus le ... u
trap [*dolon*] to the acropolis" (*Od.* 8.498); and naturally when he identifies himself in 9.19–20 he refers to his *doloi*. The *Odyssey* sustains this
traditional *kleos* of Odysseus on other occasions: allusively, for instance, when it celebrates the *kleos* Athena claims to possess for virtues
that are analogous to those of Odysseus (*Od.* 13.298) or, indirectly,
when it extols Odysseus' own *mētis* as in *Od.* 20.20–21. Whenever
characters cite Odysseus' *kleos* they refer to that *kleos*—his royal portrait, his past in the Trojan War—and accordingly Telemachus, too,
defines his father's *kleos* in Iliadic terms (*Od.* 16.242; *Il.* 9.443).

Yet the *Odyssey* is almost explicit in denying *kleos*—that is, the specifically epic fame and renown—to Odysseus' return and revenge. This
is made clear at the end of the poem when the two passages which use
kleos in relation to Odysseus' victory over the suitors both display
ironic and controversial gestures.[6] Especially in 24.192–202, the text
attributes *kleos*, "glory," "reputation," to Penelope and only through
its ambivalent syntax also to Odysseus;[7] but the grounds for his *kleos*
remains Penelope's good and honest behavior. Such a limited conces-
sion to Penelope's husband is set against the preceding celebration of
Achilles' *kleos* in its Iliadic splendor (*Od.* 24.93–94). The contrast is
striking: Odysseus' *kleos* is debased to a generic reputation for his
share and merits in Penelope's domestic virtues.[8]

The adventures of return receive a bad press in the *Odyssey*. We
have already commented on the passage, *Od.* 5.308–12, when Odysseus, imitating Achilles (or vice versa), deprecates the miserable death
at sea (*leugaleōi thanatōi*). This evaluation is confirmed by the *kakos oitos*
by which Phemius defines—in Telemachus' paraphrase—the wretch-
ed return (*lugros nostos*) of the Danaans. Odysseus of course confronts
the ghastly adventures of return and revenge with cunning (*mētis*) and
tricks (*doloi*), and the poem certainly illustrates these traditional at-

---

[6]In *Od.* 22.137–38 Odysseus is afraid that the "rumor" of the suitors' death may
spread and reach their families—with dire consequences for him and his people. He
uses the formulaic expression *kleos euru* for "rumor," and of course the reader cannot
avoid thinking of the "wide glory" the formula usually evokes. But because the *Odyssey*
accommodates the encomiastic formula in a context that rejects the encomiastic sense, it
raises suspicions about its strategy. In my view this strategy consists of ironically suggesting and then denying *kleos*.

[7]See Edwards, *Odysseus against Achilles*, p. 88, n. 36.

[8]On the mirroring of features between Odysseus and Penelope, see Helene Foley,
"'Reverse Similes' and Sex Roles in the *Odyssey*," *Arethusa* 11 (1978): 11 and passim.

tributes of Odysseus' "glorious royal portrait" (*kleos*). Yet the *Odyssey* sotto voce suggests that it would extol Odysseus' glorious portrait (*kleos*) as such, while exhibiting this hero's *mētis* and *doloi* during his return and revenge, were it possible to conceive this *kleos* in a less stern fashion than the Iliadic tradition conceives it; but as long as *kleos* implies the death of the king (*Od.* 24.93–94), it cannot be attributed to a man who is happy and prosperous at home (*olbios, Od.* 24.192). Amusingly, the *Odyssey* adds by innuendo that were *kleos* downgraded to the less demanding virtues of faithfulness and spiritual nobility (*Od.* 24.192–98), the *Odyssey* could be termed the song of *kleos* also for Odysseus.[9]

The *Odyssey*'s general downgrading of *kleos* and its relative neglect of the theme of the Muses' inspiration contrast with the strong evocation of both themes in Demodocus' song (*Od.* 8.72–73) and leaves no doubt that Demodocus sings in the wake of the heroic Iliadic tradition of the *klea andrōn*, that is, in the wake of a different thematic tradition than the *Odyssey*.

Whether the episode of the strife between Odysseus and Achilles is so well known that it has already ascended to wide heaven or whether it will become this well known thanks to its presence in the *Odyssey* remains undecidable. If the episode really were unknown the irony would be stronger,[10] but even if it is already known,[11] the formula

[9]Consequently the *Odyssey* does not constitute a poem of *klea andrōn;* and if we asked ourselves what word the *Odyssey* would use to name itself as a poem, we would certainly say *aoidē*, "song." See Andrew Ford, "A Study of Early Greek Terms for Poetry: 'Aoide,' 'Epos,' and 'Poiesis'" (Ph.D. diss., Yale University, 1981). But we should also be aware that Odysseus defines his own stories to the Phaeacians as *muthologeuein* (12.430, 450). Just as the poetics of the *Odyssey* fluctuates between the heroic and unheroic realms whose labels are *thumos* and *gastēr*, so it fluctuates between the realms of *kleos* and *muthoi*, for assuredly the Odyssean Odysseus is the man of *ainoi* and *muthoi* (see for instance, *Od.* 13.297–98).

[10]Walter Marg, "Der erste Lied des Demodokos," in *Navicula Chiloniensis* (Leiden: Brill, 1956), pp. 20–21, takes this episode as an invention of the *Odyssey*, based on the opening of the *Iliad*. Indeed, the passage in the *Odyssey* clearly alludes to the *Iliad*'s proem by certain remakings (*Od.* 8.75 ff.; *Il.* 1.1 ff.). This line of thought assumes that Agamemnon misunderstood the prophecy: Apollo actually meant the strife between Achilles and Agamemnon—that is, the theme of the *Iliad*. See also G. M. Calhoun, "Homer's Gods—Myth and Märchen," *AJP* 60 (1939): 11; and Antonino Pagliaro, *Nuovi saggi di critica semantica* (Messina and Florence: G. d'Anna, 1956), pp. 17–18, who accepts the same theory. For Jenny Clay, Demodocus' story is an "amalgam of familiar material in a new configuration" (*The Wrath of Athena* [Princeton: Princeton University Press, 1983], p. 103).

[11]It is of course consonant with the normal practice of the *Odyssey* to pick up a motif that is already traditional and to interpret it with a certain bias: see, for instance, *Od.* 5.105 ff., with my comments on p. 38, and 5.306 ff. and pp. 63–64. I therefore agree with Nagy that "there are traditional elements in the epic opening reported by *Odyssey* 8.72–82 that go beyond the scope of the opening in *Il.* 1. These elements may still be

that describes this *kleos* as "ascending to wide heaven" (*ouranon eurun hikane*, 79) still seems an amused wink at the reader (one of many in this passage). This formula is very rare in epic diction; thus, while the text implies that this lay has been repeated so many times that its fame has reached heaven, it is also suggesting that a *kleos*, "fame," that "ascends to wide heaven" has *not been repeated* that often in epic diction.[12]

Nevertheless, this ironic innuendo does not negate the influence of the Muses on Demodocus. To be sure, the text does not make it clear whether the lay Demodocus sings has become famous because the Muses have inspired each performance[13] or simply because the poets have performed it so often.[14] Whoever (Muse or poets) is ultimately responsible for the song's *kleos*, the metaphor *anēken*—with its reference to letting a horse have its head—suggests that the Muses, at the very least, stir Demodocus into singing. They program him, as it were, to sing this specific lay, then "give him his head" to continue alone.[15]

---

considered 'Iliadic' only in the sense that clear traces of them are indeed to be found in our *Iliad*. But they are not within the actual opening of *Iliad* 1; instead, they surface here and there in the rest of the composition" (*Best of the Achaeans*, pp. 43).

[12]Segal, "*Kleos* and Its Ironies," shows that this formula occurs only three other times: once in *Il*. 8.192, for the *kleos* of Nestor's shield, and twice in the *Odyssey*: 9.20, where Odysseus describes his own *kleos* and his tricks (*doloi*), and 19.108, where Odysseus extols Penelope's *kleos*. In the latter passage the *Odyssey*—and its tradition—must be at the origin of that *kleos*, for in the *Iliad* Penelope has no *kleos* at all, since she is never mentioned. Odysseus' *doloi*, on the contrary, are already famous: in *Il*. 4.338 Agamemnon attacks Odysseus as surpassing everybody in "evil *doloi*": see my comments on pp. 60–62.

[13]The evidence for the theory of the Muses' inspiration appears in *Il*. 2.484–86, where the poet invokes the Muses as his inspirers and teachers: "Tell me now, you Muses who have your homes on Olympus; For you are goddesses, you are there and you know all things [*panta*]. But we the poets hear only the rumor [or fame—*kleos*] and know nothing." The Muses see and know whatever happens in the world (*panta*) because they are present there, while the poets, by themselves, know only *kleos* ("reputation," "rumor," "fame"), and therefore they really know/see nothing. Thus in this decisive passage the *Iliad* correctly ranks *kleos* as a source of ignorance for the poets (in *Od*. 16.461 *kleos* is the "town gossip"), and does so, paradoxically, with great risk to its own internal coherence and the truth of its narrative, since the same *kleos* names the immortal fame of Achilles and the deeds of the heroes that the Muses (supposedly) know and teach to the poets. For the problems connected with this passage, see Pietro Pucci, "The Language of the Muses," in *Classical Mythology in Twentieth-Century Thought and Literature*, ed. Wendell M. Aycock and Theodore M. Klein (Lubbock: Texas Tech Press, 1980), pp. 168 ff.

[14]The final line of the episode (8.83: *taut' ar' aoidos aeide periklutos*) contains a marked repetition. It is an Odyssean formula (see *Od*. 1.325, 8.367, 521) that in the last two occurrences closes the narrative of Demodocus, whereas in 1.325 it opens that of Phemius. Note the etymological figura *aoidos aeide* and the insistence on *kleos* through the epithet *periklutos*, which qualifies *aoidos* only in these four passages.

[15]The Thamyris episode in *Il*. 2.594–600 may help us interpret Demodocus' blindness: it could be a sign of punishment for having once tried to escape the Muses'

The *Odyssey* summarizes the song of Demodocus (8.75–82), which thematically recalls the overture of the *Iliad* and remakes some lines of the proem of the *Iliad* (*Od.* 8.71b and *Il.* 1.1b; *Od.* 8.77 and *Il.* 1.7; *Od.* 8.82 and *Il.* 1.5), yet the episode itself does not appear in the *Iliad*. Unless we follow the usual explanation—that Agamemnon has misunderstood Apollo, who meant the strife between Achilles and Agamemnon (that is, the theme of the *Iliad*)—the *Odyssey* would recall the *Iliad* by pointed remakings only to make its absence from the *Odyssey* more conspicuous.[16]

Walter Marg has remarked that, with this first song, Demodocus hints at the beginning of the Trojan War and, with his last song, he covers the destruction of Troy.[17] Thus the absence in the *Odyssey* of any episode from the *Iliad*, though striking, can be explained. Because the *Odyssey* embraces the Trojan War as a whole and has Odysseus as a leading hero at the beginning and at the end of the war, from its perspective the *Iliad* seems merely a deviant episode.[18]

The *quotational* aspect of Demodocus' text is evident. Through him the *Odyssey* recalls not the Trojan War, but the "literary" tradition on the Trojan War, the texts that have made that war "famous." Accordingly, the *Odyssey* here provides the appropriate references: first, to the *klea andrōn*, the "genre" from which it digests the episode (*oimē*) of the quarrel, and then to the formal, textual indications, which suggest how the *Odyssey* wants to be read at this point.

The most teasing suggestion the *Odyssey* makes is that heroic poetry really mirrors life. When in listening to Demodocus' song Odysseus cries, he confirms what he later will state: the truth of Demodocus' song and thus its divine origin. Thanks to the Muse, the poet can have

---

control. More plausibly, however, Demodocus' blindness intimates the poet's total inability to sing without the initial inspiration of the Muses. In l. 8.64 the powerful chiasmus underlines the paradox of a Musean love (inspiring presence) that handicaps the poet and makes him unable to act alone; the adjective "sweet" (*hedeia*) for song (*aoidē*) indicates the value for which Demodocus lost his eyes. Possibly the adjective also underlines the paradox of a severe heroic song that is sweet.

[16]See the analogous case in *Od.* 5.309–10 and my comments in chap. 5, pp. 63–64 and n. 3.

[17]*Homer über die Dichtung*, p. 14, n. 9. The oracle of Apollo (*Od.* 8.79 ff.) perhaps occurred at the beginning of the war. The expression *kulindeto pēmatos archē* (*Od.* 8.81)—"the beginning of the suffering was rolling over Trojans and Danaans"—is curiously elaborated. The verb in this phrase is well represented in the *Iliad* (11.237, 19.99) and the *Odyssey* (2.163), but the expression *pēmatos archē* is unique in our epic poems. *Pēma, pēmata* are used only as subject or object. The *Odyssey* here seems to elaborate on a formula, giving it its "beginning," as it were.

[18]This Odyssean perspective is exactly that of the Sirens: recall that in the Sirens episode, too, while the Iliadic diction is evoked, the *Iliad* itself is absent, though indirectly abused.

knowledge even of distant events. The myth of the simple divine origin guarantees the myth of the truth of poetry. By the same token, however, the *Odyssey* intimates the divine origin of its own truth: Odysseus therefore—we are invited to believe—is really as he is depicted by poetry, and *kleos* is truth. Of course, all these intimations occur just where the text makes clear its quotational quality, and just as its narrative—Odysseus in the Phaeacians' land—becomes, more than ever, fabulous and its truth more and more utopian.

Following Carlo Diano's strategy of reading the Phaeacian frame as a utopian world, we might interpret the intimations of this reading scene as a wish for, or a nostalgic gesture toward, an ideal past. The fiction of the poet's control over reality would thus take on the aspect of a utopian desire. It would indeed be marvelous if the Muses (that is, tradition) did make knowledge of everything immediately accessible to the poets; but alas, in real life, as Phemius' song testifies, traditions waver and their truth oscillates so that it is postulated only through a series of blind acts that involve the collusion of poet, discourse, and readers.

In the ideal utopian world of the Phaeacians, the beginning of the war and its pathetic end in murder and destruction (*Od.* 8.487–520) produce pleasure for the Phaeacians but elicit uncontrollable tears from Odysseus. Why this difference? The Phaeacians have no experience of suffering and, being godlike readers, are immune from pity.[19] Pity arises either from our fear that the griefs we see others suffer may come to us or from our attachment to someone whose grief or loss may pain us. Without such fear or affection there can be no pity. Thus the Phaeacians can simply enjoy Demodocus' song, whereas Odysseus is deeply shaken by crying.

To understand the nature of Odysseus' uncontrollable weeping we must examine the amazing simile through which the *Odyssey*—not the Iliadic Demodocus—now compares the hero's tears to those of one of the victims of his heroic deed in the past:

> and Odysseus melted and the tears wet his cheeks beneath the eyelids. And as a woman throws herself with cries over her dear husband who has fallen before his city and the people, to ward off the pitiless day from his town and his children; and she beholds him dying and drawing breath with difficulty, as she embraces his body and cries aloud; the warriors behind her smite her with spears on the back and on the shoulders and drag her into bondage to bear labor and grief; her cheeks are

[19]In the *Iliad* the gods enjoy their view of the fighting armies and remain unmoved by the killing and the massacres.

wasted by the most pitiful pain; just so pitifully Odysseus poured tears underneath his eyelids. (8.521–31)

As Gregory Nagy has indicated, correctly, the hero who has fallen dead is definitely similar to Hector and, accordingly, "the generic situation in the simile is . . . strikingly parallel to the specific situation of Andromache at the end of the *Iliou Persis*."[20]

Through this simile Odysseus is evoked both as the doer of the victorious deeds and as the *reader* of the victorious deeds that Demodocus has described in his song. Though he weeps on both accounts, he weeps especially as a reader. For the simile reenacts one of the scenes implicit in Demodocus' narrative on the destruction of Troy. The *simile* therefore transposes a theme of the *Iliou Persis'* narrative in which Odysseus is a doer into a rhetorical mode that describes him as a listener. The narrative of deeds is changed into a rhetorical effect, the experience of doing into an artistic elaboration, and accordingly the doer is changed into one who is affected by that rhetoric.

Furthermore, Odysseus weeps out of pity, just as does the woman whose cheeks are wasted by "the most pitiful pain" (*eleeinotatōi akhei*, 529). The woman's wretchedness is "pitiful" because she must pity herself and her husband, but more conspicuously because her misery is the object of pity for her real and imaginary spectators. Odysseus once was one of her real spectators; now, through the simile, he is, with the Phaeacians and with us, one of her imaginary spectators. Though the text tells us explicitly that he weeps *like* the wretched woman and not *for* her, the adjective "pitiful" in the simile forces us to understand that he now weeps for her as well. Of course he could never have been able to destroy Troy and to enslave its citizens had he felt pity when he was doer of the deeds the simile recalls.[21] It is only now, as an imaginary spectator—that is, as a reader—that he feels pity, that the wretchedness of the woman is pitiful to him as it is to us.

The *Odyssey* gives us a lesson on what reading the Iliadic tradition ideally means. First, it tells us of the text's tremendous power of

[20]Nagy, *Best of the Achaeans*, p. 101. In this poem Andromache was enslaved by Pyrrhus. Of course Hector had already fallen, but the simile refers to a generic situation of which Andromache is emblematic. By the simplest means, a simile, the *Odyssey* so to speak wipes away the whole *pragma* of Achilles and puts Odysseus in direct contact with a Hector-like hero and his Andromache. The boldness and the consistency of this gesture are admirable.

[21]Iliadic characters usually do not feel pity for their enemies. Achilles, in book 24 of the *Iliad*, feels something close to pity for Priam, but he does so through the remembrance of his own father, Peleus. His pity for the old Peleus, whose fate will be comparable to Priam's, allows him to weep with Priam (*Il.* 24.507–52).

enticement. For Odysseus himself provokes Demodocus to sing about the destruction of Troy, notwithstanding his previous experience of morbid crying.[22] With a most lavish display of respect and admiration for the poet Demodocus, and in the course of a convivial, festive occasion, Odysseus asks the poet to sing again an epic lay.[23]

Odysseus' insistence on hearing another epic lay about himself may be read as a textual foil to his recognition, or perhaps as his desire to consolidate "the sense of himself in present obscurity";[24] the festive paraphernalia of the banquet may be intended to constitute the proper celebratory context for this recognition, and at any rate it constitutes the proper context for an epic and heroic song.[25] Despite the festive atmosphere, the epic song of the heroic Iliadic tradition, according to the *Odyssey*, bends the mind of its listener to a morbid cry.[26] The narrative of the *Iliad* therefore would leave no space for a hero/reader: either he ceases to be a reader and acts so as to obtain *kleos* (a glorious poem about himself) or he reads and becomes a mourner. This is the *Odyssey*'s lesson on the effects of reading the *Iliad*.

This may appear a crude and blunt lesson, but of course the *Odyssey*'s view need not correspond with another reader's view of the *Iliad*, or with the *Iliad*'s perception of itself. To begin with, Achilles sings the deeds of heroes (*klea andrōn*, *Il.* 9.189–90), and he derives pleasure from this song (*terpomenon*). It is true that he sings and his companions listen to him when he has decided to renounce war, and singing therefore almost serves as a replacement for real deeds, but he enjoys the singing all the same.

Furthermore, the *Iliad* shows that even when the heroes feel pity

---

[22]See the fine remark of George B. Walsh, *The Varieties of Enchantment* (Chapel Hill: University of North Carolina Press, 1984), p. 3: "The Phaeacians feel dispassionate curiosity about distant things they cannot know directly, but Odysseus has asked the poet for a song about himself, to hear what he already knows, apparently aware that his reawakened memory will be painful."

[23]Odysseus honors Demodocus with the offer of a piece of the choicest meat, the *nōtos*, "fillet" (8.479–83); the *Odyssey* puns on his name (472); and Odysseus extols the teaching Demodocus receives from the Muses (*edidaxe*, 480, 488). On the elaborate sequence of themes in the banquet see *Odissea*–Hainsworth, 2:287, ll. 469–586. These contextual features give us a hint that helps us understand the celebratory and festive occasion on which the epic poet did perform.

[24]Walsh, *Varieties of Enchantment*, p. 3. Walsh quotes the analogous scene in Vergil's *Aeneid* when Aeneas discovers painted murals representing the fall of Troy: "at Carthage too . . . there are the tears of things" (*lacrimae rerum*, *Aen.* 1.462).

[25]On the Phaeacians' recognition of Odysseus in book 9, see Bernard Fenik, *Studies in the Odyssey* (Wiesbaden: F. Steiner, 1974), pp. 5–60, especially pp. 12 and 45; and Wilhelm Mattes, *Odysseus bei den Phäaken* (Würzburg: K. Tritsch, 1958).

[26]"Perhaps Odysseus' tears more accurately figure the norm for Homer's audience as well as for Aristotle's" (Walsh, *Varieties of Enchantment*, p. 5).

for fallen companions, for themselves, or even indirectly for their enemies, they persist in their fighting, always maintaining an edge of superiority over their enemies or victims. Accordingly, even when they realize, as Achilles does, the nonsensical waste of war (for both sides), the heroes remain the victors and masters. Yet while Achilles weeps with Priam at this realization, knowing he must continue to fight, the reader may be co-opted to pity the warriors' destiny. Here the Odyssean view of the Iliadic reader finds support.

The Iliadic pity emerges as well in the display of the most brutal and ferocious feelings. For instance, when Achilles decides to kill Hector and to accept his own death, he adds:

> "Now may I win a noble glory [*kleos*] and may I induce some Trojan woman, some deep-bosomed daughter of Dardanus, to wipe her tears from her tender cheeks and lament bitterly.[27] (*Il.* 18.121b–24)

Achilles transforms his wish to kill many Trojans, and Hector in particular, into a crude image in which he contemplates the crying and despair of the innocent widowed wives over the bodies of their dead husbands. He savors revenge in the concrete form of the crudest pain he can inflict on his enemy. Simultaneously, however, the reader cannot fail to perceive in this despondent image of mourning and crying Achilles' own crying for his own irreparable loss of Patroclus. It is clear to us that Achilles' revenge allows him to transfer onto the Trojan widows the despair he feels for the dead Patroclus. Of course, this transference is the source of the gruesome comfort that revenge provides. Accordingly, the text at this point suggests for the reader an equation of despair between the conqueror Achilles and the victims of his deeds.

Here the text glances at itself, and the reader is invited to read this glance, to assess the *Iliad*'s own perception of itself as a narrative, and to recognize the pitiful wretchedness of Achilles and the Trojan women. Yet while Achilles reads his own despair in that of the Trojan widows, the glorious excitement of heroic deeds is still present. In contrast the *Odyssey*, when it presents Odysseus' weeping just like the Trojan widow and slave, intimates the absence of all splendor and prestige.

---

[27]*Adinon stonachēsai:* the expression *adinon* is connected with *hade*, "with satiety": in the *Iliad* it is always an epithet or an adverb for *funeral* lamenting, as it is obviously in this case.

Achilles' wish emerges in complicity with the funeral lamentation it evokes, since it is at the source, as it were, of that funeral narrative. The reader is made to accept that wish, for it founds the reader's stance and role. As the warriors in the *Iliad* are capable of both wrath and pity, even of self-pity, the reader of the *Iliad* is co-opted, essentially to admire and to mourn for the "beautiful" death of the hero. In this sense the *Odyssey*'s assessment of the *Iliad*'s effects on the reader, though crude, is not incorrect.

The *Odyssey* conceives for its characters the sort of pity that is congenial to the civilized world of pleasure: pity for those who are marginal to that world, for the beggars, the poor guests, the victims. Nothing like Zeus' tremendous compassion for Sarpedon and for the human destiny of death ever shakes a page of the *Odyssey*. This civilized pity, however, comprehends the pity of the reader, and accordingly the *Odyssey* stages the sort of pity a reader of the Iliadic tradition may feel. On this account the *Odyssey* reaches a high point with Odysseus shaken by crying as a reader/mourner of the Iliadic poems.

In demonstrating the powerful effects of this pity the *Odyssey* stages a discourse—what elsewhere I have called the discourse of pity— whose goal is to consolidate the sense of the self. It is no accident that it is through the display of pity that the text leads up to Odysseus' recognition. To the extent that the discourse of pity allows an *imaginary* identification of the reader (of the mourner in general) with another suffering person, it simultaneously produces a reaction in which the reader (or the pitier) perceives his difference from the other person and retrieves the sense of the self. Here Odysseus, through the imaginary identification with his victim that the text draws for him, retrieves the sense of his own *new* identity: that of a reader of the *Iliad*.[28] But of course this new identity implies a drifting image where master and victim, doer and reader coalesce in an unstable portrait.

The text of the *Odyssey* constantly forces the reader to become conscious of the act of reading as an act that establishes meaning.[29]

---

[28]For the strategy of the discourse of pity, see Pietro Pucci, *The Violence of Pity in Euripides' "Medea"* (Ithaca: Cornell University Press, 1980), pp. 21–50. The *Odyssey*'s assessment of the pity that the Trojan War and its literary tradition produces is well presented in book 4. Here, only because of Helen's magic *pharmaka* are Menelaus and his guests able to go tearless through reminiscences of episodes in that tradition.

[29]Readers of the *Odyssey* are expected to possess the same intellectual gifts as the poet and the character of the poems: otherwise they will read this amazingly subtle and complex text as a mere fable for grown-up children.

Through the song of Demodocus, the *Odyssey* has induced us to read
its own reading (of Odysseus' reading) of his other tradition and to
become conscious of the thematic continuity and difference that the
text constantly maintains with respect to the heroic tradition. Odysseus has become a fellow reader of the heroic tradition: he is no
longer a hero of that genre but is now the character whose pathos
points at the business of survival and pleasure. This business is epito-
mized by his transformation from an actor in the Trojan War into a
passionate and pitiful reader of that war's story. The synonymy of
gastēr and *thumos* accommodates a large gap in this transformation.

It is because Odysseus is such a reader that he can also become a
poet and a poet of himself. While Achilles in the ninth book of the
Iliad could only sing the *klea* of the heroes, Odysseus becomes the
pathetic autobiographer, the storyteller, of his pitiful adventures (*Od.*
9.12–15). He speaks of himself in the wake of his readings.

Odysseus takes over and, like a poet (*Od.* 11.363–68), narrates the
story of his survival and return.[30] No Muse inspires him, and yet he
charms and beguiles the Phaeacians who formerly had simply "enjoyed" Demodocus' song. He charms them so much (*kēlēthmōi d'
eskhonto, Od.* 11.334) that they add more gifts to those they have already lavished upon him (*Od.* 11.336 ff.). And they want to listen
longer:

> But let our guest suffer [*tlēto*] to stay, however much he longs for home,
> until tomorrow till I shall make our gift complete. . . .
>   The night is very long, interminable. Nor is it time to sleep in the hall.
> Tell me your wonderful deeds [*theskela erga*]. (*Od.* 11.350–52, 373–74)

Alcinous defines both the night and the deeds of Odysseus' return
with old epic epithets that mean "divine": they are not deeds (*erga*)
that give *kleos*, but ones that "the listeners applaud more" (*Od.* 1.351:
mallon epikleiousi anthrōpoi). Like men enchanted by the Sirens, Odysseus' audience falls under a sort of divine spell and would like to hear
more. One does not need any experience of suffering to fall under
the spell of a narrative that seems always to conquer the menace of
death; the Phaeacians do not fight but nevertheless they die. And so

---

[30]In this famous passage the *Odyssey* again emphasizes the terms of its poetics. Alcinous praises the beauty (*morphē*) of Odysseus' words, the skill (*epistamenōs*) of his
performance, and the truth of his story ("You are not a liar and a cheat," 363–64). But
of course Alcinous is charmed (*Od.* 11.334) and, like Telemachus, cannot perceive the
incompatibilities among these terms.

Odysseus continues his story (*muthologeuein, Od.* 12.450, 453). We cannot take *muthos* in this compound with the modern sense of "myth," but certainly we must take it with the meaning of "story."[31] The *klea* of the heroes that the poet, inspired by the Muses, tellers of truth, sings in the heroic tradition have become *muthoi* (stories); and their glorious poet sings those stories to receive the praise of the listeners (*mallon epikleiousi anthrōpoi*) as he enchants them. For of course the Phaeacians become completely oblivious of themselves. Mildly affected with pleasure by Demodocus' *truthful* song, they are *enchanted* by the *muthoi* of Odysseus; and Odysseus himself, the sensitive reader of Demodocus' song who could not avoid crying at Demodocus' recital, now could continue his own narrative endlessly. The supplement of art as emblematized by *thelgein* never stops spinning the incompatible terms that compose it.

[31]See Marcel Detienne, *L'Invention de la mythologie* (Paris: Gallimard, 1981), pp. 160–61.

21

Phemius and the Beginning
of the *Odyssey*

Like some primordial *pharmakos,* Aesop is unjustly accused and ex-
ecuted by the Delphians.

Gregory Nagy, *The Best of the Achaeans*

I am approaching the last stage of this long and polytropic journey
through the Odyssean poetics; but the reader and I know that this
journey could continue further and we would simply recross what are
by now familiar borders. In this last stage we see how some of the
traits of Odyssean poetics—truth, pleasure, and compulsion—conflict in a dramatic way when the text presents Phemius' statement and
recantation at the end of the poem (*Od.* 22.344–53).

After the massacre of the suitors, Phemius throws himself as a
suppliant at Odysseus' knees. It is at this momentous point that the
text, for the only time, calls him Terpiades[1] (*Od.* 22.330, *Terpiadēs . . .
aoidos . . . / Phēmios*), as if to evoke, at the moment of his threatened
death, the pleasure he created and for which he pays so dearly. Odysseus has just murdered Leodes, the sacrificing priest of the suitors,
and Phemius repeats Leodes' gestures of supplication.[2] The two are
guilty of analogous crimes, since the one prayed for Odysseus' failure
to return and the other sang this failure.

When Phemius is represented by the *Odyssey* as supplicating his
master Odysseus—the character in his song—and even quoting him
from the *Iliad,* he is not simply being made to ask him for mercy, he is
also represented as re-creating the character at his demand; and this

[1]On Terpiadēs, "son of Pleasure" or "pleasure-giving," see chap. 18, p. 196 and n.
15.
[2]The text has Phemius repeat the same gestures already performed by Leodes. The
lines are repeated verbatim: *Od.* 22.342–44 = *Od.* 22.310–12. Since these lines echo
closely the episode of Lycaon, Phemius too enters into that transference: "and he
[Phemius] with a rush, clasped Odysseus' knees and, imploring, spoke winged words: 'I
clasp your knees, Odysseus. Respect me and have pity on me'" (*Od.* 22.342–44).

poetic operation, of course, comes into the foreground as recantation. Here is a stunning example of a poet *performing* for his master's pleasure (and ours), treating him as a new character, under the threat of death:

"I clasp your knees, Odysseus. Respect me and have pity on me. You shall feel grief later [*autōi toi metopisth' akhos essetai*][3] if you kill [your] poet who sings[4] for gods and men alike. I am self-taught [*autodidaktos*], but the god has implanted [*enephusen*] in my mind all sorts of lays [*oimas*],[5] and I am fit to sing before you as before a god.[6] Do not wish, therefore, to cut my throat.[7] Besides, your dear son Telemachus will confirm this, that it was not by my will or wishing anything that I came often to your house to sing to the suitors in the midst of their banquets [*daitas*].[8] They were many more and stronger and brought me by force. (*Od.* 22.344–53)

The fictional presuppositions and the social implications of this passage are of mind-boggling complexity.

1. The *Odyssey* stages the recantation of the poet who has *often* sung an erroneous version of Odysseus' return. Because of this recantation the poet of *gastēr* will become a poet of praise: the contiguity between poetry of blame and poetry of praise easily and constantly spans the two realms.

[3]In *Il.* 9.249 Odysseus uses the same expression when, speaking to Achilles, he tries to assuage his wrath and resentment. Phemius, and Homer on his behalf, is devilishly accurate in his choice of quotations, for indeed Achilles eventually did pay bitterly for not having subdued his wrath in time. Another Iliadic allusion occurs in the narrative part, in line 330: *aluskane kera melainan*, for which compare *Il.* 16.47, 19.66.

[4]Note the endings of lines 345, 346: ". . . *aoidon* / . . . *aeidō.*" Phemius could then also sing theogonic poems; see Antonino Pagliaro, *Saggi di critica semantica* (Messina and Florence: G. d'Anna, 1953), p. 9.

[5]The *oimai* are interpreted differently by different critics, since neither the etymology nor the primary meaning of the word is clear. Karl Meuli, "Scythia," *Hermes* 70 (1935): 172, explains the word as "way of the song," a representation of an ecstatic voyage in the realm beyond, on the roads of the dead; Pagliaro, *Saggi di critica semantica,* pp. 34–40, opts for the same meaning "way of the song"; but others take it to mean "song," "lay": see *DE.*

[6]I translate this line in accordance with David B. Monro, *Homer's "Odyssey"* (Oxford: Clarendon Press, 1901), who discusses the other possible interpretation: "I seem in singing to you, to be singing to a god." The question, of course, is whether we should emphasize the worthiness of Phemius or the godlike portrait of Odysseus. To me it seems impossible to decide.

[7]In the *Iliad* the verb *deirotomeō* is always used in connection with Achilles, and it occurs in, among other passages, the Lycaon episode (21.89). Probably the *Odyssey* has this text in mind since, with the exception of 21.555, all the other uses of the verb refer to the killing of victims. Lycaon sees himself as a sacrificial victim, as does Phemius here.

[8]Interpretations of *meta daitas* vary: "after the banquets," or "in the midst of their feasts." See *GH,* 2:118.

A suspicion arises: What if the tradition of our *Odyssey* originates in
Phemius' recantation? Otherwise why would the *Odyssey* bother to
dramatize the scene in which Phemius promises to sing before Odysseus as before a god? This promise seems at any rate to be the fictional
event from which the song of the *Odyssey* emerges as the version that
triumphs over and silences all the others.

2. Phemius supplicates Odysseus, who happens to be simultaneously a character of Phemius' songs and the actual king (*basileus*). The
fiction the *Odyssey* sustains here intimates again that poetry (fiction)
narrates and mirrors real, historical events and persons. On this exceptional occasion, the poet Phemius is shown both begging Odysseus
for life and "singing" his recantation.

3. Many features of the text are difficult to interpret. For instance,
Phemius makes a cryptic parallelism (or distinction?) between the
ways he is self-taught (*autodidaktos*) and the ways he is inspired by the
Muses. Confronting his master, who on other occasions has praised
the poet whom the Muses "teach" *word by word*, Phemius seems to
claim some autonomy for the poet. His agricultural metaphor suggests the limits of the Muse's responsibility: "The god implanted
[*enephusen*] in my mind [*en phresin*] all sorts of lays [*oimas*]" (*Od.*
22.347b–48). The god would make an initial intervention—a programming as it were—but after that, the poet takes over and teaches
himself to cultivate the song. This statement would parallel that of *Od.*
8.44–45 when the narrative says of Demodocus: "To him the god
gave song more than to others, in order to please [*terpein*] whenever
[or however (*hoppēi*)] his heart stirs [*epotrunēisin*] him to sing," and also
that of *Od.* 8.73–74 when the Muse launches (*anēken*) the poet's song.

As we have seen, this initiatory "programming" by the Muses might
imply their limited responsibility, and it contrasts on the one hand
with the statements that make no mention of the Muses at all (*Od.*
1.346 ff., 8.260 ff., 266 ff.) and on the other with the intimations that
the Muses *teach* the poet *word by word* (for example, *Od.* 8.479–81,
497–98).

4. If this interpretation of the text is correct,[9] Phemius seems to put
himself in the middle ground between these extremes. In his first

---

[9]Not every interpreter reads ll. 22.347–48 as I do, that is: "I am self-taught and the
god implanted in my mind all sorts of lays." A.H.C., for instance, take this statement to
imply that Phemius has not learned from any school of poets and thus that everything
he knows has been implanted in him by the god. According to this reading, "self-
taught" would mean "with no [school] knowledge," and therefore "exclusively inspired" by the Muses. This interpretation would reduce the collaboration that Phemius
describes to a one-dimensional act. It is better to assume that the poet views his self-

song no Muse was mentioned; in this last one, when the poet recants, the Muse is given a limited but definite and initiatory responsibility. The *Odyssey* itself, however, knows the impossibility of this position, for there is no middle ground between truth (Muses) and fiction (*muthoi*), paralysis and seduction (*thelgein*), necessity and pleasure (*gastēr*).

I refer to these notions here because Phemius re-cants and pro-duces a new version of his song, and he produces it for the pleasure of all. Phemius, son of Pleasure (or pleasure-giving Phemius) *did* sing under the threat of death to charm the suitors (and Telemachus), and now, under the same threat of death, he promises to sing before Odysseus as before a god. The charm the song produces in the reader is derived not from the gratifying proximity to the Muses, but from the sword hanging over the poet's neck.

5. The *Odyssey* certainly invokes the Muses at the inception of the poem (1.1), and yet it reveals by numerous clues a constant striving to limit and circumscribe their responsibility. My analyses have shown that the *Odyssey* constantly activates the reader's role and responsibility in giving meaning to the text; that the text calls attention to its quota-tional, derivative nature; that it stages scenes in which Odysseus openly invents his own fiction (e.g., 14.462 ff., 18.138 ff.). All these features, of course, imperil the necessity and the coherence of the mythological representation of the Muses' role and interference. These features would in fact support the idea that for the *Odyssey*, the Muses—like the Sirens—are personifications of literary practices, of the epic tradition, rather than divine objective inspirers. But again we reach an undecidable point.

Even the unique invocation of the Muses at the beginning of the *Odyssey* (1.1) confirms this striving to limit the responsibility of the Muses and to blur the lines between the various sources of the Odys-sean song. The Muses are invited to sing of the man who

wandered very widely after he destroyed the holy city of Troy: he saw the towns of many men and he learned their mind; and he suffered many griefs in his heart during the seafaring, striving to save his life and the return of his companions. But even so, he did not save his compan-

---

training and the Muses' inspiration as two facets—human and divine—of the same process, since he must see no contradiction in his working and in the Muses' assistance.

This seems to be Phemius' view, now. As concerns the poet of the Odyssey, we have recognized sufficient signs to express the idea that the Odyssean poet leaves even more indeterminacy than Phemius about the exact relation between his and the Muses' contributions.

ions, though he wanted to. For they perished because of their foolishness, fools! who ate the cattle of Hyperion Helius. He took from them
their day of return. From some point of these events, goddess, daughter
of Zeus, tell to us too. (*Od.* 1.2–10)

The Muse is explicitly invited to tell the poet about the events that
are listed in 1.2–10 and that actually cover only books 5–12 of the
whole *Odyssey*. What about the other sixteen books? Aren't the Muses
responsible for the Telemachy (1–4) and for the story of Odysseus'
revenge (13–24)? And even for the eight books that relate the events
for which the poet asks the assistance of the Muses, a subtle fictional
strategy seems to dethrone the Muses from their place as source and
origin of the song. Books 9–12 are narrated by Odysseus himself with
the expertise of a poet—as Alcinous intimates—and, accordingly, the
Muses are implicitly removed, since no source can be closer to the
narrated events than their doer. Only when we consider that the
complete autobiographical narrative is known to the Odyssean poet(s)
through the Muse is her role fully legitimized and justified. Again, the
choice remains open to the reader's interpretation.

The contradictions, or at least inconsistency, with which the *Odyssey*
represents the Muse's activity is, however, consistent with the *Odyssey*'s
refusal to exert complete control over some of the supplementary
structures it knows are uncheckable. It is impossible to say how conscious and intentional these inconsistent strategies are: even if an
explanation can be found to legitimate the silence on the Muse's inspiration (*Od.* 1.346 ff., 8.260 ff., 266 ff.) or the mythological view of
the Muses' full presence (*Od.* 8.479–81, 497–98), these explanations
do not erase the diversity of the strategies employed. Accordingly the
Odyssey, whether consciously or not, parades the Muse's inspiration
while simultaneously undermining the metaphysical implications of
that inspiration. One could also reverse this assessment, however, and
say that, notwithstanding the frequent and localized ironies that shake
the belief in the myth of the Muses, the *Odyssey* maintains it and, by so
doing, adds to it the force of its insistence.[10]

The indecision about the specific responsibility of the Muse appears
flagrant and deep-seated in this last episode when the poet of pleasure promises to sing according to the Muse's inspiration *and* accord-

---

[10]It must be added that the impulses that press the *Odyssey* to limit the intervention of
the Muses need not be secular, rationalistic, or cynical. The recognition of how difficult
and intriguing it must be for the poets to trace the divine voice in the rich message and
sound of the tradition could also bring desire both for restraint and for responsible,
limited assumptions regarding the Muse's activity.

ing to his own self-education, and to sing before Odysseus as before a god. This obedience to such different agents and urges twists pleasure, truth, and fiction into an impossible unity.

6. The conditions under which Phemius' re-cantation occurs are troubling, especially at the point at which Phemius promises to sing of or for Odysseus: "I am fit to sing before you as before a god." This statement may imply Phemius' promise to look at the *basileus* as if he were a god, to sing about him almost as if he were a god. On the other hand, it might put the accent on *eoika:* "I am worthy to sing before you as before a god," implying his own exceeding worth: if a god finds my song worthy, you too should find it so.

Since it is impossible to decide between the two interpretations, the text presents two tantalizing views and a teasing tension. In the former interpretation, Phemius' promise would imply a commitment that, though pleasurable for Odysseus, would certainly contradict the epic knowledge and truth. If we compare the passage of Sarpedon in *Il.* 12.299 ff., where the portrait of the king is initially presented as that of a god but is finally turned into the image of a man on the brink of death, we have a concrete measure of the distance between the Iliadic truth and the Odyssean one. The *Odyssey* itself states explicitly the division between god and man, which Odysseus himself describes to Alcinous in one of the most powerful statements on the mortal condition (*Od.* 7.208–12). Phemius would then simply be adulating his new master, just as Odysseus does when he is pressed by the urges of *gastēr* and promises Antinous that he will "celebrate" him "all over the world" (*Od.* 17.418). In fact, the situations are analogous, but Phemius' is still more extreme, for he makes his promise under the threat of Odysseus' sword.

In the latter interpretation the worth of the poet is measured by the similar attention that Odysseus and the god offer to Phemius' song. Here again, however, the portrait of the king assumes analogies with that of the god: Phemius sees himself singing before two images, a human one and a divine one, as being concretely in that astonished presence that is described repeatedly in the *Odyssey*, often with a *para-* verb.[11] Accordingly, Odysseus and the god are both thought of as present at the *dais* of the *basileus*, as in Alcinous' description of the *daites* among the Phaeacians (*Od.* 7.199 ff.).

7. Phemius' last line, 353: *alla polu pleiones kai kreissones ēgon anankēi*, "They were many more and stronger and brought me by force," has the unmistakable ring of Hesiod's *ainos* (story) about the hawk and the

---

[11]See *Od.* 1.339, 17.521, *parēmenos*, said of the poet "sitting before" his audience.

nightingale. It is important to remember that in this story the hawk represents the king (*basileus*) and the nightingale the poet (*aoidos*):[12]

> The hawk spoke in this way to the colorfully necked nightingale, carrying her very high among the clouds, pierced by its claws. The nightingale pitiably lamented as it was pierced by the crooked claws. . . . To her he spoke disdainfully: "Poor thing, why do you cry out? One far stronger than you holds you fast and you shall go where I take you though you are a singer; and I'll make a meal of you or let you go as it pleases me."
> (Hesiod *Works and Days* 203–9)

Besides the very precise linguistic echoes,[13] the symbolic situation represented in this fable corresponds exactly to Phemius' real stance. Even the touch of violence in the hawk's threat to eat the nightingale conveys to us the structure of *gastēr* and of its urges, within whose frame I have been describing some aspects of the poetry of the *Odyssey*.

Leaving aside the unresolvable question of which text influences the other,[14] I prefer to speak of the *insistence* (or permanence) of the theme of the masters' dangerous control over the poets. Of course, this thematic aspect and its permanence do not deny the historically real pressure that the masters undoubtedly exercised upon their poets. The insistence tells us only that this pressure is manifested in stylized forms whose permanence and repetition could always be exploited whatever their structure of references may have been, for it is also clear that this theme may not easily have been sung whenever the poet was in real danger.

It is claimed here that Phemius could not resist the pressure of the suitors and that he sang for them, as we know well; Hesiod, on the contrary, represents himself as being able to defy the gift-eating kings (*basileis*). Since Phemius recants under the same menace that induced

---

[12]On this passage, see Pietro Pucci, *Hesiod and the Language of Poetry* (Baltimore: Johns Hopkins University Press, 1977), pp. 66 ff.

[13]L. 353, *alla polu pleiones kai kreissones ēgon anankēi*, is rightly connected by Jesper Svenbro, *La Parole et le marbre* (Lund, 1976), pp. 72–73, to the Hesiodean passage *Works and Days* 202–12. The language is without a doubt allusive: *Works and Days* 205, *Od.* 22.344: *eleon, eleēson; Works and Days* 9.208, *Od.* 22.345: *aoidon; Works and Days* 210, *Od.* 22.353: *kreissonas, kreissones.*

[14]Even if it were proved that Hesiod's text follows the *Odyssey's*—an assumption that I ventured to maintain in *Hesiod and the Language of Poetry* but that is far from being agreed upon by the specialists—no serious critical consequence should stem from this assumption: historically and empirically speaking, the tradition that lies behind the two texts may be the same, and theoretically the question of the "first one" in the epic tradition is hopelessly unresolvable.

him to sing for the suitors, we do not know whether he is now singing just what his heart and, or the Muse, or the pleasure of the listeners wants him to sing—in a word, whether he complies again with necessity. Telemachus indeed intervenes immediately in defense of Phemius and tells Odysseus that the poet is *anaitios*, "innocent" (*Od.* 22.356), and Odysseus without a word—a rare reaction in epic and for him in particular to desist from a gesture without a comment— spares Phemius. In so doing he spares the poet who initiates a new literary tradition about himself, the tale of his happy return under the *mnēmē* of Athena.

The *Odyssey* points here at its odd and painful victory over the other versions of Odysseus' return, for it explains this victory through Phemius' recantation under the sword of Odysseus. I do not imply that such an event really occurred; I simply state that by staging this event the *Odyssey* may intend to prove the truth of its own version and to reveal the violent repression of any other version.[15]

This poet who must constantly yield to necessity (*anankē*, 353) and to need (after all, he sings "in the midst of the banquets") is forced to give up the memory of the past and to obey the needs of the present. The masters for whom he sang were literally and metaphorically eating up the house of Odysseus; not exactly like the *gift-eating basileis* that Hesiod stages as corruptors of *dikē*, "justice," but similar masters. Odysseus has now rightly taken possession of his own house, and he will rule with *dikē*, "justice," but this notion does not come forward at this point to qualify Odysseus' pressure upon Phemius. The *Odyssey* leaves us with the painful realization that the correct, righteous, and pleasurable song upon Odysseus' return is somehow obtained by the same pressures that produced the wrong and pleasurable song about Odysseus' failure to return.

At each instance, therefore, the song of beguiling pleasure evokes the threatening stillness of the Sirens' island, where their voices, beguiling with pleasure, are synonymous with the silence of death.

---

[15]I have mentioned other versions or variants on Odysseus' return when commenting on Phemius' first song. See also Walter Burkert, *Homo Necans*, trans. Peter Bing (Berkeley and Los Angeles: University of California Press, 1983), p. 159.

2 2

Arte Allusiva

> Ambiguity itself can mean an indecision as to what you mean, an
> intention to mean several things, a probability that one or other or
> both of two things has been meant, and the fact that a statement has
> several meanings.
>
> William Empson, *Seven Types of Ambiguity*

The function and the status of the allusion[1] have only recently been
studied by semiologists. Oswald Ducrot has analyzed the allusion as a
specific form of "enunciation," that is, as a speech act that does something as it communicates.[2] The sense the allusion creates intertwines
with, or is superimposed upon, the "literal" meaning. The allusive
sense is somehow enigmatic, says Ducrot, or implicit—what we have
sometimes termed a "disguise" in accordance with the main thematic
points made by the *Odyssey:* it is, in fact, proposed by the allusive
sense; it is suggested and can never be fully proved to have been
intended.

The "literal" meaning communicates something about the events in
the poem and the allusive sense (Ducrot distinguishes between the
"meaning" of the phrase and the "sense" of the "enunciation"), introduces the relationship of our *Odyssey* with the *Iliad,* and accordingly
builds an intertextual sense—to be sure, one that must be further
determined.

What is then markedly typical of the allusion is that it proposes the
possibility of a sense that emerges only, so to speak, as an act of

---

[1]Giorgio Pasquali, "Arte allusiva," in *Stravaganze quarte e supreme* (Venice: N. Pozza,
1951), pp. 11–20. According to Pasquali, all the arts (literature, painting, etc.) are
marked by allusion, which for him means the recognizability in a text of an echo, or a
quotation, from the tradition. In a sense—which Pasquali probably intuited—all literature is allusive, since its language is "literary" only inasmuch as it refers to a special
language.

[2]See Ducrot's "Presupposizione e allusione," in *Enciclopedia Einaudi*, 15 vols. (Turin,
1980–), 10:1083 ff. The allusion thus constitutes a "performative," to use J. L. Austin's
term in *How to Do Things with Words*.

decodification and not of codification, as if it were not inscribed in language—or, to hold onto our metaphors, that appears in a certain recognition of textual disguise, since the text hides and exposes itself as being other than itself.[3]

Notice in fact that the literal meaning does not seem to lack anything to be understood as it is. The allusive sense is only an *additional* and *unnecessary* meaning. With what authority then are we adding an additional, unnecessary sense to the *literal*, perfectly self-contained signification? The authority comes from the fact that the notion of "literal" meaning as being perfectly self-contained is fully artificial and arbitrary: any phrase of the *Odyssey* would make poor or no sense if applied to an average Greek in a specific linguistic group of Greece in the eighth century b.c. It is only because a phrase is part of the poem, of its unique traditional language, of its conventions, of its textuality, and so forth, that it is meaningful.[4]

The allusive phrase is marked by repetition and difference with respect to another text. Accordingly, the allusion invites the reader to jump out of the present text toward another text. The allusion emerges in the act of reading and is imposed by literary language—for this language is a closed system, endlessly self-referential. No philologist has any hesitation in comparing several instances of the same words in the two poems in order to better define their meanings. However, when the same philologist refuses to make the same operation on the level of what language says it is doing when it repeats, the philologist refuses to take the text as a speech act—that is, in its living realization—and takes it as a grammatical specimen, with its "literal," "dead" meaning. But only in dictionaries are there "literal" meanings.

Finally, the decision to refuse or to include the allusive sense remains an interpretative decision. The scholars who hesitate before the allusive sense do not avoid a critical decision only because they remain on more empirical grounds than those who admit the allusive sense. They too interpret, and in a drastically reductive way.

At this point one may balk before the problem of taking all Homeric repetitions as being allusive. There are *connective phrases* that are endlessly repeated (*ton*, or *tēn d'apameibomenos prosephē*, "answering to him/her . . . said"), *noun-epithet formulas* for all sorts of animals,

---

[3]Hence the question whether the allusion is properly a linguistic or a rhetorical phenomenon still stirs the linguists; see Ducrot, "Presupposizione," pp. 1104–5.

[4]On the artificial quality of the "literal" meaning, see also Oswald Ducrot, *Les Mots du discours* (Paris, 1980), pp. 11 ff.

places, objects (ships, weapons, etc.), gestures, habits, and so forth, that occur invariably in different contexts; should all of these be compared and taken to be allusive? Evidently so, and in fact invariably we do so whenever we take them, for instance, as a mark of the heroic style and ethos in accordance with Milman Parry's explanation. Here, however, the first of the methods of classifying allusions described by Ducrot,[5] or a slight modification of it, could be useful. Ducrot writes that it is possible to ground the classification of allusion on the degree of commitment the speaker makes in relation to the implicit (allusive) sense. In other words, it is a question of the degree of explicitness and implicitness of the allusion: at one extreme the implicitness would be absolute and the allusive sense would be superimposed on the speaker's will; at the other extreme the allusive sense would be solicited by so many hints as to make the allusive commitment convincing.

The concrete analysis of the allusive sense of the formula would bring us to a description of the specific hints and features that solicit an allusive sense for any given formula. We would therefore classify these features in accordance with an increasing scale from those that suggest minimal allusive sense to those that forcefully suggest allusive sense. To give an example: it is obvious that the endless repetition of the same phrase in *connective*—that is, *unmarked* and *unspecific*—contexts constitutes a feature of minimal allusive degree and that for a reader to construe an allusive sense on this feature would mean working out a sense from an almost absolute allusive silence. At the other extreme, we have cases like *Od.* 13.254–55 and *Il.* 4.357, 339 (or *Od.* 5.222, *ekhōn telapenthea thumon; Il.* 5.670, *tlemona thumon ekhōn*), where the repetitions are several times marked: (1) by being unique or very rare and (2) by containing differences of meaning—and in *Od.* 5.222 of form, (3) they are in *specific* contexts—they qualify *exclusively* a specific theme, in this case Odysseus' virtues—and (4) the *allusive sense's* endless spectrum of possible interpretations puts one text in a textually significant relationship with another text. In other terms, the allusion has specific literary character; its doing outdoes another text. These four features of the repetition—(1) rarity, (2) marked repetition, (3) specificity of context, exclusivity of theme, and (4) textual reason for the allusion—force upon the reader the conviction that an allusion either is meant or has slipped in.

Each of these features may contain a latitude that it is hard to circumscribe. For instance, in an exclusive context (3), the terms of the second feature, that is, repetition and difference, may vary enor-

---

[5]See "Presupposizione," pp. 1102–3.

mously so that the difference may even include *allomorphs* of a formula: Michael Nagler has convincingly shown that two dogs by the
sides of a young man are an allormorphic repetition of the formulaic
motif that shows two maidens attending the young mistress.[6] And I
have shown the formulaic synonymity that in some cases is built
around *gastēr* and *thumos*. When the formulaic system legitimately
operates with allomorphs, synonyms, and such, the extension of the
different forms and replacing expressions within the repetition
scheme becomes hard to limit.

These considerations suggest the need to operate with a more flexible definition of the "formula" than that initially presented by Parry. I
hasten to add that by admitting allomorphs into the economy of the
Homeric formula, Parry suggested a more flexible working of the
formula than his definition implies.[7]

The Homeric formula cannot be conceived and outlined as an ex-
isting, precise linguistic entity that could cover a specific meaning.
The Homeric formula is a modern critical tool that allows us to understand, by a sort of retroactivation, the functioning of the patterned
strings of Homeric diction. Yet neither its specific meaning nor its
fixed patterning and metrical place can be the absolute constituent
part of the formula if each different context affects, even minimally,
the meaning of each occurrence of the formula; if the speech act may
add to each occurrence of the formula a different sense; if, finally,
even *allomorphs* are still part of the formulaic system.

Our model—the formula—is extrapolated from a diction that did
not single out the formula as its component but that endlessly created
and repeated patterns of numberless variety, composition, and structure. When we now define and outline the formula in a rigid way we
do so by a decontextualization and a simplification that necessarily
distort the process of living Homeric diction.

Yet we cannot avoid this pitfall: any scientific reconstruction of a
phenomenon brings to our knowledge that phenomenon—in our
case the specific traits of Homeric diction—and displaces it as well.
We reconstruct it *après coup* in a different environment, and the ef-

[6]Michael Nagler, *Spontaneity and Tradition* (Berkeley: University of California Press,
1974).
[7]See Milman Parry, "The Traditional Epithet in Homer," in *The Making of Homeric
Verse*, ed. Adam Parry (Oxford: Clarendon Press, 1971). On p. 72 Parry describes the
formation of new formulas in cases in which "the sounds of one expression have
suggested another one quite different in meaning." This strikes me as incompatible
with Parry's own definition of the formula as "an expression regularly used, under the
same metrical conditions, to express an essential idea" (p. 13).

fects of the *après coup* are unavoidable. We recognize these traits of the Homeric diction after they have fallen in a long and complete concealment; we presume them—that is, we assume them in advance and in the place of them through our dis-covery and re-covery. The displacing, disfiguring effects of this recognition or discovery are well known to us.

Yet the formula remains a heuristic critical tool. It aims at outlining a specific form or pattern of the *repetition* that is the generative force of Homeric diction. The description of the specific traits of the formula must remain the constant goal of critical inquiry: one definition or another must prove its validity by its operational success. It is only within this working success that the guarantee of their legitimacy can be found. Scholars should in fact constantly enlarge and simultaneously restrict the focus on the formula, by outlining definitions and modes of functioning of this form of the generative repetition of Homer's diction. This book is an attempt in this direction.

All the language of Homer is allusive: to different degrees, all the epic language plays constantly with references in a ludic display of intertextual noddings, winks, and gestures and, accordingly, puts itself on stage and acts out its own idiosyncrasies and preferences in a sort of narcissistic extravaganza while it says what it says. This signifying level, that of the allusive sense, is unknown to the characters, may also fully or in part escape the intention of the poets, and constitutes an implicit addition for the reader to decode in order to interpret the text. What we call literature is nothing else but this.

In dealing with Homeric intertextuality I have constantly applied the principle that the determination of the textual intentions, and therefore also of the allusive sense, remains speculative. Ducrot, in commenting upon the allusive sense, confirms the point. His arguments on the relative "implicitness" of the allusion and on the mythical or artificial character of the "literal," "explicit" meaning lead him to assert that in principle the possibilities of allusive interpretations are infinite.[8]

An important point follows from the implicitness of the allusion, and Ducrot defines it clearly when he alleges that to describe the diverse levels of the allusion means to describe the diverse modes according to which an individual "is constituted" by the others, since

---

[8]"Presupposizione," p. 1101. Ducrot implies in fact that the possible interpretations respond to the infinite, contradictory situations the speaker is in when he speaks: the interpretations are in accordance with whichever of these situations the interpreter *decides* to appeal to. Only in this sense, it seems to me, namely as *a decision* of the interpreter, can a precise sense of the allusion be suggested.

its "reality" takes shape only through the perceptions others have of it.[9] When we apply this principle to the literary allusions we are retrieving and describing, this means that the *Odyssey* is constituted by the readings that the *Odyssey* allows through the readings that the *Iliad* gives of the *Odyssey*, and conversely the *Iliad* is constituted by the reverse process. The *Iliad* still outlines and writes the *Odyssey* and vice versa.

Yet since these constitutive readings occur in the space of a relative implicitness—the implicitness of the sense of repetition—they are the product of a certain emptiness or vagueness of the text that the reader *desires* to fill up. In my own terms, these constitutive readings function as the acts of suspecting and uncovering a disguise in order to look for a source, an original text, a father-text. In this case too, therefore, the constitutive readings are products of a certain desire for fullness that the text provokes by itself through its gaps and its intertextual implicitness—that is, through its repetitions that hint at an additional sense rather than tell it, sham it rather than reveal it. This desire affects in the first place, of course, the reader, who constantly searches for more meaning, and for a place to anchor it. It follows that the critical operation of searching for allusion is highly ambivalent. For the intertextual analysis may be prodded by the critic's desire to efface the inconsistencies of the text, to fill its gaps, and to point to a father-text source of the full potential significance of the texts. Of course, the intertextual analysis may also, on the contrary, produce a deconstructive view of the text, as my analysis aims to do, by revealing the iridescent surface of the text, and the dissemination of its meanings and connotations.

The desire for a full appropriation of meaning and of the meaning of the other texts affects the poets also. In this sense the allusions that I have traced reveal the desire of the *Odyssey* to fully appropriate the *Iliad*, and vice versa.

As the reader's and the text's desire emerge from the mere implicitness of the text, they necessarily cannot ever rest, for this upsetting structure of things said/not said keeps on vibrating. Such a structure in fact is eminently differential, on the limit, inextricable. In my terms, the unmasking reading reveals itself as a new mask, and the discovered allusion identifies neither the original nor the originator, neither the competitor nor the outdoer.

Probably Giorgio Pasquali would not have believed it possible to speak of "allusion" in texts that he would not have defined as "learn-

---

[9]Ibid., p. 1103.

ed," (*dotti*) and certainly not to the extent that I have assumed here.
Yet my analysis has shown that allusion dominates in the Homeric
text. The reason for this lies also in the fact that the allusion is a way of
quoting in the highly conventional and stylized Homeric language.
Accordingly, the formulaic repetition—which has often discouraged
scholars from speaking of deliberate allusion—turns out to be the
very ground of a continuous intertextuality, of quotations, of incorporation, of an exchange of views or polemic arguments among the
texts.

The result is that the epic texts entertain an endless dialogue and
conversation on all the topics of archaic Greek thought. To begin with
the notion of truth in relation to the language of poetry, the *Iliad,* the
Odyssey, and Hesiod eavesdrop on each other, the *Odyssey* teasing
slightly the notion of *kleos* in the *Iliad,* the *Odyssey* providing the foil for
Hesiod's attack on the poets, *gasteres oion,* "mere bellies." In the age of
writers, a man as wise as Xenophanes is not content with attacking *by
name,* author to author, the hexametric poetry of Homer and Hesiod:
he goes on to quote, and he quotes by alluding to a line of the poet he
is condemning. So Xenophanes fragment 36, which reads *tauta dedox-
astho men eoikota tois etumoisin,* "let these things be considered to resemble truth," cannot be separated either from Hesiod *Theogony* 27 or
from *Od.* 19.203.[10] The textual parallels between Parmenides and the
Odyssey, as Alexander Mourelatos writes, "have been commonplace
for almost a century," and several incorporations of Odyssean phrases
by Parmenides' text have in recent years been shown to contain a
specific set of allusive interactions.[11]

The perception that the poetic language maintains a difficult and
problematic relation with truth belongs to all the texts in question, but
the economy of this relation and the strategies that are devised to save
the notion of truth from the contiguity of falsity are as different as are
the texts.

The question of truth (*alētheia*) in relation to being (*to on*) and to
language (*logos*) remains fundamental. Heidegger has elaborated
these questions in the Greek context beginning with *Il.* 1.70, *ta t'eonta,
ta t'essomena pro t'eonta,* in a famous essay,[12] where he defines being of

---

[10]The resemblance between Xenophanes frag. 36 and Hesiod *Theog.* 27 is evident to
some critics: see André Rivier, "Remarques sur les fragments 34 et 35 de Xénophane,"
Revue de Philologie 30 (1956): 37–61.

[11]See Eric A. Havelock, "Parmenides and Odysseus," *HSCP* 63 (1958): 133–43; and
Alexander P. D. Mourelatos, *The Route of Parmenides* (New Haven: Yale University
Press, 1970), pp. 17–34.

[12]Martin Heidegger, "The Anaximander Fragment," in *Early Greek Thinking,* trans.
David Farrell Krell and Frank A. Capuzzi (New York: Harper & Row, 1975), pp. 36 ff.

einai as presencing and connects the Iliadic *ta eonta* with Anaximander's *ta eonta.*

In the realm of "ethics" an endless dialogue develops between our texts, again through "quotations" that are made perceptible or audible by marked repetitions. The *Odyssey* and the *Iliad* never cease to confront each other in relation to their typical heroes or characters, Achilles and Odysseus, and the ramifications of these polemic views extend beyond epic to lyric poetry,[13] drama, and again to philosophy.[14] For the intuition of the Greek enlightenment about these two characters was essentially correct, Achilles being the man of *haplous muthos,* "simple discourse," Odysseus the polytropic man.[15] I have emphasized that within Odysseus' polytropy the *Odyssey* lets us glimpse the excitement of a life spent in increasing knowledge and wisdom. Odysseus is the first Socratic man, in the Nietzschean sense of "Socratic." The enlightenment missed—but we may not be sufficiently informed—the strategies that in the *Iliad* too expose and hide the notion of truth as being close to that of falsehood.

The set of notions that hinge on *mētis,* "ruse," "practical intelligence," "retorted thinking," does not find suitable territory in Greek thought after the *Odyssey* unless, as expected, in comedy. Here the plot depends heavily on machinations, deceptions, and tricks (*doloi*).[16] Unexpectedly, the word *mētis* occurs rarely in the extant plays of Aeschylus and Sophocles and never in those of Euripides, though the notions of intrigue and ruse (*doloi, mekhanē,* etc.) appear frequently.

As Marcel Detienne and Jean-Pierre Vernant write in concluding their study on *mētis,*[17] *mētis* remains excluded from philosophical thought. This exclusion is particularly clear in Plato, who in the name of truth banishes the deviating, retorted thinking of *mētis.* This conclusion is "incontrovertible," as Sarah Kofman writes,[18] and yet *mētis*

---

[13]On the relation between the Odyssean character and the lyric character, see Joseph Russo's inspiring paper "The Inner Man in Archilochus and in the *Odyssey,*" *GRBS* 15 (1974): 139–52; Bernd Seidensticker, "Archilochus and Odysseus," *GRBS* 9 (1978): 5–22; and on the several traits that unite Solon to Odysseus, see the learned book by Onofrio Vox, *Solone autoritratto* (Padua: Antenore, 1984), passim.

[14]See Hermann Fränkel, *Early Greek Poetry and Philosophy,* trans. Moses Hadas and James Willis (Oxford: Blackwell, 1975), pp. 134 ff.; and Bruno Snell, *The Discovery of the Mind,* trans. T. G. Rosenmeyer (Oxford: Blackwell, 1953).

[15]See Pietro Pucci, *The Violence of Pity in Euripides' "Medea"* (Ithaca: Cornell University Press, 1980), pp. 80–81 and 204, nn. 22–25; and A. Patzer, "Antisthenes der Sokratiker" (diss., University of Heidelberg, 1970).

[16]See the superb thesis by Séamus MacMathúna, "Trickery in Aristophanes" (Ph.D. diss., Cornell University, 1971).

[17]Marcel Detienne and Jean-Pierre Vernant, *Les Ruses de l'intelligence: La Métis des grecs* (Paris: Flammarion, 1974), pp. 301 ff.

[18]*Comment s'en sortir* (Paris: Galilée, 1983).

continues to play a cunning and hidden (of course) role even in Plato. Kofman reminds us that Eros in the Platonic myth of the *Symposium* is the son of Poros and that Poros is the son of Metis: as Eros stands for the philosopher, *mētis* still operates. Furthermore, the notions of ruse and resource are implicit in some sophistic procedures and according- ly also in the parallel ones that Socrates is sometimes shown to follow, though in his case these are intended *in bonam partem* and in order to get out of the *aporiai*.

An important religious view is presented by the *Odyssey* when Athe- na is described as *phaneisa*, "appearing" (*Od.* 16.159, *Odussēi phaneisa*) and simultaneously the text (*Od.* 16.160) alludes to *Il.* 20.131. Athena appears in book 13, in the figure of goddess of *mētis*. This mode of appearance never occurs in the *Iliad* and marks an important dif- ference. Whether the *Odyssey* is ironic or not in this presentation of the figure of Athena matters—for it engages specifically the attitude of the reader—but it is not the crucial point. Certainly the *Odyssey* stresses the arbitrariness of the divine figure, saying that Athena can look like whatever she wants. At the same time, however, in contrast with the *Iliad,* it maintains or supports the illusion or the domesticated belief in a specific visible, describable *image* of the goddess. The imagi- nary is made visible, and the temples and the theater will be quick to use the device of an *eidolon* of the god appearing in the sacred pre- cinct or in the theater.[19]

In this case, too, we cannot decide with any certainty whether the *Odyssey* represents the modern attitudes of Ionian rationalism, the ironic and skeptical view that however the gods reveal themselves, the form they take is always to some extent arbitrary, or whether it repre- sents an ancient, more respectful belief. Accordingly, it would be impossible to use this and the other features we have accounted for as evidence of an intellectual development after the *Iliad*. Any reader who would decide in favor of this view would do so at his or her own risk, for it is of course gratifying to encase the *Odyssey* in a historical movement determined by a specific *telos,* "finality," and to use the text as one piece of evidence for this *telos*. Caution, however, demands that we consider the Odyssean positions with their iridescent glow, with their vacillating rhythm (ironic/not ironic, etc.) as modes that are characterized by permanence and insistence. These positions, in other words, go through history as a specific set or structure of themes and ideas—survival of the hero, self-identity of the subject, accumulation of knowledge, return to that which is familiar, pleasure.

---

[19]A statue of Athena is recorded in *Il.* 6.273 ff.

The insistence is produced by repetition, both as the text emerges and is composed and as it is transmitted and read. Each reading—perceptive and blind at the same time—reproduces this insistence and develops it as continuity and difference without ever producing singly and simply a total "otherness," without ever jumping out of them. Thus the many-faceted, supportive, or polemic readings of the *Odyssey* are from the beginning part of its insistence.

These few hints do not claim to be even a beginning of the analysis of Greek archaic thought. They suggest only the fertility of a way of reading that activates the enunciative, allusive, quotational force of repetition. Of course the immense material this reading brings to our attention is doubly difficult and sensitive. On the one hand, it belongs to the realm of implicitness, at least to some extent; on the other, it opens up the thorny questions of intertextuality, of originality and passivity, of new and old, history and structure, change and continuity. But difficulties are the surest incentives to continue the analysis.

BIBLIOGRAPHY

Adkins, A. W. H. *Merit and Responsibility: A Study in Greek Values.* Oxford: Oxford University Press, 1960. Reprint. Chicago: University of Chicago Press, 1975.

Apthorp, M. J. "The Language of the *Odyssey* 5.5–20." *CQ,* n.s. 27 (1977): 1–9.

Arend, Walter. *Die typischen Scenen bei Homer.* 1933. Reprint. Berlin: Weidmann, 1975.

Arthur, Marylin B. "Cultural Strategies in Hesiod's *Theogony:* Law, Family, and Society." *Arethusa* 15 (1982): 63–82.

————. "The Dream of a World without Women: Poetics and the Circles of Order in the *Theogony* Prooemium." *Arethusa* 16 (1983): 97–116.

Auerbach, Erich. "Odysseus' Scar." In *Mimesis: The Representation of Reality in Western Literature,* trans. Willard R. Trask. Princeton: Princeton University Press, 1953.

Austin, Norman. *Archery at the Dark of the Moon: Poetic Problems in Homer's "Odyssey."* Berkeley: University of California Press, 1975.

————. "The Function of Digressions in the *Iliad*." *GRBS* 7 (1966): 295–312.

————. "Odysseus Polytropos: Man of Many Minds." *Arche* 6 (1981): 40–52.

Bannert, Hans. "Zur Vogelgestalt der Götter bei Homer." *Wiener Studien,* n.s. 12 (1978): 29–42.

Beck, Götz. "Beobachtungen zur Kirke-Episode in der Odyssee." *Philologus* 109 (1965): 1–29.

Benveniste, Emile. "Renouvellement lexical et dérivation en grec ancien." *BSL* 59 (1964): 24–39.

————. *Le Vocabulaire des institutions indo-européennes.* 2 vols. Vol. 1, *Economie, parenté, société.* Vol. 2, *Pouvoir, droit, religion.* Paris: Minuit, 1969. English translation, *Indo-European Language and Society.* Trans. Elizabeth Palmer. Coral Gables, Fla.: University of Miami Press, 1973.

Bergren, Ann. "Allegorizing Winged Words: Similes and Symbolization in *Odyssey* V." *CW* 74 (1980): 109–23.

————. "Helen's Good 'Drug.'" In *Contemporary Literary Hermeneutics and Interpretation of Classical Texts,* ed. Stéphane Krésic. Ottawa: University of Ottawa Press, 1981.

Bibliography

_____. "Helen's Web: Time and Tableau in the *Iliad*." *Helios* 7, no. 1 (1980): 19–34.

_____. "Language and the Female in Early Greek Thought." *Arethusa* 16 (1983): 69–95.

_____. "Odyssean Temporality: Many (Re)turns." In *Approaches to Homer*, ed. Carl A. Rubino and Cynthia W. Shelmerdine, pp. 38–73. Austin: University of Texas Press, 1983.

Bertelli, Lucio, and Italo Lana, eds. *Lessico politico dell'epica greca arcaica*. Vol. 2. Turin: Bottega d'Erasmo, 1978.

Blass, Friedrich. *Die Interpolationen in der Odyssee: Eine Untersuchung*. Halle: M. Niemeyer, 1904.

Boedeker, Deborah Dickmann. *Aphrodite's Entry into Greek Epic*. Leiden: Brill, 1974.

Burkert, Walter. *Homo Necans*. Trans. Peter Bing. Berkeley: University of California Press, 1983.

_____. "Das Lied von Ares und Aphrodite zum Verhältnis von Odyssee und Ilias." *Rheinisches Museum* 103 (1960): 130–84.

_____. *Zum altgriechischen Mitleidsbegriff*. Inaugural Dissertation der Philosophie Fakultät der Friedrich-Alexander Universtät zu Erlangen. Erlangen, 1955.

Buschor, Ernst. *Die Musen des Jenseits*. Munich: F. Bruckmann, 1944.

Cairns, Francis. *Generic Composition in Greek and Roman Poetry*. Edinburgh: Edinburgh University Press, 1972.

Calame, Claude. "Entre oralité et écriture: Enonciation et énoncé dans la poésie grecque archaïque." *Semiotica* 43 (1983): 245–73.

Calhoun, G. M. "Homer's Gods—Myth and Märchen." *AJP* 60 (1939): 1–28.

_____. "The Poet and the Muses in Homer." *CP* 33 (1938): 157–66.

Chantraine, Pierre. "Grec MEILICHIOS." In *Mélanges Emile Boisacq*. 2 vols. Vols. 5 and 6 of Annuaire de l'Institut de Philologie et d'Histoire Orientales et Slaves (1937–38), 5:169–74. Reprinted Brussels: Kraus, 1969.

Clay, Jenny. "Demas and Aude: The Nature of Divine Transformation in Homer." *Hermes* 102 (1974): 129–36.

_____. "The Planktai and Moly: Divine Naming and Knowing in Homer." *Hermes* 100 (1972): 127–31.

_____. *The Wrath of Athena: Gods and Men in the "Odyssey."* Princeton: Princeton University Press, 1983.

Codino, Fausto. *Introduzione a Omero*. Turin: Einaudi, 1965.

Collins, Leslie L. "ΝΕΙΚΕΟΣ ΑΡΧΗ: Helen and Heroic Ethics." Ph.D. diss., Cornell University, 1982.

Culler, Jonathan. *On Deconstruction: Theory and Criticism after Structuralism*. Ithaca: Cornell University Press, 1982.

_____. *The Pursuit of Signs: Semiotics, Literature, Deconstruction*. Ithaca: Cornell University Press, 1975.

de Man, Paul. *Allegories of Reading: Figural Language in Rousseau, Nietzsche, Rilke, and Proust*. New Haven: Yale University Press, 1979.

Bibliography

———. "Hypogram and Inscription: Michael Riffaterre's Poetics of Reading." *Diacritics* 11, no. 4 (1981): 17–35.

De Martino, Francesco. "Eraclito e gli efesi 'sempre ottusi.'" *L'Antiquité Classique* 52 (1983): 221–27.

Derrida, Jacques. *La Carte postale de Socrate à Freud et au-delà.* Paris: Flammarion, 1980.

———. *De la grammatologie.* Paris: Minuit, 1967. English translation, *Of Grammatology.* Trans. Gayatri Spivak. Baltimore: Johns Hopkins University Press, 1976.

———. "La Pharmacie de Platon." In *La Dissémination.* Paris: Seuil, 1972. English translation, *Dissemination.* Trans. Barbara Johnson. Chicago: University of Chicago Press, 1981.

Detienne, Marcel. *L'Invention de la mythologie.* Paris: Gallimard, 1981.

———. *Les Maîtres de vérité dans la Grèce archaïque.* 2d ed. Paris: F. Maspero, 1973.

Detienne, Marcel, and Jean-Pierre Vernant. *La Cuisine du sacrifice en pays grec.* Paris: Gallimard, 1979.

——— and ———. *Les Ruses de l'intelligence: La Mētis des grecs.* Paris: Flammarion, 1974.

Diano, Carlo. "La poetica dei Feaci." In *Saggezza e poetiche degli antichi.* Venice: N. Pozza, 1968.

Dietrich, B. C. "Views of Homeric Gods and Religion." *Numen* 26 (1979): 129–51.

Dirlmeier, Franz. *Die Vogelgestalt homerischer Götter.* Sitzungsberichte der Heidelberger Akademie der Wissenschaften, Philos.-Hist. Klasse, no. 2. Heidelberg: C. Winter, 1967.

Dubois, Jacques, et al. (Groupe μ). *Rhétorique générale.* Paris: Larousse, 1970.

Ducrot, Oswald. *Les mots du discours.* Paris: Minuit, 1980.

———. "Presupposizione e allusione." In *Enciclopedia Einaudi.* 15 vols. 10:1083–1107. Turin: Einaudi, 1980.

Dupont-Roc, Roselyne, and Alain Le Boulluec. "Le Charme du récit." In *Écriture et théorie poétiques: Lectures d'Homère, Eschyle, Platon, Aristote,* ed. Jean Lallot and Alain Le Boulluec. Paris: Presses de l'Ecole Normale Supérieure, 1976.

Durante, Marcello. *Sulla preistoria della tradizione poetica greca.* 2 vols. Rome: Ateneo, 1971–76.

Edwards, Anthony T. *Odysseus against Achilles: The Role of Allusion in the Homeric Epic.* Beiträge zur klassichen Philologie, vol. 171. Königstein/Ts.: Hain, 1985.

Edwards, M. W. "Convention and Individuality in *Iliad* I." *HSCP* 84 (1980): 1–29.

Fenik, Bernard. *Studies in the Odyssey.* Hermes, suppl. 30. Wiesbaden: F. Steiner, 1974.

Ferrucci, Franco. *The Poetics of Disguise: The Autobiography of the Work in Homer, Dante, and Shakespeare.* Trans. Ann Dunnigan. Ithaca: Cornell University Press, 1980.

Bibliography

Finnegan, Ruth. *Oral Poetry: Its Nature, Significance, and Social Context.* Cambridge: Cambridge University Press, 1980.

Floyd, E. D. *"Kleos Aphthiton:* An Indo-European Perspective on Early Greek Poetry." *Glotta* 58 (1980): 133–57.

Focke, Friedrich. *Die Odyssee.* Stuttgart: W. Kohlhammer, 1943.

Foley, Helene. "'Reverse Similes' and Sex Roles in the *Odyssey.*" *Arethusa* 11 (1978): 7–26.

Ford, Andrew. "A Study of Early Greek Terms for Poetry: 'Aoide,' 'Epos,' and 'Poiesis.'" Ph.D. diss., Yale University, 1981.

Frame, Douglas. *The Myth of Return in Early Greek Epic.* New Haven: Yale University Press, 1978.

Fränkel, Hermann. *Early Greek Poetry and Philosophy: A History of Greek Epic, Lyric, and Prose to the Middle of the Fifth Century.* Trans. Moses Hadas and James Willis. Oxford: Blackwell, 1975. English translation of *Dichtung und Philosophie des frühen Griechentums.* Philological Monographs, no. 13. New York: American Philological Association, 1951. 2d ed. rev. Munich: C. H. Beck, 1962.

———. *Die homerischen Gleichnisse.* Göttingen: Vandenhoeck & Ruprecht, 1921.

Friedrich, Rainer. "On the Compositional Use of Similes in the *Odyssey.*" *AJP* 102 (1981): 120–37.

Gentili, Bruno. *Poesia e pubblico nella Grecia antica.* Rome and Bari: Laterza, 1984.

Griffin, Jasper. *Homer on Life and Death.* Oxford: Clarendon Press, 1980.

Güntert, Hermann. *Von der Sprache der Götter und Geister.* Halle: M. Niemeyer, 1921.

Havelock, Eric A. "Parmenides and Odysseus." *HSCP* 63 (1958): 133–43.

Heidegger, Martin. "The Anaximander Fragment." In *Early Greek Thinking,* trans. David Farrell Krell and Frank A. Capuzzi. New York: Harper & Row, 1975.

Heitsch, Ernst. "Tlēmosynē." *Hermes* 92 (1964): 257–64.

Hertz, Neil. "The Notion of Blockage in the Literature of the Sublime." In *Psychoanalysis and the Question of the Text,* ed. Geoffrey Hartman. Baltimore: Johns Hopkins University Press, 1978. Reprinted in Hertz, *The End of the Line: Essays on Psychoanalysis and the Sublime.* New York: Columbia University Press, 1985.

Hesiod. *Theogony.* Ed. M. L. West. With prolegomena and commentary. Oxford: Clarendon Press, 1966.

———. *Works and Days.* Ed. M. L. West. With prolegomena and commentary. Oxford: Clarendon Press, 1978.

Hoekstra, Arie. *Homeric Modifications of Formulaic Prototypes: Studies in the Development of Greek Epic Diction.* Amsterdam: North-Holland, 1969.

Hölscher, Uvo. "Das Schweigen der Arete." *Hermes* 88 (1960): 257–65.

Horkheimer, Max, and Theodor W. Adorno. *Dialectic of Enlightenment.* Trans. John Cumming. New York: Herder & Herder, 1972.

Bibliography

Irwin, Terence. *Plato's Moral Theory: The Early and Middle Dialogues.* Oxford: Clarendon Press, 1977.

Kahn, Laurence. "Ulysse." In *Dictionnaire des mythologies et des religions des sociétés traditionelles et du monde antique,* 2 vols., ed. Yves Bonnefoy, 2:517–20. Paris: Flammarion, 1981.

———. "Ulysse, ou La Ruse et la mort." *Critique,* no. 393 (1980): 116–34.

Kakridēs, Johannes Th. *Homeric Researches.* Lund: Gleerup, 1949.

———. *Homer Revisited.* Lund: Gleerup, 1971.

Kofman, Sarah. *Comment s'en sortir.* Paris: Galilée, 1983.

Latacz, Joachim. *Zum Wortfeld "Freude" in der Sprache Homers.* Heidelberg: C. Winter, 1966.

Lesky, Albin. *Thalatta: Der Weg der Griechen zum Meer.* Vienna: R. M. Rohrer, 1947.

Long, A. A. "Morals and Values in Homer." *JHS* 90 (1970): 121–39.

Loraux, Nicole. "*Ponos.*" In *Annali del Seminario di Studi del Mondo Classico: Sezione di Archeologia e Storia Antica,* no. 4, pp. 171–92. Naples: Istituto Universitario Orientale, 1982.

MacMathúna, Séamus. "Trickery in Aristophanes." Ph.D. diss., Cornell University, 1971.

Marg, Walter. "Der erste Lied des Demodokus." In *Navicula Chiloniensis: Studia Philologia Felici Jacoby Professori Chiloniensi Emerito Octogenario Oblata.* Leiden: Brill, 1956.

———. *Homer über die Dichtung.* 2d ed. rev. Münster: Aschendorff, 1971.

Marzullo, Benedetto. *Il problema omerico.* 2d ed. rev. Milan and Naples: R. Ricciardi, 1970.

Mattes, Wilhelm. *Odysseus bei den Phäaken: Kritisches zur Homeranalyse.* Würzburg: K. Tritsch, 1958.

Mazon, Paul, ed. and trans. *Homère, Iliade.* 4 vols. Paris: Belles Lettres, 1937–38.

Mazzotta, Giuseppe. *Dante, Poet of the Desert: History and Allegory in the "Divine Comedy."* Princeton: Princeton University Press, 1979.

Meuli, Karl. "Herkunft und Wesen der Fabel." *Schweizerisches Archiv für Volkskunde* 50 (1954): 65–88. Also in *Gesammelte Schriften,* 2 vols., ed. Thomas Gelzer, 2:731–56. Basel: Schwabe, 1975.

———. "Scythica." *Hermes* 70 (1935): 121–76.

Michel, Christoph. *Erläuterungen zum N der Ilias.* Heidelberg: C. Winter, 1971.

Monro, David B. *Homer's "Odyssey": Books XIII–XXIV.* Oxford: Clarendon Press, 1901.

Moulton, Carroll. *Similes in the Homeric Poems.* Göttingen: Vandenhoeck & Ruprecht, 1977.

Mourelatos, Alexander P. D. *The Route of Parmenides: A Study of Word, Image, and Argument in the Fragments.* New Haven: Yale University Press, 1970.

Mühlestein, Hugo. "Le Nom des deux Ajax." *Studi Micenei* 2 (1967): 41–52.

Mülder, Dietrich. "Götteranrufungen in Ilias und Odyssee." *Rheinisches Museum* 79 (1930): 7–34.

Bibliography

Müller, Marion. *Athene als göttliche Helferin in der Odyssee.* Heidelberg: C. Winter, 1966.

Nagler, Michael N. "Entretiens avec Tirésias." *CW* 74 (1980): 89–108.

———. *Spontaneity and Tradition: A Study in the Oral Art of Homer.* Berkeley: University of California Press, 1974.

Nagy, Gregory. "Another Look at *Kleos Aphthiton.*" *Würzburger Jahrbücher für die Altertumswissenschaft,* n.s. 7 (1981): 113–16.

———. *The Best of the Achaeans: Concepts of the Hero in Archaic Greek Poetry.* Baltimore: Johns Hopkins University Press, 1979.

———. *Comparative Studies in Greek and Indic Meter.* Cambridge: Harvard University Press, 1974.

———. "On the Death of Sarpedon." In *Approaches to Homer,* ed. Carl A. Rubino and Cynthia W. Shelmerdine. Austin: University of Texas Press, 1983.

———. "Sêma and Nóēsis: Some Illustrations." *Arethusa* 16 (1983): 35–56.

Nestle, Wilhelm. *Vom Mythos zum Logos: Die Selbstentfaltung des griechischen Denkens von Homer bis auf die Sophistik und Sokrates.* Stuttgart: A. Kröner, 1942.

Notopoulos, James. "Mnemosyne in Oral Literature." *TAPA* 69 (1938): 465–93.

Page, Denys. *History and the Homeric Iliad.* Berkeley: University of California Press, 1959.

———. *The Homeric Odyssey.* Oxford: Clarendon Press, 1955.

Pagliaro, Antonino. *Nuovi saggi di critica semantica.* Messina and Florence: G. d'Anna, 1956.

———. "Origini liriche e formazione agonale dell'epica greca." In *La poesia epica e la sua formazione,* pp. 31–58. Problemi attuali di scienza e di cultura, no. 139. Rome: Accademia Nazionale dei Lincei, 1970.

———. *Saggi di critica semantica.* Messina and Florence: G. d'Anna, 1953.

Parry, Milman. "The Traditional Epithet in Homer." In *The Making of Homeric Verse: The Collected Papers of Milman Parry,* ed. Adam Parry. Oxford: Clarendon Press, 1971.

Pasquali, Giorgio. "Arte allusiva." In *Stravaganze quarte e supreme.* Venice: N. Pozza, 1951.

Patzer, A. "Antisthenes der Sokratiker." Diss., University of Heidelberg, 1970.

Peabody, Berkley. *The Winged Word: A Study in the Technique of Ancient Greek Oral Composition as Seen Principally through Hesiod's "Works and Days."* Albany: State University of New York Press, 1975.

Peradotto, John. "Prophecy Degree Zero: Tiresias and the End of the *Odyssey.*" In *Oralità, cultura, litteratura, discorso.* Rome: Ateneo, 1986, pp. 429–59.

Pollard, John R. T. *Seers, Shrines, and Sirens: The Greek Religious Revolution in the Sixth Century B.C.* London: Allen & Unwin, 1965.

Pucci, Pietro. "Banter and Banquets for Heroic Death." In *Beyond Aporia?,* forthcoming.

Bibliography

_____. "Decostruzione e intertextualità." *Nuova Corrente* 93/94 (1984): 283–301.

_____. *Hesiod and the Language of Poetry*. Baltimore: Johns Hopkins University Press, 1977.

_____. "The Language of the Muses." In *Classical Mythology in Twentieth-Century Thought and Literature*, ed. Wendell M. Aycock and Theodore M. Klein, pp. 163–86. Proceedings of the Comparative Literature Symposium, Texas Tech University, vol. 11. Lubbock: Texas Tech Press, 1980.

_____. "The Proem of the *Odyssey*." *Arethusa* 15 (1982): 39–62.

_____. "La scrittura dell'Odissea." Forthcoming in *Quaderni Urbanati*.

_____. "The Song of the Sirens." *Arethusa* 12 (1979): 121–32.

_____. *The Violence of Pity in Euripides' "Medea."* Ithaca: Cornell University Press, 1980.

Ramersdorfer, Hans. *Singuläre Iterata der Ilias*. Beiträge zur klassischen Philologie, vol. 137. Königstein/Ts.: Hain, 1981.

Redard, Georges. *Recherches sur* XRE, XRESTHAI: *Etude sémantique*. Paris: H. Champion, 1953.

Reinhardt, Karl. *Die Ilias und ihr Dichter*. Ed. Uvo Hölscher. Göttingen: Vandenhoeck & Ruprecht, 1961.

Rivier, André. "Remarques sur les fragments 34 et 35 de Xénophane." *Revue de Philologie* 30 (1956): 37–61.

Roscher, W. H. *Ausführliches Lexikon der griechischen und römischen Mythologie*. 6 vols. Leipzig: Teubner, 1884–1937.

Russo, Joseph. "Homer against His Tradition." *Arion* 7 (1968): 275–95.

_____. "The Inner Man in Archilochus and in the *Odyssey*." *GRBS* 15 (1974): 139–52.

Schein, Seth L. *The Mortal Hero: An Introduction to Homer's "Iliad."* Berkeley: University of California Press, 1984.

Schnapp-Gourbeillon, Annie. *Lions, héros, masques: Les Représentations de l'animal chez Homère*. Paris: F. Maspero, 1981.

Scott, W. C. *The Oral Nature of the Homeric Simile*. Mnemosyne, suppl. 28. Leiden: Brill, 1974.

Segal, Charles. "*Kleos* and Its Ironies in the *Odyssey*." *L'Antiquité Classique* 52 (1983): 22–47.

_____. "The Phaeacians and the Symbolism of Odysseus' Return." *Arion* 1 (1962): 17–63.

Seidensticker, Bernd. "Archilochus and Odysseus." *GRBS* 19 (1978): 5–22.

Shewring, Walter, ed. and trans. *The Odyssey*. Introduction by G. S. Kirk. Oxford: Oxford University Press, 1980.

Shipp, G. P. *Studies in the Language of Homer*. 2d ed. Cambridge: Cambridge University Press, 1972.

Sittl, Karl. *Die Wiederholungen in der Odyssee*. Munich: Ackermann, 1882.

Snell, Bruno. *The Discovery of the Mind: The Greek Origins of European Thought*. Trans. T. G. Rosenmeyer. Oxford: Blackwell, 1953.

Stanford, W. B. *The Ulysses Theme: A Study in the Adaptability of a Traditional Hero*. Oxford: Blackwell, 1954.

Svenbro, Jesper. *La Parole et le marbre: Aux origines de la poétique grecque.* Lund, 1976.

Todorov, Tzvetan. *The Poetics of Prose.* Trans. Richard Howard. With a new foreword by Jonathan Culler. Ithaca: Cornell University Press, 1977.

Touchefeu-Meynier, Odette. *Thèmes odysséens dans l'art antique.* Paris: Boccard, 1968.

Van Den Abbeele, Georges. "The Economy of Travel in French Philosophical Literature." Ph.D. diss., Cornell University, 1981.

Vernant, Jean-Pierre. "A la table des hommes." In Marcel Detienne and Jean-Pierre Vernant, *La Cuisine du sacrifice en pays grec.* Paris: Gallimard, 1979.

———. *The Origins of Greek Thought.* Ithaca: Cornell University Press, 1982. English translation of *Les Origines de la pensée grecque.* Paris: Presses Universitaires de France, 1962.

——— and Marcel Detienne. *Les Ruses de l'intelligence: La Métis des Grecs.* Paris: Flammarion, 1974.

Vetta, Massimo. *Poesia e simposio nella Grecia antica.* Rome and Bari: Laterza, 1983.

Vidal-Naquet, Pierre. "Valeurs religieuses et mythiques de la terre et du sacrifice dans l'Odyssée." In *Problèmes de la terre en Grèce ancienne,* ed. M. I. Finley, pp. 269–92. Paris: La Haye, 1973.

Voigt, Christian. *Überlegung und Entscheidung.* 1934. Reprint. Meisenham am Glan: Hain, 1972.

Von der Mühll, Peter. *Kritisches Hypomnema zur Ilias.* Basel: F. Reinhardt, 1952.

Vox, Onofrio. *Solone autoritratto.* Padua: Antenore, 1984.

Wackernagel, Jacob. *Kleine Schriften.* 2 vols. Göttingen: Vandenhoeck & Ruprecht, 1953.

———. *Sprachliche Untersuchungen zu Homer.* Philologische Seminar, Universität Basel, vol. 1. Göttingen: Vandenhoeck & Ruprecht, 1916.

Walsh, George B. *The Varieties of Enchantment: Early Greek Views of the Nature and Function of Poetry.* Chapel Hill: University of North Carolina Press, 1984.

Weber, Samuel. "It." In *Glyph 4: Johns Hopkins Textual Studies,* pp. 1–31. Baltimore: Johns Hopkins University Press, 1978.

Wilamowitz-Moellendorf, Ulrich von. *Die Heimkehr des Odysseus.* Berlin: Weidmann, 1927.

Willcock, Malcolm M. "Mythological Paradeigma in the *Iliad.*" *CQ,* n.s. 14 (1964): 141–54.

Wolff, Christian. "A Note on Lions and Sophocles' *Philoctetes.*" In *Arktouros: Hellenic Studies Presented to B. M. W. Knox,* ed. Glen W. Bowersock et al. Berlin: W. de Gruyter, 1979.

Zumthor, Paul. *Introduction à la poésie orale.* Paris: Seuil, 1983.

INDEX

Aatos, 60–61
Achilles:
 and death, 58, 141–42, 169–72, 225
 epithets of, 61, 146n47
 etymology of name, 65
 kleos of, 139, 217
 as ontological or polemic opposite of
 Odysseus, 18, 243
 parallels with Odysseus. *See* Allusions:
 on Odysseus and Achilles
 representative of Iliadic pity, 223–26
 See also Iliad; Odysseus
Adaēmōn, 78n3
Adkins, A. W. H., 84n1
Adorno, Theodor W., 72n24, 77n2
Aeikelios, 83n1
Aeikēs, 83n1
Aethiopis, 38, 39, 63, 64n3
Agamemnon, 36–40, 104, 106, 134, 166
Agēnōr, 158–59, 161, 171
Agnōstos, 100n6
Ainos, 150, 233. *See also Poluainos*
Ajax, 38, 41, 121, 145–47
Akhos, 65
Alaston, 199n23
Alcinous, 62n26, 101, 174
Alētheia, 99n2, 112
 relation to being and language, 242
Alēthēs (alēthea), 99n2, 103n11
Alki pepoithōs, 160
Allegorical readings. *See* Reading: meta-
 phorical vs. literal
Allusion, 18–19, 28–30, 50–53, 236–45
 critic's search for, 241
 and decodification of sense, 237
 defined and described, 18–19, 28–30,
 51–52, 236–38
 drifting chain of, 114
 Ducrot on, 236–38, 240

father-text of, 42–43, 51–53, 241
formula as means of, 239
implicitness of, 50–51, 240–41
interchangeable with "intertextuality,"
 29n30, 50
Parry on, 29, 238
playful, 42–43, 55, 104–5, 240
undecidable or unreadable sense of,
 19, 50–53, 108–9, 111–12, 143–44,
 161, 240–41
See also Disguise; Formula; Irony;
 Mētis; Poetics; Reading
Allusions:
 to Homer, by post-Homeric writers,
 242–45
 to *Iliad,* in Demodocus' song, 216,
 220
 on Iliadic and Odyssean lion similes,
 157–61
 on Iliadic and Odyssean views of return, 33–43, 128–42
 on Iliadic *mēnis* and Odyssean *gastēr,*
 78, 175–76
 on *Iliad's* and *Odyssey's* generic themes,
 205–6n30
 on Odysseus and Achilles:
 attitude toward death and mourning, 58, 141–42, 145, 168–76
 "best of the Achaeans," 38
 drowning scenes, 63–64
 epiphanies to, 41–42
 fighting *epistrophadēn,* 131–35, 143–
 44
 kleos of, 30, 217
 oizuros, 38, 57–58
 return and homecoming, 139–42
 supplication scenes, 128–42
 on Odysseus and Agamemnon, 103–
 5, 134n13

Index

Allusions (*cont.*)
  on Odysseus in *Iliad* and *Odyssey*, 33–43
  on *Theogony* and *Odyssey*, 193
Amph' Odusēa daiphrona poikilomētēn, 146n7
Anagignōskō (anagignōskein), 96, 127
Anankē, 69n16
  and *gastēr*, 178–79, 196–97
  as grammar, tradition, and textuality, 207
  of poet *(aoidos)*, 206–7, 233–35
Anaphanda-on, 114
Anaximander, 243
Andra moi ennepe, 113
Antinous, 84, 179, 186
Aoidos, 196n14
  and *anankē*, 206–7, 233–35
Aphrodite, 193
  song on Ares' love of, 55, 215–16
Aphthiton kleos, 139
Après coup (Nachträglichkeit), 43, 86, 239–40
Apthorp, M. J., 22n11
Arend, Walter, 72
Ares, 61
  song on Aphrodite's love of, 55, 215–16
Argos, 110n1
Aristotle:
  Nicomachean Ethics, 67n11
  Poetics, 89n11
Arthur, Marylin B., 165n1, 174n5, 191n1, 192n4
Athena:
  disguised as Mentor, 114–16
  epiphanies of, 16, 94–95, 102–3, 105–9, 110–23
  Ergane, 108
  goddess of *mētis* (Odysseus' tutelary goddess and divine counterpart), 16, 22n12, 23, 101–3, 105–6, 107n16
  iconography of, 105, 107–9, 130
  manipulator of disguise, 84, 99–105
  mnēmē of, 20–22
  promakhos, 108n22, 130
  represents *Odyssey*'s polytropic style, 23
  split role of, 115–16
  unreadable figure of, 105–9, 110–11, 117–23
  and wretched return of Achaeans, 199, 205
  See also Disguise; *Enargēs*; *Mētis*
Athenaeus, *Deipnosophistai*, 173n1

Austin, Norman, 34n4, 46n8, 73n26
Author, subjectivity of. *See* Text: and authorial intentions
Autodidaktos, 113, 230–31
Autolycus, 23, 25n19, 87–89

Bannert, Hans, 114, 118
Being and *logos*, 81
Benveniste, Émile, 146n6, 166n2
Bergren, Ann, 44n1, 99n3, 183n5, 192n4, 194n13, 196n15
Blame poetry and praise poetry, 163–64, 187, 193. *See also Gastēr*; *Kleos*
Boskō, 177
Burkert, Walter, 18n4, 135n16, 137n20, 235n15

Calame, Claude, 29n30
Calypso, 33–41, 53–55, 150
  compares herself with Penelope, 54
  as Concealer, 20
  and ironic misreadings, 54–55
  offers Odysseus immortality, 37, 57n4
  represents literary jealousy and textual competition, 40, 53
  textual echoes (= allusions):
    of Athena, 34–37
    of Helen, 36
    of Hera (*Il.* 14), 54
    of *Iliad*, 38n12, 39–40
Chantraine, Pierre, 46, 59nn14–15, 153n15, 174n4
Circe, 24, 194–95, 209, 211
Clay, Jenny, 22n17, 107n19, 218n10
Codino, Fausto, 68n14, 166n2, 167, 176n10
Collins, Leslie L., 94n19
Culler, Jonathan, 26nn22–23, 50n1
Cyclops, 73, 182, 183

Daiphrōn, 59–60, 146n7
Dais, 25n20, 160n7, 167n6, 168n14, 169, 174n3, 184–86, 196, 197, 235
Daptō (daptei), 146n6
Death, 17, 68, 141–42, 169, 173
  "beautiful," of hero, 212, 225
  community of, 137
  hero's contiguity with, 171–72
  Iliad allied with, 128
  and immortality, 150–54
  Odyssey aimed at cheating, 128
  and pleasure, in *Odyssey*, 186, 214
  and Sirens' song, 210–13
  uncheatable power of, 68
  See also Achilles; Odysseus

Index

Deirotomeō, 229n7
De Man, Paul, 51n4, 118n24, 122n32, 181
Demodocus, 55
  as Iliadic poet, 215–23, 226–27
  replaced by Odysseus, 186
Derrida, Jacques, 27n25, 77n2, 181n2, 182n3, 194n13
Detienne, Marcel, 16n2, 28n29, 61n20, 163, 192n4, 200n25, 227n31, 243n17
Diano, Carlo, 23n13, 184n8
Dietrich, B. C., 114
Difference(s):
  chain of, in sign, 26–27
  between figural and literal, 113–23, 181
  and sameness, within allusions, 30, 46–51
  textual attempts to hide, 80–81, 86
Dii mētin atalanton, 22n12, 35–36n6
Diogenes, 34n4
Diomedes, 41, 66, 67n10, 77n2, 131
  vs. Odysseus, as hero, 145, 147
  traditional relationship with Odysseus, 131n5
Dioskouroi (Castor and Poludeukes), immortality of, in Odyssey, 141, 152–53
Dirlmeier, Franz, 114n7, 118, 121n30
Disguise:
  of Athena, 106–9, 112n5, 115. See also Enargēs
  defined, 83, 85–87
  of Odysseus:
    permanence of, 87–88
    self-displacing effects of, 89, 93, 95–97, 106
    textual (= allusion), 103–5, 122–23, 157, 160–61, 237, 241
    unreadability of, 111–14
  See also Allusion; Athena; Epiphany; Mētis; Names and naming; Odysseus; Reading; Recognition; Text
Dolos, 34n4, 58, 60–62, 150, 217, 243
Doxa, 112
Dubois, Jacques, 118n24
Ducrot, Oswald, 50, 236–38, 240
Durante, Marcello, 58n11, 59n15, 103n11, 130n2, 216n3
Dustēnos, 58

Edō, 178n17
Edwards, Anthony T., 80n6, 216n5
Eeldomai, 54
Eidomai, 118n21
Eiskō, 95, 106–7

Enargēs, 110–23
Eoika, 106–7
Eonta, ta, 242
Epiphany:
  of gods, as birds, 114, 117–22
  grammar of, 111
  in Greek (Homeric) religion, 112, 244
  to Odysseus, in Iliad vs. Odyssey, 41–42
  of Poseidon, 121–22
  See also Athena; Enargēs
Epistrophadēn, 131–135, 143–44, 147
Epithets. See Formula; Gastēr; Odysseus; individual names
Esthio, 178
Eukhōlē, 36
Eukhomai, 36
Eumaeus, 77, 79–81, 196n14
Eupatereia, 35n6
Euryclea, 87–89

Fenik, Bernard, 88n9
Ferrucci, Franco, 105n15
Fiction:
  of Athena's epiphany, 113–22
  as disguise of truth, 98–109, 122–23
  and Odyssey's allegory of textual truth, 96–97
  See also Disguise; Mētis: textual; Poetics
Figure. See Reading: metaphorical vs. literal; Simile
Finnegan, Ruth, 27
Focke, Friedrich, 107
Foley, Helene, 59n13, 91n15, 217n8
Ford, Andrew, 218n1
Formula, 102, 197n17, 239–40. See also Allusion; Grammar; Homeric diction
Formulaic diction. See Homeric diction
Frame, Douglas, 49n16, 119n26
Fränkel, Herman, 119n25, 121n30, 243n14
Friedrich, Rainer, 146n9, 159–60n5

Gastēr:
  of beggars, 177, 196n14
  defined and described, 157, 165, 181
  epithets of, 176n8, 179
  etymology of, 165n1, 177n13
  in Iliad, 165–70
  linked to kleos and poetry, 186
  and mētis, 182–84
  and necessity, 159, 178–79, 182, 196
  Odysseus characterized by, 178–79
  in Odyssey, 173–82
  and pleasure, 186

Index

Gastēr (cont.)
  and poet, in Homer and Hesiod,
    196n14, 234–35
  of suitors, 178
  and *thelgein*, 193–208
  and *thumos*, 157–87
  undecidable force of, 181–82
Gentili, Bruno, 28n29
Gounoumai . . . su de m'aideo kai m'eleēson,
  135–36
Grammar:
  and disguise, 111, 112n5, 113
  indeterminable, 206–7, 233
  passivity of, 206–8
  See also Mētis: textual; Reading: and
    unreadability
Griffin, Jasper, 27–28, 30n33, 118n21,
  120n27
Güntert, Hermann, 24n17

Haplous muthos, 243
Havelock, Eric A., 242n11
Hector, 41, 61
  alki pepoithōs, 160
Heidegger, Martin, 242
Helen, 35, 36, 70, 94n19, 152, 206n30
  epithets of, 35n6
Hephaestus, 197
Heracles, 58, 62, 73, 151–52
Hermes, 191
  patron god of Odysseus and Auto-
    lycus, 89
  polutropos, 23–25
Herodotus *1.60,* 108n21, 109
Hertz, Neil, 52n6, 211n3
Hesiod:
  Metis in, 22n12
  and Muses, 192–93
  on relation between poet and king,
    233–35
  Theogony, 22n12, 198; *26–28,* 107,
    192–93; 27, 98n1, 242; *98–103,*
    200; *594–602,* 177n11, 191
  Works and Days, 22n12; *3–8,* 97; *24–*
    26, 196n14; 25–26, 30n34; *77–78,*
    191; *203–9,* 234
Heuron (-en) epeit' Odusēa, 145n5
Hoekstra, Arie, 67n9
Hölscher, Uvo, 185n11
Homeric diction, 26–30, 239–40. *See
also* Allusion
Horkheimer, Max, 72n24, 77n2
Hōs, 130n2
Huphainō, 65
Hymn to Aphrodite, 112, 153n14, 199n23

Hymn to Demeter, 112
Hymn to Hermes, 185n11
Iconography. *See* Athena; Disguise;
  Enargēs
Iliad:
  contrasted with *Odyssey. See* Allusions
  defined by *klea andrōn,* 216–18
  as embodiment of Achilles' *kleos,* 139
  generic plot of, 206n30
  poetics of, allied to war and death, 57,
    128, 139, 169
  representative of epic tradition, 17
  See also Allusion; *Odyssey;* Poetics
Iliou Persis, 222
Ino, 64–65
Intertextuality. *See* Allusion; Allusions
Irony:
  literary, 40–42, 53–55, 109, 147, 164
  and misreading, 50–55
  puzzling aspects of, 120–21
  secular, 116–23
  See also Mētis: textual; Parody;
    Reading
Irus, 23n14, 130n1
  and fight with Odysseus, 161–63
  and *gastēr,* 177
  See also Blame poetry and praise
    poetry
Irwin, Terence, 67n11

Kahn, Laurence, 54–55n11, 68n13,
  154n18
Kakrides, Johannes Th., 102n9, 168n16
Kalē te megalē te aglaa erga iduiē, 108
Kammoros, 58
Katakruptō (katakruptousin), 110n2
Kerdaleophrōn, 104n14
Kerdaleos, 59n13
Kerdion einai, 67, 70
Kerdos, 58–60
Khreiō and *gastēr,* 159, 178
Khrusorrapis, 23
Kleiō, 186–87, 198–99
Kleiomai, 108
Kleos:
  and *gastēr,* 186–87
  Iliad as song of, 37, 39, 128, 139, 216
  and *mnēmē,* 20n5
  and Muse-inspired song, 219–21
  Odyssean, 216–19
  Odysseus denied, 147
  of poets, 187, 198, 202
  and *thelgein,* 202
Kofman, Sarah, 191n2, 244
Kunteron, 174n2

Index

Lacan, Jacques: "Purloined Letter," 87
Latacz, Joachim, 184n7, 193n11
Leodes:
  represents *Odyssey*'s view of return, 141
  suppliant to Odysseus, 129–38
Lesky, Albin, 56n3
Leugaleos, 64n3, 217
Leukōlenos, 35n6
Logos:
  and being, 79, 81
  deceptive power of, 99
  and truth, 242
Loraux, Nicole, 60n18, 205–6n30
Lucian, *Tragodopodagra*, 173n1
Lycaon:
  represents *Iliad*'s view of return, 139–41
  suppliant to Achilles, 129–38

MacMathúna, Séamus, 243n16
Marg, Walter, 216n2, 218n10
Marzullo, Benedetto, 46n5, 47n10, 56n1, 107n19, 117n17, 159n4
Mazon, Paul, 47n9
Meilikhios, 153n15
Melanthius, 69, 78, 80, 82
Menelaus, 145, 151, 185n10
Mēnis, 175–76
Menō (meneō), 66, 71
Mermērizō, scenes, 66–75
Metaphor, 146. *See also* Disguise; Reading
Mētis:
  defined and described, 16–17, 58
  as metamorphosizing power, 101, 103
  as polytropy, 16–17, 19, 150
  in post-Homeric literature, 243–44
  and *tekhnē*, 197
  textual, 19, 65–66, 72–73, 105–6, 111, 119–23
  disguising identity, 80–86
  in relation to *gastēr*, 182–84
  voice of, 73
  See also Allusion; Irony
  unreadable figure of, 105–9
  weakness and insufficiency of, 73, 106, 182–84
  See also Athena; *Dolos;* Odysseus; Polytropy/*polutropos*
Meuli, Karl, 60n16
Michel, Christoph, 121n30
Mnēmē, 19–20
Moira, of Odysseus, 106, 183
Monro, David B., 162, 229n6

"Monro's law," 17–18nn3–4
Mühlestein, Hugo, 121n29
Mülder, Dietrich, 111n4, 116n14
Müller, Marion, 107n19, 115n9
Muse:
  and epic song, 20, 220–21
  in Hesiod (*Theogony*), 192
  and Iliadic and Odyssean poets, 202–3, 215–16, 218–21, 227, 230–35
  in *Odyssey*, 215
Muthologeuō (muthologeuein), 147, 227
Muthos, 150, 152n13

Nagler, Michael, 57n6, 239
Nagy, Gregory, 17n3, 37n9, 45n2, 65n5, 87n7, 107n16, 131n5, 151n8, 163, 198n21, 200n25, 218n11, 222n20
Names and naming, 196, 203. *See also* Odysseus: names of
Nausicaa, 35n6, 91
Necessity, 17. *See also Anankē; Gastēr*
Nestle, Wilhelm, 116n12
Nestor, 77n2, 114–16, 117
Noos and Nostos, 49, 79, 150
Nostoi, 38, 187, 197, 201, 206, 207
Nostos, 41n22
  glukus, 138, 141n7
  meliēdēs, 138
  and *noos*, 49, 150

Odysseus:
  anonymity of, 149, 183nn5–6
  as character of romance, 56
  compared with Agamemnon, 104, 106, 134n13
  compared with Diomedes, 145, 147
  contrasted to Achilles, 18, 41–42, 56, 57–58, 63–64, 68, 128–42, 166–69, 173–76, 217, 243. *See also* Allusions: on Odysseus and Achilles
  and death(s), 14–15, 57, 62, 64, 68, 71, 141, 149–54, 169, 183, 186
  denied Iliadic *kleos*, 39, 147, 216–17
  as different character in *Iliad* and *Odyssey*, 25n19, 41
  disguises of, 77–97, 149
  epithets of, 24, 34n4, 38n13, 46–47, 48n14, 57–61, 67n9, 128, 145n5, 146n7, 185n11, 197n19
  etymology of name, 23n15, 183nn5–6
  as first "Socratic" man, 243
  and Heracles, 58, 73, 152
  as hero, 45, 47, 144–45, 147
  and immortality, 34, 152
  kaleidoscopic, 15

259

Index

Odysseus (*cont.*)
  literary character of, 21
  mētis of, 15–17, 42, 56, 58–59, 73–74,
    144, 182–84, 216–18
  as model of wandering hero, 149
  names of:
    Aithon, 149n6, 197n19
    Outis, "Nobody," 149, 154,
      183nn5–6
    pun with *odussomai*, 23, 65, 183nn5–
      6
  as *oizuros*, 38n13, 57–58
  as poet, 226–27
  polutropos, 14, 24, 49, 119, 128, 149
  as portrayed in *Iliad*, 144–47
  as reader/mourner of *Iliad*, 209–13,
    222–27
  returns of, 14, 16, 37, 53, 56, 148–50
  and "self," 14–17, 76–82, 85, 88–89,
    95, 149, 154. *See also* Disguise
  as Stoic, 58, 62
  voice of, 77n2
    as allegorical voice of text, 95–97
    as illusory mirror of self, 76–77,
      79–82
    and *mētis*, 72–73, 76n2
  See also Achilles; Disguise; *Mētis; Odys-
    sey;* Polytropy/*polutropos*; Reading
    scenes; Recognition scenes
Odyssey:
  critical readings of, 13–17
  and *Iliad. See* Allusions
  and immortality, 151
  life- and pleasure-affirming poetics of,
    57, 128, 141, 169, 214
  magical and "real" worlds of, 150–51,
    154
  not a poem of *kleos*, 39, 45, 128, 169,
    216
  religious views of, 116–22, 233, 244
  thelgein as underlying principle of, 202
  See also Allusion; *Iliad;* Odysseus; Po-
    etics; Polytropy/*polutropos*
Oileus, 38
Oistros, 130
Oitos (*kakos oitos*), 198n20
Oizuros, 38, 57–58
Oral diction. *See* Text
Oral performance, 197n18
Ou nemesis, 205–6n30
Ouranon eurun hikane, 219

Page, Denys, 17n3, 22, 166n2
Pagliaro, Antonino, 48n13, 216n2
Palin d'ho ge lazeto muthon, 103–4

Pandora, 191
Pantotropy:
  of Athena, 107
  of text, 123
Parmenides, 112, 242
Parody:
  Iliadic, of Odysseus, 37n10, 42n23,
    168
  in Irus episode, 162–63
  Odyssean, of Iliadic diction, 41, 70,
    162
  See also Allusion; Irony; *Mētis:* textual
Parry, Milman, 19, 21n10, 29n31, 51n3,
    60n15, 238–39
Paskhō (paskhōn), 57, 185n11
Pasquali, Giorgio, 64n3, 236, 241–42
Pateomai, 167n6
Peabody, Berkley, 20
Peisistratus, 116, 185n10
Pēma, 220n17
Penelope, 99, 113, 148
  epithets of, 59n13
  kleos of, 217, 219n12
  mētis of, 93
  recognition of Odysseus, 89–94
  as sober reader, 198–201
Penthos alaston, 199–200
Peradotto, John 149n5
Periklutos, 197
Peristenakhizomai, 91n16
Phaeacia, 184, 221
Phainomai, 110–12, 244
Phemius:
  autodidaktos, 113, 229–30
  compared to Odyssean poet, 201–3
  recantation of, 229–35
  song of, 99, 195–208
  Terpiades, 196, 228
  See also Demodocus; Muse; Poetics;
    Thelgō
Phusizoos, 141, 152–54
Phuteuō, 65
Pity, Odyssean vs. Iliadic, 221–26
Plato:
  Laches, 67n11
  Republic, 173n1
  Symposium, 244
Pleasure, 184, 197n19
  and *gastēr*, 182–87
  and necessity, 17, 99, 207, 231
  Odyssey's affirmation of, 57, 128, 141,
    169, 214
  poetics of, 193–96, 201–4
  sexual, 55, 64
  and Terpiades, 196

Pleasure (cont.)
textual, 17, 41, 65, 68
See also Dais; Mētis: textual; Phemius;
Thelgō
Poetics:
of Iliad, 139–42, 147, 223–27
of Odyssey, 201–15, 221–27
Poikilomētēs, 59–60
Poluainos, 60
Polukerdos, polukerdiē, 59n13, 103–4
Polumēkhanos, 33–34, 46n8
Polutlas, 47n10, 78
Polytropy/polutropos, 16–17, 24, 49, 51,
119, 127–28, 149–50, 243
as pantotropy, 123
See also Athena; Mētis: textual
Ponos, 60–61
Poseidon, 49n15
epiphany of, 121–22
rage of, against Odysseus, 63, 65, 183
Praise poetry. See Blame poetry and
praise poetry
Priam, 41, 170–71
Primitivism, 27, 115–23
Ptoliporthos, 21n10
Pucci, Pietro, 20n5, 24n16, 28n30,
49n16, 57n8, 60n17, 98n1, 119n26,
151n7, 186n12, 192n4, 200n25,
210n2, 212n7, 225n28, 243n15

Ramersdorfer, Hans, 40n19, 42n23
Rationalism, 115–23
Reading:
of allusions. See Allusion
curse of, 210
establishing meaning, 225, 231
metaphorical vs. literal, 93, 95–97,
100–101, 113–14, 118–23, 181
and mimetic substitutions, 196, 204
Odyssean, 196, 214–15, 240–41
Odyssey's irony, 116
and unreadability:
of disguised figures, 105–9, 111–14
of figural or literal expression, 119–23
of Odyssey's poetics, 207–8, 233
See also Allusions; Disguise; Grammar;
Irony; Poetics; Recognition
Reading scenes:
Odysseus and Iliadic tradition, 214–
27
Odysseus and Sirens, 209–13
Penelope and Phemius, 198–201
Phemius and poet of Odyssey, 202–8
Telemachus and Phemius, 201–8
See also Recognition scenes

Recognition, 83–97
of gods in disguise. See Athena; Enargēs; Epiphany; Poseidon
of readers vs. characters, 113–14
and return, 127–28
See also Allusion; Disguise; Mētis;
Odysseus
Recognition scenes:
Eumaeus and Odysseus, 77, 79–81
Euryclea and Odysseus, 88–90
Penelope and Odysseus, 89–94
Telemachus and Odysseus, 94–97
See also Athena
Reference:
linguistic, 48n14, 108–9, 236–45
thematic:
to Odysseus' Trojan War experience, 17–18, 63–64, 67n11, 136–
37, 143, 214–27
to Odysseus' Trojan War kleos,
39n18, 185–87, 198–99, 216–17
See also Allusion; "Monro's law"
Referent:
in recognition, 113–14
in similes, 107, 118–19
See also Recognition scenes
Reinhardt, Karl, 38n12, 80n6, 107n16,
122n31, 197n17
Repetition:
and generative force of Homeric diction, 19, 30, 240
and performances of bardic songs,
197n18
and process of allusion, 18–20, 236–
38
of voice, and self-identity, 79–82
See also Allusion; Disguise; Formula;
Homeric diction
Russo, Joseph, 72n25, 84n3, 85n5,
243n13

Sameness:
and difference, in epic diction, 29
in Lycaon's return, 140
and recognition, 127–28
of self, through repetition, 80–81
utopian notion of, 14, 140
See also Allusion; Difference(s); Disguise; Repetition
Sarpedon, 151, 157–58, 225, 233
Schein, Seth L., 18n4
Schnapp-Gourbeillon, Annie, 146n9
Segal, Charles, 40n20, 148, 198n19,
219n2
Shewring, Walter, 111n4

Simile:
  of gods as birds, 114–23
  Odyssean vs. Iliadic, 132–33, 146n9,
    147n11, 157–61
  and referent, 105, 114, 146
  See also Homeric diction; Reading:
    metaphorical vs. literal; Referent
Sirens, 60, 151n7, 195, 209–13, 231
Sittl, Karl, 131n5, 132n7
Snell, Bruno, 243n14
Sophocles, *Ajax*, 112
Stanford, W. B., 61n21, 116, 120n27,
  173n1
Supplement:
  defined, 194–95
  in disguise-recognition, 87
  structure of, for *gastēr*, 93, 181–87
  structure of, for *thelgein*, 194–95,
    209–13, 227
  See also Disguise; Difference(s)
Svenbro, Jesper, 138n22, 174n5,
  185n11, 191n1

Talapenthēs, 44–55, 77–81
Tekhnē, 197
Telemachus, 89–91, 99
  as intoxicated reader, 201–8
  mediates blame and praise poetry,
    161–64
  recognition of Odysseus, 94–97
  relation to divine power, 94–95
Text:
  allegorical voice of, 96
  and authorial intentions, 113, 240
  and author's subjectivity, 113
  oral vs. written, 26–30
  scheming, 65
  as sum of its readings, 19
  textuality of, 52, 112–13, 122–23,
    157, 183–84
  See also Allusion; Disguise; Irony;
    Mētis: textual; Reading
Thelgō, 191–215, 226–27
  defined, 193–95
  in *Iliad*, 193–94
  and poet's *kleos*, 202
  of Sirens, 195
  See also Gastēr
Thelktērion, 198–201
Thumos:
  and *gastēr*, 157–87

talapenthēs thumos, 46–53, 77–81, 178–
  80
thumos agēnōr, 158–62, 177, 178
tlēmōn thumos, 46–53
Tlēmōn, 46–53
Tlēnai forms, 46–53, 66–74, 77–81
Todorov, Tzvetan, 45n3, 103n10,
  115n10
Tolmaō, 47, 78
Touchefeu-Meynier, Odette, 108n22
Truth:
  of Athena's appearances, 107–9, 111–
    12
  and *logos*, 242
  and naming, 203
  and opinion, in Parmenides, 112
  and poets' songs, 192, 203
  relation to *thelgein*, 226–27
  See also Disguise; Fiction; Text

Vernant, Jean-Pierre, 16n2, 61n20,
  116n13, 165n1, 191nn1 and 3,
  243n17
Vidal-Naquet, Pierre, 39n17, 40n20,
  138n22
Voice:
  epic, 77n2
  narrative (textual):
    and allegory of truth and fiction,
      95–97
    between characters and readers,
      115–23
  Odyssean. *See* Odysseus: voice of
  playfulness of, 104–5
  split mode of, 115
  See also Text
Von der Mühll, Peter, 42n23
Vox, Onofrio, 243n13

Walsh, George B., 223nn22, 24, 26
Weber, Samuel, 87n7
Wilamowitz-Moellendorf, Ulrich von,
  107, 108
Wolff, Christian, 146n9

Xenophanes, 98n1, 242

Zeus, 151, 172, 225
  as inspiration of poets, 206–7
  mētis of, 22n12
  mnēmē of, 20
Zumthor, Paul, 27n26

Library of Congress Cataloging-in-Publication Data

Pucci, Pietro, 1927–
    Odysseus Polutropos : intertextual readings in the Odyssey and the Iliad.

    (Cornell studies in classical philology ; v. 46)
    Bibliography: p.
    Includes index.
    1. Homer—Criticism and interpretation.   2. Homer. Odyssey.
3. Homer. Iliad.   4. Odysseus (Greek mythology) in literature.   5. Trojan
War in literature.   I. Homer. Odyssey.   II. Homer. Iliad.   III. Title.
IV. Series.
PA4037.P8   1987   883'.01   86-16798
ISBN 0-8014-1888-7 (alk. paper)